THE ECONOMICS OF LONG-DISTANCE TRANSPORTATION

Long-distance transport is carried out by various means in different countries of the world, ranging from the transport of fuel in pipelines in the intense cold of Siberia or Alaska, to the use of car and train for longer commuting journeys in the capitals of Western Europe. Not only does the climate vary, but also social and economic systems are different.

In this volume experts from centrally planned or market economies put forward very contrasting views on transport organization and objectives – for example, on how "efficiency" should be defined. In all countries, there is a desire to plan an integrated and efficient system, but stress is sometimes put on the use of commercial market pricing, and in other cases, on the proper calculation of social costs and benefits.

There are twenty-seven papers presented here, together with summaries of the discussions they prompted in Moscow, dealing with technical, economic, organizational and political aspects of long-distance transport. The book is intended to be useful to transport specialists, economists and geographers, and also to those interested in comparative studies between centrally planned and market economies.

Academician T. S. Khachaturov is one of the most distinguished of Soviet economists, and is an Honorary President of the International Economic Association.

Dr P. B. Goodwin is a leading British transport economist. He is Reader in Transport Studies and Director of the Transport Studies Unit at the University of Oxford.

THE ECONOMICS OF LONG-DISTANCE TRANSPORTATION

Proceedings of a Conference held by the
International Economic Association
in Moscow

Edited by
T. S. Khachaturov
and
P. B. Goodwin

Assisted by S. M. Carpenter

St. Martin's Press   New York

ISBN 0–312–23439–2

Library of Congress Cataloging in Publication Data

Main entry under title:

The Economics of long-distance transportation.

Includes index.
1. Transportation –Congresses.   I. Khachaturov, T. S.
(Tigran Sergeevich), 1906–   .   II. Goodwin, P. B.
III. Carpenter, S. M.   IV. International Economic
Association.
HE11.E25   1982   380.5   82-791
ISBN 0–312–23439–2   AACR2

Contents

Acknowledgements   Michael Kaser   ix

Officers of the Conference   x

List of Participants   xi

Introductory Address: Transport Development in the USSR

                                  T. S. Khachaturov   xiii

PART ONE: CHANGES IN THE RELATIONSHIP
            BETWEEN DIFFERENT MODES OF
            TRANSPORT   1

        1   Planning and Mode Split of Freight Traffic in
            the USSR   A. A. Mitaishvili   3

        2   Comparing the Efficiency of Western Euro-
            pean Rail and Road Services   Fritz Voigt 12

        3   Changes in Freight Traffic among the Modes
            of Transport, Past and Future
                                     Dudley F. Pegrum   22

        4   The Socialist Transport System – its Manage-
            ment and Planning   Hermann Wagener   34

        5   Modal Split, Efficiency and Public Policy
                                     Yukihide Okano   49

            Discussion   64

PART TWO: FUEL FREIGHT AND TRANSPORT-
            ATION IN LESS ACCESSIBLE REGIONS   79

        6   International Implications of Long-distance
            Transport of Fuels   Holland Hunter,
                                Leslie Dienes and Lee Bettis 81

            Discussion   94

        7   The Today and Tomorrow of Arctic Trans-
            portation Routes   Jerzy Zaleski   97

        8   Trunk-line Transportation in Less Accessible
            Regions   V. Burkhanov   106

9 Transportation System Planning for Alaska
Development David T. Kresge,
J. Royce Ginn and John T. Gray 112
10 Pipeline Transportation of Natural Gas in the
USSR O. M. Ivantsov 134
11 Efficient Long-distance Fuel Transportation
R. W. Lake, C. J. Boon and C. Schwier 142
Discussion 156

PART THREE: PROBLEMS OF THE OPTIMAL RE-
LATIONSHIP OF INDIVIDUAL AND
PUBLIC PASSENGER TRANSPORT 165
12 Mass Transport and Individual Transport: an
Optimum Modal Split Rezso Bajusz 167
13 The Optimum Ratio between Private and
Public Passenger Transport Services in Conur-
bations: the Experience of the German
Democratic Republic Werner Lindner 179
14 Motorisation in Japan Ryohei Kakumoto 187
15 Problems in Attaining an Optimum Ratio
between Long-distance Individual and Public
Passenger Transport H. St. Seidenfus 197
Discussion 210

PART FOUR: PROBLEMS OF INCREASING EFFI-
CIENCY OF TRANSPORT MODES 219
16 Impediments to the American Railroads'
Achieving their Comparative Advantage for
Long-distance Movement George W. Hilton 221
17 The Development and Main Problems of
International Transport Systems R. Squilbin 232
Discussion 240
18 Rational Policies for Development of
International Air Transportation
John R. Meyer and William B. Tye 245
Discussion 264
19 Time as a Factor in Increasing the Economic
Efficiency of Ports and Sea–Land Transport
Witold Andruszkiewicz 267
20 Port Congestion or Port Dysfunction
S. Wickham and N. Tien Phuc 274

21 Inland Waterways and Long-distance Freight
Traffic   D. M. Hayter and C. H. Sharp   286
Discussion   300

PART FIVE: TRANSPORT AND PRODUCTION;
             ORGANISATIONAL ASPECTS OF
             TRANSPORT DEVELOPMENT   303
22 Spatial Distribution of Productive Powers
   and Socialist Transport Policy
                      Gerhard Rehbein   305
23 Organisation of Transport Enterprises
                      H. J. Noortman   312
24 International Transportation Systems
                      Richard Burke   326
   Discussion   342
25 The Importance of Organisational Forms of
   Integration in the Field of International
   Transportation   Stefan Tsankov   348
26 Material Relations and Transport Policy in
   the Czechoslovak Social Republic
                      Karel Vitek   353
27 Principal Problems of the Development of
   International Relations in the Transport
   Sector   G. Antal   361
   Discussion   371
28 Themes and Conclusions of the Conference
   The Discussions   P. B. Goodwin   374
   The Papers   T. S. Khachaturov   377
   Index   384

Acknowledgements

The Round Table Conference held in Moscow (15–19 October 1979) of which this volume is an outcome, was organised for the International Economic Association by the Institute of Complex Transport Problems of the USSR. It represented a diamond jubilee as the sixtieth conference that the Association had arranged. The organisation was excellent, with a well-planned agenda and a social programme which was not only restorative (in the midst of a Round Table to which more papers were read than to any previous one) but also professionally informative (in a visit to a railway research establishment at Shcherbinka). The Association is grateful to the presenters, discussants and session-chairmen; to the organising committee in Moscow and its secretary Sergei Borisovich Shlikhter; to the many representatives of Soviet government departments and scientific institutions who helped in many ways, and above all to the Conference Chairman, Tigran Sergeevitch Khachaturov.

Of the leading Soviet economists who have been members of the Executive Committee of the Association – V. P. Dyachenko, K. N. Plotnikov and O. T. Bogomolov are the others – Academician Khachaturov has served for the longest period and had already presided over an earlier Round Table – on methods of long-term planning and forecasting in 1972; the Council of the Association at its triennial meeting in 1980 honoured him by nomination as an Honorary President.

The proceedings are also being published in Russian in the Soviet Union.

MICHAEL KASER

Officers of the Conference

Chairman	Professor T. S. Khachaturov
IEA Representative	M. Kaser
Organiser	Professor S. Shlikhter
Rapporteur	Dr P. B. Goodwin
Editorial Assistant	S. M. Carpenter
Secretariat	G. Belova
	A. A. Dynkin
	E. Emelyanova
	O. Laptev
	V. Malysheva
	E. Sentulyova
Interpreters	Y. Gelman
	E. Halfkin
	A. Rozentzweig
Translator	J. Curtis
Secretaries	Mrs J. Gray
	Mrs S. Boyce

List of Participants

Dr W. Andruszkiewicz, Maritime Institute, Gdansk, Poland

Dr G. Antal, Ministry for Foreign Trade, Budapest, Hungary

Dr R. Bajusz, Ministry of Transport & Communications, Budapest, Hungary

Mrs T. M. Borisenko, Institute of Complex Transport Problems, Moscow, USSR

Professor V. Burkhanov, Council for Investigation of Productive Forces, Moscow, USSR

Dr P. B. Goodwin, Transport Studies Unit, Oxford University, UK

D. Hayter, Public Sector Economics Research Centre, Leicester University, UK

Professor H. Hunter, Department of Economics, Haverford College, Penn., USA

Dr O. Ivantsov, Ministry for the Construction of Oil and Gas Pipelines, Moscow, USSR

Dr R. Kakumoto, Transport Economics Research Centre, Tokyo, Japan

Professor L. V. Kantorovitch, Scientific Council for Integrated Transport Systems, Moscow USSR

M. Kaser, St Antony's College, Oxford University, UK

Professor T. S. Khachaturov, Association of Soviet Economic Scientific Institutions, Moscow, USSR

Professor I. V. Kovalev, Institute for World Economy & International Relations, Moscow, USSR

Dr B. S. Kozin, Institute of Complex Transport Problems, Moscow, USSR

Dr R. Lake, Institute of Guided Ground Transport, Queen's University, Kingston, Canada

Dr K. Leydon, Directorate General for Transport, EEC, Brussels, Belgium

Dr W. Lindner, Zentrale Forschungsinstitut Fur Transportwesen, Berlin, GDR

Professor A. A. Mitaishvili, Institute of Complex Transport Problems, Moscow, USSR

Professor J. J. Noortman, Institute of Transport, Tijswijk, Netherlands
Professor Y. Okano, Faculty of Economics, Tokyo University, Japan
Dr N. T. Phuc, CECOTRAT, Paris, France
Professor G. Rehbein, Hochschule fur Verkehrswesen, Dresden, GDR
Professor S. Sarkisian, Aviatsionny Institute, Moscow, USSR
Professor H. St. Seidenfus, Institute for Verkehrswissenschaft, Munster University, FGR
Professor S. B. Shlikhter, Institute of Complex Transport Problems, Moscow, USSR
Dr S. Tsankov, Karl Marx Economics University, Sofia, Bulgaria
Dr W. Tye, Charles River Associates, Boston, Mass., USA
D. P. Velikanov, Institute for Complex Transport Problems, Moscow, USSR
Dr K. Vitek, Institute Manipulacnich Dopravnich Obalovych a sklado-vacich systemu, Prague, Czechsoslovakia
V. P. Vodianitsky, Institute for Complex Transport Problems, Moscow, USSR
Professor H. Wagener, Hochschule fur Verkehrswesen, Dresden, GDR
Professor S. Wickham, Université de Paris, France
Professor J. Zaleski, University of Gdansk, Poland

OTHER AUTHORS

The following authors and joint authors of papers were not able to attend the conference.
L. Bettis, Haverford College, Penn., USA
C. J. Boon, Queen's University, Ontario, Canada
R. Burke, Commission of the European Communities, Brussels, Belgium
L. Dienes, Haverford College, Penn., USA
J. R. Ginn, Cambridge Systematics, Cambridge, Mass., USA
J. T. Gray, University of Alaska, USA
G. W. Hilton, Smithsonian Institution, Washington DC USA
D. T. Kresge, Centre for Urban Studies, Cambridge, Mass., USA
J. R. Meyer, Harvard University, Boston, Mass., USA
D. F. Pegrum, UCLA California, USA
C. Schweir, Queen's University, Ontario, Canada
C. H. Sharp, University of Leicester, UK
R. Squilbin, International Railway Congress Association, Brussels, Belgium
F. Voigt, University of Bonn, FRG

Introductory Address: Transport Development in the USSR

T. S. KHACHATUROV

That the Soviet Union should have been chosen to host the Conference is not fortuitous. The role of transport in our country and in our national economy is of the utmost importance. This is because of the high level and the speed of the development of our economy, as well as the enormous size of our territory.

It is nearly 9000 kilometres from the East to the West of the Soviet Union, and nearly 4000 kilometres separate the Arctic Ocean from our Southern borders. Our frontier stretches for 60,000 kilometres. Our population is now over 260 million. The country produces 20 per cent of the world's industrial production. The national income for the current year is 14 times greater than it was in 1940. These few general statistics should explain certain characteristics in our country's huge demand for sophisticated long-distance transportation between towns.

A peculiarity of transport in the USSR, as in other socialist countries, is that it comes under a single socialist ownership (except, of course, for private cars and boats). All forms of transport therefore work in a co-ordinated fashion, as component parts of a single transportation system in accordance with the state economic plan. But as a result of the peculiar features of our country, its huge territory, and the need for transportation on a massive scale, our main form of transport is the railway. The majority of goods and passenger traffic between towns goes by rail. Our railway network, which stretches over 140,000 kilometres, carries a volume of 3.5 billion ton/kilometres, which comprises more than half of the world's turnover of goods carried by rail, and about 60 per cent of the turnover on all forms of transport in the USSR. In 1979, passenger transport on the railways numbered 335 milliard passenger/

kilometres, comprising 40 per cent of all intercity passenger transport. The density of transportation is therefore extremely high; one kilometre of railway carries per year 24.5 million ton/kilometres and 2.4 million passenger/kilometres. No other country carries such a high load on its railways.

Soviet railways have been able to cope with this heavy load due to the fact that almost the entire railway stock was switched over soon after the war to electric and diesel locomotives. Electric locomotives serve 41,000 kilometres of track – more than in any other country. Diesel locomotives serve about 100,000 kilometres of track. The introduction of modern locomotives and the modernisation of other aspects of railway technology – the switching of all rolling stock to automatic couplings and automatic brakes, the laying of heavier rails, the double-tracking of main lines, and the redevelopment of stations – all this has allowed us significantly to increase the volume of transportation by railway.

At the same time, transportation has become more economical. Thus during the period 1960–1975 fuel consumption per ton/kilometre on the railways went down four times, for sea transport it went down 40 per cent; for river transport it went down 2.4 times; and for road transport it went down 25 per cent. Productivity of labour on the various forms of transport went up by two and a half times and more.

The growth of transportation is continuing, and by the end of the century it will increase significantly. It is for this reason that it is so important correctly to determine the prospects for the further development of transport by rail, and for an even greater rise in its capacity.

Not all the possibilities for increasing rail transport have yet been fully exploited. The distances covered by the railway network will increase, though at a slower rate than the volume of traffic. It is probable that both the weight and speed of trains will increase still more. In those sectors where there is the greatest volume of transport, there will perhaps be a need to build third or possibly even fourth tracks; and in some of the places where diesel locomotives are being used they will be replaced by electric ones. But to a large extent growth in transportation will come about as the result of expanding other forms of transport, and by co-ordinating it all into a single transport system.

An extensive network of large-diameter oil and high-pressure gas pipelines has been built up in the USSR: they now stretch for 193,000 kilometres. They carry about a quarter of all the turnover in the transport network. The length of the pipelines will be still further increased, and it has proved a very economical form of transport: the unit cost is 2.5 times less than by rail and 1.5 times less than by sea.

The electricity transmission network is vast – it covers 735,000 kilometres. This network connects all the electric power stations and all energy consumers in the Soviet Union to form a single energy system, thus assuring high effectiveness in the production and transmission of electrical energy.

Road transport in the USSR is growing rapidly. At the moment its share is about 7 per cent of goods turnover; but as far as actual tonnage is concerned, road transport holds first place, carrying 82 per cent of all loads despatched (with an average distance for transportation of about 16 kilometres, as against 900 kilometres by rail). Public transport by bus accounts for 25 per cent of passenger traffic between towns, with private cars accounting for about 12 per cent. The relative proportion of road transport will increase as the number of goods vehicles and cars grows, and as the road network becomes more extended. At the moment there are 736,000 kilometres of hard-surface roads (5 times more than in 1940), more than half of these being high-grade roads with cement or asphalt surfaces. The territory of the USSR covers 22 million square kilometres. Even if we take only the economically active part of the territory and exclude deserts and tundra, it still covers 14.5 million square kilometres, so that even for that area 770,000 kilometres of road is still very inadequate: we need at least twice as much. Between 1965 and 1980 the length of hard-surface roads increased by about 100 per cent. At this rate of growth it would be possible by the end of the century to bring the length of roads up to 1.5 million kilometres. This would go a long way towards solving the task of providing the country with road transport, particularly for the transportation of goods requiring rapid delivery such as agricultural produce and so on.

Under the Soviet government a whole network of deep waterways has been created with the construction of the Moskva–Volga, Volga–Don, Volga–Baltic Sea and other canals, as well as the deepening of river channels. Navigation conditions have been improved and considerable stretches of river have been equipped with lighting. More dock facilities in river ports have been mechanised and extended. The river fleet has been considerably expanded; powerful tugs, self-propelled craft with a large freight-carrying capacity for combined river- and sea-sailing, catamaran container ships, car-transport ships, cement barges, sectional ships and so on have all been built. But river transport's share of the turnover is not great, comprising about 4 per cent. For the most part it is bulk loads which are transported in this way, such as timber, building materials, fuel, agricultural cargoes, as well as the products of factories actually situated on the river banks.

Passenger transportation by river is also not very great, forming less than 1 per cent of the overall number of passenger/kilometres travelled between towns. A significant proportion of this transport is accounted for by holidaymakers, who use river transport in their time off. This demand is met by the comfortable ships which ply the Volga and the other big rivers in the USSR.

Sea transport's share of the transportation of freight measured in ton/kilometres comprised 14 per cent in 1978; in the transportation of passengers, it comprised about 0.3 per cent. Sea transport is used principally for the external trade of the USSR, while the transporting of passengers is mainly met by coastal shipping. The tonnage of the sea-going fleet has increased considerably – it is four times greater now than it was in 1960. The fleet has been expanded with a large number of modern craft; container ships, multi-purpose ships for the transportation of general freight, ships designed for carrying timber, refrigerator ships, trailer ships and tankers. The average speed of ships has risen. In the sea ports, docks have been extended and considerably mechanised, and the ports themselves have been deepened.

A greater proportion of passenger traffic is now being accounted for by air transport, which in 1978 had acquired 16 per cent of the traffic and is still growing. Routes now cover 908,000 kilometres, including 200,000 kilometres of international routes.

As a result of the increase in goods traffic and improvements in technology, the USSR has evolved a type of transport system which is characterised by a high density of traffic, very large-scale technical resources, and low unit costs, so that transportation has become much cheaper. Between 1950 and 1975 the unit cost of transporting freight by rail dropped by a half; sea transport costs dropped 2.4 times; river costs 1.5 times; road unit costs 1.3 times, while the unit cost of passenger transport on the railways dropped 1.5 times, and that of road by 10 per cent.

In recent years the capital investment required to finance the introduction of new transport routes has risen considerably. This is because construction of new routes is at the moment being carried out principally in the East and the North of the USSR, as well as in the mountains – that is to say, in those regions which had hitherto had poor provision of transport facilities.

The USSR's development is placing greater and greater demands on the transport system. Our task consists in correctly analysing both these demands and the future paths of development of transport itself as well as continually improving its performance.

PART ONE

Changes in the Relationship between Different Modes of Transport

1 Planning and Mode Split of Freight Traffic in the USSR

A. A. MITAISHVILI

I THE ROLE OF TRANSPORT IN THE USSR

A high level of transport performance is required to assist planned economic growth in advanced socialist countries. The volume of freight traffic of all modes of transport in the USSR amounted to 6.0 billion ton/kilometres, and the volume of passenger traffic reached 1.2 billion passenger/kilometres in 1978. Every freight ton produced in the national economy travels on the trunk routes an average of 1000 kilometres from producer to consumer; citizens travel an average of more than 4000 kilometres annually.

The overall expenditure on freight traffic in the national economy of the USSR amounts to approximately 80,000 million roubles annually. The share of transport expenditure in the cost of production is now 8–9 per cent: for oil and timber 25–26 per cent; for iron ore and raw chemicals nearly 20 per cent; for coal 15 per cent. Raising transport efficiency and reducing transport expenditure are indispensable to the growth of production efficiency.

The role of transport is expanding more and more in USSR international trade. These problems can only be solved by treating the Soviet transport system as an integrated social-economic system. The USSR united transport system represents all the transport modes which are state property, each contributing to an integral co-ordinated plan of satisfying the country's demands with minimal costs.

The main characteristic of the united transport system is the organisation of an uninterrupted, highly efficient transportation process along the whole way from shipper to consumer, on the basis of co-

3

ordinated technology of all modes of transport participating in delivery of goods.

The improvement of transportation quality through the operation of specialised rolling-stock, the reduction of the number of handling operations, development of containerisation and new modes of transport considerably reduces the losses of goods in the transportation process and as a result reduces the need for the introduction of new production capacity, as well as reducing inventories.

II TRANSPORT PLANNING

Transport is always considered in the context of the whole national economy. Together with current annual plans, five-year and long-term plans are worked out. The general objective of forming such an overall transport plan is the balancing of production and transportation of goods both in the country as a whole and in the particular republics and economic regions.

The calculation of a long-term plan is always of an iterative character. Firstly, general forecasting estimates are worked out, followed by the elaboration of general trends and at last the final version of the plan appears. While passing from one stage of planning to another the extent of balancing the different aspects of the plan increases, including its countrywide and territorial aspects. Determination of the required total volumes of freight transportation is done on the basis of intersectoral balance of production and distribution of goods in natural and monetary terms. For this purpose suitable data on the specific transport requirements per ton of coal, oil, metal, timber, grain and other commodities produced are prepared beforehand. Such indices are calculated both for the transport system as a whole and for particular modes of transport – railway, inland waterways, maritime, pipelines and road transport. Thus the draft version of the transportation plan is defined more precisely and in greater detail.

The magnitude of freight traffic and its modal split depends upon the structure of the national economy, in particular, on the correlation of industrial and agricultural production, as well as mining and manufacturing industries, and the production of basic and consumer goods in the gross national product. All these and other structural and qualitative alternatives are reflected in the intersectoral balance and, therefore, may be taken into account by calculations of traffic volume together with elaboration of the balance itself.

For improvement of the modal split it is important to determine the prospective optimal inter- and intraregional transport-economic links. One of the main stages of dealing with this problem is planning the location of production over the country's area with simultaneous optimisation of transport links. At this stage reduction in transport costs is not a main task. In many cases it is more efficient for the national economy to allow some transport costs to increase, if at the same time the production costs are being reduced considerably (for example, by the establishment of large specialised industrial complexes, which supply large areas). The main criterion of transportation efficiency adopted for the planning of transport performance is the *combined* amount of economic costs of production, transportation, storage and consumption of commodities, which at the same time determines the most suitable size, specialisation and location of enterprises.

The account of combined expenditures on production and transportation confirms the efficiency of the fuel and raw materials branches located in eastern regions of the country, increasing the concentration of oil-refining and of the iron and steel industry, and specialisation and co-operation in engineering. The volume of traffic and transport expenditure increases when these measures are taken, but as a rule transport expenditures are being considerably outweighed by saving on the production and consumption of goods.

Location of enterprises in several cases depends on the transport mode being used. Thus, as a result of increases in oil production and the use of efficient pipelines for its transportation oil refineries began to be located more advantageously, not in the oil-producing regions as during the period dominated by the railway services, but in the regions of concentrated oil product consumption.

After determining the location of industry, optimal transport economic links and the traffic volume must be decided according to only a minimum summary of adjusted transport expenditure (operational expenses and capital expenditure adjusted to an annual amount by using the standard coefficient for capital investment). The territorial balances for large regions should be disaggregated. The calculations are done according to a differentiated list of goods which includes 100–120 items amalgamated into nine large groups at the final stage.

Balance calculations are done according to the following form:

(1) Economic regions, districts, autonomous and union republics
(2) Production
(3) Imports

  (4) Total resources
  (5) Distribution of resources according to use
  (6) Production operational requirements
  (7) Market fund or individual consumption
  (8) Other inputs to be specified if needed
  (9) Exports
(10) Total
(11) Surplus or deficit

Material balances of production and consumption of any product have two common parts – income (resources) and input (distribution of resources). However, a list of items in both parts, or formation (sources) of resources and their distribution for special purposes, differentiate according to the sectors of the economy, reflecting their specific features.

Income and input parts of resources accordingly represent volumes of primary shipment and arrival of goods for each territorial unit, determining countrywide the national economy's requirements in transportation services, which must be covered.

Optimisation of transport-economic links and the trunk modal split is carried out by using economic and mathematical methods and computers for the calculated (aggregated) routes network, including approximately 1000 nodes. At this stage a closed model of the transportation problem using linear programming in the network form is solved, using 'minimal adjusted transport expenditure' as the objective function; this includes operational expenditure for trains' (ships') movement, their servicing during the trip and maintenance of fixed equipment as well as capital investment in rolling stock and reinforcement of the network's technical equipment.

The specific features of modes of transport are taken into consideration, to determine the sphere of economically expedient usage of each of them – regularity, safety, movement, speed and cheapness of traffic with necessary consideration of geographical, ecological, social and other factors.

In cases when transport modes are competitive, the selection of a transport service scheme for a region or industrial complex is worked out on the basis of technical-economic calculations of comparison of variants with the utilisation of indices of unit transport expenditure, which are calculated by taking into account the following demands:

  (1) the total journey 'from door-to-door';
  (2) determination of real resource expenditure irrespective of tradi-

tional methods of planning and accounting, in particular inclusion of highways and waterways maintainance expenditure, being financed from the state budget;

(3) according to the type of problem being solved there should be consideration only of operational expenditure and capital investment in rolling stock (the current period) and moreover capital investment in the fixed assets development;

(4) the expenditure rates are represented in the form of average figures which are typical for a given mode of transport or in the form of expenditure on the particular unit;

(5) the split of expenditure according to the main operational elements of the transport process;

(6) reflection of the optimal performance conditions for each mode of transport in the unit expenditure.

The calculation of indices of unit transport expenditure is done in the following way.

(1) Ajdusted expenditure in static terms

That is for the specific year of evaluation

$$Z = C + eK$$

where Z = operating expenditure;
  K = capital investment;
  e = standard coefficient for comparative capital investment efficiency.

(2) Adjusted expenditure in dynamic terms for the whole period of expenditure

$$Z = K_0 + \sum_1^t (K_i + C_t)(1 + e)^{-t}$$

in which K_0 = the initial capital investment for construction of a transport unit;
  K_i = additional (for a certain stage) capital investment in the reinforcement of the throughput;
  t = the period of expenditure under consideration.

The full unit adjusted expenditure (in dynamics) is determined in the following way:

$$Z_f = \frac{\sum_1^t Z_t(P_t)(1+e)^{-t}}{\sum_1^t P_t(1+e)^{-t}}$$

in which Z_t = the general expenditure, corresponding to the final level of transport output:
P_t = final level of transport output.

The unit adjusted incremental expenditure (in dynamics) is

$$Z_{incr} = \frac{\sum_1^t [Z_t(P_t + \Delta P) - Z_t^0(P_0)](1+e)^{-t}}{\sum_1^t \Delta P(1+e)^{-t}}$$

in which P = the level of initial transport output;
ΔP = the increase of transport output which determines the quantity of incremental volume of traffic;
Z_t^0 = general expenditure for the initial level of transport output.

Since we consider only freight traffic in the frame of the main transport activity, we do not take into account all the expenditure, but only that which is connected with freight traffic. Expenditure related to all kinds of traffic is divided so as to specify that part which relates to freight traffic only. It is also necessary to consider other effects, for example, indirect effects on the users of freight services, terminal costs, the suitability of various modes for journeys of different lengths, and the relative traffic efficiency of the modes. This is measured as shown in Table 1.1.

TABLE 1.1

Modes of transport	Unit operating cost	Unit capital investment	kop/10t/km adjusted expenditure (E–0, 10)
Railways	2.57	19.6	4.53
Pipelines	0.75	9.2	1.67
Maritime	2.58	16.6	4.20
Roads	49.43	70.13	56.44
Inland waterways	2.55	36.3	6.18

The change in importance of different transport modes is connected first of all with the further increase of the specialised modes for oil, oil products, and natural gas delivery, especially pipelines. The share of these modes of transport now amounts to one-third of total fuel goods traffic. Due to the opening-up of the oil and gas region in the north of West Siberia a powerful system of pipelines to pump oil and gas from the Tumen region to European and eastern regions of the country is rapidly being formed.

Pipeline transport is in practice the one mode of transport capable of providing the delivery of large amounts of fuel from this almost inaccessible region, and it is also highly efficient. Capital investment and pumping costs for pipelines are 2–2.5 times lower than for railways with analogous capacity. The process of pumping can easily be automated and therefore causes a sharp decrease in the need for service staff. This is extremely important in the conditions of North Siberia with its sparse population. The effectiveness of pipeline transport increases especially with the introduction of large-diameter pipes. The specific location of the Tumen oil and gas deposits creates favourable preconditions for large concentrations of oil and gas flows. With the fivefold increase of pipe diameter (for example from 200 up to 1000 mm) the throughput increases 45 times and the unit capital investment and operating expenditure decrease 7 and 3.5 times accordingly.

The increasing use of maritime transport corresponds with the stable trend of foreign trade development; and that of road transport corresponds with the increase of transportation of building materials, agricultural and other perishable goods, small consignments and the development of non-transhipment traffic. At the same time, the share of railways and inland waterways in the total traffic is gradually being reduced, while in absolute terms.

The modal split of traffic is aimed at the relief of the USSR railways which are now reaching their maximum load. In 1977 the traffic density (per 1 km of route) amounted to 24.0 million t/km and 2.3 million passenger/km. Besides switching goods to a reasonable extent to other modes of transport (pipelines, trucks (short-run) and inland waterways) the limitation (and in some directions even reduction) of traffic density will be achieved by large-scale construction of new railway track. During the tenth Five-year Plan period approximately 8000 kilometres of new railway lines and second tracks will be built and put into operation; approximately 5000 kilometres will be electrified. The changes shown in the relative indices in Table 1.2 occurred while the traffic volume in absolute terms tripled.

TABLE 1.2

Modes of transport	Percentages	
	1960	1977
Railways	79.7	59.1
Pipelines	2.7	16.4
Maritime	7.0	13.7
Road	5.2	6.6
Inland waterways	5.3	4.1
Air (rounded)	0.1	0.1
Total	100.0	100.0

III DEVELOPMENTS IN FREIGHT TRANSPORT

The freight structure of traffic by the main modes of transport has undergone considerable changes. In particular, the share of coal and timber moved by inland water transport. Simultaneously the share of finished articles, ore and building materials is growing. The provision for traffic in regions with already developed economic structures is being solved by complex development of all (or most) transport modes on the basis of forming a "frame" of the most important trunk routes with high throughput in combination with a ramified network of local roads, providing intraregional traffic and serving as access roads to the trunk routes.

The problem of constructing roads in the North, Siberia and the Far East for the speedy development of productive forces in these regions is becoming more and more important. A typical example of such an approach is the formation of the system of transport routes in the oil- and gas-producing regions of the West Siberian plain. Inland water transport played a pioneering role here. Pipes, equipment and facilities for the construction of oil and gas pipelines were delivered by ship. The pipelines became the second mode of transport in the north of Western Siberia.

The railways—the universal 'all-weather' and mass mode of transport— have reached the Surgut regions in the last few years. A different way of opening up new regions has become possible with the creation of the Baikal–Amur trunk railway. Here the formation of economic complexes has begun simultaneously with the construction of the railway which provides stable all-year transport connections for a vast area and considerably reduces the time taken to obtain access to rich natural resources, and provides a second outlet to the Pacific coast.

Besides the utilisation of traditional transport modes the introduction of new modes of transport is planned. Thus for the reduction of short-run railway traffic volume it is planned to introduce uninterrupted modes of transport such as container pneumatic pipelines, hydraulic slurry-pipelines, conveyors, rope-ways and others. For large coal flows slurry-pipeline transport may be used for long distances as well.

Vast areas of the North and North-East cannot be provided with a network of constantly operating routes in a short time. Therefore motor-sledges and aerosleighs are used, and in future air-cushion modes will be developed. Their specific pressure on the ground is approximately four times lower than that of caterpillar cross-country vehicles, and so their sphere of implementation is much wider. Non-self-propelled platforms on air-cushions with a carrying capacity of 40 and 60 tons are already developed and have undergone operational tests. The platforms are transported behind tractors in marshes and tundra and carry heavy equipment for boring machines, pipe equipment and building materials. Amphibious hovercraft, for operation over water and ice, will also be developed.

Despite the activisation of work on the introduction of new modes of transport the main trend of increasing transport potential remains the intensive development of a network of routes by which the increase of throughput considerably exceeds the increase of the length of the network itself owing to electrification, centralisation controllers of and automatisation of movement control.

Such methods are typical for all traditional modes of transport and correspond to the course adopted by the USSR of intensification of every kind of production. Preferential development of the most progressive modes of transport, and the growth of capacity of means of trans-shipping at 'junction' points, where goods are trans-shipped from one mode of transport to the other, allow the state to rationalise the modal split and transport-economic links to accelerate the process of delivery of goods from a shipper to a consignee, to reduce the national economic expenditure for traffic, and altogether to increase the effectiveness and quality of the united transport system's performance.

2 Comparing the Efficiency of Western European Rail and Road Services

FRITZ VOIGT

I INTRODUCTION

This paper compares the efficiency of road and rail services from the point of view of the whole economy rather than of narrow financial preoccupations. It would be desirable to quantify the full macroeconomic costs and benefits of modes of transport, but this is not possible. Instead, we use a number of different indicators of quantitative and qualitative aspects of efficiency, basing the analysis on cross-section data for the year 1976, for the nine states of the EEC. These data are given in full in a large table as an Appendix to the paper. We will discuss in turn the results of the analysis of (a) traffic volumes, (b) networks, (c) vehicles, (d) quality of service (speed, capacity, origin-destination matching, reliability, frequency, safety and comfort), (e) energy, (f) environment, and (g) demand factors. Lastly we draw some conclusions for future development.

II TRAFFIC VOLUMES

Traffic volumes are given in tons, ton/kilometres, and passenger/kilometres, from which the relative importance of transport modes can be assessed (though without full consideration of economic values). In all the countries the three indicators agree in showing much lower traffic volumes on rail than road, except for goods traffic in

Belgium and Luxembourg where road and rail are closer because of the pattern of heavy industrial traffic. Average haul length on rail is two to six times as great as road (again with the exception of Luxembourg). All the countries except Denmark and Ireland have shown a shift from rail to road from 1970 to 1976. Similar patterns are seen in the passenger statistics. The strong relationship between mode used and journey distance is seen in Figure 2.1.

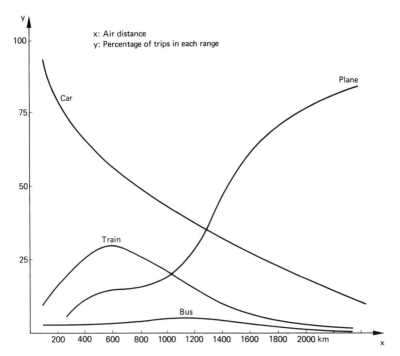

Figure 2.1   Modal distribution of trips by trip length in passenger transport

x: Air distance.
y: Percentage of trips in each range.
Source: *The Future of European Passenger Transport*, (Organisation for Economic Co-operation and Development (OECD), Paris, 1977), s. p. 139.

III NETWORKS

Traffic volume divided by the network length gives a measure of the density of traffic. This generally shows a distinct advantage of rail over road, with a much more concentrated utilisation of the system. One exception is Italy, probably due to the relatively small rail network.

IV VEHICLES

Productivity indicators are shown, based on motor vehicles, whole trains, passenger coaches, goods wagons, and utilisation of offered seat/kilometre and ton/kilometre capacity. The results show advantages of efficiency of trains over motor vehicles (and buses over cars), but this potential is not fully used because of low levels of demand.

V QUALITY OF SERVICE

Time-losses due to loading, shunting, collection and delivery offset the railway's fast line-haul speeds. As shown in Figure 2.2, door-to-door

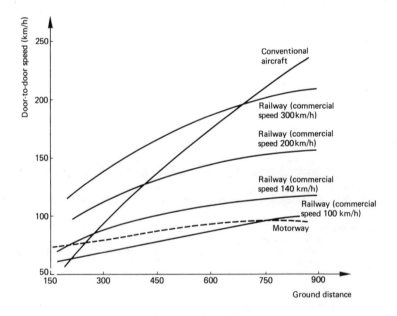

Figure 2.2   Door-to-door speed on ground distance for various means of passenger transport (km/h)

Source: *The Future European Passenger Transport*, Organisation for Economic Co-operation and Development.

speed for rail is better than road only for journeys of over 750 km (though if rail speeds were increased to 140/h, the advantage would obtain at journeys of over 150 km: speeds of 149 km/h are now being planned in at least six countries).

The ability of rail and road services to cater flexibly for mass capacity within a short time period is also an important consideration: seat and tonnage capacities clearly favour rail transport, though for short passenger trips the indicators are higher for road. This can also apply for the more valuable, less bulky types of goods traffic, which are growing. Clearly road networks are usually very much more efficient at closely linking origins and final destinations, as shown by indicators of network density per unit area or per 100 population.

Reliability (measured by variations from planned journey time) is good for scheduled railway services and long-distance passenger trips, but worse for rail goods traffic. Traffic congestion and the effects of weather affect the reliability of road services.

Considerations of frequency can favour private road vehicles (which are available at any time), though this will depend strongly on the density of the railway timetable, where considerable improvements are possible. Railway services are considerably safer than road transport, though possibly causing more damage to goods because of vibration. Comfort is important, though difficult to measure and only indirect and ambiguous evidence is available in the indicators shown.

VI ENERGY

Energy efficiency will become increasingly important towards the end of the twentieth century; railways are much less dependent on oil products, and also several times more efficient in measures of output per energy input.

VII ENVIRONMENT

It is not easy to judge whether road or rail has the overall advantage in the absorption of land-area: this will depend on the specific circumstances and type of traffic. Also, the nuisance effect of road and rail noise shows different patterns in the countries studied. However, there is a very clear advantage to rail concerning air pollution.

VIII DEMAND FACTORS

Although many of the macroeconomic efficiency indicators tend to favour rail, effective economic demand has tended to be influenced more by the flexibility and personal advantages of private road transport. For goods traffic, an important trend is the increasing amount of high-value and refined goods, which are not so sensitive to transport costs and again are greatly attracted by the flexibility and door-to-door convenience of road transport. Thus the demand factors, influenced by private costs, tend to favour road transport, at high social costs in energy, environment and safety.

IX FUTURE DEVELOPMENT

Consideration of the social costs of road traffic requires:

(1) that these social costs must be considerably reduced;
(2) that the modal split should change in favour of railways.

Efforts have been made in FRG and elsewhere to achieve these effects, though limited by the bureaucratic inflexibility of railway authorities, the commercial competitiveness of road haulage authorities, and tax concessions favouring company-owned traffic.

Future development will depend on extensive cybernetic or automatic systems to reduce railway staff costs, new capital investments, and possible new technologies (e.g. magnetic suspension). These should be evaluated by reference to the long-term optimal allocation of resources in the whole economy.

Appendix: Indicators of Road and Rail Efficiency in Nine West European Countries, 1976

	Belgium	Denmark	France	Germany (FR)	Great Britain	Ireland	Italy	Luxembourg	Netherlands
Rail goods 10^6 *tons*	62	8	235	314	178	4	53	15	19
10^6 ton/kms	6834	1892	69930	60606	20448	596	16988	624	2831
passengers 10^6	187	100	643	965	709	14	390	11	172
pass/kms 10^6	7575	3300	50834	37216	28608	788	39118	240	8218
Road goods 10^6 *tons*	307	237	1645	2183	1516	–	1037	15	337
10^6 ton/kms	9300	9850	92500	103402	95600	–	66708	684	16700
pass/kms 10^6									
public	9874	–	2500	67373	53000	–	48259	–	11400
private	46661	39700	390000	488700	359000	–	314562	–	108700
Rail Network kms									
passenger	2926	1982	24377	23904	14410	1763	15528	229	2479
goods	3983	1943	33981	28175	17091	2010	16143	274	2832
Road Network kms	114814	66515	795777	469568	345532	89006	291864	4465	86354
Rail 10^3 passengers/km	63.91	50.45	26.38	40.37	49.20	7.94	25.12	48.03	69.38
10^6 pass kms/km	2.59	1.67	2.09	1.56	1.99	0.45	2.52	1.05	3.32
Road 10^6 pass kms/km	0.49	–	0.52	1.18	1.19	–	1.24	–	1.39
Rail 10^3 tons/km	15.57	4.12	6.92	11.15	10.41	2.00	3.23	54.74	6.71
10^6 ton kms/km	1.72	0.97	2.06	2.15	1.20	0.30	1.05	2.28	1.00

APPENDIX—(Continued)

	Belgium	Denmark	France	Germany (FR)	Great Britain	Ireland	Italy	Luxembourg	Netherlands
Road 10³ tons/km	2.67	3.56	2.07	4.65	4.35	–	3.55	3.36	3.90
10⁶ ton kms/km	0.08	0.15	0.12	0.22	0.28	–	0.23	0.15	0.19
Rail av. length of travel av. journey length	110.7	248.3	300.9	195.4	121.0	168.3	323.5	39.8	152.5
av. journey length	40.5	33.1	79.1	38.6	40.4	57.9	100.3	21.2	47.9
Road av. length of travel av. journey length	30.3	41.6	56.2	47.4	63.1	–	64.3	45.6	49.6
av. journey length	–	–	–	19.4	–	–	–	–	–
% pass kms by rail 1970	15	7	13	8	9	–	11	–	8
1976	12	–	11	6	7	–	10	–	6
% ton kms by rail 1970	47	–	52	48	23	–	25	–	22
1976	42	16	43	52	18	–	20	48	16
Utilisation, Rail									
Pass kms/pass carriage kms	–	18.57	26.63	18.32	–	–	28.42	30.38	22.67
Pass kms/seat kms	–	0.30	0.39	0.27	–	–	0.41	0.35	0.36
Pass kms/train kms	115.7	89.4	183.9	97.0	83.5	123.1	178.4	82.8	87.5
Ton kms/wagon kms	–	9.48	13.23	10.11	–	7.33	8.49	–	–
Ton kms/ton kms offered	–	0.37	0.35	0.32	–	–	0.31	–	–
Ton kms/train kms	325.4	249.0	340.6	324.4	243.1	156.8	292.9	445.7	206.6
Utilisation, Road									
Pass kms/veh. kms cars	1.3	1.8	1.9	1.7	1.8	–	1.9	–	2.1
buses	24.7	–	13.9	23.2	15.1	–	25.4	–	22.8
total	1.6	–	2.0	1.9	2.0	–	2.2	–	2.3

Pass kms/seat kms cars	0.33	0.45	0.47	0.41	0.45	–	0.48	–	0.52
buses	0.69	–	0.36	0.53	0.41	–	0.57	–	0.54
total	0.37	–	0.46	0.43	0.44	–	0.49	–	0.52
Ton kms/veh kms	2.21	2.59	2.37	3.65	2.24	–	2.64	–	4.91
Ton kms/ton kms offered	0.53	0.51	0.87	0.75	–	–	0.69	–	–
Rail capacity: pass seats 10³	295	104	1069	1388	1082	22	903	8	122
seats/carriage	86.3	62.5	68.0	68.2	65.4	64.5	69.9	87.3	62.6
seats-kms 10⁹	–	11.0	130.3	137.8	–	–	95.4	0.7	22.8
wagons 10³ tons	1645	240	6958	8721	3864	95	2959	119	379
tons/wagon	34.0	25.7	36.7	30.4	20.7	14.9	27.7	34.7	28.2
ton kms offered 10⁹	–	5.1	199.8	189.4	–	–	54.8	–	–
Road capacity: car seats 10³	10800	5400	64900	76700	56200	2200	66600	500	15100
bus seats 10³	712	305	1947	2766	4162	–	2109	–	423
seat/bus	35.8	48.4	38.9	43.1	36.8	–	44.4	–	41.5
10⁹ car seat kms offered	140.4	87.6	832.0	1180.0	802.0	–	649.6	–	209.6
10⁹ bus seat kms offered	14.3	15.5	70.0	125.0	128.8	–	84.4	–	20.8
vehicles 10³ tons	1109	682	6251	6154	–	–	2870	–	1975
tons/vehicle	5.1	2.1	2.8	4.4	–	–	–	–	5.1
ton kms offered	16.9	19.2	106.3	138.5	–	–	96.7	–	–
Network density km/km²									
rail passenger	0.095	0.046	0.045	0.096	0.059	0.025	0.052	0.088	0.060
rail goods	0.131	0.045	0.062	0.113	0.070	0.029	0.054	0.105	0.069
rail 2 + track lines	0.084	0.017	0.028	0.049	0.052	0.007	0.017	0.062	0.038
road total	3.764	1.543	1.455	1.889	1.416	1.266	0.969	1.717	2.096
road motorway + main	0.392	0.108	0.060	0.156	0.065	0.037	0.165	0.342	1.296

APPENDIX (Continued)

	Belgium	Denmark	France	Germany (FR)	Great Britain	Ireland	Italy	Luxembourg	Netherlands
Network density km/1000 pdp									
rail passenger	0.299	0.389	0.461	0.389	0.257	0.551	0.276	0.572	0.180
rail goods	0.406	0.381	0.642	0.458	0.305	0.628	0.287	0.685	0.205
rail 2 + track lines	0.262	0.146	0.288	0.199	0.227	0.152	0.091	0.403	0.113
road total	11.715	13.042	15.403	7.635	6.170	27.814	5.193	11.162	6.258
road motorway + main	1.218	0.911	0.618	0.623	0.283	0.813	0.886	2.225	3.868
SAFETY									
Rail injuries	90	—	249	695	238	2	212	2	88
deaths	57	—	194	298	115	5	152	2	120
pass kms + ton kms/ injury 10^6	160.1	—	485.0	140.8	206.1	692.0	264.7	432.0	125.6
pass kms + ton kms/ death 10^6	252.8	—	622.5	328.3	426.6	276.8	369.1	432.0	92.1
Road injuries	84063	19.599	347745	480581	333103	7798	217976	2443	63304
deaths	2488	857	13577	14820	6570	525	8927	100	2432
pass km + ton km/ injury 10^6	0.783	—	1.469	1.372	1.524	—	1.971	—	2.161
pass km + ton km/ death 10^6	26.461	—	37.379	44.499	77.260	—	48.116	—	56.250
ENERGY									
Rail tonnes coal equivalent 10^3	401.6	173.6	2268.2	2790.0	1782.7	45.8	1276.3	25.4	312.2

Road tonnes coal equivalent 10³	5938	3121	34410	40130	32139	1524	24005	396	8090
Pass km + ton km/energy 10³									
rail	35.9	29.9	53.2	35.1	27.5	30.2	44.0	34.0	35.4
road	11.1	—	14.8	16.4	15.8	—	17.9	—	16.9
% rail energy from oil	48.8	81.6	31.0	28.8	58.5	100.0	15.6	44.9	18.3
NOISE									
Persons 'afflicted' 10⁶									
road	1.4	0.8	8.4	10.4	9.6	0.4	7.8	0.05	2.3
rail	0.24	0.16	1.7	2.22	2.09	0.08	1.73	0.01	0.48
Pass km + ton kms/afflicted									
road	47.0	—	60.4	63.4	52.9	—	55.1	—	59.5
rail	60.0	35.5	71.0	44.1	23.5	17.3	32.4	86.4	23.0

Sources for Appendix
Statistique internationale des chemins de fer, 1976 (UIC, Paris, 1978).
World Road Statistics 1973–77 (IRF, Geneva, 1978).
Annual Bulletin of Transport Statistics for Europe, E.C.E. (United Nations, New York, 1977).
Statistisches Jahrbuch-Verkehr, 1976 (Luxembourg, 1978).
Verkehr in Zahlen 1977 (DIW, Berlin, 1977).
Compendio di Statistiche sui Transporti, 1975 (Rome, 1978).
Krell, K. (1977) Techniche und medizinische Probleme der Umweltbelastung durch den Verkehr, in *Verkehr und Umwelt* (Koln, 1977).

3 Changes in Freight Traffic among the Modes of Transport Past and Future

DUDLEY F. PEGRUM

I INTRODUCTION

The allocation of freight traffic movements among the modes, and the changes in it, involves the respective roles of the different agencies in terms of types of traffic, distance of hauls, technical interactions or connections (i.e. intermodal traffic), the volume of traffic for each, and the revenues obtained. This paper is concerned with analysing the development of the various modes in the United States and their future trends. Geographical, economic and political contrasts between different countries mean that the pattern of freight transport in the United States will not be reflected precisely elsewhere. However, the use of modern transport technology has resulted in comparable patterns of development in the United States and other advanced, industrialised countries.

The history of transportation might be written in terms of changing technology. However, an examination of technological developments and the quantitative shifts in traffic allocation alone, would give a totally inadequate basis for understanding what has taken place and what future trends may be. Devices may be technologically possible, yet economically, politically, or socially unfeasible or unacceptable. The economic potential of the different modes depends upon the relative economic efficiency of the technology utilised by them. Institutional arrangements, however, have had a profound effect on the course of development of the modern freight-transport system of every country and the changing interrelationships among the modes.

Although this paper is confined to freight transportation, the influence of passenger traffic on transport development should be noted in passing. The prime movers of intercity passenger traffic today, in the United States, as well as in many other countries, are the private automobile and aeroplane. Both of these modes of transport developed initially as means of moving people. Heavy government participation in the provision of infrastructure facilities has had two effects: (a) the railroads have lost their passenger traffic and have suffered heavy financial losses in the transition, (b) the demands for highway facilities have provided the infrastructure for intercity freight trucking. Whether there will be a similar development in air transport remains to be seen.

Water transport in the international area has not been subject to significant competition with other modes. Ocean shipping still provides the means for moving all but a very small amount of high-value and very light shipments. Changes in the technology of shipping and in the methods of handling cargo have not been intermodal in nature and therefore have not affected the allocation of traffic among the modes. Air transport, to date, has had little impact on international water traffic. It seems to be unlikely that there will be any important change in this situation for many years to come. Discussion of interrelationships among the modes and shifts in the provision of long-distance freight movements by them can be confined, therefore, to inland traffic.

II MODAL TRENDS IN LONG-DISTANCE FREIGHT TRANSPORTATION

The years following the Napoleonic wars witnessed the application of mechanical power to land and water transport. This development made the railroads the prime agency for inland freight movement, although inland water transport benefited materially from steam power. The status of long-distance freight transportation remained this way until approximately 1920. Meanwhile, new technology which was to provide the automobile, pipelines and the aeroplane rapidly developed to the point that, in the immediately ensuing years, the five modes that constitute the present system brought about a radical change in the entire structure. Thus, 1920 may be taken as a watershed for the emergence of the modern transport system. The new developments occurred everywhere but most rapidly and dramatically in the United States.

Some idea of the developments in freight traffic may be gained from

TABLE 3.1   VOLUME OF INTERCITY FREIGHT TRAFFIC (Billion ton/miles)

	1920	1929	1954	1974
Total freight traffic	500	575	1124	2439
Railroad freight traffic	414	450	556	852

Table 3.1 and Figures 3.1 and 3.2. Growth in total freight has been accompanied by a continuous trend against the railroads, while motor and water carrier shares have remained constant for nearly twenty years and oil pipelines have taken up the railroad decline.

The change in the relative positions of the modes in the movement of freight would not, of itself, present any unique problem. The loss of the dominant role by the railroads, however, has been accompanied by a change in the composition of the traffic. This has deprived them of much of their high-grade tonnage. Some of this has gone to petroleum pipelines which now transport over 40 per cent of the ton/miles of petroleum products. The greater part of the shift, however, has gone to the trucking industry: motor carrier revenues were twice that of the railroads in 1958 and three times in 1976; $56 billion and $18.6 billion respectively in 1976 (US billion). It may be noted that the railroads hauled 35.3 per cent of the revenue ton/miles while the trucks carried only 24.4 per cent, yet received three times the revenue for this.

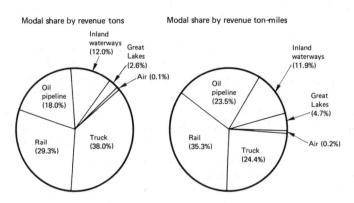

Figure. 3.1   Modal shares of freight market

Source: Reproduced from *A Prospectus for Change in the Freight Railroad Industry*, US Department of Transportation, Washington, DC, October 1978, p. 15.

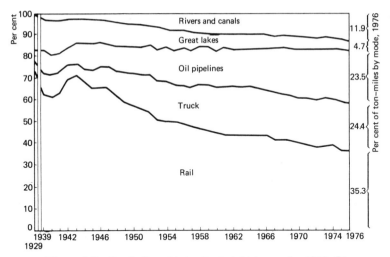

Figure 3.2   Ton/miles of intercity freight by mode, 1929–76

Source: Reproduced from *A Prospectus for Change in the Freight Railroad Industry*, US Department of Transportation, Washington, DC, 1978, p. 44.

The altered position of the modes in long-distance freight traffic is also reflected in the composition of that traffic. The railroads have become restricted primarily to bulk commodities, such as coal, grain, chemicals and metals. In contrast, trucks are carrying lighter, high-grade goods such as textiles, furniture and fabricated metal products. Over 90 per cent of shipments moving 1500 miles or more are transported by rail. The greater part of the transport market, however, is for shorter distances, 73.6 per cent of shipments of manufactures moving under 500 miles, 59.5 per cent of these weighing less than 6000 pounds. (See Figure 3.3.) The railroads are thus caught between the upper millstone of motor carrier competition everywhere for traffic of 500 miles or less, even on bulk commodities, and the lower one of severe competition for bulk traffic by oil pipelines and inland waterways.

III REASONS FOR THE TRENDS

(1) Technological development is the most obvious factor in the change in intermodal relationships. The development of the inland waterways has led to intense competition with the railroads in the eastern half of the country, especially with mechanical

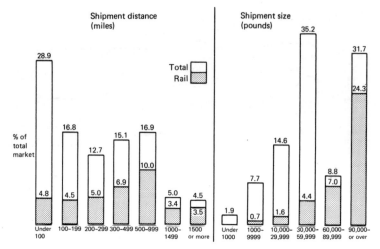

Figure 3.3   Rail freight market for intercity manufactures, 1972

Source: Reproduced from *A Prospectus for Change in the Freight Railroad Industry*, US Department of Transportation, Washington, DC, 1978, p. 18.

improvements which make tows of over 40,000 tons possible. An extensive network of pipelines over practically the whole country has diverted much of the oil from the railroads. The greatest change has been in motor trucking. The development of a high-grade system of national highways has given the trucks access to every important freight traffic point in the country.

(2) A second significant factor in the change in modal shares of freight traffic is demographic. The railroad network was built to serve a population distribution which has since changed. Not only has there been a large reduction in the rural population but there has also been a shift in population, and to a greater extent in manufacturing, from the Northeast and Northcentral regions to the South and West.

(3) A third factor of major importance affecting the trends in modal transport interrelationships has been public provision of the infrastructure for motor and water agencies. For freight transport the impact, to date, has been on rail, truck and water traffic. Public investment in highway and water transport facilities has provided the infrastructure that has made the growth of these modes possible, at the same time that it has resulted in unequal competition for bulk traffic by the oil pipelines, and inland

waterways which operate in much of the area east of the Rocky Mountains.

Total government expenditures on domestic transportation since the First World War have been estimated to be $522 billion by 1976. Total highway expenditures by the federal government from 1952 to 1976 amounted to $93 billion, by state and local authorities $288 billion, for a grand total of $381 billion. Federal receipts from user charges have amounted to $85 billion while state and local governments have collected $217 billion. Public investment has provided a highway system without which long-distance freight transport by truck would be very different from what it is today. The portion of the infrastructure expenditures which trucking should bear is a matter of severe controversy, but there seems to be a general consensus that it is not enough to equalise the cost burdens of rail and truck freight movements.

Total government expenditure on waterways from 1947 to 1974 amounted to $18.7 billion. No charges have as yet been imposed for the use of these facilities except for tolls on the St Lawrence Seaway.

(4) A fourth major influence on the development of the modes and the division of traffic among them has been regulation by the federal government. The present pattern of regulation was established by the Transportation Act of 1920 by which the railroads became completely regulated and were required to serve as common carriers only. The only important development in regulation and its administration after that date and down to 1976, was extension to cover common carriers by motor, water and air. (Pipelines for liquid products of the oil industry are controlled by the Interstate Commerce Commission if they provide transportation for producers other than the pipeline owners. The effect of the regulation has not been of significance on long-distance freight movements.)

The railroads are subject to detailed regulation on rates and rate discrimination, issue of securities, consolidation, abandonment of lines and/or services and freight car service. Common carriers by truck operate under quite similar regulatory controls, but only about 44 per cent of the intercity traffic (including contract carriers) is federally regulated. Transportation by trunk route of agricultural commodities is exempt from federal regulation. Less than 10 per cent of water transport is subject to regulation.

It is clear that the railroads enjoy much less freedom of action than the other modes. However, the effect of the restrictions in quantitative terms is a matter of vigorous controversy. It is almost impossible to give a meaningful quantitative picture of what the intermodal relationships would be in the absence of present policies. The railroads want a thorough-going relaxation of the controls under which they now operate, but they do not support similar treatment for the other modes. Common carriers by truck do not want a reduction of regulation of themselves, but rather advocate an extension of it to other trucking traffic. They also oppose reduction of regulation of the railroads. The water carriers seek the elimination of limitations on bulk commodity traffic but oppose steps toward deregulation of their competitors, especially the railroads. Thus, while there is widespread dissatisfaction with current regulatory policies there is little consensus among the modes on what should be done about it. It is evident, however, that present regulation does impose substantial limits on competition in transportation.

IV CRITERIA FOR AN ECONOMICAL TRANSPORT SYSTEM

A discussion of future trends in the interrelationships in long-distance freight transport among the modes must give careful consideration to the objectives of public policy and the means of achieving them. The amount of economic resources necessary to meet the transportation requirements of a modern industrialised society forms such a significant part of Gross National Product as to demand careful attention to economising on the provision of it. Its drain upon energy resources also gives additional emphasis to this issue. The estimated transportation bill for the economy of the United States has amounted, approximately, to 20 per cent of the GNP for each of the last twenty years. One-half of this is for freight, about 60 per cent of which is long-distance traffic. However, long-distance freight movements, and the other aspects of transportation activity in the western industrialised countries, are so inextricably intertwined, particularly in the United States, that separation of these in terms of national policy presents some very complex problems.

The transport requirements of an industrialised economy are of such magnitude that it needs the cheapest possible way of meeting them adequately. This means that it must economise in the allocation of resources to transportation as well as among the modes. If transport is to be economical, the resources devoted to it must be more valuable than if they are used elsewhere. Resource allocation among the modes must meet the same criterion. (It should be noted that what constitutes the most valuable uses depends upon the source of decision-making. If market forces are permitted to decide, the user or consumer makes the decision. If a central government controls all the facilities, it makes the decision.) If each of the modes does not meet the test of covering all of the economic costs applicable to it, then there is an uneconomical allocation of resources among them.

This abstract formulation provides the theoretical basis for an economical transport system but application of it to the real world is fraught with extraordinary complications. The total cost of the railroads by virtue of the technology can be ascertained with reasonable accuracy, and therefore the total cost of freight transport, where passenger traffic does not offer a severe problem. Given freedom of action on service and line offerings or abandonments, management can use the market place to price the traffic and thereby find the railroads' appropriate role in the transport system. This, however, assumes that the competition which they face from the other modes has to meet similar standards, an assumption which at the present time seems to be a little more than heroic for truck and water transport.

Automotive transport is the mode that presents the severest challenge today to the development of an economical transport system. This is because the infrastructure is a multiple-use undertaking provided by public investment. The intercity highways are an integral part of the total roadway system affording facilities for long-distance traffic as well as for terminal, originating and through freight. It might be possible to obtain the total costs for the infrastructure comparable to that of the railroads, and to assess that total on automotive traffic. This would present serious problems, however, particularly with the inclusion of the urban areas. A more workable approach would be to ascertain the costs of the intercity highways and to place the burden of these directly on the users. This, however, would be only the beginning of the task of equalising competition with the railroads.

Intercity highways are multiple-use projects. They are used by both passenger and freight vehicles. A considerable part of the costs of these highways is traceable to each category. A large part is simply not traceable either practically or theoretically. The allocation of the burden of these costs will probably have to be arbitrary for some time to come. Any assignment of joint or non-traceable costs between freight and passenger traffic is unavoidably arbitrary by the very nature of those costs; recovery of them on an economical basis is a matter of market price.

Intercity freight traffic has now risen to the point that some method of separating it from other traffic may have to be devised before long. If this is done, the burden on freight traffic will rise. Just how much intercity freight traffic by trucks would move this way if they had to support their highways completely is not readily discernible. Perhaps the lack of highway development in those countries where the passenger car is still a distinct luxury offers a clue. In any case, the enormous use of the passenger automobile in the western industrialised countries has provided the major impetus for the growth of automotive manufacture and transport in the automotive age since 1920. It has also created a major problem for the development of an economical system for the movement of freight.

Waterways present a situation that is very similar to that of the highways. They are commonly constructed in connection with such other projects as hydro-electric power, flood control, reclamation and navigation. Each of these purposes has its own directly traceable costs. A considerable part of the investment in these undertakings, however, involves joint or non-traceable costs. The costs of the infrastructure attributable to water transport and the operation of it constitute the minimum burden which belongs to this mode of transport. Whether the contribution by the users can or should be more than this to equalise competition among the modes is a matter of pricing policy – not cost allocation. If water transport can make a contribution to the joint costs, it is not easy to see why the other uses of the total project should be required to carry all of them. If these other uses are made to do so, they will be shouldering part of the transport costs of the country under some other guise – probably through general taxation.

V OUTLOOK FOR THE FUTURE

Trends in the relative positions of the different modes in intercity freight from 1920 to date are clearly portrayed by the traffic statistics. The railroads have suffered a relative decline, and may be an absolute one. Pipelines have become the major mode for petroleum and its products, while waterways have had a significant revival for the movement of heavy commodities. Many ingenious, and a goodly number of dis-ingenuous models and scenarios have been developed to forecast future trends. Too frequently these are based upon assumptions which will result in the conclusions which the forecasters desire. In any case they cannot evaluate in a meaningful way the unravelling of the unknowns and variables which will be crucial to future developments. All that can be done in an objective way is to point out the factors that have to be taken into consideration and the impact they may have. The relative significance of these forces and how they will be permitted to exert themselves, even for a comparatively short time ahead, is literally impossible to foretell.

Developments over the last half-century in transport and in intercity freight transport in the western industrialised world clearly indicate that we are now in an automotive age. The motor vehicle, where public supply of highways has permitted and encouraged its use, has become the dominant means of transport for passenger and freight traffic both intercity and local. Its flexibility, mobility and adaptability are unmatched by any other mode. In freight traffic, trucks are very similar to the tramp steamer. They can, and do, go wherever the market is. The other transporters of intercity freight can offer no such accommodation. The prospects of any major change in the role of the motor vehicle in the foreseeable future are not very great.

Pipelines are likely to maintain their position for the movement of petroleum products. They may become important for other bulk products if slurry lines can be developed on an economical basis. Waterways, where they are available, will probably continue to haul heavy intercity traffic.

This leaves us with the question of the future of the railroads, which seem to be in a precarious position everywhere. A good deal of criticism has been levelled at management and labour in the industry. Some of this is undoubtedly valid but the railroads have faced a major problem of readjustment to competition from the new technologies. It is scarcely surprising that they have had such difficulty in adjusting to the new situation, especially when their competitors have been supported by such extensive public investment and aid. The prospects of technological developments that will tip the scale somewhat towards the railroads are not very promising for the future – although intermodal exchange may be of some help. The future seems to rest on other matters – energy and public policy.

Transportation is the largest single user of energy in the economy. The critical issue regarding energy at the present time lies in the petroleum industry. This is stimulating the production of coal which will provide increased revenue for the railroads that are able to haul it. However, this is unlikely to divert traffic which has gone to the trucks. Furthermore, even coal traffic may face new competition from slurry pipelines and more efficient long-distance transmission of electricity, especially where the sources of coal are located at great distances from the area of use. Increased fuel costs may have some effects on the very long-distance freight traffic of the trucks but this is not likely to bring about any significant modification of the current relative positions of the modes.

The rapid technological developments of the last half-century seem to have reached a point of relative stability, such that major break-throughs are not likely to occur for the next decade at least. The most important factor influencing trends in this period will therefore be public policy. This will be concerned with two major issues: (1) the freedom of action accorded the modes to compete for the available intercity freight; and (2) the problem of calculation and assessment of the economic costs of the modes whose infrastructure is provided by public funds.

Freedom of action to compete for intercity traffic requires an equalisation of regulatory rules, such that the enterprises in each of the modes are able to obtain the traffic that they are economically most fit to haul. Competition of this sort has had only limited opportunity to exert itself in most countries in the last fifty years. In the western European countries truck competition has been restricted by policies designed to preserve the assumed appropriate role of the rail and water carriers. In those countries where intercity transport is publicly supplied, intercity freight is allocated according to centralised plans which have not notably encouraged highway development and motor transport. In the United States restrictions on freedom of competition have been most severe on railroads who have been required to act as total common carriers under complete regulation. Without doubt this has been a serious handicap on the ability of the railroads to adapt their plans to changing conditions, to adopt effectively competitive pricing-policies and to attract investment for modernisation. Federal authorities now seem to be aware of the distortions in public regulation, but what steps will be taken to correct them is not clear at the present time. What would be the effect of affording the opportunity for thorough-going com-petition among the modes is something that cannot be ascertained until that competition has emerged. Of itself, however, it is not likely to be decisive on the direction of trends.

Allocation of intercity traffic among the modes on the basis of economic efficiency requires that each of them be assessed with its full economic costs. Calculating the total for each, at least within workable limits, is perhaps not too difficult a task. Ascertainment of those costs for particular users or groups of users and recovery from those users is another matter, however. Even though more accurate cost calculations for the principal intercity highways may be obtained, the problem of the other parts of the highway system still remain, in addition to that of the urban terminal areas where passenger traffic and local and intercity freight are inextricably intermingled. In those countries where highways are constructed primarily, or almost exclusively, for freight purposes, these complexities are not present. If, however, these countries reach the stage where the passenger automobile becomes the prime means of personal travel, they will face the same difficulties. Even now they face somewhat analogous issues with regard to the development and use of multipurpose inland waterways.

VI CONCLUSION

The dominance of the motor vehicle in the movement of intercity freight in the United States and the western industrialised world is clearly established. The railroads predominate in a large amount of the long-distance bulk traffic but they have lost the rest. Intermodalism may help them regain some of this, but how much is open to question. The real issue is how much they can retain of what they have and whether even this will continue to sustain them as economical undertakings. It cannot do so unless they are able to eliminate unprofitable lines and services and unless their competitors are required to bear their full economic costs. It is doubtful that either of these conditions will be met adequately. Railroad transport will probably continue for a long time, but only with government support. Economical public expenditure will probably persist as a critical issue for the indefinite future. Transportation is unlikely to reflect its true economic costs in the years that lie ahead. The best that can be hoped for is some improvement on that score – a somewhat forlorn hope in light of past experience everywhere.

4 The Socialist Transport System – its Management and Planning

HERMANN WAGENER

I INTRODUCTION

In all developed industrial countries, demands for the further development of transport systems increase continually. These arise from the existence of different methods of transport which differ in their suitability for various functions, and from increasing concerns with their integration and co-ordination so that social requirements for transport are met systematically.

This demand should be met by considering transport as an objective part of the processes within society, and by balancing the particular interests of different transport enterprises against national economic considerations or plans. But in countries with market economies, the principles of the free market system, in which market laws are subject to capitalist production conditions, present a barrier to the broader objective. This is in contrast to systems in centrally planned economies, in which the objective forms a more natural part of the general processes of production planning and socialist intensification.

A socialist transport system comprises all the different transport enterprises and sectors, and these elements co-operate within the overall system to meet the requirements of the whole country (Autorenkollektiv, 1977, p. 112). Within the overall national system, subsystems can be identified which have particular functions or cover particular geographical areas (Shafirkin, 1977). In co-ordinating the system as a whole, attention is paid to the following features:

   (i) technical (e.g. network planning, resource allocation);
   (ii) technological (e.g. freight handling);

(iii) economic organisation (e.g. pricing policies, demand management);
(iv) managerial and legislative (administrative and legal regulation).

Emphasis is on long-term strategy, a 'complex process developing in
several stages, comprising the whole period of socialist construction and
that of the creation of the material-technological basis of communism'
(Transport, 1971). Quick responses are also required towards changes in
demand and technology.

II THE TRANSPORT SYSTEM IN THE GERMAN DEMOCRATIC REPUBLIC

Transport systems in different socialist countries are organised
differently: the system in the GDR is described here as one example. This
is planned and co-ordinated by the state and various organs of transport
management, which represent 'the Alpha and Omega of socialist
transport policy' (Arndt, 1975).

Internally, the system comprises all forms of overland transport:
merchant shipping and aviation provide international transport, so their
role is relatively independent. Table 4.1 shows the relationships of
different transport sectors to the national system, with reference to
transport shares, performance, volumes and states of development.
From the table, it is clear that rail and road transport form the main
parts of the system.

III TRANSPORT PLANNING AND MANAGEMENT IN THE GERMAN DEMOCRATIC REPUBLIC

While each part of the system is independently organised economically,
the system is organised as a whole at a national level: Figure 4.1 shows
the organisational structure. Through the GDR Council of Ministers,
the Ministry of Transport is responsible for enforcing a unified policy of
transport and transport management. The task requires considerable
and complex managerial co-operation which is ensured by:

(1) Central management by the Ministry of Transport of the main or
more specialised transport sectors (railways, shipping, inland
waterways, aviation).

TABLE 4.1   COMPOSITION BY MODE OF TRANSPORT IN THE GDR, 1977

Transport	Transport volume			Transport performance		
			Goods transport			
	Absolute (million t)	1950 = 100%	Percent-age	absolute (million t km)	1950 = 100%	Percent-age
Railway[a]	299	234	28.0	52 174	346	66.0
Road transport[b]	714	821	67.0	20 048	1031	25.4
Inland navigation[a]	15	150	1.4	2 215	140	2.8
Pipe installation[a]	38	+	3.6	4 585	+	5.8

| | Passenger traffic | | | | | |
| | | | Urban and business traffic | | | |
	(million persons)	%	%	(million p km)	%	%
Local urban traffic	1952	109	65.0	7 792	118	28.5
Road transport[b]	759	+	25.2	13 330	+	48.8
Railway	295	40	9.8	6 212	66	22.7

| | Other passenger traffic | | | | | |
	(long-distance traffic)					
Railway	336	154	32.4	16 138	176	63.9
Public motor traffic	700	+	67.6	9 107	+	36.1

[a] Including international transport carried out on national transport network.
[b] Public motor traffic and works transport service by means of motor vehicles.
+ No usable statistical data available.
Source: Statistiches Jahrbuch 1978 der Deutschen Demokratischen Republik (Berlin 1978).

(2) Decentralised management of motor transport by regional councils, and urban traffic by town councils, in accordance with general policy determined by the Minister of Transport and as supervised by specialised departments within the Ministry.

(3) The Minister of Transport has responsibility for issuing orders relating to problems of the transport-political development of

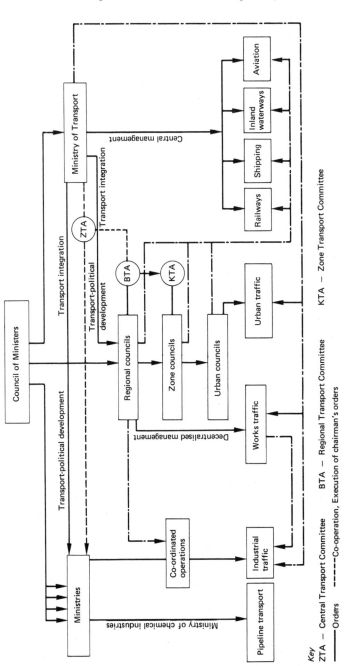

Figure 4.1 Management of the combined transport systems of the GDR

Key
ZTA – Central Transport Committee   BTA – Regional Transport Committee   KTA – Zone Transport Committee
———— Orders
— — — Co-operation, Execution of chairman's orders
········ Co-ordination, Contingency, Balancing, Approval (long-distance)
———— Guidance, Control

works transport, and its integration within the transport system as a whole. These must be observed by all fifteen ministries among which are allocated responsibilities for the various enterprises that operate works transport services.

(4) Transport planning and transport operations are managed through the authority of local bodies.

(5) Liaison between transport and transport management bodies at all these levels is maintained through a system of joint committees (GB1.I, 1973).

The methods by which the transport system is organised and developed are these:

(1) The planning and balancing of social transport needs, of the distribution of traffic among sectors of the system and of development or expansion.

(2) Legislative and administrative control of the utilisation of transport resources, co-ordinating the actions of different decision-making units.

(3) Comprehensive systems of organisational or contractual co-operation between transport enterprises and reloading enterprises) and transport customers.

(4) Active assistance of workers, within a framework of discussion of plans and socialist competition.

The development of the transport system is also stimulated by means of economic measures. The transport customer is interested in the choice of the most efficient transport means in terms of the transport price, while the transport enterprises are concerned with lowering transport costs, on the basis of economic accountancy. Though at present the stimulating effect of economic means in socialist transport practice is low, and does not correspond to their intrinsic objective possibilities, it will never be the principal method of putting the transport system into practice under socialist conditions, even with further development and improvement.

The activity of co-ordinating the development of the transport system is performed in several different spheres:

(1) The first sphere of co-ordination refers to the total transport system of the GDR including, above all, the functions of general divisions of labour, and the co-ordination of railway and road

transport, as well as the efficient integration of inland navigation into the transport system. As with goods transport, the respective principles have been fixed in a transport ordinance and made obligatory (GB1.I, 1973). According to this, transport duties must be assigned to transport branches in such a way that the goods transported put the transport system to the lowest cost and the customer to the lowest possible charges. As a general rule:

(i) large quantities tend to be transported by railway, especially over long distances;

(ii) bulk goods may best be transported by inland navigation if the distance to be covered is very great and the transport route coincides with the waterway.

It should be noted, however, that the so-called critical motor traffic distance, beyond which motor traffic becomes uneconomic as compared with railway transport, has increased mainly as a result of improved technical and economic efficiency of road haulage. Table 4.2 shows current mean values of critical road distances in the GDR.

TABLE 4.2   CRITICAL ROAD DISTANCE (IN KM)

| *Vehicle type* | *Type of transport* | | |
(lorry)	*Direct railway transport*	*Transport with one transhipment*	*Transport with two transhipments*
Normal vehicles	12	78	143
Special vehicles	39	69	197

Transport expenditure is not considered in determining the most appropriate functions for different transport sectors with respect to the type of goods transported. Adequate methodological tools, including the initial data, have yet to be produced and adapted to the practical problem of determining the precise function of each transport subsystem. At present, adherence to the most appropriate fields of utilisation is still made difficult because of capacity limits, especially in railway transport, and by differing regulations with regard to the obligation to carry. Contradictions may possibly arise from the demand for the lowest transport charges to be paid by the customer on one hand or highest receipts of the different transport enterprises on the other.

(2) In the second sphere the co-ordination of road transport takes place, i.e. the co-ordination of public road haulage, with 25 per cent of load transported and 47 per cent of transport performance, and works transport services, with 75 per cent of load transported and 53 per cent of transport performance in road transport. At present this co-ordination task cannot be fulfilled by economic means but only by planning and balancing of road haulage (GB1.I, 1975), by integrating works transport services to fulfil public transport tasks, by arrangements between the public transport system and big enterprises operating a works transport service (VMMV, 1971 and 1974), by fixing quotas for vehicles and fuel and by special authorisation of long-distance runs.

(3) The third sphere concerns the co-ordination of motor traffic, for example to avoid 'dead runs' and generally to ensure efficient utilisation of personnel, thus reducing transport costs. One way of achieving this is by directional long-haul traffic, organised according to state guide-lines (VMMV, 1978). Road haulage performed between two regions is assigned to the motor traffic concern which generates the most important goods flow. In general the concern in question takes over all loads transported in the opposite direction too. (A schematic diagram illustrating these principles is shown in Figure 4.2.) Other methods include agreements between motor traffic trusts to co-operate over transport operating practice (such as agreements on driver rotation in the case of joint transport operations, in order to save working time and to avoid overnight stopovers). These also work to improve the working and living conditions of the driving staff. The principle is shown in Figure 4.3.

(4) The fourth sphere of co-ordination involves planning for the mutual co-ordination and partial specialisation of vehicle pools in particular regions. This is done by organising contractual works-transport communities (TVA, 1978). The aim is to achieve more efficient common transport operations by maximising the usage of all transport capacities of enterprises performing works-transport services.

(5) With respect to passenger traffic, longer-distance traffic is co-ordinated, in principle, by a concerted carriage offer of railways and motor traffic. Urban and suburban traffic is co-ordinated in accordance with regional conditions, by means of co-ordinating networks involving different transport enterprises, together with standardising fares. Because of the extremely low rates and fares,

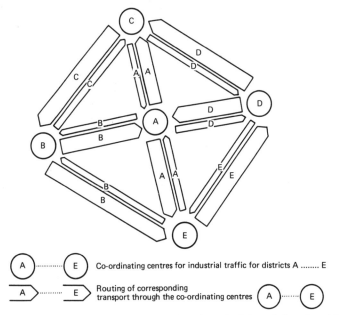

Figure 4.2 Schematic diagram illustrating the principles of directional long-haul traffic

and high levels of state subsidy, economic measures do not affect either the transport enterprise or the customer.

Policies promoting the development of a uniform transport system also differ in terms of time-scale. In particular, three types of objective may be distinguished:

(1) The long-term development of a uniform transport system, over a period of about 10 to 15 years, aimed at step-by-step adaptation of the uniform route network according to its length, density, configuration, junctions, and at changing the utilisation of the vehicle pool. The optimisation criterion for long-term transport system development is given by the minimisation of the operating and total transport costs at the end of the planning period, but with due regard to the time difference between expenditure and effect, i.e.:

$$K + I_F \cdot e_N + I_A \cdot e_N \longrightarrow \text{minimisation,}$$

where K = operating costs;
I_A = investments in transport routes and stationary installations;

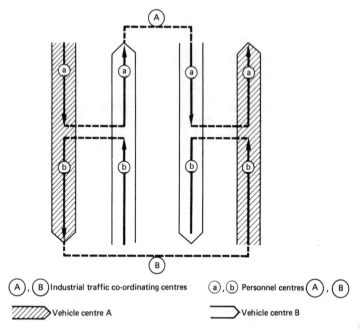

(A), (B) Industrial traffic co-ordinating centres   (a), (b) Personnel centres (A), (B)

▨▨▨▨▶ Vehicle centre A   ▭▭▶ Vehicle centre B

Figure 4.3   Schematic diagram illustrating the principles of personnel rotation in joint transport operations through two co-ordinating centres for industrial traffic.

I_F = investments in rolling stock;
e_N = normative coefficient for efficiency.

The method of determining these criteria consists mainly of forecasting traffic development. These forecasts are made by order of the Council of Ministers, under the direction or at the responsibility of the Ministry of Transport and in co-operation with certain other economic planning agencies. A system of long-term draft outlines and plans is also referred to: these form the basis of long-term economic-political, transport-political and scientific-technological decisions which also include investment policy. A description of the system of long-term draft outlines referring to the GDR transport system is given in Figure 4.4 (Schleife and Lindner, 1977). At present these are prepared up to the years 1990/2000, and they are regularly (within the stages of five-year plans for instance) taken over into the plan 'from the bottom' meaning always for the next five years to come. At the same time, they are specified in terms of their substance, and

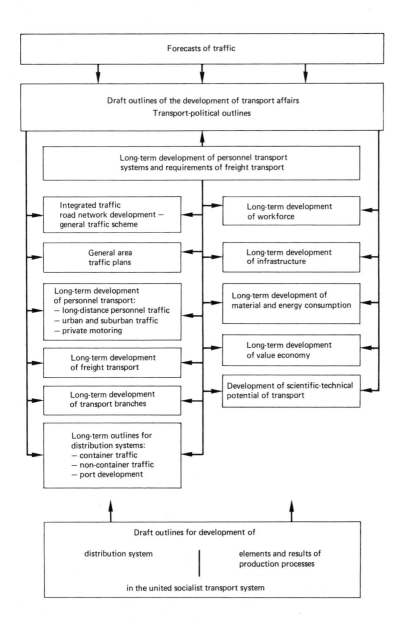

Figure 4.4   The system of long-term draft outlines referring to transport in the GDR.

projected 'towards the top' by the following five years. They ensure that the material and technological basis of transport meets the demand for transport on a long-term basis and that the uniform transport system is able to cover its requirement in an efficient way.

(2) Medium-term transport co-ordination over the period of a five-year plan aims mainly at adjusting the size and specialisation of the rolling stock. Objectives are the optimum utilisation of existing transport capacities, and the optimum distribution of transport tasks among the different transport sectors.

Here, the optimisation criterion consists of minimising operating costs and investment costs of rolling stock $(K + I_F \cdot e_N \longrightarrow$ minimisation). In the medium-term investment costs of transport infrastructure do not, as a rule, affect the system. The chief methods of medium-term transport co-ordination are through five-year plans, investment policy, vehicle procurement policy (involving domestic production or foreign trade) and also vehicle distribution or the establishment of quotas.

(3) Short-term transport co-ordination involves annual planning. Its main aim is the optimum utilisation of all existing transport capacities in order to cover social transport requirements. The choice of the most appropriate type of transport in each case permits a minimisation of operating costs $(K \longrightarrow$ minimisation), or the decision to choose other transport capacities if negative capacity is evident in the balance sheet of the transport branch originally selected. The most important aspect of short-term transport planning is the definition of the most appropriate use of transport sectors by the Ministry of Transport (GB1.I, 1973) and planning the transport requirements of the most transport-intensive sectors of the economy. Further aspects include balancing capacities of the different transport sectors and of works transport services, in monthly (operative) transport planning, in the work of transport committees and in arousing the economic interest of transport customers by fixing costs to influence the choice of the appropriate transport means.

A description of short-term transport co-ordination of goods traffic by means of a plan – which is the most important co-ordinating instrument under socialist conditions – is given in Figure 4.5. The management system of the uniform GDR transport system (see Figure 4.1) demonstrates the planning

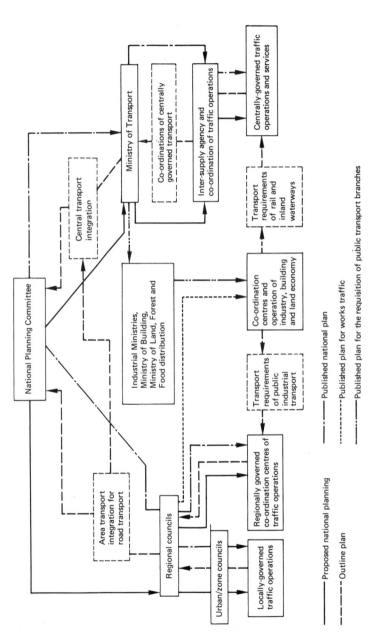

Figure 4.5 Planning progress of freight transport requirements and its implementation

sequence of goods traffic requirements and the way these requirements are met in the GDR transport system.

From this follows:

(1) Enterprises of other economic sectors which have a transport
    requirement of at least 1000 t per year establish their own transport
    requirement plans as part of their enterprise plans on the basis of
    their production and marketing plans.
(2) Enterprises with a vehicle pool of a payload of 10 t and more
    decide which portion of their transport requirements will be
    covered by their own works vehicle pool and then draw up a
    capacity balance sheet. Thus about 80 per cent of the total works
    transport services are covered. Transport requirements to be
    covered by public transport branches are submitted to transport
    enterprises by forwarders, taking into consideration the most
    appropriate fields of utilisation of transport means in accordance
    with transport regulations (GB1.I, 1973).
(3) The regional transport balance sheet is then drawn up for road
    goods traffic including works transport service at a regional level
    and the Ministry of Transport combines it with the transport
    balance sheet of the Deutsche Reichsbahn and inland navigation
    to form the central GDR transport balance sheet, which becomes
    part of the state balance sheet for the first time.

On the basis of this central transport balance sheet, targets (balancing
decisions) are submitted to sectors of industry with respect to their
transport requirement and to the transport sectors and the works
transport service regarding the transport volume to be carried.

It goes without saying that, in applying the three optimisation criteria
of transport co-ordination and transport system configuration mentioned above, the whole transport expenditure including expenditure on
transport infrastructure, creation and maintenance (independent of its
financing by transport enterprises or state budget) and, if appropriate,
the indirect expenditure or gain in other social fields must be taken into
account according to a uniform method valid for transport sectors. At
present neither the methodological tools necessary for it nor the data
base required are fully secured. Therefore detailed economic evaluations
of the transport system have not yet been developed.

But, all things considered, one can see above all from the example of
goods traffic that in the German Democratic Republic the main features

of the socialist transport system are developed according to actual possibilities, an achievement which could only be obtained in socialism and by utilisation of its fundamental advantages.

IV FURTHER DEVELOPMENTS IN SOCIALIST TRANSPORT PLANNING

A further improvement of socialist transport system requires:

(1) Further developments in determining the individual elements of transport requirements.

(2) Further development in the economic evaluation of transport sectors with unification and comparability of economic accountancy with respect to both services on the other. This includes economic stimulation in order to use transport capacities to their full extent (also, if necessary, taking over any transport which is unprofitable from the viewpoint of operation economy but becomes necessary due to labour-division principles) and the development of appropriate evaluation criteria and data.

(3) Specification of real national economic transport expenditure which now is only imperfectly reflected in prime cost, which is the main criterion of labour division especially when the proportional infrastructure expenditure is included.

(4) Further development of economic incentives, above all of transport prices and transport expenditure statements in customers' accounts to arouse the interest of customers regarding the choice of the most appropriate type of transport.

(5) Further development and standardisation of organisational forms and the legal foundation of the socialist transport system, e.g. uniform freight regulations, and the system of indicators and of forms of labour division and co-operation applied by transport enterprises (e.g. by planning, as a transport community of legally autonomous transport enterprises on a contractual basis, through assignment of transport tasks by the forwarding agent or formation of a special transport organ requiring all loads to be notified and assigning them to transport branches according to available capacities and most appropriate utilisation fields). In the different socialist countries a variety of experience has been gained relating especially to the forms   and methods of labour division and co-operation of transport enterprises. GDR transport scient-

ists are endeavouring to make further contributions to the development of a scientific methodology as the basis for a socialist transport system.

REFERENCES

Arndt, O. (1972). Die Beschlüsse des VIII. Parteitages und die Aufgaben des Verkehrswesens im Jahre 1972. *DDR-Verkehr*, Heft 1.
Arndt, O. (1975). Planmassige Arbeitsteilung mit den anderen Verkehrstragern. *Schienen der Welt*, Brussels, March.
Autorenkollektiv (1977). *Okonomie des Transports, Band I*, Berlin.
GBl.I (1973). Verordnung uber die Leitung, Planung und Zusammenarbeit beim Gutertransport, *Transportverordnung*, nr. 26.
GBl.I (1975). Anordnung uber die Transportbedarfermittlung und Transportbilanzierung, *Transportbilanzanordnung*, nr. 23.
Shafirkin, B. I. (1977). Yedinaya transportnaya syet i vzaimodyestvye razlichnych vidov transporta, *Vasshaya Shkola*, Moscow.
Schleife, H. W. and Lindner, W. (1977). Weiterfuhrung der langfristig konzeptionellen Arbeit im Verkehrswesen der DDR, *Report-Schriftenreihe des Zentralen Forschungsinstitutes der DDR*, 4, Jahrgang, Heft 13.
Transport (1971). *Transportnaya sistema mira*, Moscow.
Tarif-und Verkehrsanzeiger (TVA) (1978). Richtline uber die *Bildung, Organisation und Tatigkeit von Werkfahrgemeinschaften*, nr. 9.
Verfugungen und Mitteilungen des Ministeriums fur Verkehrswesen-*VMMV (1971). Vereinbarung uber Zusammenarbeit und Koordinierung der Transportaufgaben zwischen dem Ministerium fur Verkehrswesen und dem Ministerium fur Handel und Versorgung*, nr. 2.
VMMV (1974). *Vereinbarung uber die Grundsatze der Zusammenarbeit und Aufgabenabgrenzung zwischen dem Bauwesen und dem offentlichen Kraftverkehr*, nr. 11.
VMMV (1978). *Richtlinie uber die Durchfuhrung des richtungsweisen Guterfernverkehr mit Kraftfahrzeugen*, nr. 1.

5 Modal Split, Efficiency and Public Policy

YUKIHIDE OKANO*

I INTRODUCTION

Governments always pay keen attention to the demand for transport as a whole and the modal split among different forms of transport, whether or not they adopt a policy of extensive and strong intervention in the transport market. This is because the government is generally responsible for providing transport infrastructure such as roads, harbours, airports and, to varying degrees, railways. In transport planning, either at national or local level, modal split is regarded as a very important factor in determining the allocation of resources among the various methods of transport.

Most transport infrastructures are long-lived and transport investment based on incorrect forecasts of total demand and modal split would bring about a serious waste of resources. If the investment in transport infrastructure in the past turns out to have been misallocated, the government tends to intervene in the transport market in order to make the modal split adapt to the present provision of infrastructure, on the pretence of efficient utilisation of the existing facilities – even if misallocation has arisen from wrong forecasts produced by the government. This is likely to entail tremendous welfare loss to the society. Furthermore, free choice of the means of transport, one of the targets of government transport policy of most countries, tends to be sacrificed by the government itself.

The fact that the present modal split is not determined by the free market under government regulation is often overlooked. Many

* The author is grateful to Ian G. Heggie, former Director of Transport Studies Unit, University of Oxford, who read the first draft and made comments and suggestions.

economists, in particular those who specialise in pure theory, are apt to regard the 'poor' performance of the transport market (whatever that means), as an outcome of market failure. It is certainly true that there exist scale economies and externalities which, in theory, justify intervention in the market by government. However, this does not mean that the 'poor' performance will be removed by such intervention, because 'poor' performance of the market is not an outcome of the failure of the free market, but an outcome of a regulated market.

The purpose of this paper is to examine how modal split on long-distance, inter-urban transport is determined and how government policy affects it. The study is based on recent observations in Japan.

First, the structure of the transport industry in Japan is briefly described. The general trend of changes in the transport industry is similar to that experienced by most developed countries, though there exist some differences because of Japan's socio-geographical character. Secondly, the reasons for the recent changes in modal split in long-distance transport are discussed. Thirdly, the way in which government regulation of railways is responsible for the recent loss of patronage of Japanese National Railways, in particular its high-speed railways (the Shinkansen), is examined. Finally, the public policy which the Japanese government is launching – even stricter government-enforced cartelisation – is criticised.

II THE STRUCTURE OF THE TRANSPORT INDUSTRY IN JAPAN

The structure of the transport industry of developed countries can be characterised by the decline in market share of railway transport and the dominance of road transport, in both passenger and goods transport. Japan is no exception to this, although the decline of rail transport started much later than in the United States and Great Britain.

Goods transported by Japanese National Railways (JNR) reached their peak in 1964, in tonnage terms, and in 1970, in ton kilometres. Thereafter both have been steadily decreasing, despite the increase in the total goods transported. Naturally the JNR's market share of total goods transport has also decreased, while the market shares of road transport and coastal shipping have increased.

The passenger transport market has increased with national income. Figure 5.1 shows personal consumption expenditure in real terms and

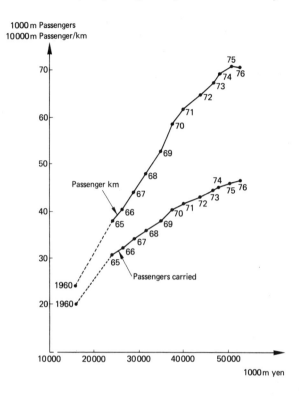

Figure 5.1 Passenger transport and real personal consumption expenditure (1970 Price).

passenger transport from 1960 to 1976. During this period the structure of passenger transport has also significantly changed. Travel by private cars and air increased rapidly; on the other hand, passenger travel by JNR has been stagnating, in spite of its success with the Shinkansen, which started operation in 1964 (Table 5.1). The market share of JNR steadily decreased from 51.0 per cent in 1960 to 28.1 per cent in 1977, in terms of passenger kilometres. The increase in passengers carried by JNR between 1960 and 1975 was 37.5 per cent, while this increase in passenger kilometres was 73.5 per cent. This is attributed to the increase in demand for long-distance journeys caused by technological innovation: the opening and extension of the Shinkansen, though the shift of relatively short-distance journeys from rail to private cars should

TABLE 5.1   PASSENGER TRANSPORT IN JAPAN

	1960	*1965*	*1970*	*1975*	*1976*	*1977*
Total: thousand million passengers	20.3	30.8	40.6	46.2	46.7	42.5
			Per cent modal split			
Rail:						
JNR	25.3	21.8	16.1	15.9	15.4	14.9
Private railways	35.3	29.5	24.2	22.8	22.3	22.5
Road:						
Public service vehicles	36.4	41.1	35.9	27.1	26.2	25.2
Private vehicles	2.6	7.2	23.3	34.4	35.7	37.0
Coastal shipping	0.5	0.4	0.4	0.3	0.3	0.3
Air:						
(regular flight)	–	–	–	0.1	0.1	0.1
Total: thousand million passenger km	243.3	382.5	587.2	710.5	709.4	710.8
			Per cent modal split			
Rail						
JNR	51.0	45.5	32.3	30.3	29.7	28.1
Private railways	24.8	21.3	16.9	15.3	15.3	15.8
Road:						
Public service vehicles	19.7	22.1	17.3	13.5	13.3	12.3
Private vehicles	3.1	9.5	31.1	37.3	38.9	39.6
Coastal shipping	1.1	0.9	0.8	0.9	0.9	0.9
Air:						
(regular flight)	0.3	0.8	1.6	2.7	2.8	3.3

Source: Statistics of Transport Economy, Ministry of Transport

also be taken into account.[1] However, passenger kilometres by JNR began decreasing after the peak of 1974. Even the number of passengers carried by the Shinkansen has decreased since 1975, when the extension of the line to Hakata was completed and both passengers carried and passenger kilometres reached their peak (that is, 157.2 million passengers and 53.3 thousand million passenger kilometres respectively).

[1] Private cars are not so dominant in Japan for long-distance travel. This is probably due to the relatively bad condition of the roads, traffic congestion and high tolls on expressways.

III DEMAND FOR PASSENGER TRANSPORT AND MODE CHOICE

It has been suggested that the demand for passenger transport, like the demand for goods transport, is a derived demand of the household's activities, such as visiting relatives or historic monuments and of business activities, such as meetings or sales negotiations (Becker, 1965; Grounau, 1970). According to this argument, long-distance holiday travel, one of the household's activities, involves the combination of goods purchased in the market, such as hotel accommodation and meals, and the time provided by the participants in travelling. The advantages of this approach are that: (i) time is explicitly taken into account as an input to the production of activities; and (ii) the possible substitution between a transport-intensive activity and a less-transport-intensive one is explicitly taken into consideration.

In passenger transport the consumer desires the greatest possible speed and comfort (as well as other factors), at the lowest price, and the history of the industry is one of progressive improvements in these standards (Gronau, 1970). When a faster transport facility becomes available without any considerable increase in fares, people consume more transport services not only by increasing the frequency of travelling but also by taking longer journeys. Generally speaking, the value placed on time increases with the household's income and the higher the consumer's income, the more his tendency to use a faster transport facility. Probably the fact, shown in Figure 5.1, that the rate of increase in passenger kilometres has been larger than that in passengers carried could be explained by the relatively larger increase in long-distance travel, due to the development of faster transport facilities or because of constant travel time budgets.

The opening of the Shinkansen between Tokyo and Osaka (553 km) in 1964 brought about tremendous changes in the transport market. New traffic on rail was created and also quite a few passengers shifted from air to Shinkansen. As shown in Table 5.2, passengers carried by air over a thirteen-month period from October 1964 to October 1965 decreased by 21 per cent between Tokyo and Osaka, and by 55.1 per cent between Tokyo and Nagoya. Travel times by rail between Tokyo and these two cities were very much shortened; from six and a half hours to four hours for Tokyo–Osaka, and from four hours and ten minutes to two and a half hours for Tokyo–Nagoya. In November 1965 speeds on the Shinkansen were increased and journey times were again reduced substantially. As a result the number of passengers carried by air

TABLE 5.2   CHANGES IN PASSENGERS CARRIED BY AIR

Passengers carried per month	*Tokyo–Osaka (553 km)*	*Tokyo–Nagoya (366 km)*
Oct. 1963–Sept. 1964	115,002 (100)	19,160 (100)
Oct. 1964–Oct. 1965	90,588 (78.8)	8,602 (44.9)
Nov. 1965–March 1966	81,227 (70.6)	3,814 (19.9)

decreased further (see Table 5.2); although some of the decrease in air travel may be due to a reluctance to travel by air after the accidents in Japan in early 1966.

Given the initial success of the Shinkansen, why has JNR's share of the long-distance travel market decreased since 1975? The depression of the Japanese economy after the oil crisis in 1973 discouraged demand for passenger transport. However, the decrease in patronage of JNR can be mainly attributed to the increases in its fares between 1974 and 1976.

These consecutive increases in tariff rates and supplementary charges significantly affected the patronage of JNR in long-distance transport in two ways. The fare increases stimulated passengers to change their mode of transport, that is, from rail (JNR) to air and to a lesser extent to private cars. The fare increases also stimulated households to change their consumption activities from highly transport-intensive activities to less transport-intensive ones.

An analysis of the development of the Shikansen also allows certain conclusions to be drawn about the value of time. It was observed that passengers preferred the Shikansen for journeys of up to three or four hours, but beyond that limit they preferred air, although the fares of both modes are relevant. For journeys of over 600 km, the time saved by travelling by air rather than by the Shikansen increases at a faster rate than for shorter journeys (Table 5.3). The choice of mode appears to be consistent with the traditional theory of the value of time, which assumes a constant value per unit of time-saving. However, a more detailed examination of the data shows that this assumption does not hold.[2] It seems that the disutility of travelling and the non-linearity of the value of time should be taken into account, though it is difficult to

[2] Heggie pointed out that the value of time-saving is not linear, that is, the unit value of small time-saving is less than that of large. His comment on short-distance travel seems to be applicable to long-distance travel too (Heggie, 1979).

TABLE 5.3 UNIT PRICE OF TIME-SAVING AND CHANGES IN PASSENGERS: RAIL vs. AIR

	Travel time by rail (1) (min)	Travel time by air (2) (min)	Time saving by air (3) = (1)-(2)	Rail fare (4) (yen)	Air fare (5) (yen)	Difference in fare (6) = (5)-(4) (yen)	Unit price of time-saving (7)=(6)÷(3) (yen/min)	Change in rail passenger (8) (%)	Change in air passenger (%)
Tokyo–Nagoya (366 km)	121	50	71	3,890	6,800	2,910	41.0	-5.4	19.6
				5,700		1,100	15.5		
Tokyo–Osaka (533 km)	190	55	135	5,510	10,400	4,890	36.2	-9.1	16.3
				8,300		2,100	15.6		
Osaka–Hakata (624 km)	225	55	170	6,110	10,300	4,190	24.6	-16.9	13.8
				9,300		1,000	5.9		
Tokyo–Hakata (1,177km)	416	100	316	9,010	20,100	11,090	35.1	-23.3	24.5
				14,000		6,100	19.3		

Notes:
(i) No access time is included in travel time (1) and (2).
(ii) Figures in column (4) show the fares (tariff plus supplementary charges) before and after the fare increase by JNR in November 1976.
(iii) Columns (8) and (9) represent percentage changes in rail and air passengers in the 1977 business year compared with those in the 1976 business year.

separate the two effects. Passengers on the Shikansen reported an increasing marginal disutility of travelling (boredom, fatigue) on journeys over three hours. Furthermore, people tend to value large time-savings more than proportionately to the increase in time-saving. This is mainly due to the adjustment of activities by a traveller. If the time-saving is large, then a traveller may be able to decrease travelling days without any loss in his utility of travel, or he may be able to take part in an additional activity such as sightseeing. There are various activities which require several hours at least, and only become feasible when time-savings are large.

There is some evidence to support the hypothesis that the value placed on time-saving is not linear. When the Shinkansen began operation in 1964 air passengers between Tokyo and Nagoya (366 km by rail) decreased much more than those between Tokyo and Osaka (553 km), though the value per unit of time-saving by air for the former was smaller than the latter.[3] Other more notable evidence is the effect of fare increases by JNR in 1976 on the passengers carried by air and the Shinkansen.

As shown in column 6 of Table 5.3, the price per unit of time-saving by air significantly decreased because of the large increase in fares by JNR. As a result, the Shinkansen has become much less competitive and passengers carried by the Shinkansen decreased while those using air increased, as shown in columns 8 and 9 of Table 5.3. Both the rate of decrease in rail passengers and the rate of increase in air passengers among the four city pairs are largest between Tokyo and Hakata, though the unit price of time-saving by air between them is largest, at 19.3 yen per minute. The rate of decrease in rail passengers is smallest for the nearest pair of cities – Tokyo and Nagoya – although the price per minute of time-saving is as large as that for pairs of cities farther apart.[4]

These facts support the hypothesis that the unit value of time-saving is not constant, but is larger for large time-savings than for small ones. It seems that there are thresholds, that the marginal value of time saved

[3] The price per minute of time-saving was 25.0 yen/minute for Tokyo–Nagoya and 29.8 yen/minute for Tokyo–Osaka.

[4] The rate of increase in air passengers between Tokyo and Nagoya is larger than for Tokyo–Osaka and Osaka–Hakata. This may be due to the restraint on the number of flights landing at and departing from Osaka Airport for the purpose of reducing noise pollution. The average load factor between Tokyo and Nagoya was less than 50 per cent in 1976 and a little over 60 per cent in 1977. On the other hand, the average load factors between Tokyo and Osaka and Osaka and Hakata were 40 and 70 per cent respectively in 1976 and 83 and 81 per cent in 1977.

increases as travel time (or journey length) increases, and this is probably due to the time threshold of activities. The larger the time-saving, the more additional activities become feasible.

In concluding this section, the following points are emphasised concerning modal split, in long-distance transport: Firstly, the valuation of large time-savings must take account of the consumer's adjustment of his activities. Secondly, the value of time is not linear but dependent on whether the time-saving is large or small; in addition, there is some threshold point at which large time-savings arise. And thirdly, fare policy must take much more account of the consumer's ability to adjust his activities as a whole, instead of concentrating on mode choice alone and assuming other activities are fixed.

IV EFFICIENCY AND PUBLIC POLICY

In this section the change in modal split resulting from the consecutive increases in tariff rates and supplementary charges by JNR is evaluated from the viewpoint of efficiency. As described in Section III, the large fare increases between 1974 and 1976 brought about the loss of patronage on JNR, particularly on the Shinkansen. Figure 5.2 shows the operation-km, passengers carried and load factor (the ratio of passengers carried to the total number of seats provided) of the Shinkansen for 1970–77. Operation-km increased from 552.6 km to 1176 km. Passengers carried increased by 86 per cent in the five years after 1970 and then sharply decreased in 1976 and 1977.

Load factors, which had remained at 65–70 per cent until 1975, also sharply declined to 50 per cent in 1977. Now many trains are no longer full. The decrease in passengers carried can certainly be attributed to the fare increases. In spite of this decrease the operating ratio of the Shinkansen has still been low; that is, 62 per cent in 1975 and 60 per cent in 1976 and 1977, though it is not so low as it was in 1973 (46 per cent). A low loading factor, combined with a low operating ratio, is a typical phenomenon of the inefficiency of monopoly. The low operating ratio (and probably high profit rate) and underutilisation of the capacity of the Shinkansen is the outcome of government regulation applied to JNR, which is a public enterprise.[5]

Since 1964 JNR has made operating losses every year and these losses

[5] Generally speaking, low operating ratio does not necessarily mean high return rate of capital.

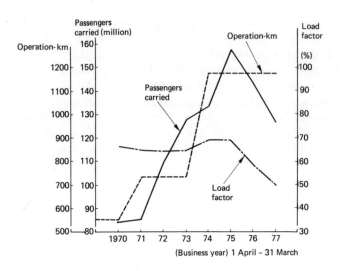

Figure 5.2   Operation-km, passengers carried and load factor of the Shinkansen.

have accumulated progressively. At the end of the 1975 business year the JNR's debt in the Treasury was written off. At the same time the government required JNR to become profitable and to offset the rest of the deficit carried over within a few years. The aim of consecutive fare increases was simply to increase fare revenues. However, railway goods transport had been no more competitive with road transport and coastal shipping than its passenger counterpart and, consequently, JNR was obliged to meet its objective by increasing passenger fares.

Under the Japanese National Railway Rate Law JNR must achieve a yearly balanced budget, combined with extensive cross-subsidisation under the uniform tariff rates across the nation. In addition, it is necessary to get the approval of the Diet (Parliament) for tariff rates increases, although increases in supplementary charges only need the approval of the Minister of Transport.

Neither the government nor the JNR correctly understood the changes in the transport market which had begun with the period of economic growth since the early 1960s. The government railway policy failed to make JNR adjust to the changes in the market. The above-mentioned regulations, which were apparently obsolete, were not changed at all until 1977.[6] Since increases in tariff rates were often suppressed by the Diet simply for political reasons, JNR has come to rely on increases in supplementary charges instead of increasing tariff rates. In fact, an increase in supplementary charges was certainly an effective measure for increasing revenues, because passengers' preference for faster services was increasing their incomes. The Shinkansen was regarded as the most reliable revenue source. Over the last few years the revenue of the Shinkansen accounted for more than 40 per cent of the total passenger revenues (excluding season ticket revenue). The increase in tariff rates and supplementary charges in 1974 brought about a 46.8 per cent revenue increase in the following year, partly because of the increase in passengers due to the extension of the Shinkansen to Hakata in 1975 and partly because of the fare increases of air transport in 1972 and 1974. Before the increase in supplementary charges in 1975, the Shinkansen was just as competitive as before the fare increase of JNR in 1974. However, the increase in supplementary charges by 24 per cent in 1975, followed by a 50 per cent increase in 1976 led to a drop in passenger kilometres of 10 per cent and 12.4 per cent respectively. The price elasticity tends to become larger as the difference in fares between the Shinkansen and air decreases, and it becomes more and more difficult to increase revenue by increasing fares, unless air fares are also increased.[7]

JNR is not free from criticism about its X-inefficient management, which caused larger operating losses. Though it is hard to measure this, some sources of X-inefficiency which are more or less intrinsic to a public enterprise certainly exist within JNR. First, as the organisation responsible for the national railway network, JNR is not allowed to die. Secondly, the public enterprises which are expected to carry out non-economic functions, or – as they are usually phrased – social functions, may continue to survive at public expense. Where an enterprise carries out 'social functions' it is likely to create a situation in which high costs are used as a rationalisation for high X-inefficiencies. Thirdly, the nature

[6] In 1977 the regulation on tariff rates slightly changed and JNR only needs the approval of the Minister of Transport for rate increases within the limit of cost increases.

[7] When JNR increased fares in 1976 both the government and JNR anticipated that air fares would be increased in the near future. But ironically enough, an unanticipated shift of passengers from rail to air helped the airlines improve their financial results. Then the airlines no longer needed to apply for a fare increase. The average load factor of All Nippon Airways, the largest domestic airlines, increased from 66 per cent in 1976 to 72.1 per cent and 73.5 per cent in 1977 and 1978 respectively.

of public enterprises – even in a competitive environment – does not lead to organisational structures which allow appropriate changes to be introduced without a considerable time lag (Leibenstein, 1978).

Fourthly, the management of public enterprises, particularly those subsidised by the government, is vulnerable to political interference.

According to an international comparison of railway efficiency, JNR is highly efficient (HMSO, 1976). But comparisons of efficiency in physical terms are misleading because the measures of efficiency (such as passenger kilometre per carriage, tonne kilometre of paying traffic per tonne capacity stock and passenger kilometre plus tonne kilometre of paying traffic per employee) are likely to depend more on market demand than on the efficiency of railway management. Efficiency is better measured in terms of cost of production rather than as physical productivity. If JNR were really efficient in this sense, then the last three fare increases could have been smaller and the loss of patronage would have been less.

However, as far as the Shinkansen and the main trunk lines are concerned, government railway policy (or regulation) must be mainly responsible for the loss of rail patronage. Due to changes in the market it has long been impossible for JNR to achieve a yearly balanced budget, combined with extensive cross-subsidisation under the uniform tariff rates across the nation (Ponsonby, 1969). Since 1968 the abandonment of extremely unremunerative local lines has been proposed again and again, but only 121 route km out of 2600 km which were proposed for closure at that time have been abandoned so far. There were thirty-two local lines where operating ratios were over 1000 per cent in 1977 and on seven of these the ratio was over 2000 per cent. In 1976 the government began subsidising the operation of local loss-making lines, but subsidies have been too small to compensate fully for their operating losses. Whether or not the government abandons local lines or expands subsidies, the present cross-subsidisation must be abolished and the uniform tariff rates across the nation must be deregulated, so that those lines which still have inherent advantages can be more efficiently used. Except in the big urban areas, where railways are still monopolistic because of severe road congestion, rates should be deregulated or at least relaxed.

V DEREGULATION vs. STRICTER REGULATION

When the transport market became more competitive, what policy should have been adopted? Some countries, like Great Britain,

Australia and Canada have abandoned traditional regulations on railways and road haulage and deregulated the transport industry to a considerable degree.

However, the Japanese government seems to be moving in the opposite direction and is proposing an even stricter regulation: a thorough government-enforced cartelisation under the name of a 'comprehensive transport policy'. This title is nothing but eyewash. The government has tried to rehabilitate JNR through expanding subsidies and removing past debt burdens; however, all measures have failed. This is not surprising, because they were not only distorted by politics but also based either on wishful anticipation of the future transport market or excessive expectations about the railway's performance.[8] The government has finally realised that under the present competitive market conditions, JNR would not be able to reduce its financial difficulties by increasing fares. So the government has decided to make the market favourable to JNR, to enable it to improve its financial position by increasing fares, instead of deregulating JNR. The measures under discussion include:

(i) suppressing private cars and own account road haulage, through discriminatory heavy taxation against them, in order to prevent the market for public transport from being invaded by private transport;[9] and then

(ii) allocating the market among public transport undertakings so that all undertakings would be financially viable, through entry regulation and rates control.

Various reasons are given as a rationale for these measures. For instance, railways are an energy-saving means of transport, and in comparison with automobiles, public transport is more efficient than private transport. However, the data which are used to justify these statements are misleading. A notable example is the comparison of efficiency between public road hauliers and own account operators. The average load factor (i.e. the ratio of tonne kilometres to capacity tonne kilometres) of public hauliers in 1977 was 58.7 per cent, which was larger than that of own account operators (53.4 per cent). Based on this comparison, the Ministry of Transport concluded that public hauliers

[8] The forecast of rail traffic in the future in which investment in transport infrastructure was based turned out to have been overestimated since 1970.

[9] Own account operators are prohibited by law from transporting goods for reward.

were more efficient than own account operators. If we take account of the regulation which prohibits own account operators from transporting goods for reward, however, the difference in load factor between public hauliers and private operators is quite natural and seems to be smaller than one would expect. If own account operators were allowed to transport goods for reward their load factor would certainly improve.

This kind of government-enforced cartelisation will obviously aggravate the efficiency of the transport sector and bring about tremendous losses to the society, in several ways.

Firstly, discriminatory heavy taxation against private transport will impair free choice amongst modes of transport, which is one of the targets of government transport policy.

Secondly, artificially high fares on public transport, and the lack of incentive in the undertakings to save costs under the cartel, bring welfare losses to the public. People would be forced to reduce their consumption of transport services and their choice of mode would be distorted by artificially determined fares which might not reflect the true cost of each mode.[10]

Apart from the welfare losses mentioned above at least two further points concerning policy implementation must be noted.[11] First, the decision-makers may not be capable of allocating the market among the various means of public transport in the way they regard as the best. It is doubtful whether they could understand consumers' mode choice correctly and manage to determine the fares on each mode which would bring about what they wanted to achieve. Secondly, the decision-making process is subject to political pressure. It is true that, in principle, the efficiency of the transport sector can be attained by a regulatory policy. However, in practice, regulatory policy does not achieve efficiency, but only aggravates market performance. If it had been allowed to, the transport sector would have always been efficient.

Even if the Ministry of Transport (the regulatory agency) were disinterested, it would always be under the political pressure of interested groups. As a matter of fact, the idea of the government-enforced cartelisation mentioned above is the result of a compromise among the various public transport undertakings, who want to protect their market from private transport. But there are no reasons to suppose that the 'fruit' of the cartel — exploited profit — would be distributed

---

[10] The Ministry of Transport seems to assume that the total demand for transport (either passenger or goods transport) is price-inelastic.
[11] Not only the Ministry of Transport but also some economists support the government-enforced cartelisation.

among public transport undertakings in the way the Ministry of Transport would expect. Sharing cartel profit among them is formally under the discretion of the Ministry of Transport through rates control; although this does not necessarily happen in practice. Some evidence can be produced to support the view that regulation or tax policy is vulnerable to political pressure and could easily be distorted, even if its original aim were right.

For instance, in 1971 the vehicle weight tax was introduced in order to place road and rail on an equal footing with respect to track costs. The tax was proportional to the weight of vehicles and accordingly the tax was borne more heavily by buses and heavy lorries. In 1974, when the rate of tax was raised, the new tax rate was applied only to private vehicles. At present, own account operators pay a vehicle weight tax which is more than twice as much as public hauliers for a lorry of the same weight. The vehicle weight tax for private vans between 0.5 tonne and 1 tonne is more than that for public hauliers' lorries of 4 tonnes. The original aim of the tax has thus been completely ignored.

Another example shows how regulation by licensing does not work. Licensed public hauliers are required not to overload as a condition of their licence. Recently the National Police Agency enforced a stricter road traffic law which penalises not only the operators and their supervisors but also the shippers who are responsible for overloading. As a result the demand for rail goods transport suddenly increased. Although an overall increase in demand for goods transport due to the recovery of the economy must be taken into account, the demand for lorries also suddenly increased, which shows how much overloading has been prevalent.

It should be noted that the poor performance of the transport market cannot simply be regarded as the outcome of market failure, in its true sense. Poor performance of the market must be, to a certain extent, attributed to government failure, because the transport market is not a free market but a market which is regulated by the government.

REFERENCES

Becker, G. S. (1965). A Theory of Allocation of Time, *Economic Journal*, September.

Gronau, R. (1970). *The Value of Time in Passenger Transportation: The Demand for Air Travel*, NBER.

Heggie, I. G. (1979). Economics and the Road Programme, *Journal of Transport Economics and Policy*, January, 59–62.

HMSO (1976). *Transport Policy, Consultative Document*, Volume 1.

Leibenstein, H. (1978). *General X-inefficiency Theory and Economic Development* (Oxford University Press).
Ponsonby, G. J. (1969). *Transport Policy: Co-ordination through Competition*, Hobart Paper 49, Institute of Economic Affairs.

Discussion of Papers by Professor Mitaishvili, Drs Pegrum and Voigt, Professors Wagener and Okano

The discussion was opened by introductory statements from *Professor Seidenfus* and *Dr Tye*. First, *Professor H. St Seidenfus* said that the three reports that he had to present, by Mitaishvili, Pegrum and Voigt, dealt with past and future changes in the modal transport structures in the USSR, the USA and the Countries comprising the European Community; they thus offered a general survey of the long-distance transport situation in a large part of the industrialised world. They permitted the conference at the same time to analyse the common factors and the differences that characterised long-distance transport in various economic systems and under various geographical, demographic and historical conditions. Furthermore, they showed the different opportunities available to economists of supplying directions for a more efficient application of measures to political decision-makers in the sphere of transport.

Professor Mitaishvili illustrated in his paper that, in a planned economy system, the transport function was always to be regarded in close connection with the entire national economy. It was derived in short- and long-term planning from the territorial material balances of production and consumption. The transport policy did pursue aims of its own too, e.g. increased transport capacity, improved capacity utilisation, reduced unit expenditure, etc., but there was no isolated significance inherent in these aims. They rather entered into an integrated calculus that sought to fulfil the aims of production and distribution plans at optimal cost. There was thus a possibility of transport expenditure playing a secondary role, particularly in decisions on the location of new industrial complexes. In Professor Mitaishvili's words: 'The main criterion for transportation efficiency adopted for the planning of transport performance is the combined amount of national economic costs of production, transportation, storage and consumption of commodities, which at the same time determines the most suitable site, specialisation and location of enterprises'. When the regional

* Dr Pergrum and Dr Voigt were not present at the Conference.

distribution of resources had been ascertained, the optimal transport routes and the modal split were determined by means of linear programming. In contrast to the situation in the Western countries, modal-split planning in the USSR was aimed at relieving the railway system, which was operating at the limit of its maximum capacity. This was achieved on the one hand by a comprehensive programme of supplementation and expansion of the existing railway network – such as, for example, the Baikal – Amur trunk railway –but on the other hand, by a deliberate shift to other modes of transport, i.e. to pipelines, trucks and inland waterways.

This change in the transport structure, illustrated by Professor Mitaishvili in Table 1.2 of his report, was strengthened by changes on the production side – e.g. increase of the finished product proportion in the gross national product – that lent other modes of transport a more than proportionally increasing significance.

One of the most typical features of postwar development in transportation in the USSR was the enormous increase in significance gained by pipeline transport, which at present accounted for one-third of all fuel transportation. Particularly in the transport-related opening-up of the north and the extreme east of the USSR and of Siberia, the pipeline had played an essential role, just as the opening-up of those regions represented altogether an interesting and unique example of stepwise application of various transport modes to exploit the specific advantages. The formation of the system of transport routes in the West Siberian regions, for example, was started with inland waterways along which the material for pipeline construction was brought. Pipeline systems thus became the second mode of transport there; and it was only in the past few years that the railways advanced to these regions. Although new goods transport technologies had also been developed owing to the special nature of the ground in vast areas of the USSR (swamps, tundra) – he referred in this connection to the interesting account by Professor Mitaishvili on pages 10–11 of his report – the main aim of goods traffic development would continue for a long time to be an increase in the efficiency of conventional modes of transport.

The fact that the economic application of the resources made available to cover the demand for transportation was an aim independent of system, so that it also determined transport policies in countries with a free market economy, was illustrated in the papers presented by Dr Pegrum and Dr Voigt. Dr Pegrum formulated it as follows:

The transport requirements of an industrialised economy are of such magnitude that it needs the cheapest possible way of meeting them adequately. This means that it must economise in the allocation of resources to transportation as well as among the modes. If transport is to be economical, the resources devoted to it must be more valuable than if they are used elsewhere. Resource allocation among the modes must meet the same criterion. (It should be noted that what constitutes the most valuable uses depends upon the source of decision-making. If market forces are permitted to decide, the user or consumer makes the decision. If a central government controls all the facilities, it makes the decisions.) If each of the modes does not meet the test of covering all of the economic costs applicable to it, then there is an uneconomical allocation of resources among them.

As was illustrated by Dr Pegrum in his time-series analysis for the USA – see Figure 3.2 of his report, for example – and by Dr Voigt in his cross-section analysis for the member countries of the EEC – see the Appendix of his report – road transport had been able to attract shares of the traffic volume at the expense of the railways in those countries with a free market economy.

Dr Pegrum gave four reasons for the American variant of this trend which was valid with certain modifications, however, for the West European countries as well;

(1) The most important factor in the change in transport structure to the detriment of the railways was technological development. The development of inland waterways and the establishment of pipeline networks had absorbed part of the bulk traffic from the railways, whereas the enormous development in the highway infrastructure – originally stimulated by the increase in individual passenger traffic – had drastically deteriorated the competitive position of the railways as opposed to highway goods traffic – particularly with regard to high-grade commodities and transport quantities not comprising a full wagonload.

(2) Demographic development also had had an adverse effect on the railways. It was above all the superproportional growth of urban conglomerations that had favoured road transport.

(3) Another reason for the intermodal changes in transport volume was the unequal financial treatment of the transport modes. Expenditure on road and waterway projects had been high, but the cost burdens for using the transport routes were not the same.

(4) Finally the railways (in the USA and in West European countries to a varying extent) were impeded by state regulations in making decisions on production and pricing that were adequate to the free market economy system.

According to Dr Pegrum it was doubtful, on the other hand, whether an adjustment in the last two, politically oriented, factors named could give any of the lost freight back to the railways; the question for him was rather how much they could retain of what they had and whether even this would continue to sustain them as economical undertakings. It was furthermore to be assumed that a policy striving for an increase in overall economic efficiency in the transport sector by reducing the 'social costs' arising mainly from road transport could lead at least to a partial rehabilitation of the railways. This was one of the demands made by Dr Voigt in connection with a comparison between the efficiency of road and rail transportation in Western Europe. As the manifold problems relating to, for example, data collection and charging of costs made any determination of actual costs and benefits impossible, Dr Voigt formulated a series of efficiency indicators with which the specific traffic volume was set in relation to certain quantitative and qualitative features of transport production and to its external effects.

With regard to utilisation of the different traffic routes it was shown that in all EEC countries the transportation performance related to one route unit attained the highest value for rail transport, both in passenger and in long-distance goods transport. On the other hand, the transportation efficiency of road transport with regard to the 'speed' characteristic currently surpassed even that of rail transport, although changes could be expected here in the future. Whereas road traffic was being restricted more and more in its maximum speed for safety and energy-saving considerations, considerable possibilities for increasing transportation speed were being opened up by the construction of new high-speed railroad-routes (see the survey on page 14 of Dr Voigt's report). These gains in time, on the other hand, would be of advantage to passenger traffic rather than to goods traffic, the time required by the latter being determined largely by reloading the shunting operations.

According to Dr Voigt, the ability of a transport mode to form networks covering a whole region could be measured with an indicator relating the length of the network to the area or the population of a region. It was evident, and was verified in the Appendix of Dr Voigt's report, that this indicator was a great deal higher for road transport than for rail transport in those regions that were as densely populated as the west European countries and that this gap was likely to widen in the future. With regard to the characteristics of 'reliability' and 'operating frequency', too, road transport was superior to rail transport, at least where the goods side was concerned.

A different result was shown, on the other hand, on analysis of the 'safety aspects' of different modes of transport. In the West European countries the number of persons killed in road accidents was 4 to 17 times higher than that of those killed in rail accidents, related to one unit of traffic volume.

Outstanding advantages were displayed by rail transport under the aspects of 'energy consumption' and 'effects on the environment' too. It was not only the fact that road transport was 100 per cent dependent on crude oil, whose availability and price in the future were still highly uncertain, but also the better utilisation of the applied energy that spoke for higher energy-related efficiency in the railway sector; in this connection Dr Voigt determined an energy-specific productivity indicator for rail transport that was 1.7 and 3.6 times higher than that for road transport in the various EEC countries. In the various components of environmental damage, too – absorption of area, noise and air pollution – railway transport showed, on average, considerable advantages over road transport.

If the road had become the preferred mode of transport in Western Europe despite these great advantages displayed by rail transport, this was due above all to the fact that, in decentralised transport decisions, microeconomic efficiency considerations were dominant, considerations in which the primary factor taken into account was that the flexibility of transport by truck with regard to speed, to frequency and to the ability to form networks surpassed rail transport – which frequently failed to meet even the minimum demands of the potential customer – by no small margin. A change in the modal split in favour of the railways could therefore be attained in the West European situation, according to Dr Voigt, only by increasing the attractiveness and flexibility of rail transport, but not by market-regulating measures.

Professor Seidenfus was of the opinion that all three of these papers gave important information on what reasons determined the shift in the modal split in the course of time and how these intermodal trends could be supported by transport policy decision-makers to help attain maximum transport efficiency. To his mind, this point raised the following questions for discussions:

(1) Were there any indications that the railways in the Western countries were likely to regain significance due to exogenous

influences, for example by:
(a) environmental policies;
(b) energy policies;
(c) infrastructural policies?
(2) Were there any indications that endogenous processes of inter-modalism, i.e. different forms of combined transport, would create the need to expand the capacity of the railroad network?
(3) What were the criteria for measuring the efficiency of transport modes
(a) to decide on the best use of existing capacities?
(b) to decide on the best development of future capacities?

Dr W. Tye opened by saying that he wished to add some general comments to the papers by Professor Wagener, dealing with transport management in a centrally planned economy, the German Democratic Republic, and by Professor Okano, dealing with questions of transport efficiency in a market economy, Japan.

It was interesting to contrast the experience described in Professor Wagener's papers (and also that of Professor Mitaishvili) with the problems faced recently in the United States – especially in three respects which influenced the criteria by which infrastructure decisions were made. The first was the very large financial cost of making new investments. The second was the environmental impact. The third was the problem of demand forecasting – then subject to a crisis of confidence in the US, with many of the established techniques discredited because of their failures. Other experience had also been of the inadequacy of maintenance expenditure, compared with investment, and the difficulty of abandoning uneconomic facilities.

Clearly such contrasts may in part be due to the difference between 'socialist' and 'mixed' economies – but this was not always the case. For example, Professor Mitaishvili's proposals for measuring benefits were very similar to the techniques of social cost-benefit analysis which had been developed for use in market economies.

There seemed to him to be some questions regarding Professor Wagener's approach. First, was it not very misleading to use average indicators, such as fuel/tonne-mile? Certainly in demand forecasting they had found it necessary to use very disaggregated measures and approaches. Secondly, how could one assess the effects of the transport sector on other sectors of the economy? Thirdly, was it possible to develop good definitions of the 'level of service' which was a very complex concept?

Turning to Professor Okano's paper, it seemed to him that the critical relationship was that between investment and pricing policy: these two could not be separated, for example by dividing responsibility between two agencies, without bad policy results. He would raise one question here. Why were governments involved in transport at all? The usual arguments were that there were economies of scale, externalities and public benefits requiring government intervention. But the practical effects of this intervention were often not in line with the theory.

For example, they had to assess the value to consumers of the savings in travel time brought about by transport policies. This value was probably related to the length of the trip, and was not linear – i.e. bigger time-savings had a greater unit value. In addition, there might be important threshold effects, such as the great value when a journey was shortened sufficiently to eliminate an overnight stay. Further, there had been suggestions that consumers had a fixed 'time budget' spent on travel. If this were valid, then it meant that changes in speed would not result in time 'savings' but rather in a different pattern of activities.

Finally, it was most interesting to contrast Professor Okano's approach with that of Professors Wagener and Mitaishvili. Professor Okano favoured economic incentives, rather than comprehensive transport planning, to solve such problems as the relative inefficiency of own-account vehicles.

It was Dr Tye's last point – about the balance between economic incentives and comprehensive planning – that was the dominant theme in the following general discussion, underlying questions of definition, techniques, pricing and administration. But the discussion was not really about such differences between centrally planned and market economies – rather it was about the best choices to be made within the planned economies.

Professor Kantorovitch said that it was quite clear that the analysis of intermodal split was a topical question requiring considerably more research. The central problem was that the ordinary 'economic' indicators, such as profit, income, revenue, etc., might in the transport sector not reflect the true costs to the economy as a whole. In this case, regulation by the State was necessary.

Dr Bajusz wished to speak of Hungarian experience in using a combination of economic and administrative methods. First, it was necessary to assign specific transport objectives for each mode on the basis of an optimal 'division of labour' between the modes. This optimum was calculated using mathematical models which were, as far as possible, disaggregated and incorporated some elements of wider economic considerations such as the importance of transport costs in the costs of population of various sectors (though this was very small: using input-output analysis suggested that transport formed about ½ per cent of total costs in 85 sectors of the Hungarian economy, and between 2 and 12 per cent in the other 11 sectors). Then tariffs and maintenance costs were both included into a unified – and comparable – calculus of costs for roads and railways, with the intention that costs and prices were closely in line (and an aim of a 6 per cent 'profit' projected with assumed average wage levels in transport and the national economy).

However, these economic levers were not enough in themselves to orient transport authorities to select the optimal balance between modes (for example, because other differences in quality of service between modes were about equally influential as price in determining the mode used). So administrative measures must also be used, such as the control of long-distance tariffs.

Mr Antal suggested shifting the balance in favour of greater use of tariffs and pricing levers, but still not to the point where they would be dominant, in a socialist economy. This should be directed at an increased use of rail, because of energy and speed advantages, though this would require improvements in the quality of service especially for transloading, using the 'rail-sliding' (*anschlussleiter*) system, and improvements in the usually bureaucratic organisation of railways.

Professor Khachaturov argued that the important point in discussing centralised control was to distinguish between socialist and private economies. Professor Okano was critical of the 'poor performance' of Government control – but this was a conclusion based on the attempt to control within a market economy and perhaps was due to the bureaucratic way in which such control was exercised. Even within such an economy the conclusion might not be true – for example, many Japanese railway operations were, as Professor Okano showed, unprofitable. But 'unprofitable' did not mean the same thing as 'economically inefficient' for which the effects on the whole national economy must be considered. An operation could be efficient and unprofitable. But there were also important differences between socialist countries, for example between the GDR and the USSR. In the GDR the rail and motorway networks had largely been completed, while in the USSR new extension was still necessary. Then also there were differences in organisation and management – for example, in the GDR one Government department (the Ministry of Communications) was responsible for the whole transport sector. This used to be the case in the USSR, but only for a brief period in the first stage of Soviet power after

1917 – but there were difficulties in connection with the huge dimensions of the whole transport system and therefore the separate management of each mode of transport was preferred. At the same time the planning of the whole transport sector was kept centralised in the state planning Committee.

But there were still unresolved questions. How was it possible to ensure that the sort of formulae and indicators discussed by Professor Mitaishvili represented the actual costs borne by the economy? Even if this were solved, how could the use of such indicators be reconciled with a greater role of railway revenue, income and profit as levers? (On the use of indicators generally Professor Khachaturov disagreed with Dr Tye's general preference for disaggregate quantities – sometimes the average values were very useful.)

Professor Kovalev drew quite a different conclusion from Professor Khachaturov about the period when Lenin had set up a unified Ministry of Rail and Communications for the USSR, including all modes of transport (even horses) and with links with the central committee for planning and various conferences with consumers. They just could not ignore the problems of integrating the administration, management and maintenance of transport. Integration was particularly important in the 'junction points', i.e. interchange between modes, where there had to be a nationwide system of transhipment schedules, including the State Government, the transport operations and the Planning Branch. Otherwise transport was chaotic, not harmonious.

Dr Andruszkiewicz supported Professor Mitaishvili's argument. The main task of transport planning was to optimise the use of all modes with respect to the whole economy. But this required a fairly long time horizon – for example in Poland river transport was now on a very small scale, but the Poles were planning for it to become very much more important in twenty years, with a large-scale investment programme (500 billion zlotys over twenty years). The calculations made to assess this investment included estimates of the overall economic effect.

Mr Vitek raised some problems of control in market economies. There were experiences with the Inter-State Control Communion in the USA – a central body helping to develop the American transportation system. Without this intervention, the very intense competition would probably destroy the railways. This experience demonstrated the necessity of central management – even in a market economy – in integrating the transport system.

Professor Wickham spoke of a related argument currently being waged in Western countries, especially Britain, France and the United

States. Here the key word was 'deregulation'. It was important to understand that deregulation was not necessarily hostile to any sort of central planning: there should be a central choice about investment on infrastructure. However, it was necessary to remove bureaucratic administration involving central control over one mode of transport. For the main method of control over transport operations you should really choose between planning or competition: 'limited competition' was ineffective.

Dr Lake took up this theme. Canada deregulated the railways some 12 years ago, but this had been widely misunderstood. In Canada, it meant sweeping away a large number of very detailed specifications and regulations, replacing them by easier, more general regulations. Of these, the most important was the pricing rule:

The tariff must be no lower than the variable cost and no higher than $2\frac{1}{2}$ times the variable cost.

In practice, the process was only invoked when a customer (or a competitor) complained about a breach of the rule – and the result had actually been to *increase* effective Government control over planning, since it was now possible to consider strategic questions.

Some other, more detailed questions were raised about the papers. Both *Mr Kaser* and *Mr Vitek* were interested in a new economic incentives system in the USSR (announced on 29 July 1979). How did it affect the arguments in Professor Mitaishvili's paper? What implications were there in this approach for the integrated transport system in the GDR outlined by Professor Wagener?

Professor Khachaturov asked about the importance of new modes of transport (especially pipelines, monorails, hovercraft) and he and *Mr Kovalev* both questioned Professor Wagener's use of 'critical distances' – how were these calculated? Should they not be different for different modes and commodities? *Dr Kakumoto* queried the Unit Capital calculations. *Dr Antal* introduced developments in the theory of transhipment (which was further discussed later in the conference).

Profesor Okano replied to some points in the discussion. He accepted that there was an economic argument in favour of a shift to the railways – but this would require a change in the *physical* system, not just in tariffs and pricing policy – for example, in handling merchandise. The key question was what was the cost of these changes, since this must be offset against the benefit. He agreed with Professor Wickham on deregulation, but the transport market was not a free market.

Professor Mitaishvili first answered a number of detailed questions. Railways would remain the dominant mode, but with some development of pipelines for transporting coal, ore, mineral building materials and other dry bulk goods. Depreciation costs, or replacement cost for new investment, were integrated into current costs. A rate of banking 'interest' was incorporated if the project finance was produced by bank credit.

Now to the main themes of the debate. It was important to form an optimal *system* of modes, considering them together even if they *were* dealt with by various organisations. This meant that some general criterion of efficiency was required, defined in terms of minimising adjusted costs – but this would be handled at two levels. The highest level involved minimising the *combined* cost of production and transport and consumption, and could only be achieved by a development socialist economy with a unified system of planning.

At this level it was necessary to have a planning horizon of ten to twenty years – and it would be quite wrong to try and use short-term tariffs to achieve such long-term goals. For example, the optimal location (and relocation) of production, depended on the transport of goods in the distant future. The second level, which would be operated in the context of five-year planning, could involve the transport costs being derived from the tariffs for the predetermined pattern of production and consumption.

In practice, such calculations should take into account the technical and operating characteristics of each mode, the estimated volume of freight and passenger traffic, the effects of transport costs on the cost of production, and the costs of interchange. It also implied the use of indicators that should reflect the 'end product' of transport, and a unified system of management.

What role did this leave for profit? In his opinion it was wrong to judge the success of a transport operation by the amount of profit it made, for two reasons. First, what was the source of money profits? Only other economic bodies. Secondly, transport was necessary for production, but did not itself create products – it did not increase the benefits available to the consumer.

From this point of view, transporting goods added only to their cost without adding to their value, and it was therefore necessary to use an economic indicator that focused attention on minimising cost, rather than making profit, though a transport enterprise, as a commercial unit, had a minimum necessary profit level. The point he made was that profits on transport in a socialist economy differed both from profits on other sectors of the economy and from profits in other systems. As far as formulae in his report were concerned they had been proposed for the calculation of adjusted unit transportation cost at the stage of surveying the region's industrial complexes transportation schemes, provided the competitive transport modes were available. These formulae made it possible to determine current as well as capital costs taking into account the coefficient for comparative capital investment efficiency. Thus, we were dealing with real transportation costs rather than with 'costs caused by the economy' or with tariffs. Generally speaking one should not mix up these concepts.

Lastly, *Professor Wagener* replied to the discussion. Many of the questions raised were connected with the transport policy of the speakers' own countries and therefore the answers would be different in countries with different social systems. But in his opinion transport policy in economically developed countries had reached a point of reorientation of its subject matter, aims and methods, because social production was growing enormously, requiring a permanent increase of transport, especially goods transport. It would be necessary to reduce the goods transport expenditure per unit of final social product. Under socialist conditions this might be reached by:

(i) a reduction of the amount of goods movement by means of improved regional co-operation, by relocating users closer to production sites of raw materials and transport-intensive products, and by a general conservation of material;

(ii) a reduction of transport distances by means of transport optimisation, and only then

(iii) a rationalisation of the actual transport process.

Therefore transport policy should begin by influencing long-term location policy and by reducing the need for transport. Lower specific transport costs released national income, thereby promoting further social development.

In addition, as economic processes became more complex, and required more co-operation between different branches of the economy, it became more and more sensitive to troubles caused by transport: stability and reliability of transport provision became crucial. Now the development rate of transport capacities – especially that of infrastructure – went ahead more slowly than that of transport needs. And at the same time non-commercial transport services and private passenger car traffic were rapidly growing.

As a result, transport policy increasingly had not only an effect on public transport branches but also on carriers, non-commercial transport services, and private passenger car traffic, and it became increasingly important that policy decisions should be seen from the viewpoint of the whole national economy, all transport branches and regions.

Next he made some remarks on *transport forecasts*. Due to the time necessary to develop transport infrastructure and its sluggish reaction to technical and economic changes, transport required long-term forecasts. The forecasting problems in a socialist economy were rather different from those which caused Dr Tye such difficulty – for example, long-term forecasts were based on processes free from economic fluctuations and there were reasonably reliable forecasts of the general development of the economy, since that itself was planned. In practice a reliability of ± 10 to 20 per cent was generally achieved using relatively simple forecasting methods. Greater deviations only occurred when the details of developing other economic branches had not been forecast correctly (e.g. energy development) or when they were guided by 'technical enthusiasm'.

In his opinion the most important thing in further forecasting would be the collection of data suitable for forecasts as well as a better hypothesis as to underlying developmental laws. This was more important than the development of ever new sophisticated forecasting models.

One other consequence of the long-term nature of infrastructure development was that it must be the State which was financially responsible for it. As a result, infrastructure costs were not a current component of transport costs and prices. More work was necessary to solve the problem for pricing caused by the different expenditure required for infrastructure for different modes.

However, even in advance of solving this problem co-ordination of different modes of transport was essential, and in this both averaged and disaggregated data were useful.

His country too, he added, welcomed the development of transport prices in freight transport adequate to costs. (For reasons of social policy fares in passenger transport were intentionally fixed in such a way that they remained beneath the cost level.)

Nevertheless their effectiveness in actually influencing the customer's choice of appropriate transport mode became less and less, because as the goods to be moved grew in value, transport costs became proportionately less. He thought, therefore, that the stimulating action of transport prices on the selection of transport means was limited. In addition some choices were fixed by administration, and transport branches had the right to refuse inconvenient loads.

It would be better to ask the transport customer for information about his transport order (origin, destination, timing, type of commodity, etc.) and then leave the selection of the most appropriate transport mode to a transport organisation. This would ensure that decisions were based on national economic aspects and on utilisation of all capacities available.

Finally, co-operation between centralised and decentralised *management* had been treated in his paper in detail. He would like to refer to one additional aspect.

Under the conditions of a small country like his and by applying modern computational and data transmission techniques they had begun to introduce centralised co-operation of long-distance transport of some types of goods being carried by lorries in order to reduce empty trips. This was a case of central co-ordination integrated with the work of independent economic units. It seemed to him that modern computational techniques tended to stimulate a trend for more, rather than less, centralisation.

PART TWO

Fuel Freight and Transportation in Less Accessible Regions

6 International Implications of Long-distance Transport of Fuels

HOLLAND HUNTER, LESLIE DIENES AND LEE BETTIS

I INTRODUCTION

The long-distance transport of fuels and energy supports the foundations of every major economy in the world today. This is true in part because, for several centuries, cost-reducing innovations in transport have encouraged and facilitated the investment in transport required for interregional specialisation and exchange. Now, in a period of substantial fuel and energy cost increases, this paper uses recent Soviet economic experience to examine the potential role of the transport sector in alleviating the resulting problems confronting most of the world.

We start by summarising a well-known theoretic framework for placing transport activities in the optimal organisation of all economic activities. We next review some special features of the fuel and energy sector reflecting the non-renewable nature of fossil fuels. Then, to illustrate the importance of transport in making low-cost energy available for use, we offer a case study of recent Soviet experience, since the USSR is a world leader in both the production and the transport of fossil fuels. Finally, the paper suggests a series of research tasks in this area that could appropriately be considered by members of the International Economic Association for joint international investigation.

II THEORETIC FRAMEWORK

1 Transport costs as a part of total costs

For every commodity, total delivered costs are the sum of producing costs plus transport costs (Khachaturov, 1939; Losch, 1954). For some commodities transport costs are negligible, but for others transport is a major element in total costs. Often this is true for fuels. In the USSR in 1966, for example, transport costs made up 44 per cent of the total cost of gas; the share was 28 per cent for oil extraction and 23 per cent for coal (see Arthur L. Moses' analysis in Treml, ed., 1977). Moreover in looking at any final good, we recall that total transport costs are the sum of direct and indirect transport costs, i.e. of transport costs incurred in moving all the intermediate components entering into the final good. (Leontief, 1951; Isard, 1956). Each specific transport charge equals distance from shipper to receiver times a freight rate (price) per ton-kilometre. The transport service has important qualitative characteristics as well: speed, reliability, freedom from damage, etc., which heavily influence choices among rival modes of transport (Meyer *et al.*, 1959).

2 Short-run efficiency in minimising total costs

Efficient production in the short run involves selection of commodities and producers (at specific locations) so that demands (at specific locations) can be met at minimum total costs (taking account of both production and transport costs) (Kantorovich, 1939; Lange, 1963; Dantzig, 1963). These total costs, moreover, involve not only current inputs but an appropriate share of fixed capital (Hicks, 1939; Khachaturov, 1946; Dorfman *et al.*, 1958).

3 Optional output expansion paths

The expansion of commodity output should draw on least-cost alternatives among input combinations and among production locations. Similarly, transport capacity expansion should be based on least-cost choices of input combinations and transport modes. For an economy-wide optimum, the two problems should be solved jointly. Since unit production costs frequently decline as scale increases (implying longer shipping distances to some customers), and since transport costs for multiproduct carriers depend on how total costs are assigned to individual commodities carried, solutions are not easily determined. Using contemporary theory and methodology, however, recent research is yielding useful results (Takayama and Judge, 1971; Meyer, 1971; Goreux and Manne, 1973; *Tipovaia*, 1977).

III SPECIAL FEATURES OF FUEL TRANSPORT

1 Transport of natural resources in general

The costs incurred in using natural resources include finding costs, extraction costs, processing costs, transport costs and opportunity costs (location rents) for favourably-located resource deposits. The relative size of these components of total costs varies greatly from one resource to another, one region to another, and one period to another (Khachaturov, 1973). For present purposes it is sufficient to note that wherever resource users are separated from natural resources by substantial distances, efficient transport can make an important contribution to minimising total costs. Economies with growing demands for natural resources have tended to reach out for supplies from more and more distant locations, so the transport element in costs has tended to become increasingly significant.

Sometimes transport costs can be reduced if the resource is processed at its initial location or at some intermediate point on the way to its final user; moving the processed resource may be far more economical than moving the raw material. Long-distance transmission of electric power generated from coal is a familiar illustration of the point. Thus the minimisation of transport costs can involve location decisions for intermediate processing (Kantorovich and Zhuravel, 1974). In the long run, final consumption locations too may be pulled toward natural resource locations unless restrained by other factors like arable land, water supplies or a hospitable climate.

2 Transport and non-renewable resources

The use of non-renewable natural resources like oil and gas is influenced by an additional cost element that has recently gained in importance. This is scarcity rent, a cost that reflects the exhaustibility of the resource. Efficient allocation of an exhaustible resource over the period until it runs out requires that the deposit be assigned a value in each period, and that this value should increase (per ton) at an annual rate equal to the economy's rate of return on other equivalent capital investments. Since the value of the natural resource deposit is also the present value of all the expected future receipts it will earn it as it is extracted, the expected net earnings of the resource deposit must be increasing at a rate equal to the economy's going rate of return on assets whose use involves a similar degree of risk (Hotelling, 1931; Solow, 1974).

This scarcity-rent cost factor, rising exponentially, may be a negligible part of total costs if supplies are abundant relative to demand, while extraction, processing and transport costs are high. Moreover the impact on total costs of rising scarcity rent may be offset, or more than offset, by the discovery of additional supplies and by cost-reducing innovations in extraction, processing or transport. Over the last three centuries, technological progress has lowered the real cost of exhaustible resources to a remarkable extent, and improvements in transport have played an important role in the process.

But if demands increase more rapidly than supplies, and if easily extractible, easily processed, nearby deposits are exhausted, then scarcity rents begin to push up the total unit costs of the remaining exhaustible natural resource. Alternative resources, previously un-exploited because of high costs, come into use. Ultimately a 'backstop technology' (solar energy?) sets a limit to the rise in costs (Nordhaus, 1973; Manne, 1974).

3 Potential contributions of technological progress in transport

How can technological progress in transport hold down the real cost increases for fuel and energy that have spread across the world in recent years? The question is important and answers are complex. Four general points seem clear. The first is that transport improvements are especially significant for consumers who are far from fuel and energy supplies. Major industrial centres have typically grown up near fuel and energy deposits, but in Europe and North America one observes that old centres inevitably exhaust nearby supplies, thus requiring imports from more distant locations. Hence transport savings can help hundreds of millions of people who live far from their fuel and energy needs.

Secondly, transport progress can play at least a small role in dealing with the problems of environmental disruption (air and water pollution) involved in the modern use of fossil fuels. Intermediate processing of coal, oil and gas can take place before old centres are reached, with subsequent transport of a reduced volume of, for example, refined oil products or electric power. Of course transport itself disrupts the environment (air pollution by passenger cars and trucks, oil spills by tankers), so here too technological innovations can make a contribution.

Thirdly, long-distance transmission of electric power makes it easier to choose locations for nuclear power facilities that will minimise the consequences of nuclear accidents, problems of waste disposal, etc.

Fourthly, improved domestic (and international) management of transport activities, through efficient modal choice, rational route selection, and optimal capacity utilisation can maximise the productivity of the transport sector as a whole. Huge investments are involved, so gains in effectiveness can make a notable contribution.

IV SOVIET LONG-DISTANCE FUEL TRANSPORTATION: A CASE STUDY

1 Basic features of Soviet energy uses and sources

Table 6.1 presents estimates for 1975 comparing the USSR, Western Europe and the USA in the principal forms of their energy use. Much diversity lies behind these summary figures, but they convey an accurate overall indication of the Soviet stress on using fuels and energy primarily for electric power and industry, to a greater extent than in Western Europe or the USA. The relatively small share going to transport in the

TABLE 6.1   GROSS DOMESTIC ENERGY CONSUMPTION, 1975, IN THE USSR, WESTERN EUROPE AND THE USA, BY USING SECTOR

| | (*in quads*) | | | (*per cent shares*) | | |
| | | *West* | | | *West* | |
	USSR	*Europe*	*USA*	*USSR*	*Europe*	*USA*
Electric power	13.5	12.7	19.9	33	29	30
Industry	11.3	10.9	14.2	28	24	21
Transport	2.4	6.5	16.2	6	15	24
Residential and Commercial, Construction, Agriculture	7.0	10.4	11.2	16	23	17
Non-energy uses	1.8	1.5	1.6	4	3	2
Own use and losses	5.2	2.6	4.0	13	6	6
Total	41.2	44.6	67.1	100	100	100

Source: Robert Campbell, *Soviet Energy Balances* (Report – Rand Corporation – R-2257-DOE), Santa Monica: RAND, December 1978, p. 16.
Note: For value of 1 quad, see note to Table 6.2.

USSR as compared to the USA reflects the limited presence of passenger automobiles in the USSR. The fuel sector itself uses more energy in the USSR than in the West

Table 6.2 presents a similar set of estimates for 1975 covering the sources side of the picture. The USSR has been shifting from solid fuels, primarily coal, to oil and gas, but in 1975 solid fuels still contributed some 37 per cent total gross domestic energy consumption, as contrasted with 10 per cent in Western Europe and 13 per cent in the USA. Western Europe has become heavily dependent on oil; the USA draws heavily on both oil and natural gas. Hydroelectric and nuclear power figure modestly in all three regions, playing a greater role in Western Europe and the USA than in the USSR. In addition to these differences in fuel types, the regions differ significantly in their degree of self-sufficiency. The USSR in 1975 was a net fuel exporter, able to export amounts equal to almost 6 per cent of Soviet gross domestic consumption. By contrast, Europe had to import 25 per cent of its energy needs, and the USA imported 10 per cent of its gross domestic energy consumption.

The transportation of fuel and energy is the largest single responsibility of the Soviet transport system (Hunter, 1957; Dienes, 1979). Movement of coal makes up some 18 per cent of total railroad freight ton-kilometres (1977 data) and rail movement of petroleum in tank cars added another 15 per cent. The movement of oil and gas in pipelines has

TABLE 6.2   GROSS DOMESTIC ENERGY CONSUMPTION, 1975, IN THE USSR, WESTERN EUROPE AND THE USA, BY PRIMARY SOURCE

| | (*in quads*) | | | (*per cent shares*) | | |
| | | West | | | West | |
	USSR	Europe	USA	USSR	Europe	USA
Petroleum	14.4	24.9	29.2	35.0	55.9	43.5
Solid fuels	15.2	9.6	12.8	36.8	21.5	19.1
Gas	10.2	5.9	20.5	24.8	13.2	30.6
Hydroelectric	1.2	3.2	2.9	2.9	7.2	4.3
Nuclear	0.2	1.0	1.7	0.5	2.2	2.5
Total	41.2	44.6	67.1	100.0	100.0	100.0
Net trade as a per-						
centage of consumption	5.5%	25.1%	10.0%			
	(exports)	(imports)	(imports)			

Note: 1 quad = 36 million tons of 'standard fuel' (USSR) or 25.2 million tons of 'oil equivalent' (OECD).
Source: Campbell (1978), p. 13.

grown very rapidly, though less rapidly than oil and gas production, while internal waterway and maritime movement of fuels continue to be significant. Table 6.3 presents estimates for 1975 of the long-distance fuel transport accomplished by each major mode, measured in tons and ton-kilometres. Note that if the long-distance transmission of electric power could be put in commensurable units, it would add appreciably to the transport contribution to Soviet (and Western) fuel and energy movement.

TABLE 6.3   FUEL TRANSPORT IN THE USSR, 1975, BY FUEL AND MODE

Petroleum and products	*Tons originated (millions)*	*Average haul (kilometres)*	*Ton-kilometres (billions)*
Pipelines	498.3	1 336	665.9
Railroads	389.0	1 238	481.4
Maritime	91.4	3 723	340.0
Internal waterways	22.9	2 010	46.0
Gas Pipelines	319.0	1 237	394.6
Coal and coke			
Railroads	752.1	701	527.4
Internal waterways	23.4	415	9.7
Maritime	9.2		

Sources: Derived from data in TsSU, *Nar odnoe khoziaistvo SSSR v 1977 g.*, 308–18, supplemented by I. Ia. Furman, *Ekonomika magistralnogo transporta gaza* (Moscow, 1978), 78, and some average hauls for earlier years.

Soviet domestic fuel transport is further complicated by a substantial flow of exports, primarily westward across European Russia to Eastern Europe and to the world market. Major oil and gas pipelines extend from Western Siberia and the eastern edge of European Russia some 3000 kilometres into Eastern Europe. Oil is also exported from Soviet ports, including Nakhodka in the Soviet Far East, to which a major new combined rail-and-pipeline connection is being built, all the way from West Siberian oilfields, some 6500 kilometres (4000 miles) away (Shabad and Mote, 1977).

2 The changing geography of Soviet energy uses and sources

As one would expect, Soviet energy use is concentrated in the main centres of industry and population (Dienes and Shabad, 1979). These include the Moscow region, the region around Leningrad, the eastern Ukraine and the Volga Valley – all in European Russia. The Urals region and parts of West Siberia are also centres of heavy industrial energy use. Moscow and Leningrad have always had to import the fuel and energy, but the other centres have been able to draw on local or nearby sources.

Again, the locational details are complex but the crucial fact is that the old centres in European Russia are becoming increasingly dependent on imported fuel and energy. Rich deposits of coal, oil and gas have made their contributions over the last century and one by one are nearing exhaustion. The USSR is fortunate in having very large additional reserves of fossil fuels, though they lie in the east and north, at substantial distances from major centres of use. Thus from a transport point of view, it is apparent that import dependence (and with it an increased sensitivity to transport costs) now characterises not only Western Europe and the USA but the USSR as well. The European part of the USSR is already importing from the Asiatic part of the USSR very large quantities of oil, coal and gas, for overland distances that add very substantially to delivered costs. The theoretic problems sketched in Section II above are confronted now in very practical terms by Soviet resource managers, whose decisions therefore provide empirical evidence of great general interest.

3 Cost factors and technological uncertainties

The Soviet fuel and energy situation is influenced by a number of technical problems to which emerging technology may provide adequate answers, though the prospects are very uncertain. We note them here under the headings of extraction, processing and transport, merely to stress the range of issues on which detailed analysis is necessary.

Major extraction problems characterise the rich oil and gas deposits of Western Siberian lowlands which are roadless swamps in the summer, lying over hundreds of metres of permanently frozen subsoil. Establishing and maintaining drilling rigs is difficult and expensive. Here, as in the older Volga–Ural fields, water flooding requires the use of sophisticated submersible pumps. Far to the east, the new coal deposit at Neryungri in Yakutia is plagued by winter temperatures so low that the teeth on the shovels of dragline excavators break off.

Problems in processing are serious, for example, with the vast Kansk–Achinsk deposits of low-grade coal, which is too powdery to be transported in rail gondola cars and which tends to self-ignite. This deposit and others under consideration for new mines will require massive beneficiation, ash-removal and sorting facilities to make their coals cost-effective. Very different problems of processing arise at nuclear power stations, where adequate provisions against accidents are likely to receive more attention since the Three Mile Island accident in the USA. Moreover many cost and technical uncertainties surround the mining, processing and safe handling of nuclear fuel, not least the ultimate disposal of spent fuel.

Cost-reducing and capacity-expanding innovations in long-distance transport of fuels and energy show substantial promise in the USSR (Bokserman, 1978). If transmission losses on extra-high-voltage long-distance electric power lines can be overcome, westward transmission of Siberian energy to users in European Russia will be much more feasible. Soviet mastery of the technology involved in the manufacture of reliable, high-quality pipe and pumping equipment for large-diameter oil and gas pipelines will greatly facilitate delivery of eastern oil and gas to users in the European part of the USSR and in Eastern Europe. Coal slurry pipelines are under investigation as alternatives to the expansion of carrying capacity on the main rail exits carrying westbound coal from West Siberia and Kazakhstan to users in the Urals, the Volga Valley and other old centres in the European USSR. Unit coal trains, and unit tank-car trains on the Baikal–Amur trunk line when it comes into operation, can hold costs down in moving fuels long distances overland.

It must be noted, however, that these innovations involve expensive capital facilities dedicated to a single use which must bear all the costs, by contrast with the classic contribution of a railroad carrying diverse freight and passenger traffic capable of sharing these costs. The specialised transport facility requires high volume and continuous demand in order to be cost-effective, and may lose its usefulness when a fuel deposit is exhausted, unless other deposits can be linked to the route.

It must also be noted that technological and cost uncertainties introduce risk factors that inhibit change. Both government and private decision-makers properly hesitate to commit resources to large-scale, long-lived projects whose estimated costs and benefits involve major uncertainty. Thus under these circumstances painstaking research to reduce the range of error is a precondition for sound action.

4 A reconstructed fuel shipments pattern for 1975

A study using linear programming and transportation models was used to determine alternative energy flows based on existing and new technologies and different price structures (Bettis, 1979). The transportation model was intended to determine interregional flows of organic fuels in six regions (Southern, Kazakhstan, West Siberia, East Siberia, Central Asia and Far East) and the rest of the Soviet Union in 1975 and 1980.

Each of the six regions studied was self-sufficient in steam and coking coal in 1975. Four of these regions, Southern, Kazakhstan, West Siberia and East Siberia, shipped a total of 151 million metric tons of steam coal to the rest of the Soviet Union.

Interregional flow of fuel oil among the six regions and the rest of the Soviet Union was significant in 1975, totalling 15 million metric tons in standard fuel equivalents. Only West Siberia, East Siberia and Central Asia were self-sufficient.

The Southern and Kazakhstan regions imported, respectively, 3 and 2 million metric tons of fuel oil from the rest of the Soviet Union. The Far East obtained one additional million metric tons of fuel oil needed to meet requirements from East Siberia. The rest of the Soviet Union supplemented its fuel oil requirement with imports from West Siberia and Central Asia.

Every region except East Siberia and the rest of the Soviet Union was self-sufficient in natural gas in 1975. East Siberia imported 3 million metric tons of natural gas from West Siberia. The rest of the Soviet Union was supplied with 155 metric tons of natural gas from the Southern region Kazakhstan, West Siberia and Central Asia for supplementing its requirements.

5 A hypothetical optimal fuel shipment pattern for 1980

The pattern of interregional fuel flows in 1980 is similar to that described above for 1975. Again, all regions except the rest of the Soviet Union were self-sufficient in steam and coking coal.

With respect to fuel oil, regional interdependence, in general, was reduced from 1975 levels. The Southern region reduced fuel oil imports from the rest of the Soviet Union by 67 per cent to 1 million metric tons in 1980 compared with 1975. The Far East achieved self-sufficiency in fuel oil in 1980, joining West and East Siberia and Central Asia who were also self-sufficient in 1975. Only Kazakhstan among the six regions studied increased fuel oil imports to 3 million metric tons. This was supplied from Central Asia. In 1975, however, Kazakhstan supplemented its fuel oil requirement with imports from West Siberia. The rest of the Soviet Union was the overall major importer of fuel oil in 1980, drawing supplies from Kazakhstan, but especially from West Siberia.

Natural gas supplies in each of the six regions were sufficient to fulfil regional requirements in 1980 except in East Siberia. This region increased its import of natural gas from 3 to 4 million metric tons. The source of this gas was West Siberia. This region and Central Asia were the major suppliers of natural gas to the rest of the Soviet Union in 1980, shipping 178 and 119 million metric tons, respectively. The Southern region and Kazakhstan shipped one million tons each to the rest of the Soviet Union.

Data were not available to validate the results of this model. However, it is planned to link the transportation model with a dynamic optimisation production model with feedbacks, which will enhance the analytical power of these programming techniques as guides for planning energy, industrial and transportation development in the USSR.

V SUGGESTIONS FOR FURTHER RESEARCH

1 Identify the major determinants of currently-optimal patterns for fuel production and transportation

In each major region (Western Europe, USSR and Eastern Europe, North America, etc.), detailed studies along the lines sketched above can throw light on optimal patterns of regional fuel production, transportation and use. Such studies can display the relative size and importance of the key cost and technical parameters that influence choices among fuels, production sources and transport modes. Computed solutions can be compared with actual flows and differences can be evaluated. The indicated interregional imports and exports will have important international implications.

2 Investigate impending and prospective cost changes within this structural context

Subject to all the uncertainties associated with the future, economists can select from numerous current analyses the most plausible estimates for three kinds of cost change. Fuel costs will *increase* at particular locations as supplies become exhausted or require greater extractive effort. Conversely, fuel costs will *decrease*, at least the scarcity-rent element should decrease, whenever substantial new deposits are brought into use. Most importantly, total unit costs can be lowered through technological innovations in fuel extraction, processing and transportation, like those that have had such a powerful impact in the past. The potential significance of each should be evaluated within this integrated context, taking account of interaction effects, so that investments can be focused on the most productive projects.

3 Analysis of the long-run implications for transport

Wise decisions concerning the expansion of transport capacity, mode by mode and link by link, while not solely determined by the needs of the fuel and energy sectors alone, should nevertheless be sensitive to the implications of analyses like those suggested above. In the background, even more fundamental decisions will be under consideration, namely those concerning plant location and individual choice of residence. Interactive scenarios deserve attention.

Finally, changes in regional patterns of fuel and energy production, transport and use have import implications for future international trade. Both the levels and directions of international trade in fuel and energy will shift as domestic opportunity costs change. Again, long-distance transport of fuel and energy will come into play, partly as transport costs determine feasibilities and partly as trade demands determine traffic levels. As capital costs and scarcity costs rise, new energy technologies become feasible, and some of them (perhaps solar energy?) may reduce the need for long-distance transport of fuel in interregional trade.

REFERENCES

Bettis, L. (1979). *A Process Analysis of the Soviet Energy System*. Paper presented at New Haven, Connecticut meeting of American Association for the Advancement of Slavic Studies.
Bokserman, I. U. (1978). On New Progressive Types of Transport, *Planovoe Khoziaistvo*, nr. 11, 19–29.
Campbell, R.W. (1978). *Soviet Energy Balances*. Report – RAND Corporation R-2257-DOE (Santa Monica: RAND).
Dantzig, G.B. (1963). *Linear Programming and Extensions* (Princeton: Princeton University Press).
Dienes, L. (1979). Discussion paper on Soviet resources transport, Association of American Geographers project on Soviet Natural Resources in the World Economy (Syracuse: Syracuse University (processed)).
Dienes, L. and Shabad, T. (1979). *The Soviet Energy System* (New York: Halsted Press).

Dorfman, R., Samuelson, P.A. and Solow, R.M. (1958). *Linear Programming and Economic Analysis* (New York: McGraw-Hill).

Goreux, L.M. and Manne, A.S. (eds.) (1973). *Multi-Level Planning: Case Studies in Mexico* (Amsterdam: North-Holland Publishing Company).

Hicks, J.R. (1939). *Value and Capital* (New York: Oxford University Press).

Hotelling, H. (1931). The Economics of Exhaustible Resources, *Journal of Political Economy*, April.

Hunter, H. (1957). *Soviet Transportation Policy* (Cambridge, Mass.: Harvard University Press).

Isard, W. (1956). *Location and Space-Economy* (Cambridge: MIT Press).

Kantorovich, L.V. (1939). *Matematicheskie metody organizatsii i planirovaniia proizvodstva* (Leningrad: Leningrad Gos. Universitet).

Kantorovich, L. and Zhuravel, A. (1974). The Role of the Transport Factor in the Location of Production, *Voprosy Ekonomiki*, nr. 3, 79–90.

Khachaturov, T.S. (1939). *Razmeshchenie transporta v kapitalisticheskikh stranakh i v SSSR* (Moscow: Sotsekgiz).

Khachaturov, T.S. (1946). *Osnovy ekonomiki zhel. – dor transporta* (Moscow: Transzheldorizdat).

Khachaturov, T.S. (1973). Natural Resources and National Economic Planning, *Voprosy Ekonomiki*, nr.8, 16–29.

Lange, O. (1963). *Introduction to Econometrics*. 2nd edn. (New York: Macmillan).

Leontief, W.W. (1951). *The Structure of the American Economy, 1919–1939*, 2nd edn., (New York: Oxford University Press).

Losch, A. (1954). *The Economics of Location*, translated from the second, revised edition of *Die raumliche Ordnung der Wirtschaft* (1944) (New Haven: Yale University Press).

Manne, A.S. (1974). Waiting for the Breeder. Symposium on the Economics of Exhaustible Resources, *Review of Economics Studies*, 47–65.

Meyer, J.R. et al. (1959). *The Economics of Competition in the Transportation Industries* (Cambridge, Mass.: Harvard University Press).

Meyer, J.R. (ed) (1971). *Techniques of Transport Planning* (Washington, DC: The Brookings Institution). Vol. 1: *Pricing and Project Evaluation*, by Meyer, J.R. and Straszheim, M.R. Vol. 2: *Systems Analysis and Simulation Models*, by Kresge, D.T. and Roberts, P.O.

Nordhaus, W.D. (1973). The Allocation of Energy Resources, *Brookings Papers on Economic Activity*, nr.3, 529–76.

Shabad, T. and Mote V.L. (1977). *Gateway to Siberian Resources* (The BAM) (New York: Halsted Press).

Solow, R.M. (1974). The Economics of Resources or the Resources of Economics, *American Economic Review*, may, 1–14.

Takayama, T. and Judge, G.G (1971). *Spatial and Temporal Price and Allocation Models* (Amsterdam: North-Holland).

Tipovaia (1977). Tipovaia metodika raschetov po optimizatsii razvitiia i razmeshcheniia proizvodstva v perspektive, *Ekonomika i matematicheskie metody*, nr. 6, translated in *Matekon*, 1978, XV, nr.1, 75–96.

Treml, V.G. (ed) (1977). *Studies in Soviet Input-Output Analysis* (New York: Praeger).

Discussion of paper by Professor Hunter, Dr Dienes and Dr Bettis

Professor Wickham, opening the discussion, said that the relationship between transport and energy had for a long time been a theme of the authors of this paper: overall the main conclusion was that there was more to gain from internal improvements within each mode than large-scale shifts from one mode to another.

The transport of energy generally took about one-third of national transport resources. The question that arose was – how far was the paper's argument specific to the USSR? In some ways, conclusions might not be transferable to Western European countries – for example, transport of electric power was very expensive (and involved a 20 per cent loss of current during transmission) in spite of its apparent economy of physical movement. There were also differences due to the substantially smaller role of private traffic, and motorways, in the USSR.

The questions that appeared to him to be the most interesting in the paper were:

(1) The evidence in Table 6.3 for a specialisation between the modes of transport, as shown for example in the longer average distance of river and pipeline hauls.
(2) The apparently small discrepancy between actual allocation and an optimal allocation between energy-producing and consuming regions of the USSR, calculated with a linear programming model. (Though there might be larger discrepancies if the same comparison were carried out in France, where the greater importance of light industries, and cars, would reduce the chances of achieving an optimum allocation.)
(3) The use of oil prices as an internal regulator of national consumption of fuel for transport – comparable to the use of interest rates to regulate the capital market. He believed that the price of petrol to consumers was still too low to encourage efficient energy use.

Dr Kozin gave primary importance to the need to save energy. There were difficulties in finding the optimal balance of modes; for example, we were not going to eliminate private transport, but it must be admitted that cars were the biggest consumers of energy. Railway transport was the most energy-efficient and had the additional advantage that, with electrification, it was possible to use alternatives to oil: even the USSR's huge reserves of oil would not last for ever, and they were therefore trying to reduce the use of oil for transport.

On two points he disagreed with the paper. There was a mistake in Table 6.1, where energy expended on transport should be 10 per cent, not 6 per cent in the USSR. And the scope for reducing cost by technical innovation in transport was considerably less than the increased requirements due to the growth in output of the power-producing industries.

Professor Seidenfus took up the point of the scope for energy-conserving policies. Apart from countries such as the USA, Canada and Australia, the domestic transport sector accounted for a relatively small proportion of total energy (W. Europe 15 per cent, Japan 13 per cent , versus the USA 25 per cent). Private road transport was by far the largest part of total transport (70 per cent in USA, 53 per cent in W. Europe, 51 per cent in Japan). All transport markets were almost completely geared to liquid fuels. The energy intensity for moving freight was, roughly speaking, lowest for water transport (waterways, coastal and ocean), approximately equal for rail and road (with – depending mainly on the distance and possible load factor – a slight advantage for rail), and highest for aviation. These proportions had applied for a very long time: for this and other reasons the regional and urban infrastructures had developed in such a way that the various forms had now largely confined themselves to those fields of operations where their competitive advantage was greatest. The scope for conserving energy by shifting freight from one mode of transport to another was therefore rather limited within the existing regional and urban infrastructures. The issue most frequently discussed/debated was that of shifting freight from road to rail; but various studies and trials (e.g. USA, UK, France and West Germany) had shown that resultant energy savings would not be large enough to warrant enforcing such a shift. (There could, of course, be other overriding considerations such as road damage and traffic congestion.)

In commercial freight transport, energy costs had long been recognised as an important part of total costs (around 30 per cent). Hence significant efficiency improvements had already been made, e.g. the high proportion of diesel engines in the commercial transport market in W. Europe and Japan. The energy per ton-mile for ocean bunkers had almost been halved in the period 1960–75. A significant part of this was attributable to the rapid growth of the share of very large crude carriers. This growth rate would, of course, be significantly slower in future.

Lastly, there could be some thought of regulatory improvement of load factors for road freight. However, such measures could easily become counter-productive (e.g. filling up with ballast to provide an apparent full load) and a more rational scheduling of freight operations could automatically be expected from the rapid development of information processing.

Professor Noortman questioned whether it was in fact wise to try to change the transport system to accomplish the broader aims of energy policy.

Professor Khachaturov argued in favour of treating problems of transport and energy conservation together, and on a global scale, and also over a fairly long time scale. Experiments were in progress in the USSR on nuclear, solar, tidal and geothermal energy sources, and these were likely to have major impacts not only on transport but also on production and the environment.

Professor Hunter replied to the discussion. The era of Mother Nature's generosity was coming to an end. As part of a universal law, we must recognise that 'matters would be difficult everywhere'. In the USSR as in other countries, there was a contradiction between social requirements and productive capacity; as a consequence society must find ways to induce its members to be 'economic', which in this case involved some restraint of demand, and much more careful consideration of the costs of alternative plans.

In accomplishing this there were three main problems. First, transport infrastructure in a sense lasted too long, that is its physical life was longer than its service life, and its economic life was even shorter, due to technical progress. Secondly, the unpredictable speed and direction of technical progress was the enemy of long-term forecasting. Thirdly, organisational structures would themselves need to be changed. All this meant that we would have to accept very drastic changes in our expectations and planning approaches.

7 The Today and Tomorrow of Arctic Transportation Routes

JERZY ZALESKI

I INTRODUCTION

Transportation difficulties are a major problem in reaching Arctic regions, and especially in the economic development of these regions. The extreme climatic conditions in the polar area pose special technical problems, and investment costs and the operation and maintenance of the infrastructure have to be considered in a special light. The current development and future prospects of different transport modes in the Arctic region are considered in this paper.

II THE DEVELOPMENT OF ROAD AND RAIL TRANSPORTATION

The areas of the European Scandinavian and Soviet North are serviced comparatively well by road and rail. The situation is a much more difficult one in the Asiatic subpolar areas of the USSR, in Alaska and the extreme northern regions of Canada. Greenland – from this point of view – is nearly a total desert for transportation purposes.

In the USSR a new trans-Siberian railway route of 4500 km is being built to the north of the existing line. It will open up the southern areas of Yakutia, especially because it will provide a connection with the Lena river, and the highways, especially those from Newer and Magadan to the centre of Yakutia. Further to the west, the railway line under construction from Igarka to Workuta will give Norylsk a railway connection with Leningrad and Moscow. A new road, built in the 1970s, is of great importance to the Tchukotsk National District, as it links the coastal settlement at Egwiekinot with Yultin, Pewek and Zelonyj Mys.

The winter roads called *zimniki*, with a total length of about 11,000 km, which run along the frozen river beds, perform an important role in the Soviet sub-Arctic areas. Transport is performed by trucks with a very large carrying capacity of up to 20 metric tons.

The major railway in Alaska runs from Seward to Anchorage, Fairbanks and Fort Yukon, thus linking the Kenai peninsula with the centre of the state. The Alaska Highway, from British Columbia to Fairbanks, is the pivot of the road system in Alaska.

The Canadian North has a very scarce network of transportation connections owing to the great distances and particularly difficult environment conditions. The major roads are the Mackenzie Highway, from Peace River to Yellowknife, and a road which was built from Dawson Creek parallel to the Mackenzie Highway. In the Canadian Arctic, seasonal winter roads are used which run along river beds. The cost of building 1 km of a road of this sort is $1500, compared with $100,000 per kilometre for a normal highway.

III PIPELINE DEVELOPMENT

Transportation infrastructure in the American-Canadian and Soviet North has changed considerably during the 1970s, due to the discovery of rich sources of crude oil and natural gas. The specific transport technology of these raw materials has given rise to a rapid development of a special means of transportation – the pipeline. A wide range of projects have been undertaken over vast areas of tundra. The largest one of them is the Trans-Alaskan Pipeline running from Prudhoe Bay to the Valdez Port on the Pacific. The work was started in 1975. The Alaska Pipeline, 1284 km in length, crosses three mountain chains, in some sections 1400 m above sea level, and 350 water obstacles. The crude oil is heated to 80°C and travels at 11 km/hr.

The bold project of a pipeline system connecting with the planned exploitation of natural gas in northern sector of the Canadian Arctic – the Trans-Canada Pipeline – is being realised. The western section of this system, the Arctic Gas Pipeline, 3860 km long, is to transport the gas from the sources in the delta of the Mackenzie River to Calgary in south Alberta along the Mackenzie River valley. The gas from Melville Island is to be transported by a branch of this pipeline up to Toronto and Montreal. This pipeline is 4820 km long, running along the coasts of the

Hudson Bay to establish Port Churchill as the main centre of the chemical industry in Canada.

At the end of the 1960s, great investments were also started in the Soviet North, in connection with the exploitation of abundant sources of crude oil and natural gas in Siberia. In the extreme north, two pipelines have been constructed: from Workuta to Miedwiezje, and from Messo-Jacha on the Gydan Peninsula to Norylsk. Eastern Siberia is being covered by a network of gas and oil pipelines. Gas from the Yakutia fields is transported to ports: Olga on the Japanese Sea, and Magadan on the Okchotsk Sea.

IV RIVER AND SEA TRANSPORT

The powerful rivers of Alaska, Canada and Siberia play an important part in solving transport problems, especially in the expansion of river – sea shipping. However, their role is limited because of the short navigation season.

The problem with the use of the Arctic Sea routes is due to the thick layer of ice which covers part of the Arctic Ocean for the whole year, so conventional ships cannot be used. No ship sailing the waters has covered the whole of the Arctic Ocean along the chord of the polar circle. It is true that in August 1977 the Soviet icebreaker *Arktika* with a nuclear propulsion of 75,000 HP reached the North Pole, breaking the ice sheet up to 6 m thick – but that was an experimental cruise of a special unit, and not of a transport vessel.

The greatest danger a ship encounters in the Arctic is not – as it would seem – the uniform ice sheet, but ice floes, which exert pressure on the hull, and may crush a ship. It is most dangerous when 70 per cent of the water is covered by ice floes, especially when the ship encounters a mass of thick broken ice eroded partly by the sea waves. Sharp submerged projections cut the sheet metal of the hull and break off the blades of the propeller.

The specially adapted ships which operate in the Arctic areas are reinforced with powerful icebreaking equipment. The Soviet Union has applied this form of shipping on the Northern Sea Route with success, the Americans and Canadians on the North-West Passage.

The North-East Passage, more often called at present the Northern Sea Route, leads from the Atlantic Ocean along the northern coasts of Europe and Asia to the Pacific Ocean. The route from Arkhangelsk to the Bering Strait is about 6500 km long. In the sixteenth century,

English explorers initiated the search for this passage. Among the many later expeditions, the most famous was led by S. I. Diezniew, and set out in 1648 from the mouth of the Kolyma and reached the Anadyr Bay on the Bering Sea. That proved the existence of a sea passage between the Arctic Ocean and the Pacific Ocean, today called the Bering Strait.

A. E. Nordenskjöld was the first man to cross the Northern Sea Route on his ship the *Vega*, in 1878–79. The first ship that conquered that passage during one navigational season was the Soviet icebreaker *Sybiriakow* in 1932. As a result it was shown to be possible to operate this route along its whole length and not only on particular sections. The Northern Sea Route is of specific importance for the Soviet Union, but may also be an interesting variation of operation for West European shipowners. In June 1967 the Soviet Union government announced the availability of the route for all ships, although a part of the route runs across the territorial waters of the USSR. The assistance of the Soviet icebreakers and pilots guarantees safe shipping. That decision coincided with the closing of the Suez Canal and was closely linked with that event. To prove that the route was an advantageous variation of the routes from West Europe to the Far East, the Soviet ship *Nowoworonez* (3700 GRT) sailed in July–August 1967 from Hamburg to Yokohama, covering 7670 sea miles in 20 days. The route through the Suez Canal would have been 11,440 sea miles long, and would have taken five weeks.

The Northern Sea Route does not at present perform an international role owing to the short navigational period and to the high costs arising from the assistance of icebreakers. Neverthless, it may gain great importance in the future since the introduction of submarines or more powerful icebreakers will reduce the seasonality of operations and thus a voyage will be more profitable. This is a matter of the future.

The Northern Sea Route is not the only way of crossing the Atlantic to the Pacific Oceans by means of the Arctic route. The alternative is in the western direction around the northern coasts of America, the so-called North-West Passage leading from the Davis Strait to the Beaufort Sea and through the Bering Strait to the Pacific Ocean. The numerous shoals, straits and rocky islands of the Arctic Archipelago, the almost deserted areas and harsher climatic conditions than those in the east are the reason that the Passage is of a lesser importance. It was not until 1903 that Amundsen conquered the North-West Passage, although attempts had been made for three centuries.

The year 1940 opened a new chapter of its history. The Canadian police schooner *St. Roch* (80 tons displacement) sailed the whole way from the west to east within two seasons and in the following year returned through the Prince of Wales Strait within one season. In the 1960s a comparatively regular local service was initiated. Its aim was to supply the increasingly numerous polar posts growing up there.

The utilisation of the North-West Passage as a transportation route may be of great importance not only for the coastal shipping of the United States and Canada but for international shipping as well. The opening of a regular shipping service on this route allows a considerable reduction in distance. This reduction depends on the port of destination, and amounts to from 30 to 55 per cent. The route from London to Tokyo around Africa is 14,650 sea miles long, while through the North-West Passage it is only 8600 sea miles. The same route through the Suez Canal is 11,200 sea miles long.

The problem of carrying cargo on a large scale along the North-West Passage did not emerge until the rich sources of crude oil, gas and metal ores were discovered. The discovery was the result of intensive geological research carried on outside the north polar circle by the Americans and Canadians. The leading oil companies Humble Oil, Atlantic Richfield and British Petroleum decided at the end of the 1960s to carry out an experiment with a tanker that could be operated all the year round. The largest American tanker, the *Manhattan*, was bought, and rebuilt at a cost of $40 million. Her carrying capacity was increased to 115,000 tons and her displacement to 150,000 tons. The experiment was not, however, completely successful. It appeared that the tanker-icebreakers would have to be larger (up to 300,000 tons carrying capacity), and more powerful (up to 150,000 HP), and the hull should be similar to traditional icebreakers. The cost of building a ship of that kind would be very high and the economic effects less advantageous than in the case of investing in the construction of a pipeline to a non-freezing port on the Pacific Ocean. The idea of transporting crude oil from Prudhoe Bay by giant tankers has been rejected for the present.

This does not mean that the idea of using the North-West Passage has been abandoned. In Alaska and the Canadian Arctic Archipelago there are, apart from the crude oil and gas, strata of coal, copper, lead, zinc and iron ores, and these cannot be transported by pipelines. In 1974 the Americans brought into service the icebreaker *Polar Star* with a displacement of 12,000 tons and 60,000 HP. It is the most powerful icebreaker in the world with a turbo-gas propulsion which can proceed when the ice cover is 1.8 m thick, and the maximum thickness of the ice it breaks is 6.4 m.

In order to service the drilling platforms, when ice conditions are easier, and to help the ships that have been trapped in the ice by breaking a way for them, a special Arctic Supply Vessel (ASV) has been built in the USA, of 3900 t displacement, and 11,000 HP, which can break ice up to 2m thick. A special bulk carrier for the Arctic waters has been designed in Canada. This ship, of 28,000 tons carrying capacity, is to carry lead and zinc ores, fulfilling at the same time the role of an icebreaker in the Canadian Arctic Archipelago straits.

V AIR TRANSPORT

The first flight to the polar zone was performed by a Pole in the service of the Russians, J. Nagorski, in 1914, and since then there has been great progress in this area. In the second half of the 1920s Nansen initiated a wide programme for the exploration of the Arctic by means of airships, designed by the international society the Aeroarktika, with its seat in Berlin. It was not until 1957 that regular flights were established on this route with direct air communication over the North Pole on the route Copenhagen – Tokyo – London – San Francisco. Since then the number of trans-Arctic connections by air has increased many times. Many international airports have been built in small settlements among the icefields and snows of the North, such as Gander in Newfoundland, Keflavik in Greenland and Anchorage in Alaska. Other airports which are in fact military aviation bases (e.g. Goose Bay in Labrador, Thule in Greenland) are also adapted to receive civilian planes in case of emergency.

Aviation performs an unusually important role in domestic connections. The dense network of regular and chartered air connections has covered Alaska, Northern Canada, Scandinavia and the northern areas of the Soviet Union. Some companies are of the international carrier type. The Alaska International Air Co., for example, is the most important carrier for local deliveries but also takes cargo to any place on the globe. Since 1969 this enterprise has been able to deliver any type of cargo on board the DC 103 Hercules planes as pallet cargo. Gliders and hydroplanes perform an important role locally, particularly in Alaska.

Air transport in the Soviet North has developed to an impressive extent. There are regular connections by air to all the more important settlements outside the polar zone and with the more important administrative-economic centres of the USSR. The aeroplane has become almost a monopolist in the carriage of passengers, mails and valuable goods.

VI FUTURE TRENDS

Most experts are unanimous as to the thesis that the possibilities in the field of communication will determine the future development of the Arctic regions. New concepts are multiplying in the field of land transport. They deal both with the improvement of conventional means and with solutions that are totally unconventional.

The possibility of utilising heavy road vehicles is entering a new phase. Trucks of a large carrying capacity (Tatra, Ural, KRAZ) are being operated in the Soviet North. These vehicles are equipped with caterpillar tracks instead of rear wheels and they can be replaced by wheels or runners. Thus one has a mud-snow vehicle which can penetrate anywhere. Greater interest has been roused by combined methods of transport. The Boeing company has proposed to use air-cushion vehicles to transport lighter goods. These could be utilised across the flat tundras and in the corridors of the river valleys in any season. With turbine propulsion, a vehicle of 150 tons carrying capacity can reach a speed of 130 km/hr.

New approaches to pipeline connections are developing. The Institute of Research on permafrost in Yakutsk is working on the interesting project of transporting gas under pressure in channels drilled in the permafrost.

The future development of the trans-Arctic sea routes is a separate problem. Much attention is devoted to it and this will be appreciated if one considers that the first conquering of the North-West Passage, in the 47-ton motor-sail cutter *Gjoa*, took Roald Amundsen three years (1903–6); the tanker *Manhattan* (1969) needed two weeks; and the submarine *Scorpion* (1962), with nuclear propulsion, covered this route in three days, remaining submerged.

The possibilities revealed by the American military submarines were the basis of the trials to utilise this form of shipping by submarine merchant ships. The submarine variant has a great advantage over the surface one owing to the possibility of operating the ships all the year round, as well as considerably shortening the route. Sailing under the ice and the technical problems connected with it have been mastered.

As is well known, nuclear reactions do not require the presence of oxygen so that the vessel does not need to surface as is the case of a submarine with a diesel motor and electric propulsion. Modern sounding apparatus allows exact information about the thickness and distribution of ice to be obtained at any moment, and inertial navigation takes advantage of signals transmitted by artificial satellites.

The problem which until recently was a troublesome one – submarine communication – has now been successfully solved.

The advantages of submarine shipping are various. A ship can proceed constantly at maximum speed along the shortest route, bears almost no losses owing to the weight of fuel and can be in operation all the year round. The Canadians are interested in the possibility of exploiting the newly discovered layers of ores on the Arctic Archipelago and the transport of these ores by means of submarines either to the non-freezing Bay of Godthåb on the coast of Greenland, and from there by surface ships to Rotterdam or Dunkirk, or by submarine units directly to Rotterdam or Milford Haven in Great Britain. In England, in co-operation with the American firm Atomics, Inc., a technical design of a submarine vessel to serve this route has been presented, corresponding to the results obtained from the Norwegian and Soviet investigations, which indicate that the bulk carrier, that is a ship to carry dry bulk cargoes, can be successfully used on the Arctic routes in submarine shipping.

American experts quoting the laws of hydrodynamics indicate that ships for the carriage of liquid cargoes (even ores of metals as slurry mixtures) are the type which, in perspective, has the greatest chance of being applied in submarine merchant shipping on the Arctic routes. In the years 1960–75 more than 50 theoretical projects were elaborated for solving this problem, particularly in the USA, France and in Japan. The design office of the General Dynamics Co. even elaborated a concrete conception of a 170,000-ton submarine tanker and offered to build a series of such ships for the carriage of crude oil from the American and Canadian Arctic to the Atlantic ports. The number of designs of new solutions is constantly growing. Among them there is for example, a submarine 'train' composed of segments from four to eight in number (a total carrying capacity from 360,000 to 720,000 tons) hauled by an independent propulsion section of 44,000 HP with a 33-knot velocity. The loading module, 400–500 m, width 60–65 m, of a flattened construction (height 7.5 m) would not have a great draught and could be loaded in shallow coastal waters.

It has been stressed that the risk associated with nuclear vessels is not as great as it might seem. Two American nuclear submarines have been lost (the *Thresher* in 1963 and the *Scorpion* in 1969) but no higher radioactivity was observed where they had sunk. Nevertheless, the DSRV project is to organise a special division of salvage ships, which will have the ability to prevent any dangerous effects from the loss of a vessel, even if it occurs under a thick ice crust.

The essential problem on the combined river – ocean routes is to extend the navigation season. This can be attained either by using exceptionally powerful icebreakers or by preventing the rivers freezing by heating them. Plans to use nuclear energy for the purpose have not yet materialised, owing to the very high costs, but technically they could be feasible. The opinion of biologists would have to be taken into consideration since they warn against such an inconsiderate change of natural conditions that may prove disastrous for the organisms living in the ecosphere.

Many other ideas have been proposed, which would involve far-reaching environmental effects. One plan, which is discussed from time to time, is to close the Bering Strait or to direct the warm waters of the Atlantic current to melt the Arctic ice. There are more projects of this kind, most of which are still in the realms of fantasy. More important, they do not seem to take into consideration the danger of destroying the climatic equilibrium as well as the hydrological and biological balance of the Earth, and these may bring about incalculable consequences.

8 Trunk Line Transportation in Less Accessible Regions

V. BURKHANOV

I TRANSPORT A NECESSITY FOR DEVELOPMENT

The majority of Northern Arctic regions of our planet are regarded as almost inaccessible from the transportation point of view, but the richest deposits of mineral raw materials – oil, iron ores, coal and non-ferrous metals, are located in the Arctic regions. Of about 250 billion tons of the estimated world deposits of oil 40 billion tons are believed to be located in the Arctic regions. Over twenty oil and gas basins are being explored along the continental shelf of the Arctic seas, and five deposits have been discovered.

But large-scale industrial development of most mineral deposits in the Arctic regions has been restricted until now by the transportation problem – lack of cheap transport to export raw materials.

Potential reserves of oil, gas, coal, about 60 per cent of economically feasible hydropower resources, numerous deposits of non-ferrous and rare metals that play an important role in the development of most engineering industries, electrical engineering, and above all branches that determine technological progress (radioelectronics, computers, etc.), and large deposits of iron ore, chemicals and other raw materials are concentrated in the Northern regions of the Soviet Union.

High rates of industrial growth are characteristic of the development of the North. Over fifteen years have passed since we began to develop large-scale raw material resources in our country, not only in the eastern regions, but also in the North. The development of the Soviet economy in the long run will be achieved successfully due to the utilisation of Northern industrial resources. Raw power resources of the North provide the possibility of increasing the share of the most economical types of fuel – oil and gas – in the fuel and power balance, and thus improve considerably the economic efficiency of social production.

New power bases of the national economy are being formed and old ones enlarged in the North of the country. In the future there will be a possibility of developing new oil and gas provinces between the Yenisei and Lena rivers and in other regions of Eastern Siberia and the Far East. Transportation is one of the key problems in the progressive development of the productive forces of the Northern zone. The development of transportation in the North is the immediate organisational and economic task, the solution of which will determine the degree to which particular resources may be mastered in certain regions of the North, the level and rates of economic growth and the economic effectiveness of the development of the productive forces.

Transport construction in the North is developing rapidly, but up to now it has not met the growing demands of the national economy. At present the railway network that provides reliable economic ties the whole year round covers only the European North of the country and is represented by several routes within the range of the so-called Nearer North, Siberia, i.e. a belt that borders upon the developed industrial zone. The rest of the territory of the Asian North still lacks permanent communications that could provide reliable functioning of economic centres and complexes.

Problems of providing transportation are key problems in all of the newly developing regions. But in the conditions of the North they are at the same time the most complex problems, caused on the one hand by the vast terrain, and on the other by difficulties of construction, due to unfavourable climatic and soil conditions, and the complex topography of many regions. It is technically difficult to overcome these conditions, as they multiply the costs of construction.

II AN INTEGRATED TRANSPORTATION STRATEGY

Transport problems of the North require the development of a united system of trunk lines for this zone, that could provide reliable ties between separate northern regions, and with the main transportation network of the country. It should be formed on a system of basic railway trunk lines designed in conjunction with the development of other transportation routes – rivers, the Northern sea route, interregional overland transport and systems of one-purpose (pipeline) transportation.

The future transportation concept as an integral part of the programme for the development of the productive forces of the North as a whole should be considered from a broad national economic viewpoint, in close co-ordination with all principal projects of development in other sectors of the economy.

The general outline of the basic transportation system must first be elaborated: the 'transportation grid' primarily designed for the economic development of principal Northern resources in the foreseeable future, the economic development of priority regions and successive consolidation of the transportation of these regions with the railway network of the country. At the same time it is necessary to pay attention to the possible development of the productive forces of the Northern regions in the long run and consider trunk routes, lines and sections, under construction and planned as part of a powerful, broad and complex future transportation system.

This transportation system will include as its main elements:

(1) A latitudinal transcontinental railway trunk line, that will cross the territory of the Nearer North of Siberia and the Far East. The eastern section is under construction already (the BAM), and in the western part separate sections (Surgut–Nizhnevartovsk, etc.) are being planned or are under construction. Besides its interregional role, this trunk line forms the basis for the development of regional and local lines that are successively formed according to the priority of the development of particular regions.

(2) The Northern sea route system. Its transportation significance will grow with the construction of new transportation means (superpowerful icebreakers, submarine transportation means, etc.).

(3) Principal rivers of the North which form binding links between the Northern Trans-Siberian railway line in the south and the transit sea route in the north.

(4) The system of principal pipelines that provides the flow of oil and gas from the northern regions to the west, south and east.

In the long run the construction of another latitudinal railway trunk line may be forecast, that would cross the Middle North of Siberia and the Far East.

The Baikal–Amur mainline that crosses the territory of the Nearer North of Eastern Siberia and the Far East (3150 kilometres long), is at present the principal project under construction in the national economy, the greatest of the century. It has great economic significance for the development of the northern Transbaikal regions and regions of the Nearer North of the Far East. It will provide for the industrial development of new natural resources – the Southern Yakutian coal basin, the Aldan iron ore deposits, the Udokan copper ores and many other resources that are at present undergoing industrial assessment and geological studies. The utilisation of forest resources of the Far East will grow considerably. Simultaneously the BAM will link the industrial regions of Siberia with the Pacific sea ports that will considerably intensify international relations in Siberia and the Far East.

III THE SEA ROUTES

The organisation of a system of sea outlets for natural resources and industrial commodities of the northern regions is also one of the most important transportation problems. Its solution is combined with the further improvement and development of the Northern sea route.

The Northern sea route forms the extreme northern latitudinal transportation mainline of the Northern zone, uniting the outlets of separate northern regions of the European part of the country, Siberia and the Far East that have navigable rivers, and the longitudinal railways in the European North. In the future longitudinal railway links with the Northern sea route will be constructed in Siberia.

At present, the Northern sea route, particularly its western section, is one of the most important transportation trunk lines connecting Arctic regions of Siberia, above all the Norilsk industrial node with industrial regions of the European part of the country. It provides for the development of fuel resources of the Arctic regions of the West Siberian Plain and the Timano-Pechorsk province (through Naryan-Mar), and also provides important local ties for industrial centres in the North. Simultaneously the principal Arctic ports of the European part of the country – Murmansk and Arkhangelsk – provide broad international links for the USSR with many countries of the world.

In the future the possibilities of using the Northern sea route will grow considerably due to scientific and technological progress. The construction of powerful atomic icebreakers, and later of super icebreakers will allow the period of navigation in the Arctic to be extended considerably, will increase the reliability of navigation in even the most difficult ice conditions, and will also increase the speed of convoys along the entire Northern sea route, including the most difficult eastern section.

The development of submarine routes may become another area of technological progress, where ice conditions have minimum impact. The construction and use of large submarines is one of the progressive areas in the development of transportation for bulk cargo in the Arctic Ocean.

IV THE BASIC NETWORK

Thus the 'transportation grid', i.e. the basic network of transportation trunk lines in the Northern zone, is viewed as a combination of railway trunk lines latitudinally crossing the Near and Middle North, of longitudinal and sublongitudinal railways going from south to north from the economically developed zone of the country into the Arctic regions of the Northern zone, a system of river routes along the Ob, Yenisei and Lena Rivers, and the Northern sea route, which, given new technological means, will become a permanent transportation trunk line.

Parallel to the development of this principal transportation system, the formation of a system of pipelines, the organisation of a large-scale flow of oil and gas along these original 'power bridges' from the Arctic regions to the main fuel-deficient regions of the country, will be of paramount importance for the economic development of the North.

At present the principal directions of these flows have been formed. The main volume of oil and gas extracted in the Northern zone is exported from the Timano-Pechora and West Siberian regions to the west and south-west, to the most important industrial regions of the European part of the USSR, and through them to the European socialist countries.

V THE PROBLEMS OF INTRAREGIONAL TRANSPORT

Besides the principal systems of transportation trunk lines, one of the most pressing problems of the economic development of the North is the development of intraregional types of transport. An important problem is to overcome the difficult natural and climatic conditions of the North with a rational combination of permanent and seasonal types of transport, the use of different types of transportation – overland, river (including small rivers) and air transport, and the use of various types of transportation means specially designed for northern conditions.

The construction of permanent highways in northern regions requires a special technical approach and high investment costs. In spite of this the network of highways with an improved surface is constantly growing in the North. Experience confirms the economic effectiveness of undertakings such as the new systems of autotrains with large capacity sledge-trailers.

Much attention should be paid to the use of the river system, particularly the small rivers. In summer new types of shallow-draught ships (on air-cushions, hydrofoils, amphibia) could make regular passages for cargo and passengers. In the winter season roads could be laid along large or small river beds, and this would speed up and cheapen construction compared with the building of permanent highways. Landing-stages may also be used to provide a service for such winter roads.

New types of transportation means designed especially for the North include air-cushion vehicles, tracked vehicles, etc. Experience shows that in the conditions of the West Siberian Plain these machines can successfully cross vast territories of deep swamps and very weak soils.

An important role is played by air transport in the North. At present it is the main type of passenger transport. The economic development of the majority of remote regions would have been impossible without the rapid progress of air transport. The trend in the growth of the carrying capacity of planes has a favourable economic impact on the growth of freight carried by air. In the future the cost of freight by large planes will be equal to that by motor transport. Thus it is quite natural that the role of air transport in carrying freight in the North is constantly increasing. Valuable commodities and perishable goods are already profitably delivered by air to remote regions in the North. Besides planes, helicopters are gaining economic significance for geological surveys, in construction and other work.

Technical knowledge is now being directed to the construction of new airships. New types of dirigibles are designed to carry bulky freight. New types of machines, combining the principles of a dirigible and a helicopter, are being designed in our country and abroad. They will be in use in the very near future.

Thus further development of the northern regions with the help of transportation means depends to a great extent on scientific research and development, which will determine new approaches to the solution of transportation problems in the North.

9 Transportation System Planning for Alaska Development

DAVID T. KRESGE, J. ROYCE GINN AND JOHN T. GRAY

I THE ALASKA SITUATION

Petroleum development is the dominant force determining the shape of Alaska's economic future in general and of its transport needs in particular. Alaska is, and will continue to be, an important source of petroleum for the United States, as a result of the discovery in 1969 of 10 billion barrels of oil at Prudhoe Bay on Alaska's North Slope and the completion of the trans-Alaska pipeline in 1977. About 1.3 million barrels of oil a day are currently flowing through the pipeline to the port of Valdez for shipment by tanker to refineries in the continental United States. The Prudhoe Bay field, although likely to remain the dominant element in the Alaska situation, is also proving to be the start of a series of related developments. Lease sales and exploration activities are now scheduled or under way in the Beaufort Sea north of Prudhoe Bay, in the National Petroleum Reserve west of Prudhoe Bay, and in various offshore areas in the Gulf of Alaska. Although estimates of recoverable petroleum reserves in Alaska are much lower than they were just a few years ago, it is conceivable that the areas now being explored could increase Alaska's reserves by as much as 60 to 70 per cent. The exploration and development of these fields together with the construction of a natural gas pipeline from the North Slope would obviously add substantially to the strong economic growth already being stimulated by the Prudhoe Bay production.

The inherent uncertainties in the petroleum development process and the large scale of the projects involved pose particularly difficult problems for transport planners in Alaska. These problems are compounded dramatically by the harsh climate, difficult topography, and the great distances over which commodities have to be moved, both within the state and between Alaska and other parts of the United States. With a small population spread over a large land area, Alaska's transport network is very sparse; the links are typically long, costly to construct, and carry relatively low volumes. New transportation investments often represent major changes in the structure of the system and can result in drastic shifts in the pattern of commodity flows. In this type of system, inappropriate transport decisions can be both costly and very difficult to correct. Clearly, there is a significant pay-off to effective long-run transportation system planning.

The movement of petroleum itself does not pose the most difficult problems for systems planning in Alaska because petroleum tends to be shipped by separate facilities such as the trans-Alaska oil pipeline. Instead, the difficult planning issues involve the transport of materials required by the petroleum development process and the commodities needed to support the economic growth generated by that process. This paper reports some of the initial findings of a project designed to develop and apply system simulation models to the analysis of Alaska transport planning issues. The methodology and models are described in the following section. The models are then used to project the demands on the transport system that would be generated by two possible levels of petroleum development. The analysis includes an evaluation of the performance of the system and identifies points where the increased demands are likely to require investment in additional facilities. In particular, the need for additional capacity at the port of Anchorage is evaluated in some detail. The paper also evaluates the effects, and desirability, of investing in a proposed railroad that would run through Canada to connect Alaska to the rest of the United States.

II MODELS OF ALASKA'S ECONOMIC AND TRANSPORT SYSTEMS

1 The economic model

The economic environment within which transport planning takes place is represented by the Alaska economic/demographic model developed from the research conducted since 1973 as part of the Man in the Arctic Program (MAP). The structure of the MAP model is outlined in simplified form in Figure 9.1. A more complete description of the model

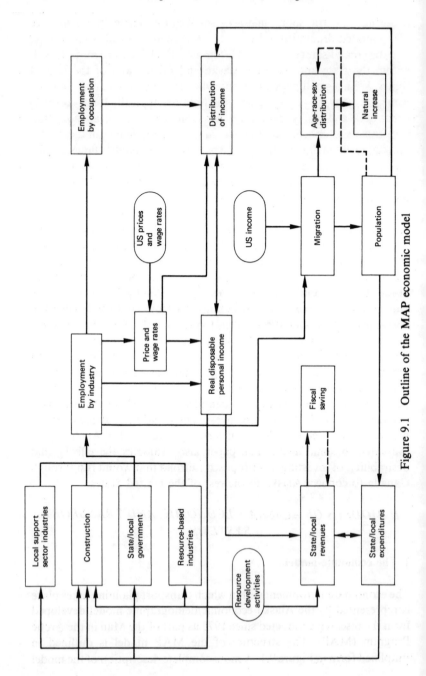

Figure 9.1   Outline of the MAP economic model

is given in Kresge, Morehouse and Rogeo, 1977 and Goldsmith, 1979. Although a regionalised model is used for the transport analysis, the basic structure is the same as the statewide model shown in Figure 9.1.

Resource development activities, particularly in petroleum, provide the primary driving force underlying the growth process. Some industries such as construction are stimulated directly by the investment in facilities for the production and transportation of petroleum. Other industries, such as trade and services, are stimulated indirectly by the increase in regional income caused by the resource development. This expansion in support sector employment will cause the total gain in regional employment to be some multiple of the direct employment in resource development.

Migration and natural increase are dealt with separately in projecting the growth in regional population, with the analysis carried out on the basis of detailed age, race and sex groups. Net migration is related to the growth in Alaska employment and to relative per capita income. When there is a relative gain in Alaska incomes, this induces additional migration and, over time, will bring Alaska back into line with the US average. The free movement of commodities and workers also tends to establish stable relationships between prices and wages in Alaska and prices and wages in the rest of the US.

The final component of the MAP model deals with the fiscal relationships in state and local government. Both revenues and expenditures are analysed on a highly disaggregated basis so that the model can accurately incorporate the appropriate causal variables, tax structure and policy instruments. As a particularly important policy option, the fiscal model recognises that the state may want to accumulate funds during petroleum boom periods which can then be used to sustain Alaska's growth in later years.

2 Transport model

The Alaska Transport model is designed to be used in conjunction with the regional economic model of the state. Figure 9.2 outlines the sequence of modelling steps required to proceed from the initial input of economic data to the output of transport system performance measures. Economic measures such as regional population, personal income and industrial output are used in empirically derived relationships to determine the demands for transport of consumer goods and industrial output. This demand is then aggregated into six commodity classifications, which are defined so that the commodities included within each

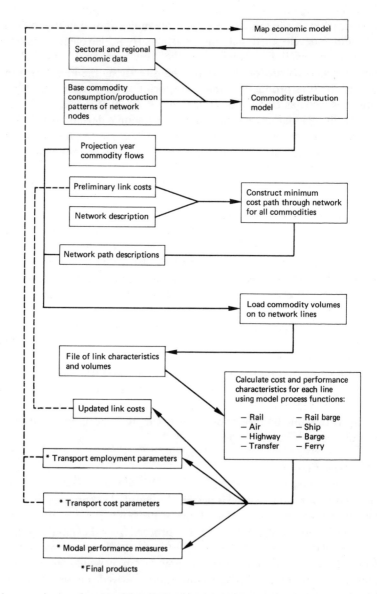

Figure 9.2   The Alaska Transport model

class have fairly homogenous tariff, time-sensitivity and handling characteristics.

At this point the model translates the basic production/consumption data into network flows using a two-stage procedure. The first step requires the determination of a set of minimum cost paths between all origins and destinations for each commodity type. The basic network over which these paths are traced is a standard type of formulation which makes each town or junction a node and the transport modes which connect these nodes the links. Each link is assigned an initial estimate of the total per ton cost of transport which is a weighted sum of tariff rates, time of transit and probability of loss and damage for each commodity type. Each town node is disaggregated into an additional set of links and subnodes representing intermodal transfers and any interface with the consumption/production system which may take place at that location. These transfer links are assigned preliminary transit costs similar to those of the modal links. After the total network has been assembled, the tree-building model finds the shortest origin-destination path using Moore's algorithm. The second stage loads the volumes for each commodity type between each origin and destination on to the shortest path determined in the first stage.

Obviously, it is unlikely that these initial estimates of shortest paths and link volumes will represent a completely realistic assignment. To improve the estimates it is necessary to iterate the model system using more realistic operation and time costs as established by modelling the operations required to serve the volume loaded on each modal link. This is done by using a set of modal engineering process models. There are eight of these models representing the air, rail, rail-barge, ship, barge, highway and car-ferry modes and the transfer process. Each of these uses as input parameters values of vehicle capacity for each commodity type, crew size and costs, fuel consumption and costs, loading and unloading requirements, vehicle costs, minimum service frequencies for each route and speed of travel. Additionally, each model contains such other parameters as may be necessary to define properly specific technologies or, in the case of the overland modes, route descriptions. These, together with estimates of overhead and maintenance requirements based on Alaska practice, are used to obtain two sets of output statistics. One of these, the revised set of link transportation costs, is directed back to the tree-building model as the internal iterative linkage in the transport modelling process. The remaining product is not used until this iterative process has been completed.

The transport model's iterative steps are completed when the transport costs which are produced by the modal models are within some predefined difference when compared to those which had previously been input to the tree-building model. For a network as sparse as that of Alaska, it is unusual for this convergence to require more than two complete iterations. With experience in use of the components and in design of the initial estimates of transport costs, it is frequently possible to use only one complete cycle.

With convergence, the remaining output set of the modal models becomes meaningful. This product contains a number of measurements of transport performance which provide sufficient detail to allow the user to focus on several levels of aggregation. These range from fairly specific project analyses on a particular link to systemwide evaluations. The latter, in the form of total network transport costs and employment statistics, are used as the feedback linkages between the transport model and the economic model. The changes in unit transport costs are used to estimate changes in Alaska's cost of living due to the impact of transport network performance. These implied differences are entered into the economic model which may then be rerun. Should substantive changes be noted in the values of the predictive measures used by the transport commodity distribution model, it is appropriate to rerun the transport model series to refine the final system performance and impact measurements. One run of the sequence will normally suffice for this refinement.

3 The Alaska transport network

In comparison with the rest of the United States, Alaska's transport network is characterised by heavy reliance on non-overland modes. All the major population centres, apart from the Fairbanks region, have access to ocean transport, and seasonal river transport is available for most areas of the interior. Air transport is most important for passengers and for the movement of high-value goods to isolated areas in the interior.

The transport network is also characterised by the flow imbalance which results in low backhaul rates. Exports are mainly bulk resource materials, while imports consist of manufactured goods and food. Thus, one vehicle type is usually not compatible with both flow directions. These two considerations have disaggregated the import commodity flows into relatively small shipment sizes and have prevented the development of a modern, efficient transport infrastructure in most areas. In most of the state, only the most rudimentary cargo-handling facilities are available and this has resulted in a severe constraint on the types of vehicles which can be used in a particular service, one which is made even more restrictive by the limited number of modal options available.

Three areas of the state have, for differing reasons, more highly developed transport networks and facilities. These areas are the Southeastern region of the state, the central 'Railbelt' corridor, and the Southwestern Peninsula and islands (see Figure 9.3). The Southeast network is primarily oriented toward the forest products industry, with several moderate sized population centres, which are not connected by overland transport. The area depends heavily on containerised tug-and-barge service for the movement of raw materials and manufactured goods. Foreign export of products is mostly to Japan by breakbulk shipping. Passenger travel is almost exclusively by air with small amounts moving on the state ferry system.

The central 'Railbelt' area more closely approximates transport patterns of the remainder of the nation. Extending 750 kilometres south

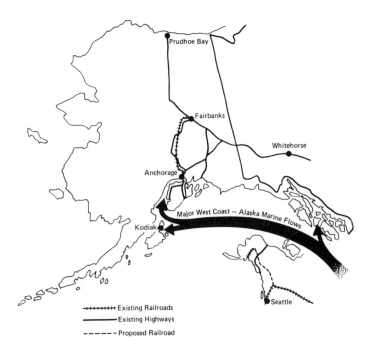

Figure 9.3   The Alaska Transport Network

from Fairbanks through Anchorage to the southern coast, it includes almost 75 per cent of the state's population. Within the corridor rail and highway dominate all except long-distance passenger movement. Exports from the region include crude petroleum, chemicals and petroleum products which are produced primarily on the southern coast or are pipelined to that area and exported by tanker, while imports of manufactured goods and food move into the region through the ports of Anchorage and Whittier. Anchorage, the state's largest port, is served by carriers based in Seattle and is a highly efficient container and roll-on-roll-off facility with direct connection to the regional highway and rail systems. Whittier serves the Alaska Railroad exclusively and provides a terminal for railcar barges, also from Seattle. Most materials moving to the North Slope and Kenai Peninsula crude production areas transit these ports.

Southwestern Alaska is like the Southeastern area in that it is also almost totally dependent on marine transport for freight movements. The system is based at the island container port of Kodiak, from which a feeder service system of barge and small ships serves the largest seafood-producing area of the state. The volume of imported manufactured items is considerably exceeded by the volume of exported fish products. This export excess is used partially to offset the empty backhaul generated by the 'Railbelt' area imports by creation of a triangular Seattle–Anchorage–Kodiak container trade system.

The remainder of the state is characterised by the use of seasonal, small-capacity surface transport, when available, and air movement under all other conditions.

Thus, given the sparseness of the network even in relatively developed regions, it is obvious that any facility additions or changes or any flow volume changes have the potential of impacting major portions of the system. The relatively small traffic volumes also make the term 'major change' refer to projects of commodity quantities which would be regarded as incremental improvements or flow diversions in more highly developed regions. This argues for a systemwide model as the most appropriate tool for establishing a basis for decision-making in the transport sector.

Based on these perceptions of the Alaska transport system, it is a fairly straightforward procedure to translate the network into a working model. A principal difficulty lies in resolving a number of possible competing links in the marine and air modes into a representative set of corridors between the major transport demand areas. For example, while it is possible in reality to obtain barge service between any coastal origins and destinations, modelling such a condition would make it impossible to trace corridorwide transportation patterns or to determine the interactions of barges with other transport modes or major commodity distribution points. It would also require a sensitivity to individually negotiated transport costs and shipment sizes far beyond the capability of any systemwide model.

The other structural issue involved the rationalisation of a large number of very small flows into a small number of aggregate origins and destinations which provide sufficient movement between them for meaningful analysis. This was accomplished by combining the flows into and out of several small points into one regional flow. Since in all cases where this was done there was almost no intraregional movement, the process proved to be entirely satisfactory.

The second major set of issues involves the characterisation of the transport modes using the link. Even at the relatively disaggregate level at which the Alaska system has been modelled, it is necessary to make some compromise in technological description. Specifically, the modal capabilities must be described so as match the level of aggregation of the network links and modes. Inevitably, this becomes an interactive process between the model and modeller, as assumptions concerning network performance are either accepted or discarded. It is also perhaps the most important step in the modelling process, as it is during this stage that it is possible to gain an appreciation of the model's capabilities and limitations in realistically describing the system.

III PROJECTED DEMANDS ON THE ALASKA TRANSPORT SYSTEM

1 A moderate growth scenario

Alaska is projected (using the MAP economic model) to show quite modest, though sustained, growth through the year 2000 just on the basis of its existing resource developments. As shown in Figure 9.4, Alaska's population under this moderate growth scenario is projected to increase steadily from 400,000 persons to reach about 520,000 in the year 2000. The scenario assumes that, except for minor extensions of existing fields, there are no new petroleum developments and there are only slight increases in the production of Alaska's other resources.

The demands on the transport system, however, increase much more substantially even in the context of this limited expansion in the Alaska

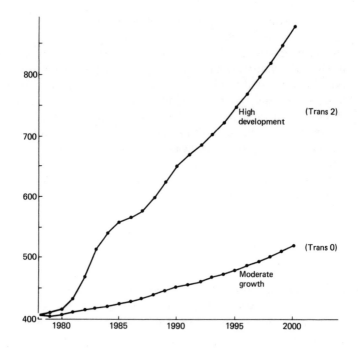

Figure 9.4   Projected Alaska population

economy. Total tonnage moving over the system increases by 83 per cent between 1978 and 2000, an average annual growth rate of nearly 3 per cent. As shown in Table 9.1, over two-thirds of the freight movements on the Alaska transport system are shipments into and out of the state, which account for nearly 80 per cent of the projected growth in freight tonnage.

There are a number of factors which account for this dominance of long-distance shipping relative to intrastate freight. First, there are almost no products which are produced in Alaska for consumption within the state. Most resources are located at sites with easy access to ocean shipping, thus exports involve little or no movement over the intra-Alaska part of the transport network. Secondly, about half of Alaska's population lives within the Anchorage area, and thus the movement of a large proportion of consumer goods finishes there.

It should be noted that this discussion (and the data in Table 9.1) excludes the movement of crude oil through the trans-Alaska pipeline and its shipment by tanker to the United States, as the transport facilities for that crude oil are completely separate from the rest of the transport

TABLE 9.1   MODERATE GROWTH SCENARIO TRANSPORT
SYSTEM TONNAGES (millions of tons)

	Total	Intra-Alaska	Into Alaska	Out of Alaska[a]
1978	11.97	3.78	3.48	4.71
1980	12.83	4.00	3.68	5.15
1983	13.88	4.16	3.93	5.79
1986	14.98	4.36	4.25	6.37
1989	16.36	4.66	4.70	7.00
1992	17.73	4.93	5.09	7.71
1995	19.18	5.23	5.55	8.40
2000	21.96	5.87	6.51	9.58

[a] Excluding movements of crude oil through the trans-Alaska pipeline and by ship to the United States.

network. On the other hand, the production and export of petroleum products are included in the analysis and, in fact, account for a substantial portion of the growth in export tonnages shown in Table 9.1.

For these reasons, freight movements into and out of Alaska are much larger and growing more rapidly than movements within the state. It is only during petroleum boom periods when interior sites like Fairbanks are used as staging areas that intrastate freight movements take on increased importance, and these booms are, however, only temporary.

Given the excess capacity present in the current network, the results of the transport model were not unexpected. They showed that with one exception, the Port of Anchorage, the present infrastructure and services are capable, with limited incremental improvements, of providing satisfactory service through the remainder of the century.

However, the results emphasise the necessity of carefully evaluating the full range of plausible economic futures before undertaking an investment from which an adequate return is dependent upon the promise of either rapid growth or the diversion of a significant portion of a flows in a relatively small market.

2 A high development scenario

It is clear that Alaska has the potential for much greater development than that shown in the moderate growth scenario. To see what additional demands might be placed on the transport system, a high development scenario is constructed which assumes that a greater proportion of Alaska's potential is exploited. It is assumed that some additional oil gas fields are brought into production north of Prudhoe Bay and in the Gulf of Alaska. In addition, a gas pipeline is constructed from Prudhoe Bay and a petrochemical complex and liquefied natural gas plant are constructed. Even more importantly, it is assumed that the state and federal governments take steps to produce much more rapid growth in Alaska's agriculture, forestry and fisheries industries. The projected expansion in these industries is taken from Scott (1979).

Under the high-development scenario, Alaska's population is projected to exceed 880,000 by the year 2000, more than double its current level; see Figure 8.4. Tonnages being shipped over the Alaska transport system increase even more rapidly, shooting up by 43 per cent in just five years after 1978 and then increasing another 85 per cent between 1983 and 2000. As in the moderate growth case, over two-thirds of the increase in traffic is due to shipments in and out of the state.

Perhaps the most striking feature of the transport system performance is that transport costs do not increase nearly as rapidly as tonnages. Real transport costs per ton fall by 10 per cent over the projection period. Real transport costs fall by 24 per cent by 2000 relative to real personal income (which is a good indicator of the overall growth in the Alaska economy) and, more importantly, fall by 20 per cent in just the first five years. The more rapid economic growth, particularly in the early years, would indeed lead to lower unit transport costs, since the increase in traffic permits the transporters to utilise the system's capacity more efficiently.

The increase in traffic does require that more transport workers be employed on the system. Thus, the improvement in capacity utilisation is accompanied by an increase in the labour/capital ratio. Under these conditions, increases in the demand for transport services will generate really large increases in transport employment.

Both the reduction in unit transport costs and the increase in transport employment have substantial impacts on the projected growth path for the Alaska economy. These effects are included in the results reported here through the feedback linkages which provide the economic model with measures of transport system performance. It is estimated that the reduction in unit transport costs in the high-development scenario could reduce the cost of living in Alaska by 3 to 5 per cent.

This reduction in prices together with the increase in transport employment have the net effect of increasing Alaska's employment by 25,000 jobs and real person income by $400 million (in 1967 prices) by the year 2000. Therefore in the high-development scenario as much as 10 per cent of Alaska's growth between 1978 and 2000 may be attributable to the changes in transport system operating characteristics and efficiency.

The higher growth rates in this scenario have somewhat more impact on the transport network than do those in the more moderate projection. However, most of these effects appear to indicate a relationship to a specific growth sector or location rather than a generalised overloading of the network. Specifically, forestry and fisheries growth requires considerable expansion of port facilities and petroleum development causes some congestion when it occurs at points relatively remote from presently existing facilities. However, in the core of the network (the 'Railbelt' area), once again it is only the Anchorage port facility which requires expansion. This expansion differs little from that required by the more moderate case. Otherwise, in only two corridors would carriers be required to absorb a high degree of volume expansion. These are the West Coast-to-Anchorage and Anchorage-to-Fairbanks corridors. Even in these instances, the capacity expansion required is well within the capability of current carriers with only normal incremental investment.

To understand the degree of change implied by these two scenarios, it is useful to undertake several specific comparisions. The differential effects of moderate and high development are shown in Tables 9.1, 9.2 and 9.3, and it can be seen that total movements in 2000 for the moderate case will approximate those of 1989 in the high-development scenario. This implies a considerable impact on project investment timing decisions that might be dependent on the analysis of these growth ranges.

Table 9.13 disaggregates the total volume into the impacts on three selected corridors while the movement in the West Coast–Anchorage corridor grows by 97 per cent in the moderate case, the change in the high case is 188 per cent. In the Anchorage–Fairbanks corridor the changes are 67 per cent and 112 per cent for the moderate and high cases respectively. This reflects the difference in projected higher growth rates for the Anchorage and Southcentral areas when compared to the interior region. The projected change between growth rates in the West Coast to Western Alaska corridor shows a change of 91 per cent for the moderate case and 301 per cent for the high case. This dramatic difference is attributable entirely to the much higher rate of growth projected for the fisheries industry in the second scenario.

TABLE 9.2   HIGH-DEVELOPMENT SCENARIO: TRANSPORT
SYSTEM PERFORMANCE TRANSPORT SYSTEM TONNAGES
(Millions of tons)

Transport system tonnages	Total	Intra-Alaska	Into Alaska	Out of Alaska[a]
1978	12.35	4.09	3.63	4.63
1980	13.22	4.36	3.87	4.99
1983	17.67	5.49	5.77	6.41
1986	19.00	5.96	5.77	7.27
1989	21.76	6.68	6.89	8.19
1992	24.05	7.43	7.43	9.20
1995	26.95	8.28	8.46	10.21
2000	32.65	10.09	10.50	12.06

[a] Excluding movements of crude oil through the trans-Alaska pipeline and by ship to the United States.

TOTAL TRANSPORT COSTS BY MODE:[b]
(Millions of 1977 dollars)

	Total System	Overland (including transfers)	Marine	Air
1978	1606.8	664.3	790.3	152.2
1980	1668.8	670.0	843.8	155.0
1983	2175.5	877.5	1106.4	191.6
1986	2293.4	922.6	1179.2	211.2
1989	2648.8	1053.8	1362.4	232.6
1992	2870.1	1119.8	1498.1	252.2
1995	3176.6	1234.4	1668.6	273.6
2000	3784.3	1470.2	1996.8	317.3

[b] Transport costs as used here include the costs associated with transit time and probability of damage as well as direct tariff costs.

TABLE 9.3   COMPARISON   OF   DIFFERENTIAL   EFFECTS   OF
MODERATE AND HIGH-DEVELOPMENT SCENARIOS

Commodity	West coast to Anchorage corridor thousands of tons/year					
	1	2	3	4	5	6
1978	356.0	159.9	198.7	159.7	210.1	372.3
2000 (Base rate)	741.0	273.8	350.3	311.0	463.5	722.8
2000 (High growth)	1231.3	1131.5	534.0	455.4	717.3	1119.8

TABLE 9.3   (*Continued*)

Commodity	Anchorage to Fairbanks corridor thousands of tons/year					
	1	*2*	*3*	*4*	*5*	*6*
1978	262.0	31.8	103.8	18.1	44.0	86.1
2000 (Base rate)	483.8	39.2	122.5	30.9	82.6	150.8
2000 (High growth)	608.5	46.1	146.2	37.8	134.1	186.9

Commodity	West coast to Western Alaska thousands of tons/year					
	1	*2*	*3*	*4*	*5*	*6*
1978	116.8	98.6	17.5	20.3	12.6	53.2
2000 (Base rate)	234.0	166.0	34.7	45.2	26.1	98.2
2000 (High growth)	560.2	282.0	66.8	82.4	56.7	220.0

1. Commodity codes: *1.* Bulk liquids
   2. Bulk solids
   3. Machinery and metal products
   4. Forest products
   5. Food products
   6. General cargo, otherwise unclassified
2. All tonnages represent through movements and do not include local traffic within each corridor.

IV PROPOSED TRANSPORT IMPROVEMENTS

1 A rail link through Canada

A transport topic of regularly recurring interest in Alaska is the construction of an overland link between the Alaska Railroad and the transcontinental railhead in northern British Columbia. A facility such as this would represent a major investment in transport infrastructure and, since it would provide an alternative routing for the state's major import and export flows, it could be expected to have impacts on a systemwide basis. Since the evaluation of this type of question is ideally suited to the capabilities of the Alaska Transport Model, an experiment was conducted to test the potential of the proposed project.

Current proposals for the route involve construction of 1600 kilometres of railroad between Fairbanks and Dease Lake, British Columbia, the projected terminus of the British Columbia Railroad's latest extension. Estimates of capital outlays, exclusive of rolling stock, are approximately $7 million per kilometre using 1977 costs. For the purposes of this exercise, construction is timed to begin in 1986 with completion and commencement of service in 1992. The overall demand for transport is assumed to be that described by the high-growth scenario.

With this background as the basis, two operational cases were considered. In the first, it was assumed that tariffs on the new route would be set so as to return all operations and maintenance costs and provide a surplus sufficient to service the construction debt at current rates available to the State of Alaska. Under these conditions, the route proved unable to attract any movement other than minor local tonnages.

In the second case, the rates were adjusted to direct operating costs only with the implicit assumption the annual maintenance-of-way and capital charges would be assumed by a public agency. Under this assumption, the rail link captures approximately 900,000 tons per annum in 1992. This tonnage represents diversions from rail barges and ships operating on a for-profit basis between the West Coast and Southern Alaska ports and from intra-Alaska trucking and rail services. Dominating flow on the link is traffic moving from Midwest and Eastern

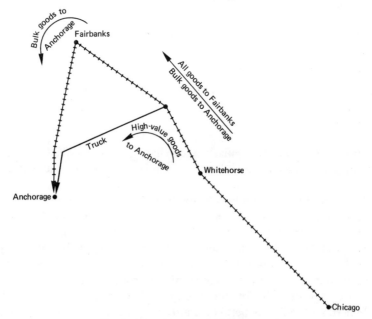

Figure 9.5 Canadian rail link use:
Chicago to Fairbanks and Anchorage

United States to Anchorage and Fairbanks. Figure 9.5 schematically displays the patterns of this movement. Of the total, about 70 per cent is destined for Anchorage.

Since the route to Anchorage is 500 kilometres longer than that of Fairbanks, the rate structure must be designed for the longer, larger market if sufficient tonnage is to be attracted to maintain operations. As a result, the much smaller, less rapidly growing Fairbanks market becomes the largest beneficiary of the investment. Table 9.4 compares total per ton transport cost from Chicago to Fairbanks for a network containing the rail link and that used for the otherwise identical high growth scenario. The costs of moving consumer goods show decreases of 50 per cent to 90 per cent with the rail link in place.

TABLE 9.4 CHANGE IN TOTAL TRANSPORT COST FOR GOODS MOVING FROM CHICAGO TO FAIRBANKS (AND NORTH) WITH AND WITHOUT CANADIAN RAIL LINK

Commodity	1	2	3	4	5	6
Rail network	164	247	420	140	96	34
Original network:	215	260	457	298	765	801
Decrease/ton:	51	13	37	158	669	767
Per cent reduction:	24	5	8	53	87	96

1. Commodity codes:
   1. Bulk liquids
   2. Bulk solids
   3. Machinery and metal products
   4. Forest products
   5. Food products
   6. General cargo other unclassified

2. Transport tariffs included in these costs represent only direct operating costs and are not designed to cover expenditures for maintenance-of-way or debt service.

The aggregate reduction in total transportaion cost for the second experiment with the rail link in its first full year of operation was found to be $87 million, equivalent to $39 million in 1977 dollars. After deduction of $17 million (based on per-mile average from 'Annual Report on the Alaska Railroad', fiscal year 1977) for maintenance-of-way expenditures, the balance of $22 million represents the direct cost savings attributable to the rail link. While this is not an insignificant amount, it should be recognised that to generate it, the state had to invest an excess of $1 billion in construction costs. This and benefit distribution questions raised above clearly call for a much more elaborate analysis of the general economic and social benefits, to evaluate properly the desirability of making a public investment of this magnitude. However, the transport model has demonstrated its ability to identify and give preliminary dimension to the questions.

2 The Port of Anchorage

In an undeveloped transport system, it is often the case that performance on one or a few critical links can influence the flexibility and capacity of the entire system. Such is the case in Alaska with the key element being the Port of Anchorage. The port has sophisticated container and roll-on roll-off capabilities in addition to breakbulk and petroleum facilities. The two general cargo berths can operate in any of the three modes mentioned while the petroleum products facility has only the single capability. Productivity of the present general cargo berths is high with each exceeding 500,000 tons throughput per year. However, the growth scenarios tested in this project indicate that under any set of assumptions, the demands on the facility will, by the year 2000, be of considerably greater magnitude than they are at present. Even under the moderate scenario, they could be expected to double while the high development assumptions would require a tripling of throughput. Under these types of demand expectations, some congestion might be anticipated if no additional capacity were installed.

A significant feature of the transport model is its ability to locate network constrictions which are acting as inhibitors to goods movements. The user can then focus on the operating and cost characteristics of the constraining link(s) in considerable detail. The model located the congestion outlined above during its initial runs. Using this information, a series of experiments were designed to determine the details of the port's performance under both development scenarios, with and without added capacity. In the early stages, it was found that the movements generated by the moderate case were within 8 per cent of those of the high case if the Canadian Rail Link is installed in the latter. Therefore, the two were combined for this analysis.

A summary of the results is shown in Table 9.5. It compares the operation of the system for both traffic situations and the addition of zero, one or two berths. All costs in this table use a 1977 base. They indicate that the addition of one berth would generate annual returns of 36 per cent and 18 per cent for the high and moderate cases respectively. However, addition of two berths could only produce a return of 6.6 per cent or 2 per cent for the second facility for the two cases. Thus, a third general cargo (container) berth appears to be an attractive investment on a strictly commercial basis under almost any plausible economic

TABLE 9.5 YEAR 2000: PORT OF ANCHORAGE

High Growth Case (no Canadian rail link)
Tons/day through container port = 9019

Alternative	Number of container berths	Average operating	*Costs per ton* Delays to commodities	Vehicle delays	Total	Savings in year 2000 (incremental)
0	2	12.96	2.95	7.05 =	22.96	0
1	3	13.06	2.91	3.15 =	19.12	3.84
2	4	13.15	2.90	2.36 =	18.41	0.71

	Incremental annual savings (1977 dollars)	Incremental construction cost				Annual return on investment
Add 3rd Berth	$3.832 million	10.66 million				36%
Add 4th Berth	0.709 million	10.66 million				6.6%

Moderate Growth Case & High Growth Case (with Canadian rail link)
Tons/day through container port = 6637

Alternative	Number of container berths	Average operating	*Costs per ton* Delays to commodities	Vehicle delays	Total	Savings in year 2000 (incremental)
0	2	13.03	2.62	5.39 =	21.04	0
1	3	13.16	2.60	2.73 =	18.44	2.60
2	4	13.28	2.60	2.26 =	18.14	0.30

	Incremental annual savings (1977 dollars)	Incremental construction cost				Annual return on investment
Add 3rd Berth	$1.91 million	$10.66 million				8%
Add 4th Berth	0.22 million	10.66 million				2%

scenario, while justification of a fourth facility would seem to be much less so.

It is interesting to note the non-linear relationship between tons handled and annual savings. The tonnage using the port in the moderate case is about one-half. This is partially due to a change in commodity mix between the two alternatives and partially to scale economies generated by more intensive usage of facilities.

While either set of development criteria indicates the requirement for a third berth, the timing of the investment decision does vary between the two. For the high-growth assumption, construction should begin by 1984 to meet the projected tonnage requirements. However, it is reasonable to delay five to seven years if the more moderate conditions are presumed. This decision would also be based on what the port's owner, the Municipality of Anchorage, would consider an acceptable rate of return for the facility.

V SUMMARY OUTLOOK FOR THE ALASKA TRANSPORT SYSTEM

While the Alaska Transport Model continues to be developed, it has reached a stage at which it is possible to draw meaningful preliminary conclusions about the state's transport system and its interactive effect on the Alaska economy. From the present work, several observations on both emerged as being of particular importance.

The existing network possesses considerable excess capacity, both in terms of facilities and the ability of carriers to provide services. With a moderate rate of growth there should be little need to invest in additional capacity. Even with high development rates, the capacity of the system is generally adequate to handle anticipated impacts apart from a few specific resource-related exceptions and the Port of Anchorage. Expansion at the port is necessary in this case and would probably be desirable in the moderate case.

A major structural addition to the network would be likely to result in an addition to the excess capacity problem. In the case of the Canadian Rail Link in which initial public investment would be large and a substantial continuing subsidy could be expected, the project would require evaluation on the basis of broadly conceived social objectives to determine its ultimate value to the state.

Finally, the improved utilisation of capacity which would accompany more rapid development could substantially reduce transport costs through increased efficiency. This can contribute significantly to the general development process.

REFERENCES

Goldsmith, O.S. (1979). *Man-In-The-Arctic-Program Alaskan Economic Model: Documentation* (University of Alaska).
Kresge, D.T., Morehouse, T.A., and Rogers, G.W. (1977). *Issues in Alaska Development* (Seattle: University of Washington Press).
Scott, M.J. (1979). *Southcentral Alaska Water Resources Study* (University of Alaska).

10 Pipeline Transportation of Natural Gas in the USSR

O. M. IVANTSOV

I EARLY BEGINNINGS

The energy problem is one of the greatest problems facing the current century. Natural gas, as shown in Table 10.1, takes the first place in the USSR's energy balance.

The development of the transmission pipeline transportation industry, in its turn, greatly affects the development of the oil and gas industries. The USSR now operates 183,000 km of transmission pipelines, including 120,000 km of gas pipelines. The total power of all the operating pump and compressor stations is 15.4 million KW. Pipeline transportation takes second place to the railways with respect to transportation capacity.

TABLE 10.1   SOURCES OF ENERGY FOR THE GENERATION OF HEAT IN THE USSR (Million tons coal equivalent)

Energy sources		Years 1975	1980
Fuel oil		215.2	265.2
Natural gas		353.4	507.4
Coal		374.8	373.4
Miscellaneous		286.6	276.6
	Total	1230.0	1422.6

Note: Fuels used as motor spirit, coking coal or chemical raw material etc. are excluded. One ton of coal equivalent is 7 million kcal.

The first oil pipeline was built in 1878, but the construction of the Saratov–Moscow gas pipeline between 1944 and 1946 is considered as the beginning of the transmission pipeline era in the USSR. This gas pipeline was mainly built by manual labour, but automatic welding, designed by the Electric Welding Institute, was used for the first time in the world in the construction of the Dashava–Kiev–Bryansk–Moscow pipeline.

II THE CAPACITY OF THE PIPELINES

Growth in the consumption of natural gas and the discovery of new gas fields in Central Asia, Komi ASSR, and later in Western Siberia have stimulated the development of gas pipeline systems and an increase in the unit capacity of the pipelines.

Table 10.2 shows the increase in the diameter and capacity of gas pipelines: 55 kgf/cm^2 remained the maximum pressure level for a long period of time. The transition from 1220 mm to 1420 mm diameter pipelines, and an increase in pressure to 75 kgf/cm^2, were made in 1973.

The discovery of gas fields in the Tumen District has caused an especially rapid development of the natural gas transportation industry. The first gas pipeline was constructed in this district in 1964, but at the present time, West Siberian gas fields are connected with the Centre and other areas of the USSR by the powerful gas pipeline systems.

TABLE 10.2   THE DEVELOPMENT OF GAS PIPELINE DIAMETER AND CAPACITY

Development period/years	Diameter mm	Operating pressure kgf/cm²	Total length thous. km
1941–45	300	up to 55	
1946–50	300	ditto	0.788
	500	ditto	2.30
1951–58	700–800	ditto	6.30
1959–65	up to 1020	ditto	30.00
1966–70	up to 1220	ditto	24.00
1971–75	up to 1420	up to 75	68.60
1976	ditto	ditto	6.80
1976–80	ditto	ditto	54.70
1980	ditto	itto	10.3

aSource: I. Ya Furman, *Ekonomika magistcalnogo transporta gaza,* (Moscow, 1978).

The average transportation distance of natural gas supply has increased continuously in the USSR, as shown in Table 10.3. Certain gas pipelines have a length of from 2500 to 4500 km. Large-diameter gas pipelines of 1220 and 1420 mm now constitute more than 30 per cent of total pipeline length.

TABLE 10.3 DEVELOPMENT OF AVERAGE TRANSPORTATION DISTANCE OF NATURAL GAS

Year	Average transportation distance (km)
1960	589
1965	656
1970	917
1972	962
1974	1126
1976	1341
1978	1580
1980	1899
1981–85	2099

Source: For 1960 to 1976 I. Ya Furman, *Ekonomika magiscalnogo transporta gaza* (Moscow, 1978) and official report on the development of The Gas Industry in 1981–90.

III PROBLEMS OF THE NORTHERN AREAS

The construction of gas pipelines in the northern areas of the USSR is complicated by extremely severe natural and climatic conditions. The areas around the Ob river, where gas pipelines are under construction, are flooded and covered with swamps. The Punga-Vuktyl and Uhta-Torjok northern routes, and many others, have large areas of swamps to overcome. In these areas, pipelines can only be built during the winter, and this requires great concentration of equipment and labour resources.

For a long time, an increase in the capacity of pipelines was associated with an increase in the pipeline diameter. The increase in pipeline diameter from 300 mm to 1420 mm means that capacity has increased in proportion to pipeline diameter by a factor of 2.5, and that the consumption of steel per unit volume of gas to be transported has been drastically reduced.

Optimisation calculations which have been carried out recently, taking into account factors such as steel quality, gas-chilling temperature, pipeline weight, reliability, modern construction equipment and capital investments in associated sectors of the economy, have shown that the optimum pipeline diameter is 1420 mm at the current level of technological development.

The construction of the northern gas pipelines requires high capital investment and labour input. Corridors for pipeline construction are narrow, and the probability of emergencies resulting from interaction with the environment and the likelihood of defects in the pipeline due to construction or operation are proportional to the length of the pipeline. However, an attempt is always made to attain the maximum capacity.

Where there is a high level of waterlogging, an increase in pipeline diameter not only increases the weight of the pipeline, but also leads to an increase in the surface of contact between the pipeline and the soil (or the permafrost in the extreme North). This contributes towards the beginning of deformations at the curved portion of the pipeline, which are caused by interacting forces of temperature and pressure. Taking this into consideration, a further increase in pipeline capacity should be provided by increasing operative pressure and by gas chilling, but not by increasing pipeline diameter. Table 10.4 shows variations in pipeline capacity with increased operating pressure and gas chilling.

TABLE 10.4   PIPELINE CAPACITY UNDER VARIOUS CONDITIONS

Operating pressure kgf/cm²	Pipeline capacity / billion m³ / year / at a temperature of				
	15° C	0° C	−17° C	−70° C	−120° C
55	–	–	–	–	101.5
75	36.0	37.2	40.0	51.4	–
100	48.0	50.6	55.0	76.5	–
120	54.6	59.0	64.6	90.7	–

Gas-pipeline capacity may also be increased by optimum spacing of compressor stations and by reducing the roughness of internal pipe surfaces. Therefore, pipeline capacity is, to a certain extent, associated with improving the quality of gas-field treatment. Under existing conditions, gas temperatures near to a compressor station can exceed 80° C, and unless the gas is cooled at every station, these will increase along the line. Such temperatures are unacceptable with the larger-diameter pipelines. Further design problems arise from the need to ensure physical stability of the pipeline and protection against corrosion. The intensity of ground-corrosion effects increases at higher gas temperatures, while protective coatings (like those based on poly-ethylene) are unsuitable for operations above the 60° C level.

In recent years, however, effective new methods of gas-cooling have been investigated and implemented in the USSR. Currently, compressor stations for high-pressure, large-diameter pipelines are equipped with air-cooling devices to lower the starting temperature of the gas. The resolution capacity of air-cooled installations is, however, limited, so gas is cooled to ambient temperatures (of less than 10° C) by means of machine-chilling. By chilling the gas to a certain temperature level, the reliability of the system can be improved, capacities considerably increased, and soil-corrosion processes retarded. Thus, chilling to between −2°C and −3°C is done, to prevent the permafrost from thawing. Chilling to between −17°C and −23°C obtains, due to the 'throttle effect', a temperature of −30° at the suction inlet of each next compressor station and this allows substantial increases in pipeline capacity. These particular operating temperatures are appropriate for multilayer pipes made from low-alloy steels, or pipes made from control-rolled steels alloyed with niobium and molybdenum, which are now in widespread use throughout the pipeline construction industry. Further gas-chilling to −70°C, and transportation of the liquefied natural gas at temperatures between −100°C and −120°C can further increase pipeline capacities, as well as reducing steel consumption, but here, special and more expensive steels become necessary.

Complex scientific, engineering and economical problems are of course associated with the processes of chilling, transporting and recovering huge volumes of natural gas. An alternative means of increasing pipeline capacities would be to construct many pipelines in parallel, but this would necessitate considerable consumption of steel, huge expenditure on labour inputs, and deleterious effects on the environment together with decreasing reliability of operations in the case of long-distance systems.

Although transmission pipelines, viewed externally, appear to be simple structures, they differ drastically from other steel structures in their complicated patterns of acting forces, their considerable un-certainty in stress-strain states, and their greater size and practical susceptibility to defects. The impossibility of visually inspecting buried pipelines, and diagnosing their stress-state while in operation, further increases risks of failure. So it is not surprising that no single type of steel structure has met with failure rates as high as these transmission pipelines. The huge scale of welding and coating operations means that some degree of eventual failure is inevitable:in 1978, 2.5 million erection joints and 9000 continuous kilometres of multilayer jointings were welded into the USSR's transmission pipeline system. The total surface area of lines annually put into operation constitutes 35–50 square kilometres. This huge surface area is of course subject to soil-steel corrosion, despite applications of coatings and cathodic-protection systems.

Because failures are inevitable, and in order to control the structural reliability of gas pipelines, it is necessary to forecast an operational reliability on the basis of statistical results of quality-control measures taken during pipeline construction. On the basis of the predetermined level of operational reliability, design standards are devised for the structures, the construction technology and the raw materials (pipes, coatings, electrodes, etc).

IV NEW DEVELOPMENTS

At the present time, new approaches are being taken towards defining the 'workability' of the system. The operating parameters of the transmission pipelines must now be designed with reference both to the actual workability of pipelines and the capacity of pipe-fabricating mills. Account is taken of the increasing danger of fractures with increased diameter and pressure, and design criteria are now set out for determining the crack propagation characteristics and for defining steel resistance towards ductile and brittle fracturing. Crack propagation characteristics make it possible to specify design criteria with respect to impact strength and ductility. The temperature of transition from the ductile to the brittle state is measured, during full-scale pipe testing procedures: a crack is artificially initiated, and the system then run over varying temperatures within a specified range. The minimum operating temperature of the gas pipeline, taking into account the air-chilling and throttle-effects provided by compressor stations along the line, is set at the −15° C level.

More reliable technical designs for northern gas pipelines are being sought in the development of improved steels, better methods for controlled heat treatment of plates, and the use of heat-hardening processes as well as in the design of new pipe structures. An entirely new approach in this field is the development of two-layer, spiral-welded and multilayer pipes. Multilayer pipes fabricated from separate shells, twisted into an Archimedean spiral from an original strip of 4–5 mm, have shown a high resistance to cracking during tests. Their temperature of transition from ductile to brittle states is 30°C higher than that of traditional pipes constructed from the same grade of steel, and their strength is 10–15 per cent more than that of sheet steel of similar grade.

The reliability and efficiency of transmission pipelines depends, to a great extent, upon the quality of their design. Maximum efficiencies, at the predetermined levels of operating reliability, can only be achieved by using an optimum designing method. Computer models for the optimum design of pipeline routes are therefore built, which take account of the characteristics of the terrain. Using this approach, the best designs can be achieved while at the same time the entire design process can be fully automated. The use of the optimum designing method has provided an average reduction of capital investments in pipeline construction of between 8 and 10 per cent. Moreover the designing process itself is simplified so that labour inputs are greatly reduced.

The USSR's transmission gas pipelines have cathodic protection over 91 per cent of their total length. The power of cathodic protection stations continuously increases: it is now between 5 and 10 KW. Stations are automatic, with independent power supplies and thermo-electric generators. Long-distance belt protectors are also in use.

The maximum efficiency of transmission gas pipelines can only be achieved by attending design capacity within a short period of time. This is done by improving equipment, designs and construction technology, which results in faster erection of compressor stations. The locations of stations over the pipeline are determined after hydraulic calculations have been made. Under the USSR's arctic conditions, stations are very often located far away from industrial regions, railways, roads and settlements, on swamp or permafrost areas that are impassable in the summer. Under these conditions, all their structural elements must be made small and light. Delivery often requires the use of helicopters during suitable seasonal periods. They need to be erected by the minimum of manual labour, especially in the northern areas which suffer a deficit of labour supply.

Further improvements to methods of constructing and erecting pump and compressor stations have been realised through package-construction methods, which have been developed over the last decade. Considerable volumes of materials and assemblies are transferred to their sites direct from the construction plants. Package-modules comprising equipment, piping and control instruments are installed within prefabricated buildings, to be mounted and connected on site. Full use of package-construction was made in the new industrial complex within the Tumen district. Here, it proved possible to halve the total weight of all structures. Labour savings amounted to between 30 and 50 per cent, and construction time was reduced by a factor of two.

In addition to increasing the capacity of gas pipelines, the unit power of compressor sets can also be increased. Collarless compressor sets with a power of 25,000 KW are now being tested, and the first station equipped with ship-driven compressor sets has already been built. New sets are more reliable and efficient than the traditional types. Their modular packaging allows construction time for a station to be reduced by 1.5 to 2 times. Design stages for the creation of full-head sets are now complete, and these will allow simpler, parallel piping of sets to replace the in-series systems.

Treatment of natural gas in the field is of paramount importance for the efficient operation of gas pipelines. Packaged, automatic, high-capacity gas treatment facilities are now in use, alongside absorption-treatment plants with a capacity of 3 million m^3 per day. Similar systems are currently being designed to a capacity of 5 million m^3 per day. Also in current use are low-temperature separation-flow-sheets which inject an absorbent into the gas stream. These make use of new absorbents capable of operating at low temperatures, and the systems use natural zeolites within a new apparatus which operates both as a separator, absorber and glycol-filter. The experimental prototype of this turbo-expanding system has a capacity of 5 million m^3 per day, and designs for gas-chilling have been tested.

Finally, automisation methods have been introduced throughout the industry, on a broad scale: 65 compressor stations and 10 gas-treatment facilities were automised during the current five-year period, and over the last ten years the volume of gas pumped by pipeline has increased by a factor of 2.4. According to current estimates, the transportation volume of gas pipelines will constitute 813 trillion m^3 km in 1980. Meanwhile, the USSR's gas pipeline transportation industry will continue undergoing further developments.

11 Efficient Long-distance Fuel Transportation

R. W. LAKE, C. J. BOON AND C. SCHWIER

I INTRODUCTION

One of the most difficult tasks facing the transportation analyst is the economic analysis of new service or new infrastructure investment proposals, particularly the determination of the transportation mode or combination of modes most appropriate for the provision of a particular transportation service. Since its 1971 study of the railway alternative to the pipeline and marine transport of Alaskan crude oil, the Canadian Institute of Guided Ground Transport (CIGGT) has been involved with an almost continuous series of modal and system investment alternative evaluation studies, most of them involving the railway or pipeline transportation of fuel. All but the latest of these – a comparison of alternative high-speed passenger systems between Toronto and Montreal, a distance of approximately 600 km – can be classified as long-distance transportation.

This paper reviews these studies with an emphasis on the development of our approach to the economic evaluation problem for increasingly complex sets of alternatives. This should be of more general value than our study conclusions, since experience has shown that generalisation from the economics of specific transportation circumstances is perilous. Consequently, the coverage given to the individual study frameworks and technical details is too scanty to permit adequate understanding, although in each case, a more thorough treatment has been, or will be, published.

II GENERAL EVALUATION ISSUES

Most of the studies were conducted on behalf of, and from the vantage point of, government, but consistent with recent Canadian transportation policy thinking, commercial viability rather than economic efficiency dominates the evaluation criterion. Thus financing and taxation were included as active parameters, with governmental (crown corporation) carriers treated as if they were private profit-seeking firms.

The three most difficult problems CIGGT faced in the development of a suitable modal-alternative economic-evaluation procedure are of more universal interest.

(1) Some modes must, by their nature, be dedicated to a single product, or narrow range of products. A large-diameter crude oil pipeline, for example, can handle batches of different crudes, but it certainly could not accommodate natural gas. As was the issue in the Canadian Mackenzie Valley transportation corridor concept, a highway in the short term, followed by a natural gas pipeline, an oil pipeline, and a few years later a railway dedicated to the carriage of mineral products, when overall a multipurpose railway would have proved the optimal initial transportation mode, would have been an unfortunate solution.

(2) The choice of a mode dictates a particular level of capital (initial capital investment) intensity, and with it an inverse relationship between capital intensity and transportation unit cost vulnerability to the impact of inflation. Pipelines are generally the most capital-intensive mode and hence the least exposed to operations cost escalation. Particularly when system construction is financed (in part) by borrowed funds, debt service (interest and capital repayment) cash flow requirements and depreciation procedures, combined with even a modest level of general cost and price inflation, lead to a decreasing real requirement for revenue or real transportation unit price over time. This effect is demonstrated in Figure 11.1, where transportation unit costs – really the annual cash flow required to support the system – computed for a mine railway extension are compared to the trucking alternative unit cost which was presumed to escalate at the general inflation rate.

(3) Beyond capital intensity and the inflation rate considerations are difficulties posed by differential cost escalation. The prices of all productive inputs do not normally escalate at the same rate. In the case of transportation system alternatives under current economic

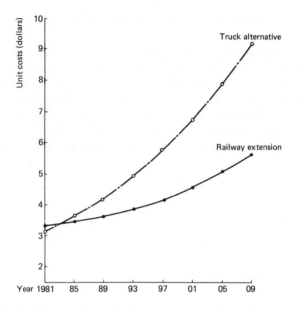

Figure 11.1   Computed unit charges – increase over time

conditions, there are two dominant effects; the persistent real increase in price of labour (which will presumably continue indefinitely), and the rapid escalation in the real price of petroleum fuel (which should decrease over the longer term as input substitution is forced).

While, strictly speaking, these concerns are not restricted to the transportation system or modal investment decision, they are much more acute in the transportation context. Investments are large and very long-term, and gradual technological or modal changes are rarely practical. The implementation of a technological stage change (Corneil, Lake, Law *et al.*, 1976) – from diesel to electric railway operation, for example – is not readily reversible, while the highway/pipeline/railway decision is even more permanent. CIGGT experience has led to an evaluation procedure that we feel does a reasonable job of treating the problems of modal comparisons, differing levels of capital intensity and differential input price escalation, but there are still important factors it does not accommodate. The subsequent sections of this paper review some of our evaluation projects, particularly those concerning the railway or pipeline decision, and discuss those issues for which we have developed some form of solution, as well as those for which a practical means of quantification as yet eludes us.

III CANADIAN CIRCUMSTANCES

Canada is a large country, and virtually every major market for Canadian natural resources requires long-distance movements over land. Canada's position is not unique – the United States, Australia and the Soviet Union face similar problems – but Canada's situation is probably the most acute, since Australia and the US are considerably smaller than Canada, and the US and Soviet Union produce proportionately more for domestic than export markets. Where world markets are far removed from the producing areas, the total transportation cost (price) can constitute a large proportion of the delivered price. Thus, not only is selection of the most appropriate transportation mode of great significance to the profitability of the remote resource development, but accurate prediction of the transportation charges required to support the transportation system investment is a crucial input to the resource-development economic-viability decision. Depletion of a non-renewable resource always involves a national cost that does not show on the financial statements. Exploitation and export of scarce resources at net economic loss – and as Canadians we have done our share of this – is to be avoided if at all possible.

IV RAILWAY TO THE ARCTIC

In 1971 CIGGT, under contract to the Canadian Ministry of Transport, undertook a preliminary study of the technical and economic feasibility of a railway to move crude oil from Prudhoe Bay, Alaska, along the Arctic coast and up the Mackenzie Valley (see Figure 11.2) to a pipeline terminus located at the southern limit of significant ice-rich permafrost, (Law, Corneil, Lake and Helmers, 1972). From this point the oil would have been moved via pipeline to markets in the US Midwest, nominally in the Chicago area.

Canadian governmental interest in moving American oil from one point in the United States to another might seem unusual, but the US plan involved a pipeline across Alaska and tankers south along the Canadian coast to a terminus within sight of the border. Any oil spills would, Canada contended (and it has since unfortunately been proved),

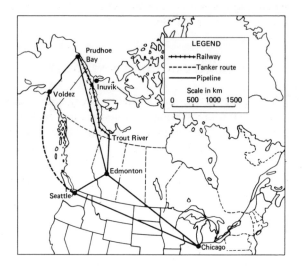

Figure 11.2   Alternatives for the movement of Prudhoe Bay oil

foul the Canadian coast. The British Columbia coast, in addition to its scenic and recreational value, has by far the richest salmon fishery in the world, and hence Canadian representations against the pipeline/tanker route were made at the highest level. As part of its programme of providing the Americans with alternatives, the government commissioned the railway study.

Because the input data were simple – a single quantity of a single product moved from a single origin to a single destination over a dedicated railway – the economic evaluation procedure required for this study was also reasonably simple. Capital and operating costs for the system were estimated, and appropriate commercial financing and equity return parameters were determined (pursuant to the commercial viability objective). Combined with the statutory taxation and capital consumption allowance rates these constituted the input data. It only remained to compute a unit tariff. The discounted cash flow equation

$$\text{Present value} = \sum_{t=0}^{\infty} (\text{Revenue}_t - \text{Cash Outflow}_t)\,(1+k)^{-t}$$

where k is the required return on the equity investment, was solved for the annual revenue capable of supporting a zero present value. This procedure has been preserved in the Institute's approach to subsequent studies. With a single annual volume of a single product, translation to a unit cost or estimated tariff presented no problem.

V ARCTIC OIL AND GAS BY RAIL

Although in one sense the Railway to the Arctic Study was a failure – the Americans approved the pipeline/tanker route without serious consideration of Canadian alternatives – in another, it was surprisingly successful. As a transportation mode in flat regions of ice-rich permafrost (the Arctic coast and Mackenzie Valley are characterised by extremely mild grades and high soil moisture content) a railway was competitive with an oil pipeline. Technical feasibility was not a serious issue (the Hudsons Bay line has operated over worse terrain for some fifty years). The computed tariff seemed reasonable, and most importantly, the government was impressed by a railway's ability to move a multiplicity of products in both directions, and by the massive carrying capacity of a double-track, low-gradient, low-curvature railway.

Out of this official interest arose the 'Arctic Oil and Gas by Rail' study (Maughan, Smith, Lake *et al.*, 1974) which focused on the transportation of Canadian resources to Canadian and American markets. The carriage of Alaskan oil or liquefied natural gas was considered secondary. This study, conducted in 1973 by a team drawn from the Canadian National and Canadian Pacific railways and CIGGT, was much more detailed technically (particularly concerning geotechnical conditions and construction materials), and developed charges applicable to thirty-two hypothetical product/volume/origin/destination circumstances. A procedure for defining feasible product/origin tariff ranges to allow realistic railway/pipeline modal comparisons while precluding hidden cross-subsidisation was developed, and is reported elsewhere (Lake and Macdonald, 1978). The crucial aspect of the study, however, was its non-comparative nature. Pipeline economic feasibility studies existed, but did not apply to the same set of circumstances, so that comparisons could not readily be made.

VI RAILWAY AND PIPELINE TARIFFS

The Institute initiated a comparative study (Engelbloom and Lake, 1977) – again at the behest of the government – in 1976. The multiple origins were eliminated, and pipeline and railway study data updated to develop figures for comparable systems (although these systems were hypothetical, in the sense that no organisation was proposing to build them). In effect modal costs were re-estimated from the physical system design data, using consistent estimating assumptions, to produce a reasonable level of comparability.

Unfortunately (from the point of view of the study), it was decided to delay any further Mackenzie Valley transportation system development, and the study was suspended after only the gas pipeline option had been costed. This evaluation did, however, incorporate a significant evaluation methodology improvement. The Arctic Oil and Gas by Rail analysis did not provide a means for capturing the effects of varying capital intensities on the unit transportation charges required to support the system – charges which would change over the life of the system. Prior to the Railway and Pipeline Tariffs study, the evaluation model was expanded to incorporate the impact of cost escalation.

Since the impact of inflation on total system costs depends on the different capital investment requirements and the relative capital intensity of each option, cost escalation – both capital and operating – must be explicitly addressed. Although adequate for most applications, the constant dollar approach to cost escalation is not appropriate for the selection of a transportation mode, since modal choice itself dictates the level of capital intensity. As various cost elements – especially those related to debt and capital consumption allowance tax savings – flow from escalated capital costs but do not escalate in themselves, the constant dollar approach ignores certain aspects of the impact of cost escalation.

In the model (Lake, Schwier and Macdonald, 1979) cash flow estimates are taken at current price levels and subdivided into operating costs, capital investment (by asset class), and proceeds from asset disposal. These are then escalated to the levels that would prevail in the year of expenditure. From these cost projections, the legal dollar[1] flows (debt financing, debt repayment and interest) – are calculated.

From these cash flows – except interest – a constant dollar charge rate is calculated in a manner similar to the computation of the unit cost discussed earlier. A schedule of annual legal dollar unit costs is then obtained by escalating the constant dollar change rate. Annual interest

[1] A legal dollar is defined here as a bank note equivalent, while a constant dollar is defined as the purchasing power equivalent. Although they would be somewhat ambiguous in the context of this paper, the terms current and real are frequently used.

expense per unit is directly assigned against each year's traffic, the annual charges reflecting the book value of the capital assets concerned.

In essence, while return on equity (dividends) is expected to keep pace with inflation, debt service charges and capital consumption allowance are based on the book value of the infrastructure capital assets (that is, historical cost less straight line depreciation).

The unit cost schedule is simply a description or forecast of how transportation unit charges are expected to behave over time.

VII MODAL SELECTION FOR WESTERN COAL

In 1977, a preliminary or prefeasibility study of the movement of coal (or coal derived energy) from Alberta to markets in the industrial region of Southern Ontario was completed (Boon, 1978) – largely as a pilot project for a more detailed treatment that is yet to be conducted. The four alternatives were: a rail lakeboat system, with trans-shipment at Thunder Bay Ontario; a slurry pipeline/lakeboat system, again with Thunder Bay trans-shipment; a High-Voltage, Direct-Current (HVDC) transmission system, linking mine-mouth generators with the existing Ontario electrical power grid; and a system of coal gasification plants, feeding existing natural-gas pipelines supplying gas-fired thermal generating stations located in Ontario.

Although the cost data developed for the analysis cannot be regarded as definitive, they were sufficient for a preliminary study. Consistent with a pilot project the emphasis was on detailed cost enumeration rather than precision, and an evaluation methodology suitable for a more thorough study was used. The fundamental comparison involved one relatively more labour-intensive and three capital-intensive alternatives, but differential cost escalation was not considered a major issue (at least at the time of the study).

The analysis established that (as shown in Figure 11.3), two of the systems – high-voltage direct-current transmission and coal gasification – were far more costly than either the rail/lakeboat or slurry pipeline/lakeboat alternatives. Further analysis then centred on the railway and slurry pipeline components of the two remaining systems.

This work demonstrated that while the unit train alternative would be preferable through the year 2000, its advantage decreased steadily over time. Further, the development of the system 'tariffs' was based on minimum incremental capital and operating costs, and this approach

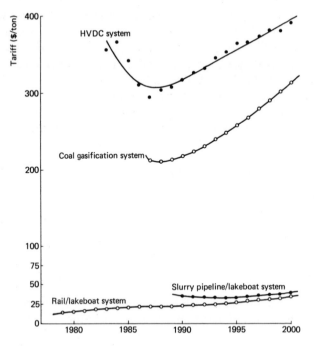

Figure 11.3 Annual systems 'tariffs', per ton of coal or the equivalent in coal-derived energy, delivered to Ontario for use

does not consider allocated costs that would, or could, be charged against the service. These basic rates only provide for the recovery of all direct capital and operating costs, plus a reasonable rate of return on the marginal investment.

Since the marginal and total capital outlays are nearly identical for the slurry pipeline, the effect of allocated costs on the competitive position of the unit train is the major issue. The railways would not price the service at the minimum (marginal) rate represented by the calculated 'tariff'. Rather, the price would be set at the highest level that would capture the traffic while satisfying all regulatory considerations, with the additional revenue providing a contribution to system-fixed costs (overhead) and possibly a margin of real economic profit. (Cross-subsidisation is a characteristic of Canadian railway transportation, but it is the minerals, including coal, that subsidise agricultural products.)

Remembering that, consistent with Canadian transportation policy, the chosen evaluation procedure is as much a model of the pricing process, with financial (cash flow) viability in the forefront, as it is a measure of economic preference, the candidate carriers' vantage point within the national economic picture is relevant. Figure 11.4 shows the limits of an evaluation model when viewed from the carriers' perspective (Schwier and Lake, 1977). In that case, the discounted cash flow was one developed to measure the incremental present value of benefits of railway electrification under conditions of differential cost escalation and volume growth.

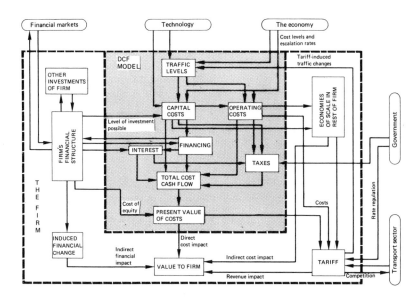

Figure 11.4   Canadian railway electrification study evaluation model in the context of the corporate decision

Seen in this context, it was necessary to perform a broad sensitivity analysis as part of the prefeasibility study. The results in Figure 11.5 demonstrate that if the total railway costs were to increase by 25 per cent, while the total costs for the slurry system decreased by 25 per cent (and these are possible margins of error) then the preference for rail would be reversed. This is not the only combination of changes that could result in a decision reversal, but it is representative.

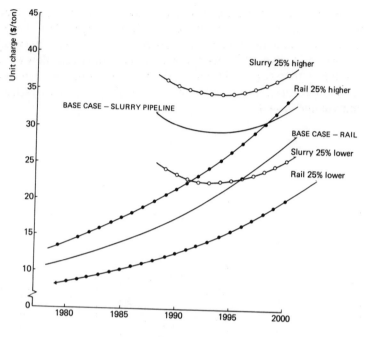

Figure 11.5 Railway/slurry pipeline sensitivity to changes in total systems costs

VIII DATA COMPARABILITY PROBLEMS

Being a pilot study, and unlike the other studies the Institute has conducted, the Western Coal study leaned heavily on costs generated and reported elsewhere. Almost without exception, a strong study-specific bias could be detected. Surprisingly, this phenomenon, expected in the case of corporations promoting a development from which they intended to earn a profit, was equally troublesome in the case of governmental institutions where the motivation was less obvious.

The range of costs attributed to a given mode was quite spectacular, even allowing for inflation and cost escalation. Further, there was a tendency on the part of some authors to cost portions of the relevant system, rather than all components, then compare these partial costs to the full costs of other modes. Also, in some instances, it was difficult to ascertain just what elements were in fact included in the stated costs.

In analysing the four systems selected for study, an attempt was made to follow a middle course between high and low estimates, but this did not always prove possible.

For example, two sources of cost data were available for the high-voltage direct-current system, and both apparently overstate the costs. The figures developed by Canadian Arctic Gas Study Limited were derived to justify the position that there was no preferable alternative to a Mackenzie Valley gas pipeline. On the other hand, the costs developed by Ontario Hydro (a provincial government agency) lack this intentional upward bias, but the conservatism inherent in such an organisation provides a strong incentive not to underestimate costs, especially in the preliminary stages of project costing.

The approach taken in the Arctic Oil and Gas by Rail study, where virtually all component costs were developed from first principles by an independent study group, gives the internal control over the costing process necessary for a reliable modal comparison. However, this approach is expensive.

IX TORONTO–MONTREAL HIGH-SPEED PASSENGER STUDY

While neither related to fuel transportation nor, at 600 km, really long-distance, the current comparison of proposed corridor passenger modes – high-speed electric railway, high-speed diesel railway, air and a magnetically levitated (Maglev) vehicle system – is significant because it forced an extension to the modal evaluation model that will be applied to the anticipated more detailed railway or slurry pipeline coal study. The air mode is characterised by relatively low infrastructure capital costs (as a result of indirect subsidisation), high labour and fuel costs, and high operations (variable) capital costs for aircraft. An electrified railway, on the other hand, is characterised by high infrastructure capital cost, modest labour and low energy costs, and relatively low rolling stock capital costs. The composition of the diesel rail and Maglev costs are similarly diverse.

For such a study, an evaluation procedure that fails to accommodate differential escalation is ignoring the basic premise that governs such decisions as electrification – that the real price of petroleum fuel will escalate. To this end, system expenditures, both capital and operating, have been segregated into reasonably homogeneous categories (civil construction, electrical systems, state-of-the-art vehicles, operating labour, diesel fuel, electricity, etc.) for which cost escalation indices are available or can be developed. Modification of the model to accommodate both differential escalation and the effects of general inflation caused a few algebraic difficulties. The selected procedure involves separate treatment of each escalation rate cost category, and aggregation to obtain total cash flows and calculated transportation unit charge.

This methodology holds distinct advantages for those future evaluations of energy transportation alternatives in which CIGGT anticipates involvement.

X PROSPECTIVE DEVELOPMENTS

The problems discussed and CIGGT's approach to their treatment do not constitute any advance in economic theory, but hopefully our experience with the practical problem of evaluating alternative modes from the perspective of the unit costs or charges, that could be necessary to support them, will be of some use.

There are two additional considerations we believe will require attention. The first innovation that must be considered is some form of probabilistic treatment. Secondly, differential escalation – at least in some circumstances – is a transitory phenomenon. Applied over a long period, even a small geometric growth rate differential can lead to ridiculous results, with the presumed (model) price of one input vastly higher than other readily substitutable inputs. Clearly, the differential must decrease over time. For the Canadian Railway Electrification Study, this was modelled as exponential decay analogous to the electrical or spring damping contexts. (Exponential functions are also used by econometricians.) The present value criterion adopted for the electrification study does not, however, present the difficulties that must be addressed before this feature can be treated in the modal comparison context.

XI OBSERVATIONS ON LONG-DISTANCE FUEL TRANSPORTATION

The dominant conclusion from the Institute's studies of the long-distance transportation of coal, oil and natural gas is that no single mode is clearly superior over a wide range of circumstances. There are however some general observations that follow from our studies.

For natural gas, over all but the longest land distances, vapour phase pipelining is cheaper than the modes that require liquefaction, but the geotechnical problems posed by the Canadian Arctic substantially shorten the distance over which pipelining has an advantage. Natural gas in the liquid phase is more valuable than the gaseous product. It can be stored readily, and it can be used as a portable transportation fuel. Liquid-phase transportation economies (once the liquefaction cost has been sustained) are substantial.

Crude oil pipelines are approximately as energy-efficient as the railway equivalent, and much more so than natural gas lines. Pipeline operation involves less labour (the cost of which escalates persistently) than rail, but it is less flexible. Volume (sufficient to warrant a dedicated system) and long life (as limited either by the field or by supply and demand patterns) govern the economics of both crude oil and petroleum products pipelining. National security (defence) considerations markedly favour the railway option, while the oil companies' desire for vertical integration favours pipelining.

The slurry/pipeline/railway decision for coal is very complex, and particularly situation-specific. The presence of existing good quality trackage is a major factor, as is the ability to dispose of the polluted water at the pipeline destination. The coal or coal-derived energy circumstance is further complicated by the different form in which the energy reaches the point of consumption. The finely ground wet material recovered from a slurry system is less valuable than the dry railway-delivered product. Of course synthetic natural gas and electricity are progressively more valuable. The relative values vary with local conditions at the point of consumption. Under such circumstances one must be prepared to modify the evaluation methodology to accommodate the important characteristics (differences) of the relevant alternatives.

REFERENCES

Boon, C. J. (1978). *A Preliminary Analysis of Factors Affecting the Movement of Western Canadian Coal to Ontario*, CIGGT Report 78–6.

Corneil, E. R., Lake, R. W., Law, C. E. *et al.* (1976). *Canadian Railway Electrification Study: Phase 1*, CIGGT Report 76–2.

Engelbloom, G. M. and Lake, R. W. (1977). *Railway and Pipeline Tariffs Applicable to Mackenzie Delta Crude Oil and Natural Gas*, CIGGT Report 77–1.

Lake, R. W. and Macdonald, J. A. (1978). Tariff Rate Determination Under Common Cost: The Cross-Subsidisation Criterion in Practice, *AIIE Transactions*, December.

Lake, R. W., Schwier, C. and Macdonald, J. A. (1979). Evaluation of Model

Alternatives on the Basis of Transportation Unit Cost Schedules, *Logistics and Transportation Review*, 15, No. 2, March.
Law, C. E., Corneil, E. R., Lake, R. W. and Helmers, H. O. (1972). *Railway to the Arctic*, CIGGT Report 72-1.
Maughan, R. G., Smith, J. S., Lake, R. W. *et al.* (1974). *Arctic Oil and Gas by Rail*, Information Canada. (See especially Vol. 6, *Cost Data and Analysis.*)
Schwier, C. and Lake, R. W. (1977). Criterion of Economic Evaluation of Canadian Railway Electrification, *Canadian Transportation Research Forum*, TRF, XVIII.

Discussion of Papers by Professors Zaleski and Burkhanov; Drs Kresge, Ginn and Gray; Drs Ivantsov, Lake, Boon and Schwier

Professor Hunter introduced this group of papers. The papers by Professors Zaleski and Burkhanov had dealt with problems at the frontiers of applied science. The technical difficulties of transport in the inaccessible, unbelievably cold conditions of the far North were enormous. For example, if railroad track were laid across permafrost territory – where only the top two or three metres of soil thawed out each summer – the track would be in danger of being swallowed up as the ground thawed and being pushed out as the ground froze. Problems with lubricants that froze, delicate tundra that could be ruined for decades, seismic regions east of Lake Baikal, and hostile living conditions generally led to very high construction, maintenance and operating costs. So it was worthwhile considering all possible options: overland, large-tyred vehicles, pipelines, even transport under the ice of the Arctic Ocean. However, he would query Professor Burkhanov's target of an approximately rectangular grid arrangement with railways East–West and never North–South. Was this really economic? Generally the minimum-cost route over three-dimensional terrain was not a straight line.

Turning to the paper by Drs Kresge, Ginn and Gray, he saw an analysis combining a model of the whole economy of Alaska with a submodel of the transport sector: this was new ground in theoretical modelling, about which many practitioners were sceptical. But his view was that the careful inclusion of operating costs – even terminal and interchange costs – made the model a useful one. Its conclusions were that with a modest rate of economic growth less expansion of the transport system was called for than might have been expected: a third berth at the port at Anchorage would be justified, but a Canada–Alaska railroad probably not.

Drs Lake, Boon and Schwier had considered the feasibility of a railroad from Alaska – first using the coastal route, then inland. Their analysis argued that the railroad was economically competitive, though in the event the US favoured a pipeline in the Northern stretch and then tankers (at the expense of damage to fisheries along the coast). This raised wider questions of the depletion of non-renewable resources generally, which was a cost to the economy not shown on the accounts of enterprises. Another important analytic point was that the impact of inflation on capital costs was likely to differ from its impact on labour and other variable costs, depending on how capital charges were treated in the accounts.

Dr Ivantsov showed the supreme importance of the transport of natural gas, compared with oil and coal, especially in the European part of the USSR. What was extremely interesting here was the interaction among the technological factors influencing pipeline transport: as the diameter of the pipe increased, costs went down – but the danger of rupture and problems of bringing and fixing the pipe increased. This set an upper limit of 1420 mm diameter. There was a related problem on the optimum temperature at which the gas should move, since cooling reduced corrosion of the pipe – which was obviously easier in the far North.

There were two general issues, *Professor Hunter* argued, considering all the papers together. First, it was interesting to look at the importance (and difficulty) of modelling. In some ways the USSR was well ahead of the West in mathematical modelling methods for these problems.

Secondly, there was the problem of the proper consideration of costs – especially over a long time period. What period indeed was appropriate – the lifetime of the infrastructure; the exhaustion of the field; the duration of present demand patterns? An optimal time path of use of a non-renewable resource could be achieved by increasing the price, year by year, up to the initial cost of the next best substitute when the last ton was used. Similarly, they should consider geographical as well as temporal opportunity costs, especially when there were worries about the export of non-renewable national resources.

These two themes raised by Professor Hunter were taken up in the general discussion, as were additional questions on the relative advantages and technical problems of railway development, roads, pipelines, submerged vessels and other modes of transport.

There was considerable interest, especially from Western delegates, in Soviet mathematical modelling methods – which had been referred to in the papers, and by Professor Hunter – but not explained in detail.

Professor Seidenfus raised this question, as also did *Mr Kaser*, and *Dr Lake*. *Professor Burkhanov* argued that no transportation problem was resolved without mathematical modelling, and for that reason there had been substantial development of models in the USSR. For example, some hundreds of variants for the construction of railways on permafrost had been tested, using a mathematical model. *Mrs Borisenko* briefly mentioned the use of minimax and probability methods, for example to optimise selection of oil fields, and for pipeline design. In general, Soviet models were optimising rather than descriptive. However, details were not discussed.

The first theme in this discussion was the relationship between transport costs and resource development, initiated by *Professor Zaleski* who argued that in some cases, costs were not 'economic' but 'necessity' – i.e. there were no alternatives but the provision of, say, a railway route. *Dr Lake* made a similar point about Canadian development of Arctic coal and iron ore: this was really a decision about the whole economy – at the present stage, the choice was 'rail, or no development at all'. *Professor Seidenfus* said, 'but there is the alternative *not* to develop'. (Laughter from many delegates.)

Professor Khachaturov said that Professor Burkhanov's argument was good but did not go far enough. Consider the importance of the resources in the Soviet sector of the Arctic – i.e. gold, non-ferrous ores, gas, oil, and further South, timber. These resources were going to become more and more valuable – surely we ought to include this increase in value in the economic analysis of the transport developments without which we could not obtain the resources.

Professor Seidenfus argued that just because gold was discovered in the earth, there was no *necessity* to bring it out – they had still to consider whether the returns would exceed the costs. *Professor Hunter* supported the point: they should not assume that the resources were 'valuable' simply because they were costly to recover.

Professor Burkhanov agreed with Professor Khachaturov that the value of natural resources was one of the elements of the economic efficiency of transport development, and this was especially important in the little-known territory of the far North, where the value of resources appeared unlimited – for example, the Russians had oil there which was cheaper than in the Baku oilfields. He thought that Professor Hunter misunderstood the argument in his paper – he would certainly not advocate building a network of railways simply to fit a pattern. Routes were selected by a strict approach, and the rate of return (including the value of the material resources) was used to assess which alternatives to adopt. Calculations had shown cases where very high returns were provided – for example in Western Siberia the return had already paid for the investment three times over.

The conference also discussed the effects of inflation. *Dr Tye* questioned Dr Lake's treatment of it. It was of particular importance because of the increase in inflation rates in the US and other Western countries. Ideally, the expectation of inflation should not effect either the real (nominal minus inflation rate) rate of return on a project, nor the decision as to the most appropriate investment project. All costs and revenues should be properly indexed or deflated so that the 'best' project did not depend on the expected rate of inflation.

Unfortunately, this was not always the case. Two alternative views had been expressed. In one, high rates of inflation justified more capital-intensive projects because loans were paid off with future dollars that were worth less than present dollars, and capital expenses did not increase as fast as operating expenses during periods of high inflation. By the same token, of course, high inflation rates put a front-end load on projects, requiring very heavy interest charges in the early years, in some cases too heavy to permit the project to go ahead in light of the projected pattern of cash flow. This was of course, an example of a more common problem, that standard accounting practices might assign revenue requirements over the years for a project in a manner unrelated to throughput volume.

This problem pointed to the need for more innovative financing techniques to ensure that the economically best projects went ahead regardless of the expected rate of inflation. His research pointed to the need for a 'reproduction cost new less depreciation' rate base rather than the familiar 'original cost' rate base, where this approach was feasible, as the preferred approach. Under this concept earnings kept pace with inflation rather than decline in real terms over the life of the investment, making the rate of inflation 'neutral' with regard to project selection.

Dr Lake said that national differences between the US and Canada might cause them to differ in this point. For example, if Canadian projects were financed with money borrowed from financiers in the US then they might have a financial constraint which forced them to treat costs in money terms rather than real terms.

Dr Tye agreed that this was conceptually correct given the constraints – but it showed the need to educate the financing authorities, because otherwise economically viable projects would be rejected because of problems caused by the *method* of financing rather than the true economic costs.

Dr Leydon thought there was no unique, textbook answer to Dr Tye's and Dr Lake's problem – rather it was necessary to consider the problem at three levels, corresponding to the 'actors' involved. At the first level, the enterprise must consider its commercial viability, its money profits and losses, whether in a socialist or free market economy. The second level was that of the 'national interest', where one could use wider definitions of economic costs, opportunity costs, etc. The third level would involve a regulatory agency, responsible for ensuring 'fair competition'. Different definitions of cost would be appropriate at the different levels.

The discussion then passed on to other questions, without further elaboration of what this might mean in practice or (to the regret of some delegates) contributions on the issue of inflation from delegates from centrally planned economies.

The papers had not come to a simple unanimous conclusion that one mode of transport was most appropriate for very cold, distant regions, and this question occupied many delegates.

Professor Wickham questioned the role that railways were able to play. A general rule was surely that infrastructure costs were likely to be very high – and railways required particularly extensive infrastructures.

Professor Khachaturov supported this point in relation to the very coldest regions of the far North. Attempts to build a railway to the East in these conditions were unsuccessful due to the destructive natural forces. Pipelines, as discussed by Dr Ivantsov and Dr Lake, had advantages because it was possible to organise 'continuous" transport without any empty return haul. For gas, transmission by pipeline was probably only one-third of the cost of transport by rail. However, on the investment side pipelines were not cheap.

Professor Hunter pointed out that the continuous character of pipeline use might nevertheless involve complications. For example, the use of slurry pipelines to transport coal required an ample supply of water where the coal originated. One such proposed system from Montana (East of the Rocky Mountains) southeast to New Orleans aroused much opposition because of competing demands for water to meet the needs of agriculture and various cities. In other situations, of course, a coal slurry pipeline might at the same time deliver water from a surplus to a deficit region!

Dr Lake said that an Alaskan study with which he was involved concluded that for *general* resource development, rail was by far superior. However, this depended on specific circumstances. For example, in Canada with surplus capacity on the rail network, the *incremental* cost was low compared with the total cost of a slurry pipeline. But for new development, the pattern was – how could you afford initially to pay for the investment? For natural gas, a pipeline was generally cheapest; liquefaction was usually too expensive, but often viable where there were small quantities of gas and economies of joint production. For crude oil, also, a pipeline was usually cheapest unless railway capacity was provided for other products also. He did not believe that the water consumption of slurry pipelines was significant – though disposal of polluted water could be a problem. *Mrs Borisenko* and *Professor Khachaturov* both contrasted the Canadian situation with that of the USSR, where there was no spare railway capacity. In these conditions slurry pipelines were nearly always advantageous if the alternative was building a new railway. *Dr Andriuszkiewicz* reported a slurry pipeline in Poland, which gave no great difference in the cost of transporting coal some 40 km compared with rail.

Mr Kaser suggested dividing the resources in 'inaccessible' regions into three categories. First, there were energy sources (such as coal, oil and gas) which had a low value/weight ratio and often occurred in high concentrations. Pipelines seemed to be the ideal form of transport for these resources. Secondly, there were certain products (such as nickel, diamonds and gold) which had a very high value/weight ratio. For these, an intensive air service including helicoptors (already widely used) would be enough. Resources which had a low or not very high value/weight ratio and did not occur in high concentrations were a third category which would not be exploited, thus not requiring the building of railways or roads. If one compared the road map of the USSR with, say, that of Canada, one found no road connection even along the line of the Trans-Siberian railway, whereas in Canada the Trans-Canada Highway and later the Alaska Highway were important developments. He asked what the prospects were for road transport across the North Asian continent.

Professor Zaleski argued the case that in the longer term the future of trans-Arctic routes lay in submarines or semi-submerged ships. These had a great advantage over surface ships, because of *reduced* resistance of water: about 80 per cent of the resistance in a conventional ship was a 'frontier' effect, with energy being wasted in making waves. A submarine below about 50 metres felt only the much smaller resistance due to the density of water and even this could be reduced by a stream of hot water. Thus high speeds could be obtained – even up to 80 knots or more. Nuclear power was still uneconomic, but for the future the potential was very great.

Professor Burkanov first took issue with Mr Kaser. It was true that gold, for example, could be carried out efficiently by air. But first it was necessary to extract it, and for this supplies, construction material, labour, machines, etc. had to be transported. As a result of various calculations they had decided to transfer a few commodities to air transport, but for ores the most efficient method was rail, especially where year-round transport was required. (The rivers could only be used in summer.) Concerning *road* transport, then it must be remembered that the road maps would generally show only those routes of high enough quality to be used by passenger cars. There were other roads (e.g. Vladivostok–Moscow) which could be used by more robust vehicles.

He made a more general point about new railway development. This would often be a matter of timing – at present, some development was not worthwhile because the level of demand was not high enough. In these cases, they would wait until the estimated level of demand was higher before starting to build. And in some cases, railways would not be economic. But overall the problem was not as frightening as it appeared. There was a lot of profit on a lot of routes and they expected to continue expansion.

Mention was made, but without great discussion, of the present or future importance of hovercraft, new forms of sledges, helicoptors used to lay pipelines, ice-breakers, access roads to mountain railways, pneumatic container freight in capsules, containers, under-sea pipelines, and the use of frozen paraffin or concrete piles sunk into permafrost to provide foundations. The general picture that emerged was one of continuous technical innovation to solve a wide range of transport problems, but the reader is referred to the appropriate technical journals for further details.

However, one technical issue proved to be intensively discussed by some of the delegates (to the bemused fascination of the rest): it related to the design of pipelines.

Mr Kaser asked about problems of safety: there were reports three years ago of a major rupture of a pipeline: were there dangers involved in running at an 'optimal' level? *Professor Wagener* asked about recent developments in the USSR. *Dr Bajusz* queried the water requirements.

Dr Lake was astonished at figures suggested by Dr Ivantsov: he noted that Ivantsov recommended 1420 mm pipe as optimal, with a pressure of 120kfg/cm^2 (equivalent to 54" and 1700 psi) and transmission at $-70°$C. This gave a throughput twice as high as the maximum that had ever been proposed in North America – and about *four* times higher than what was normally considered the optimum. Did he really mean that this was the 'optimum', from an economic point of view, or was it rather a monument to technical achievement? What was the optimisation procedure? On Mr Kaser's point, he was also worried about safety. A pipe full of methane under these conditions had the compressive energy of a large bomb. In a Canadian study of which he was a member five years ago they recommended against pressures of $120\,kgf/cm^2$ at temperatures of below $0°C$. Were they too timid?

Professor Khachaturov pointed out that even larger diameter pipe had been proposed and designed up to 2500 mm – although not with great success.

Mrs Borisenko explained some of the technical considerations of pipeline design. First, the 'rigidity' of a pipe increased proportionally to the third power of diameter, and of course there was a related problem of the stability of position with large pipes. Temperature increased every time a gas entered the compression chamber but then fell as the gas flowed along the line. 'Laminary' or multilayer pipes did allow the temperature to be brought down for pumping to an absolute minimum of $-30°C$. Power consumption, metal consumption and other factors tended to cause an optimal temperature of about $-20°C$, though this varied from case to case. Such a temperature required heat insulation, even though pumping could be managed through uninsulated pipelines. Pressures of $120\,kgf/cm^2$ were admissable with unlaminated pipes, and two-layer pipes had withstood test pressures up to 230 atmospheres. In addition extra factors had to be considered for solid or liquid products, such as the optimum mix of coal and water: this was 50:50 by weight, equivalent to 43 per cent coal 57 per cent water by volume.

The Russian optimisation procedure took account of all these factors, modified if necessary by considerations of safety and reliability – it was these factors that were most influential in deciding on 1420 mm pipes. However, the optimisation was done in economic terms, using 'summary costs' or 'total costs'; 1200 mm pipe cost (in an average environment) 400,000 roubles per kilometre, including pumping stations. 1420 mm pipe used for gas (which contained 630 tons of metal per kilometre) cost about 450,000 to 500,000 roubles per kilometre. She asked Dr Lake, what *he* considered were the optimum pressures for gas, slurry and oil pipelines?

Dr Lake replied that for gas, it seemed to him that the Soviet 'optimum' was about the same as his 'absolute maximum'.

PART THREE

Problems of the Optimal Relationship of Individual and Public Passenger Transport

12 Mass Transport and Individual Transport: an Optimum Modal Split

REZSO BAJUSZ

I INTRODUCTION

The 'homo sapiens' of the modern age is forced to travel often and regularly even if his dwelling place remains unchanged. To this end he mostly uses one or more of the various means of transport. Different means of transport offer services of different qualitative characteristics: speed, safety, comfort, etc. As a result of socio-economic development a certain horizontal and vertical division of labour has developed among them. The future development of the modal split is an important task of transport policy. Such development necessitates a certain amount of intervention.

The aim of intervening in the development of the division of labour in passenger transport is to emphasise social interests, consider given economic possibilities of the society and accordingly influence the passenger in his choice of means of transport. The basic task of Hungarian transport policy is to ensure that the transport system effectively fulfils the demands for passenger transport deriving from socio-economic development and the widening of international relations.

Different demand forecasts and surveys have shown that the demand for passenger transport will grow more slowly than in the past. This should be taken into consideration in transport policy. The rise in living standards and changes in the way of life have resulted in growing demands for a high-quality transport system. The joint role of mass and individual transport is of increasing importance in meeting these demands. The rational division of labour should be subject to the development and operation of a passenger transport system which is advantageous from the point of view of traffic. Beside high-priority investments, mass transport should also be further developed with measures aimed at a better organisation of traffic. The pace of growth of car ownership should be fixed according to the capacity of the economy and aspects of the living standard policy, foreign trade and finance. The aim should be that the problems connected with the use of cars do not grow significantly. It is a basic task that, taking international experience into account, the breakdown of the transport system should be avoided, especially in big towns.

With these aims of transport policy in mind, it is clear that priority is given to mass transport. At the same time the scale and pace of the development of individual transport and its role in the division of labour are not defined so categorically, as they depend on many preconditions.

II THE DEVELOPMENT OF PASSENGER TRAFFIC IN HUNGARY

The development of mass and individual transport and the division of labour between them should be considered from the 1960s, when the rapid development of individual transport started. Table 12.1 shows the development of mass and individual transport, the increase in population, the national income and the number of vehicles between 1960 and 1975. It should be added; that according to the practice in Hungary the category 'other transport by road' includes not only cars, but also motor-cycles and non-public buses.

Certain basic tendencies are obvious in the table: the growth of the participation of the railways in intercity mass transport has stopped, but that of bus transport has accelerated. Within local mass transport there is no significant change in the total performance of the means of mass transport in Budapest, as a result of the rapid development of the underground railways and the network of buses and the parallel decline of the performance by the tramways. The development of transport in other towns is very dynamic. Within 'other transport' the development of transport by cars and non-public buses is most pronounced. The increase in the performance of motor-cycles is slowing down.

To sum up: performance and share of 'other transport' are gradually increasing. It might be concluded that, contrary to the goals of transport policy, the development of mass transport has no priority. This is not the case.

TABLE 12.1 THE DEVELOPMENT OF PASSENGER TRANSPORT PERFORMANCE, POPULATION, NATIONAL INCOME IN $ᵃ AND THE NUMBER OF VEHICLES BETWEEN 1960 AND 1975

(thousand million passengers)

Kind of transport	1960	1965	1970	1975	1975, 1960 %	Distribution %
Intercity mass transport						
Railways	13.20	15.25	15.15	14.75	111.7	19.8
Buses	3.60	5.30	7.20	10.40	288.9	14.0
Waterways	0.08	0.07	0.05	0.06	75.0	0.1
Air transport	0.07	0.18	0.45	0.54	771.4	0.7
Total	16.95	20.80	20.85	25.75	151.9	34.6
Local mass transport						
Budapest total	9.05	9.75	8.75	8.80	97.2	11.8
of which: Suburban railways	1.10	1.10	1.15	1.05	95.5	
Underground	–	–	0.25	0.95	–	
Tramways	5.60	5.65	3.60	2.50	46.6	
Trolleybuses	–	–	–	0.20	–	
Buses	2.15	3.00	3.75	4.10	190.7	
Other towns, total	1.40	1.95	2.25	3.30	235.7	4.4
of which: Tramways	0.60	0.70	0.50	0.40	66.7	
Trolleybuses	–	–	–	–	–	
Buses owned by the towns	0.30	0.25	0.35	0.60	200.0	
Buses owned by the firm VOLÁN	0.50	1.00	1.40	2.30	460.0	
Total	10.45	11.70	11.00	12.10	115.8	16.2

TABLE 12.1 (*Continued*)

Kind of transport	1960	1965	1970	1975	1975, 1960 %	Distribution £
Mass transport, total	27.40	32.50	33.85	37.85	138.1	50.8
of which: Rail	20.70	22.70	20.65	19.85	95.9	31.2
Buses	6.55	9.55	12.70	17.40	265.6	
Other (waterways, air-transport)	0.15	0.25	0.50	0.60	400.0	
Other transport by road, total	4.30	9.15	17.95	36.55	850.0	49.2
of this: Cars	1.55	4.65	10.05	23.95	1545.2	
Number of cars (thousands)	31.3	99.4	240.3	586.5	1873.8	
Non-public buses	0.40	0.50	1.90	5.10	1275.0	
Motor-cycles	2.35	4.00	6.00	7.50	319.1	
Passenger transport performances, total	31.70	41.65	51.80	74.40	234.7	100.0
of which: Rail	20.70	22.70	20.65	19.85	95.9	
Road transport	10.85	18.70	30.65	53.95	497.2	
Other (waterways, air-transport)	0.15	0.25	0.50	0.60	400.0	
Population, thousand	100.06	101.60	103.54	105.72	107.5	
Passenger km total/$	7.80	8.40	7.50	7.95	101.9	
Thousand passenger km/capita	3.17	4.10	5.00	7.04	222.1	
Mass transport passenger km/$	6.74	6.55	4.90	4.04	59.9	
Thousand passenger km/capita	2.74	3.20	3.27	3.58	130.7	
Cars/$	7.70	20.04	34.78	62.66	813.8	
Cars/capita, thousand	3.13	9.78	23.21	55.48	1772.5	

a National income was calculated on the basis of the 1960 exchange rate.

In Hungary specific transport performances are very much higher than those in Europe generally. This is shown in Table 12.2. It should be added that the specific supply of mass transport services is especially high but the specific performance by cars hardly reached 50 per cent of the European level in 1975.

TABLE 12.2 TRANSPORT PERFORMANCE IN HUNGARY AND WESTERN EUROPE

Year	Specific transport performance 1000 pass. km/capita		Hungary as % of W Europe
	W. Europe	Hungary	
1960	2.3	2.8	121.7
1965	3.1	4.1	132.3
1970	4.4	5.0	113.6
1975	6.1	7.0	114.8
1975/1960	262	250	94

III THE DEMAND FOR CARS

The further development of mass and individual transport requires much research. As a result of the concentrated research undertaken over five years, the development strategy derived from complicated interrelations is gradually taking shape. This strategy will serve the development of mass and individual transport and the division of labour between them. On the basis of investigations it seems to be very clear that, taking into account the character of the function and the development requirements of transport and its role in socio-economic development and while resources are in limited supply, priority should be given to mass transport, especially in the capital as well as in other towns and their suburbs, and to improving the quality of transport. Beyond solving these top priority problems the supply of cars can be increased only according to material resources. According to economic forecasts of the development of the per capita national income, the increase in living standards will be such that the per capita income will be doubled in fifteen years and tripled in twenty-five years. This will certainly lead to realistic demands for an increase in the supply of cars.

The possession and use of cars – both of them are hardly replaceable – are preconditions for realising a higher living standard.

Cars represent a higher quality method of meeting demands for transport. In this respect cars are positively evaluated by society. But general evaluation is motivated also by the infrastructural needs of motorisation (road network, parking facilities, additional services, etc.) and how harmful effects on the environment (air pollution, noise, congestion and the risk of accidents, etc.) can be limited. These are all really harmful side-effects of the wide use of cars, although they can be limited. In our experience these factors do not basically influence the positive attitude towards cars (there is no other alternative) and this attitude can only become more widespread. Due to this phenomenon the evaluation of cars is different in urban transport – because of the concentration of harmful effects – and in long-distance transport. Therefore it has to be taken into account that the importance of cars in meeting transport needs will diminish after a quick growth initially in inner parts of the towns. Thus preparations have to be made by developing mass transport.

The positive social evaluation of automobilisation will remain unchanged although the growth of harmful impacts has to be considered. As far as the effects of social evaluation are concerned, they will not hinder development. From the social point of view the process of motorisation, apart from its harmful effects, corresponds to the basic intention of the socialist society to fulfil objective needs at the highest possible level. Furthermore, its positive impact on economic growth cannot be neglected.

The development of road transport on the other hand is a significant burden on the economy and huge cost items cannot be covered by the transport operators. Within the limits of material possibilities, taking into account social needs and the order of importance of social objectives, the main tasks influencing living standards should be regulated by economic and living standard policy concepts. Corresponding to these priorities the development of road transport and the increase of the supply of cars should be preceded by services with top priority for society (housing, public utility works, public health, education, etc.). On the other hand it should be clear that costs related to the development of road transport in most cases have nothing to do with the increase in the number of cars privately owned, hence independently of car ownership a modern road network is always indispensable, although maybe with reduced capacity.

A socialist society cannot ignore the increase in the supply of private cars. But on the basis of priorities established by the living standard policy within the limits of material possibilities, road transport must not be allowed to develop without control and at a pace dictated only by the consumers. Planned and proportional development should ensure that motorisation takes place smoothly, without harmful effects, and that society is prepared to absorb a higher level of road transport development.

IV FUTURE DEMAND FOR PASSENGER TRANSPORT

The future demand for passenger transport has been defined by various investigations. The following aspects were taken into account in different forecasts:

(1) future increase of the population, changes in its composition and location, characteristics of employment;
(2) development of the economy and living standards, possible changes in the way and the conditions of life;
(3) development of the regional division of labour and the network of settlements, future directions of regional development;
(4) geographic and weather conditions;
(5) characteristics of transport of today and tomorrow, development of tariffs and costs;
(6) development of tourism and automobilisation, etc.

According to the investigations and calculations, needs for passenger transport within national income as a whole will diminish by 40 per cent during the period 1975–2000 and by 20 per cent by 1990. Travelling per capita on the other hand will increase by 60–70 per cent during the next fifteen years and 90–110 per cent by the year 2000. Comparisons were made between specific passenger transport performances in Hungary and in other European countries. This was possible because there is a close correlation between the per capita passenger km and the per capita national income figures, with time as the second independent variable.

The European trend can be characterised by the following model:

Trend function of the specific degree of the supply of cars in capitalist countries:

$$y = \frac{520}{e\left(\frac{1500}{x-100} - 0.35\sqrt[3]{0.067 \cdot n}\right)} + 2/\text{vehicle/capita, 1000/}$$

Trend function of the specific degree of the supply of cars in socialist countries:

$$y = \frac{330}{e\left(\frac{1750}{x-100} - 0.35\sqrt[3]{0.067 \cdot n}\right)} + 2/\text{vehicle/capita, 1000/}$$

European trend function of specific passenger transport demand: (passenger km/capita):

$$y_n = \frac{20000 - \frac{10\,000}{1 + 0.05 \cdot n_1}}{e\left(\frac{1450 \cdot /1 - 0.01 \cdot n_1/}{380 - 7.4 - n_1 + x}\right)} + 600/\text{passenger km/capital/}$$

Where:

x = specific national income; \$/capita
(1960 rate of exchange);
$n = i - 1960$ and $n_1 = i - 1950$;
i = calendar year.

As a result of development it can be expected that travel demands will approach the European trend. Thus per capita travel, despite the relative backwardness in car use, will be 5 per cent above the European trend in 1990 and will reach the level of the European trend at the turn of the century, see Figure 12.1.

The need to meet the demands for local and urban transport will make it necessary for mass transport to grow by about 28 per cent by 1990 and by 35–40 per cent by 2000. The demand for urban mass transport will grow in the capital by 4 per cent and 2–10 per cent, and in all other towns by 94 per cent and 97–140 per cent by 1990 and 2000 respectively.

The main features of the demand for passenger transport will be:

(1) Parallel to the rise in living standards, the growth of leisure time and the number of cars there will be an increase in the need for individually motivated travel especially as far as national and international tourism is concerned.

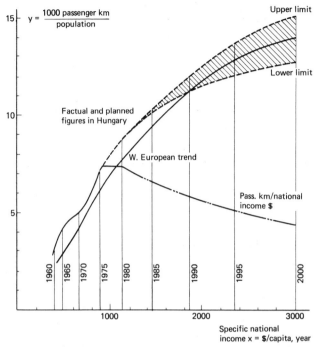

Figure 12.1 Relation of the per capita passenger transport performance to national income – European trend and domestic factual and planned figures

(2) Taking into account changes in the regional distribution of production and the process of urbanisation there will be no significant alteration in the proportion of commuter traffic related mainly to production, which today represents the most important travel purpose.

On the basis of the development trends of the two main categories (personally motivated and commuter traffic) and depending on the growth of car ownership, demands for travel will increase by 65–75 per cent and 89–124 per cent during the coming fifteen and twenty-five years respectively. As a result of the development of automobilisation, passenger transport performances by cars will increase most quickly: in the next fifteen years by 2.6–3.1 times and in the next twenty-five years by 3.4–4.8 times. (The same figures will be lower if besides cars, motor-cycles and non-public buses are also considered as individual means of transport: in the next fifteen years by 2.1–2.3 times and in the next twenty-five years by 2.5–3.4 times.) Demands for mass transport will increase more moderately: in the next fifteen years by 23 per cent and in the next twenty-five years by only 20–23 per cent.

Changes in different sectors of transport can be seen in Table 12.3. Different changes in individual transport sectors will lead to significant modifications of the division of labour in transport. Most characteristic are the expected proportional changes between individual and mass transport: in comparison to its 50 per cent share of traffic in 1975, traffic by individual means of transport will reach 61–65 per cent in 1990 and 65–73 per cent at the turn of the century, while the performance by passenger cars comes to 32, 51–56 and 58–68 per cent for the respective years, and the share of mass transport diminishes from 50 per cent in 1975 to 39–35 per cent in 1990 and 35–27 per cent at the turn of the century. Looking at the composition of transport demands from another point of view, i.e. the infrastructure used, the following results were obtained: the share of the performance by road transport vehicles grows from today's 73 per cent to 81–83 per cent in 1990 and 83–86 per cent at the end of the century; the share of other kinds of transport declines from 27 to 19–17 per cent and 17–14 per cent respectively.

The question is whether the goals in view, defined on the basis of forecast performances by cars and the increase in the number of cars

TABLE 12.3.   FUTURE DEVELOPMENT OF TRANSPORT

Kind of transport	Passenger km, 10^2			1990 1975 %	2000 1975 %
	1975	1990	2000		
Railways	14.75	13.9–13.1	13.3–11.7	94–89	90–79
Urban railways	5.10	7.0–6.7	7.5–7.7	137–131	147–137
Air and water transport	0.60	2.2–2.8	4.0–5.0	367–467	667–833
Bus transport	17.40	24.4–22.2	24.2–20.3	140–132	139–117
Mass transport total	37.85	47.5–45.5	49.0–44.0	125–120	129–116
Cars	23.90	63.0–73.0	81.0–114.0	264–305	339–477
Motor-cycles	7.50	5.2–4.8	4.0–3.3	69–64	53–40
Non-public buses	5.10	7.3–6.7	6.5–5.5	143–131	127–108
Individual transport total	36.50	75.5–84.5	91.5–122.5	207–232	251–336
TOTAL	74.35	123.0–130.01	40.5–166.5	165–175	189–224
From this:					
road transport	53.90	99.9–107.41	15.7–142.8	185–199	215–265
other transport	20.45	23.1–22.6	24.8–23.7	113–111	121–116

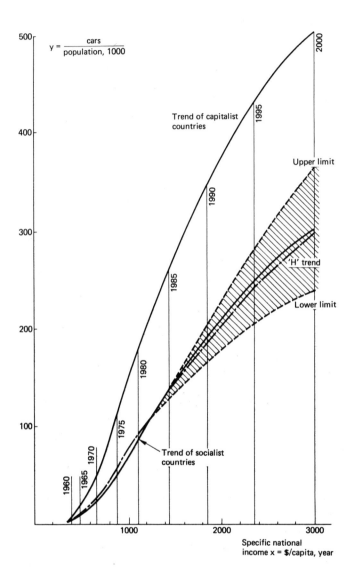

Figure 12.2 Relation of the number of cars to national income (trends of socialist countries, capitalist countries and domestic factual and planned figures)

necessary to achieve such performances, are not exaggerated. The author believes they are not. While defining the role of transport by car the whole set of conditions for their operation (roads, fuel, services, spare parts, manpower, etc) and the socio-economic effectiveness of individual transport was considered. Having taken into account these factors the pace and scale of development were fixed. Requirements deriving from the priority of social needs really did make their influence on the forecasts. It is hoped that this can be seen in Figure 12.2.

V CONCLUSION

As a conclusion the answer should be given to the question, whether the planned division of labour in Hungary between mass and individual transport can be called optimal. If the answer to this question is approached from the system of preferences of socio-political targets and economic possibilities it can be said: yes.

Further qualitative development of mass transport and the planned increases in service quality will fulfil the basic demands of society for transport. The development of individual transport, though not as spectacular as in the countries of the West, will be free of extremities and in harmony with the capabilities of individuals and the society. The conclusion may be drawn, that with the realisation of these goals the optimum socio-economic effectiveness of the division of labour between mass and individual transport will be approached step by step.

In the context of the brief forecast of the development of passenger transport in Hungary it should be added that the forecasts of development are naturally based on today's knowledge and the government has not yet taken a final position.

Forecasts made on the basis of thorough research work generally prove the soundness of the tasks of the transport policy concept. Experience of the present five-year plan, economic and political ideas for the sixth five-year plan now under consideration and the developments approved by the government up to 1990 make it probable that the expected development is not going to be very much different from the forecasts.

13 The Optimum Ratio between Private and Public Passenger Transport Services in Conurbations: the Experience of the German Democratic Republic

WERNER LINDNER

I SOCIALIST TRANSPORT POLICY

The principle of meeting the requirements of a socialist society in an optimal and effective way applies to the fulfilment of all social needs, including specific transport needs. The major strategy of socialist transport policy is the optimum distribution of functions between different sectors of transport and between public and private transport (Arndt, 1975). For example, since 1963 about 2000 km of secondary railway lines carrying light traffic have been closed because of their inefficient performance from the point of view of the national economy and the public transport service for these sections has been transferred to nationalised road transport.

The problem of effectively organising passenger transport in conurbations and large cities has been discussed all over the world, and these discussions are still continuing. Within the GDR, the development of a complex transport system to serve cities and conurbations has been

179

closely integrated into the planned, systematic organisation of the socialist society as a whole.

The following figures give an idea of the scale of the GDR transport system:

108,179 km² area;
17 million inhabitants;
1079 million tons volume of freight traffic in 1977;
4051 million passengers carried in 1977;
4160 bus lines serving 97 per cent of all towns and communities;
2.8 to 3 million flats will be built or modernised in the period between 1978 and 1990.

The planned development of regional distribution of productive forces and the consistent implementation of the housing construction programme show convincingly how the integration of regional, town and transport planning into one system of overall state planning brings about an efficient and reasonable organisation of transport, especially in conurbations and cities, for the benefit of the whole population of and the national economy (Autorenkollektiv, 1979).

Comprehensive scientific research will be carried out continually with a view to development and the relationships between economic growth and population as well as to the necessary communications. Based on the central state plan, the regional development plans and the long-term traffic plans are the fundamental elements for the management and planning carried out by local state organisations as representatives of the people of the regional unit (district or town) concerned (Lammert, 1976).

The joint aim of town and traffic planning is rational locational planning of regional investments. Locational planning incorporates traffic planning, too. Location planning which co-ordinates the needs of people and the requirements of the economy will reduce transport in general. Efforts aim at an optimum distribution between a rational supply network and the necessary passenger transport service. An important intensification factor for the territory concerned is rational locational planning which may be achieved by co-ordinating various functions (Autorenkollektiv, 1976, and Rehbein's paper in this volume). The optimum proportion of private and public passenger transport will be achieved if, with a minimum of economic expenditure the transport demand – or in other words the traffic requirements – may be satisfied at a socially accepted level of quality. It is understood that social expenditure does not only mean a first and final investment but also the current costs (Wagener's paper in this volume).

In order to secure the social interests of the socialist society as a whole and those of its citizens, an adequate public passenger transport service is required. Inefficient and economically unjustifiable private transport which does not meet the requirements of a town organism and is ineffective with regard to the highway network may not be accepted. To obtain an optimum proportion of private and public transport, planned steering and incentive measures in accordance with the economic and social interests of the socialist society have to be taken.

Past experience in the GDR has shown that a planned development of private and public passenger transport services, especially in towns and conurbations, demands a reasonable division of labour among transport sectors and a co-ordination or unification of regional, town and traffic planning. The possibilities of solving these diverse problems are given within the framework of a socialist planned economy. The form and solution of this complex policy have impacts on and connections with long-distance traffic because conurbations and towns are both origin and destination for long-distance transport.

II THE PAST DEVELOPMENT OF PRIVATE AND PUBLIC TRANSPORT IN THE GDR

The development of private and public transport in the GDR (Arndt, 1979) shows the importance of the following three factors: the co-ordination of traffic requirements and the necessary capacities, the organised allocation of functions to different modes and the role of operating plans (Lindner, 1977).

TABLE 13.1   DEVELOPMENT OF CARS AND BUSES IN THE GDR

Year	Total buses	Total cars	Cars/1000 inhabitants
1950	1,925	75,710	4.4
1960	9,365	298,575	17.6
1970	16,686	1,159,778	60.2
1975	20,983	1,880,478	110.6
1977	23,824	2,236,702	131.6

Table 13.1 shows the increase in the numbers of cars and buses in the GDR, and the importance of bus transport can be seen.

The increase in passengers carried, shown in Table 13.2, has been achieved by improved public transport in conurbations and in long-distance passenger transport. Intensive housing construction followed the rebuilding of areas destroyed during the war and the construction of smaller new residential areas on the outskirts of towns. This produced higher figures and transport distances in suburban transport as well as an increased number of lines. The systematic development of the bus and car stock and the extension of the public transport network has led to growing numbers of passengers (Table 13.3).

TABLE 13.2   INCREASE IN NUMBERS OF PASSENGERS CARRIED
(million persons)

Year	Railway	Road transport	Long-distance transport	Suburban transport	Total
1950	954	111	1065	1758	2823
1960	943	668	1611	1967	3578
1970	626	1107	1733	1714	3447
1975	634	1298	1932	1843	3775
1977	631	1409	2040	1952	3992

TABLE 13.3   DEVELOPMENT OF THE NETWORK OF PUBLIC
TRANSPORT

Year	Number of lines	Network length km
1975	16,743	567.397
1976	17,210	607,713
1977	17,552	600,866

III MEASURES, EXPERIENCE AND EXAMPLES WHICH INFLUENCE THE RATIO BETWEEN PRIVATE AND PUBLIC TRANSPORT

The basic principles of a uniform socialist transport policy and its results (illustrated in Sections I and II) reveal that all activities in the GDR have always been aimed at improving transport and making it a highly efficient factor of productivity and economic growth within the socialist reproduction process by developing the passenger transport system in such a way as to meet the transport demands of the population. For this reason the necessary transport structures, systems and methods have been elaborated and these will be continued in future, too. The preparation of a research strategy of long-term drafts and rationalisation programmes, the concentration of scientific-technical tasks on the main points of development and rationalisation complexes are in this connection important instruments of socialist transport management and planning.

The most economic transport mode will be identified on the basis of socialist production and property relationships, and by means of effective socialist management and planning activities and the support of the population. This refers to public transport sectors as well as to the interrelationship between them and private transport. The capacities required for that purpose will be integrated into plans and submitted.

Further essential measures are adequate tariff and legal incentives for passengers and commuters. Guidelines and operative measures within the framework of general traffic planning and transport concepts and the activities of transport commissions and their passenger and commuter traffic organs are put into practice, too. The elaboration of general traffic plans relating to the different regions and the co-operation between local and central organs is stipulated by law.

Good results have been achieved with a big share of public transport within total passenger transport and the ratio between private and public transport has been influenced by the following measures:

(1) the introduction and realisation of efficient railway connections in industrial and urban conurbations for coping with commuter traffic and traffic peaks, and the planned development of park-and-ride systems;

(2) systematic support for and promotion of public transport by advantageous short-distance tariffs subsidised by the State;

(3) the utilisation of railway identity cards or combined tickets for railway and suburban transport;

(4) co-operation between transport sectors within a certain region, e.g. by co-ordinating routes, timetables, advertising and travel information;

(5) operational preference for public passenger suburban transport on roads, bus lanes, green light co-ordination, inclusion of trams in green light timing;

(6) restriction of parking times in city centres, reduction of parking

space supply by car-park permits, introduction of parking charges;

(7) changes in the building and functional structure of towns and measures of traffic stabilisation.

The different measures will be outlined and comprehensively developed in the general transport plans and general building schemes and realised by the Five-Year and annual plans.

Investigations and calculations relating to the capital of the GDR, Berlin, have for example shown that the daily output of passenger transport will increase by 25 per cent in the period between 1975 and 1990. Each citizen of the capital would then use transport means twice a day.

Above all the increase in traffic volume will be produced by growing private motorisation. From 1975 to 1990 the car stock will have doubled, leading to a proportion of four inhabitants per car. To maintain the function of the centre of Berlin and high-density working areas, restrictions on the use of private cars are necessary. High quality public passenger transport services offer an alternative solution. The ratio between public and private transport is planned on the basis shown in Table 13.4 (daily, working days). Public passenger transport will be extended and travelling times reduced to 45 minutes with regard to 90 per cent of local commuter traffic.

TABLE 13.4   TOTAL PROPORTION OF DAILY TRANSPORT IN
BERLIN (GDR)

Year	Public passenger suburban transport	Private transport[a]
1970	62.8 %	37.2 %
1990	60.0 %	40.0 %

[a] Private transport with car, motor-cycle, moped.

For a great part of the commuter service between town and outskirts travelling times should not exceed 60 minutes. New housing areas in the outskirts should therefore be provided in the vicinity of high-speed roads. The intervals between trains on these sections will be shortened.

Based on these transport policies the following basis for public passenger suburban transport in Berlin has been outlined.

(1) High-speed services like the city railway (S-Bahn) and the underground railway (U-Bahn) form the basic network of public passenger suburban transport. The existing basic network will be extended and completed to guarantee a fast connection between large residential areas and the town centre and important working areas.

(2) The tram (high-speed tram) will operate on less frequented radial arteries. Buses will serve links with lighter traffic and carry out feeder traffic functions for the basic network especially in the town centre.

(3) The rolling stock in Berlin will be reconstructed and new types of vehicles provided. The age structure of buses will be improved.

(4) Radial and tangential routes of the public suburban transport network will be interconnected by means of comfortable and well-timed changes.

(5) Entrances of public suburban transport have to be comfortable and direct. This requires the construction of second entrances for some 'S-Bahn' stations.

(6) The information system for public passenger suburban transport has to be improved, especially in the event of operating troubles.

(7) In the outskirts, especially at the termini, parking areas for cars, motor-cycles, mopeds and bicycles should be provided at appropriate places.

(8) The density of trains and the sequence of coaches during peak commuter traffic should be increased to at least five minutes in the town centre and ten minutes in the outskirts.

(9) To develop the surroundings of the town a combined regional network of rail and road transport will be further extended with the capital as the central point.

In commuter transport in the towns of the GDR, the ratio between public suburban passenger transport and private transport by car, motor-cycle and moped has changed from 90 per cent to 10 per cent in 1960 to 70 per cent to 30 per cent at present. With increasing motorisation this ratio will continuously change in favour of private motor transport unless special regulations are brought in. From the view of economic profitability, however, a proportion not exceeding 60 to 40 per cent, in extreme cases 50 to 50 per cent can be accepted. The provision of more space for stationary traffic in town centres, mainly for long-time parking, can be neither realised nor accepted.

With regard to GDR towns, transport policy is based on the fact that road traffic networks must be provided for a maximum of 40 per cent of transport movements and the remaining 60 per cent should be served by adequate, appropriate public passenger suburban transport. This above-mentioned share of 60 per cent is the basis for assessing public transport facilities in towns because public passenger suburban transport must be capable of meeting requirements in all eventualities. The town also has to maintain its functions in the event of energy supply difficulties. Events prove that in highly motorised countries where public passenger suburban transport covers 20 to 30 per cent, it is not able to cope with unexpected increased transport demands.

REFERENCES

Arndt, O. (1975). Planmässige Arbeitsteilung mit den übrigen Verkehrsträgern, *Schienen der Welt*, 3.

Arndt, O. (1979). Hervorragende Leistungen der Werktä tigen des Verkehrswesens – tä glich 11 Millionen Fahrgä ste und 3 Millionen Tonnen Gü ter, *DDR – Verkehr*, 1.

Autorenkollektiv (1976). *Territorialplanung* (Berlin: Verlag die Wirtschaft).

Autorenkollektiv (1979). *Komplexe Verkehrsentwicklung im Territorium* (Transpress Verlag).

Lammert, U. (1976). Erfahrungen der DDR bei der Koordinierung von Verkehrs-und Stadtplanung. *Report of 2nd ECE Seminar*, Washington, June 1976.

Lindner, W. (1977). Zur Einheit von zentraler und territorialer Leitung und Planung des transports, *DDR-Verkehr*, 6.

14 Motorisation in Japan
RYOHEI KAKUMOTO

I THE RAPID GROWTH OF MOTORISATION AFTER 1960

The history of motor vehicles in Japan dates back to the beginning of the twentieth century. Popularisation began at the turn of 1960. As the income level rose to a certain point, more and more passenger motor vehicles came into use. In the middle of the 1960s, the income per capita increased to 70 per cent of the price of a popular passenger motor car. During the period from 1960 to 1975 real GNP rose by a factor of 3.57 and the number of motor vehicles increased by a factor of 8.56, while the number of motor cars increased by a factor of 33 (Tables 14.1, 14.2). Their share in domestic traffic and highway investment has also increased. (Tables 14.3, 14.6).

Motor vehicles were a means of transport that man had long desired. For all their merits, they have had their disadvantages too. Traffic accidents, environmental disruption, the increase in energy consumption, aggravation of the financial conditions of public transport and congestion were all triggered by the increasing number of motor vehicles, and these consequences have been experienced by every nation. The extent of these adverse effects, however, has varied in each country, depending upon its specific conditions. Japan is a densely populated, insular, mountainous country. No matter how fast car ownership grows, the use of cars is restricted, and the role of public transport still remains of vital importance in passenger service.

In Japan the number of people killed in traffic accidents reached its peak in 1970 with 16,765. In 1978 the number went down to 8782 (Table 14.7). Many measures to protect the environment have been taken and strict regulations are in force against air pollution by exhaust gas. No measures have yet been taken with respect to energy consumption (Tables 14.8, 14.9) or improving the financial position of public transport.

TABLE 14.1   ECONOMIC GROWTH AND TRAFFIC VOLUME
(1960–75)

	1960	1975	'75/'60
Population (000)	93,419	111,940	1.20
GNP(real) (in 1970 price) (in billions yen)	26,183	93.389	3.57
National income per capita (yen)	142,084	1,148,034	8.08
Consumers' commodity price index	33.2	100.0	3.01
Freight tonnage exported (000)	14,167	72,358	5.11
Freight tonnage imported (000)	94,418	553,123	5.86
Crude oil imported (in thousands of kl)	31,121	263,374	8.46
Domestic passengers carried (000,000)	20,291	46,176	2.28
passengers-km (in billions)	243.3	710.4	2.92
Domestic freight tonnage carried			
(000,000)	1,533	5,030	3.28
freight ton-km (in billions)	138.9	360.8	2.60
No. of motor vehicles (000)	3,404	29,143	8.56
passenger cars[a] (000)	440	14,822[b]	33.69
trucks[a](000)	1.322	7,381[b]	5.58

[a] Not including four-wheeled motor vehicles with less than 550 cc engines and buses
[b] If four-wheeled motor vehicles with less than 550 cc engines are added, nos. of passenger cars are 17,378,000 and nos. of trucks are 10,213,000.

TABLE 14.2   GROWTH OF MOTOR VEHICLES (1955–77)
(in thousands)

	Total	Passenger motor cars	Buses	Trucks	Vehicles for special use	Small two-wheeled cars	Less than 550 cc engine cars
1955[a]	1,502	158	35	693	34	51	531
1960	3,404	440	58	1,322	74	50	1,460
1965	8,123	1,878	105	2,870	164	48	3,058
1970	18,919	6,777	190	5,460	352	172	5,968
1971	21,223	8,173	197	5,792	404	220	6,436
1972	23,869	9,965	206	6,263	461	238	6,737
1973	25,963	11.598	214	6,721	515	262	6,654
1974	27,870	13,207	219	7,058	557	277	6,553
1975	29,143	14,822	220	7,381	596	257	5,867
1976	31,048	16,206	222	7,758	631	277	5,954
1977	32,965	17,569	224	8,023	671	292	6,185[b]

[a] At the end of each fiscal year (31 March the following calendar year).
[b] Of the less-than-550-cc engined cars, 2,373 are 4-wheeled passenger cars, 3,345 4-wheeled trucks, 466 2-wheeled and 2 3-wheeled. In the 'passenger cars', these 4-wheeled passenger cars are sometimes included. (19,942,000 cars for 1977).

TABLE 14.3 DOMESTIC PASSENGER TRAFFIC VOLUME[a]
(1960–1977)

	Total	National rail	Private rail	Bus	Auto	Air	Water
1 Passenger (000,000)							
1960	20,291	5,124	7,166	6.291	1,610	1	99
1965	30,793	6,722	9,076	10,557	4,306	5	126
1970	40,606	6,534	9,850	11,812	12,221	15	174
1971	42,010	6,659	9,836	11,634	13,687	16	178
1972	43,275	6,724	10,061	11,711	14,572	19	188
1973	44,563	6,871	10,185	11,390	15,922	24	171
1974	45,080	7,113	10,476	11,206	16,105	25	155
1975	46,176	7,048	10,540	10,731	17,681	25	151
1976	46,668	7,180	10,402	10,231	18,679	28	147
1977	47,548	7,068	10,699	10,189	19,416	33	143
2 Passenger-km (000,000,000)							
1960	243.3	124.0	60.4	44.0	11.5	0.7	2.7
1965	382.5	174.0	81.4	80.1	40.6	2.9	3.4
1970	587.2	189.7	99.1	102.9	181.3	9.3	4.8
1971	617.8	190.3	99.7	100.8	211.0	10.3	5.0
1972	648.2	197.8	102.5	108.2	220.3	12.7	6.7
1973	673.8	208.1	104.8	111.7	225.7	16.0	7.4
1974	693.3	215.6	108.5	115.8	228.4	17.6	7.5
1975	710.4	215.3	108.5	110.1	250.8	19.1	6.6
1976	709.4	210.7	108.8	98.7	264.5	20.1	6.5
1977	710.8	199.7	112.6	104.6	264.0	23.6	6.3
(DO, Ratio)							
1 Passenger (%)							
1960	100.0	25.3	35.3	31.0	7.0	0.0	0.5
1965	100.0	21.8	29.5	34.3	14.0	0.0	0.4
1970	100.0	16.1	24.3	29.1	30.1	0.0	0.4
1971	100.0	15.9	23.4	27.7	32.6	0.0	0.4
1972	100.0	15.5	23.2	27.1	33.7	0.0	0.4
1973	100.0	15.4	22.9	25.6	35.7	0.1	0.4
1974	100.0	15.8	23.2	24.9	35.7	0.1	0.3
1975	100.0	15.3	22.8	23.2	38.3	0.1	0.3
1976	100.0	15.4	22.3	21.9	40.0	0.1	0.3
1977	100.0	14.9	22.5	21.4	40.8	0.1	0.3
2 Passenger-km (%)							
1960	100.0	51.0	24.8	18.1	4.7	0.3	1.1
1965	100.0	45.5	21.3	21.0	10.6	0.8	0.9
1970	100.0	32.3	16.9	17.5	30.9	1.6	0.8
1971	100.0	30.8	16.1	16.3	34.3	1.7	0.8

TABLE 14.3   (*Continued*)

	Total	National rail	Private rail	Bus	Auto	Air	Water
1972	100.0	30.5	15.8	16.7	34.0	2.0	1.0
1973	100.0	30.9	15.6	16.6	33.5	2.4	1.1
1974	100.0	31.1	15.6	16.7	32.9	2.5	1.1
1975	100.0	30.3	15.3	15.5	35.3	2.7	0.9
1976	100.0	29.7	15.3	13.9	37.3	2.8	0.9
1977	100.0	28.1	15.8	14.7	37.1	3.3	0.9

a Includes both intercity and urban.

TABLE 14.4   DOMESTIC FREIGHT TRAFFIC VOLUME*a* (1960–77)

	Total*b*	National rail	Private rail	Truck	Water
1 Tonnage (000,000)					
1960	1,533	195	43	1,156	139
1965	2,625	200	52	2,193	180
1970	5,259	199	57	4,626	377
1971	5,434	193	58	4,796	387
1972	5,877	182	57	5,203	434
1973	5,716	176	53	4,912	575
1974	5,085	158	48	4,377	501
1975	5,030	142	43	4,393	452
1976	5,000	141	45	4,356	458
1977	5,102	132	43	4,456	470
2 Ton-km (000,000,000)					
1960	138.9	53.6	0.9	20.8	63.6
1965	186.3	56.4	0.9	48.4	80.6
1970	350.7	62.4	1.0	135.9	151.2
1971	361.9	61.3	1.0	142.7	157.0
1972	389.1	58.6	1.0	153.6	175.9
1973	407.1	57.4	0.9	141.0	207.6
1974	375.8	51.6	0.9	130.8	192.4
1975	360.8	46.6	0.8	129.7	183.6
1976	373.4	45.5	0.8	132.6	194.3
1977	386.9	40.6	0.7	143.1	202.3
(DO Ratio)					
1 Tonnage (%)					
1960	100.0	12.7	2.8	75.4	9.1
1965	100.0	7.6	2.0	83.5	6.9
1970	100.0	3.8	1.1	87.9	7.2

TABLE 14.4 (*Continued*)

	Total[b]	*National rail*	*Private rail*	*Truck*	*Water*
1971	100.0	3.6	1.1	88.2	7.1
1972	100.0	3.1	1.0	88.5	7.4
1973	100.0	3.1	0.9	85.9	10.1
1974	100.0	3.1	0.9	86.1	9.9
1975	100.0	2.8	0.9	87.3	9.0
1976	100.0	2.8	0.9	87.1	9.2
1977	100.0	2.6	0.8	87.3	9.2
2 Ton-km (%)					
1960	100.0	38.6	0.7	15.0	45.8
1965	100.0	30.3	0.5	26.0	43.3
1970	100.0	17.8	0.3	38.8	43.1
1971	100.0	16.9	0.3	3.9.4	43.4
1972	100.0	15.0	0.2	39.5	45.2
1973	100.0	14.1	0.2	34.6	51.0
1974	100.0	13.7	0.2	34.8	51.2
1975	100.0	12.9	0.2	36.0	50.9
1976	100.0	12.2	0.2	35.5	52.0
1977	100.0	10.5	0.2	37.0	52.3

[a] Includes both intercity and urban.
[b] Includes air transportation.

TABLE 14.5 TONNAGES BY NATIONAL RAIL TRUCK BY DISTANCE (1977)

	Tonnage (000)		*Percentage (%)*	
	NR (Carload)	*Truck*	*NR (Carload)*	*Truck*
1–50 km	27,573	3,701,963	22.6	83.0
51–100	17,028	375,306	14.0	8.4
101–200	28,970	198,388	23.7	4.5
201–300	15,879	61,818	13.0	1.4
301–400	9,324	43,650	7.6	1.0
401–500	5,429	24,312'	4.5	0.5
501–	17,816	51,006	14.6	1.2
Total	122,020	4,456,443	100.0	100.0

TABLE 14.6   TRANSPORTATION INVESTMENTS (1960–77)
(in billions of yen)

	National railways	Private railways	Highways	Ports and harbours	Airports
1960	116.4	54.7	211.3	23.6	n.a.
1965	348.9	101.8	699.1	66.5	n.a.
1970	478.6	219.9	1,597.9	155.8	19.8
1975	1,024.3	398.3	2,955.0	268.8	90.2
1976	976.3	419.5	3,390.4	289.2	100.4
1977	1,207.7	414.8	4,290.4	341.6	130.1

TABLE 14.7   HIGHWAY FATALITIES (1926–77)

	Pollution (000)	No. of motorcar[a] (000)	Fatalities[b]	Fatalities per million of population	Fatalities per thousand of motorcar
1926	60,210	n.a.	2,035	34	n.a.
1930	63,872	106.6	2.536	40	23,79
1940	71,400	217.2	3.241	45	14.92
1950	83,200	387.5	4,202	51	10.76
1955	89,276	1,463.7	6,379	71	4.36
1960	93,417	3,453.1	12,055	129	3.49
1965	98,287	7,897.5	12,484	127	1.58
1970	103,704	19,586.5	16,765	162	0.90
1975	111,934	28,934.0	10,792	96	0.37
1976	113,086	30,903.1	9,734	86	0.32
1977	114,154	32,853.1	8,945	78	0.27

[a] At the end of each calendar year.
[b] Death only during 24 hours after accident.

TABLE 14.8   RATIO OF ENERGY CONSUMPTION BY DOMESTIC
MEANS OF TRANSPORT (1977)

	Traffic volume (psgr-km or ton-km) (%)	Energy consumed (%)	(For comparison) Kcal per transport unit in 1974
1 Passenger			
Rail	43.9	10.4	83
Bus-commercial	10.2	4.1	123
Bus-private	4.6	1.2	
Auto-commercial	2.1	6.9	698
Auto-private	35.0	66.1	

TABLE 14.8 *(Continued)*

	Traffic volume *(psgr-km or ton-km)* *(%)*	Energy *(%)*	*(For comparison)* Kcal per transport unit in 1974
Air	3.3	6.0	953
Water	0.9	5.2	n.a.
2 Freight			
Rail	10.7	3.4	196
Truck-commercial	20.7	20.5	546
Truck-private	16.3	55.6	1,893
Water	52.3	20.5	256

TABLE 14.9 INTERNATIONAL COMPARISON OF ENERGY
CONSUMPTION PER PERSON (1960–75)
(converted in coal kg)

	World	Japan	France	West Germany	United Kingdom	USA	USSR
1960	1,405	1,164	2,402	3,651	4,920	8,013	2,847
1965	1,594	1,782	2,968	4,239	5,121	9,202	3,597
1970	1,892	3,215	3,794	5,239	5,377	11,077	4,345
1971	1,947	3,478	4,060	5,446	5,462	11,146	4,619
1972	1,984	3,251	4,153	5,396	5,398	11,611	4,767
1973	2,050	3,601	4,389	5,792	5,778	11,960	4,927
1974	2,054	3,839	4,330	5,689	5,464	11,485	5,252
1975	2,028	3,622	3,944	5,345	5,265	10,999	5,546

II FINANCIAL DIFFICULTIES OF THE JAPANESE NATIONAL RAILWAYS (JNR)

Railways and bus routes are operated in Japan by private railways and municipalities, as well as by JNR. Private railways have closed some of their lines and reduced their freight services as motorisation has increased, and they continue to operate those lines where operation on a self-supporting basis is feasible. Lately they have been given state aid for those lines where the traffic is especially light. Against this JNR and other public transport enterprises are continuing to operate their lines almost without any cuts.

Of late, the tariff income of JNR has amounted to only about 6 per cent of its expenditure (Table 14.10). One of the main factors accounting for the deficit is the freight service, where the rates have been kept excessively low, so that the transport cost in 1975 reached 3.12 times (1.74 times in the case of direct cost alone) as much as the tariff income. Even at these rates, it was not possible in the 1970s to prevent the dwindling of freight traffic volume (Table 14.11). To cover the deficit, passenger fares and charges have been raised, only to debilitate the competitive power of long-distance passenger service by rail against that by air. JNR produced deficits from 1960 to 1975, and no solution is in sight as yet.

TABLE 14.10 EXPENSES AND REVENUES OF JAPANESE
NATIONAL RAILWAYS (1960–77)
(in billions)

	Expenses	*Passenger and freight revenues*	*Miscellaneous revenues*	*Non-operative profit*	*State aid*	*(Profit) Deficit*
1960	399.3	393.7	13.8	−2.7	–	(5.5)
1965	757.1	610.4	23.7	0	–	123.0
1970	1,300.6	1,100.7	32.7	3.2	12.2	151.7[a]
1971	1,420.7	1,109.6	38.2	8.3	30.3	234.2
1972	1,594.4	1,161.2	42.6	8.6	40.5	341.5
1973	1,840.7	1,230.3	54.6	7.3	94.2	454.4
1974	2,232.9	1,365.7	57.6	10.7	148.1	650.8
1975	2,744.4	1,556.7	66.4	8.8	197.9	914.7
1976	3,100.6	1,807.0	71.2	8.4	299.9	914.1
1977	3,395.3	2,130.7	79.6	11.7	339.3	833.9
(DO, percentage)	*(%)*					
1960	100.0	98.6	3.5	−0.7	–	(1.4)
1965	100.0	80.6	3.1	0	–	16.2
1970	100.0	84.6	2.5	0.2	0.9	11.7
1971	100.0	78.1	2.7	0.6	2.1	16.5
1972	100.0	72.8	2.7	0.5	2.5	21.4
1973	100.0	66.8	3.0	0.4	5.1	24.7
1974	100.0	61.2	2.6	0.5	6.6	29.1
1975	100.0	56.7	2.4	0.3	7.2	33.3
1976	100.0	58.3	2.3	0.3	9.7	20.5
1977	100.0	62.8	2.3	0.3	10.0	24.6

[a] Up to 1970, the balance before depreciation was profit.

TABLE 14.11   REVENUE AND EXPENSES OF JAPANESE
NATIONAL RAILWAYS (1960–75)

	1960	1975	'75/'60 ('60 = 100.0)
(1) Operating revenues (in billions of yen)	407.5	1,820.9	446.8
(2) Operating expenses[a] (in billions of yen)	399.3	2,744.4	687.3
(3) Operating ratio ((2)/(1) × 100)	98.0	150.7	
(4) Passenger revenues[b] (in billions of yen)	224.2	1,315.1	586.6
(5) Freight revenues[b] (in billions of yen)	169.5	241.5	142.5
(6) Passenger-km[c] (in billions)	124.0	215.3	173.6
(7) Freight ton-km[c] (in billions)	53.6	46.6	86.9
(8) Income per passenger-km[c] (yen)	1.59	5.71	358.5
(9) Cost per passenger-km[c] (yen)	1.37	7.25[d]	529.3[e]
(10) (9) − (8) (%)	86	127[d]	
(11) Income per ton-km[c] (yen)	3.07	4.98	162.5
(12) Cost per ton-km[c] (yen)	3.29	15.55[e]	472.9[e]
(13) (12) − (11) (%)	107	312[e]	

[a] Includes depreciation cost and interest payments.
[b] Includes revenues by buses, trucks and ships.
[c] Only by rail.
[d] Includes cost for baggage and parcels. Computed by the writer.
[e] Computed by the writer.

III POSSIBLE SOLUTION

During the 1960s, in the face of the rapid increase in motorisation, fair competition between railway and road transport was hotly debated, and the conclusion was that road transport is given financial support, whereas the railway is compelled to carry on on a self-supporting basis. From 1970 on, however, the situation was completely reversed. As is seen in Table 14.10, JNR has received financial aid, while since 1975 the tax revenue from motor vehicles has begun to exceed the investments on highways (Table 14.12). Furthermore, there is a growing opinion that motor vehicles should bear the financial cost of increasing public transport.

IV CONCLUSION

Many of the problems caused by motorisation demand solutions. And, very much to our relief, in our small country the growth of motor traffic

TABLE 14.12   TAX INCOMINGS FROM MOTORCARS AND
HIGHWAY INVESTMENT (1971–77)
(in billions of yen)

	Tax incoming[a] (A)	Investment[b] (B)	(A)–(B) (C)
1971	1,338.8	1,605.9	−267.1
1972	1,596.3	2,011.8	−415.5
1973	1,793.1	2,168.6	−375.5
1974	2,008.5	2,219.1	−210.6
1975	2,434.8	2,203.3	231.5
1976	2,899.7	2,371.9	527.8
1977	3,043.3[c]	2,901.8[d]	141.5

[a] All the taxes borne by motorcars.
[b] Includes highway maintenance cost and excludes investment to tollroads.
[c] Initial budget.
[d] Budget after the supplement.

is nearly at a standstill. Motorisation in Japan has reached the stage of maturity, and no notable changes are foreseen in the transportation set-up during the 1980s.

15 Problems in Attaining an Optimum Ratio Between Long-distance Individual and Public Passenger Transport

H. St. SEIDENFUS

I INTRODUCTION

Were Phineas Fogg to be alive today, with his passion for betting, his health and his riches still intact, he would have no difficulty in completing his journey around the world in eighty hours. He would make extensive use of the aeroplane as a means of public transport and might well make private arrangements for the journey to and from the airport. This would represent an optimum ratio between private and public transportation for his purpose, though naturally a less attractive one than on his first attempt described to us with the vivid imagination of Jules Verne. This reminiscence of past adventures in the world of literature may illustrate the enormous development undergone by long-distance traffic during this century; whether for consumer or business purposes, it has become a mass phenomenon whose significance is reinforced by the increasing international relations that are an essential consequence of an institutionally organised international economy and growing co-operation in the spheres of politics and culture.

The increase in consumer demand – mainly holiday and weekend traffic – has resulted from the rising standard of living that enables people to use part of their spare money and time to leave their immediate environment temporarily in order to gain a first-hand impression of other countries, cities and people. But business tours too have undergone a marked increase as the result of growing interregional and international work specialisation and co-operation. Travellers for both consumer and business purposes have at their disposal a range of traffic modes whose technical, economic and organisational diversity does justice to the varying demands made by the potential consumer with regard to time, price and quality. Unfortunately, continental long-distance journeys have shown that the realisation of the demand – at least in many Western industrialised nations – leads to a modal split involving considerable disadvantages: some railway systems operate at a loss, bottlenecks occur on many overland routes, and the population suffers from the inconvenience of noise caused by road and airport traffic when dense settlement makes it impossible to create adequate space between traffic and residential areas. The question thus arises of whether – and, if so, by what means – the prevalent modal split can be modified towards an optimum as yet to be defined.

The following points are therefore to be investigated in this paper:

(1) What role is played by transport mode selection in the process of traffic development?
(2) What determinants influence the transport mode selection?
(3) What criteria can be applied to assess a given modal split?
(4) What strategies are available to modify a modal split?

In this analysis a reference to certain aspects of local traffic is inevitable, since long-distance and local traffic on road and rail operate in the same network and it is only their cumulation that generates a large number of the negative effects under discussion.

II DEVELOPMENT, EVALUATION AND MODIFICATION OF THE MODAL SPLIT

1 The role of transport mode selection in the process of traffic development

Since the unbalanced modal split of passenger transportation has developed into a problem, traffic researchers have been endeavouring to throw light on the principles by which traffic users base their decision for or against specific modes. In order to recognise any causal inter-dependencies at all in the manifold, even diffuse, structure of traffic, it was initially believed that the selection of the mode used could be isolated by way of a consecutive structuring of the decision process.

The different roles to be filled by an individual in society – as a resident, worker, recreation-seeker, etc. – necessitate interspatial changes. The 'homo oeconomicus transportans' was thus suspected to determine first the destinations for his activities and then to select a type of transportation and a route. Each of these process sequences was supposed to be determined by different factors that could be ascertained on the basis of geographical units as exogenous variables correlating with the observed traffic phenomena. But as a correlation is known to be no guarantee of causality, it is hardly surprising that existing situations could be illustrated in a differentiated way with this concept; but that those causalities decisive for the explanation of that situation and the forecast of future conditions were not detected. Behaviour-oriented investigations into individual transportation decisions then showed too that the determinants of origin and destination, mode and route have to be interpreted not as successive steps of several processes but as a simultaneous result of one single decision process. If one nevertheless wishes, as in the following, to reach conclusions on the significance of individual variables for the modal split, one must bear in mind that these determinants are merely modules in individual decision processes that are weighted in single cases by concrete spatial, temporal and personal factors.

2 The determinants of transport mode selection

As a rule, selection between transport modes does not represent an alternative between 'public' or 'private' transportation for the traveller but is a selection from modes differing in performance, costs and quality, modes that are evaluated differently according to the predisposition of the potential consumer. Apart from the purpose of the journey, it is above all the distance that enters into this predisposition of the potential consumer: for relatively short distances, the car is just as unrivalled as the aeroplane for very long ones. On the other hand the distance is likely to be the sole determinant only in the extreme instances of 'very short' and 'very great' and to be considered rather as the travelling time in other decision situations. This factor of time naturally depends too on the available traffic network which – looking, for example, at the West European region – still features considerable national variations. Figures 15.1a and 15.1b may illustrate this point: Figures 15.1a shows the distance-dependent modal split yielded by a sample survey of business travellers in nine West European cities; Figure 15.1b shows the

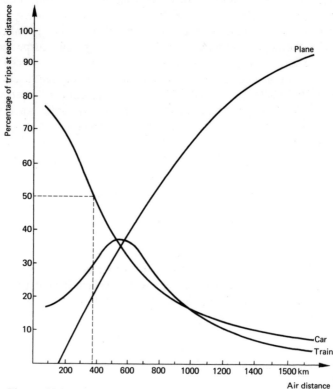

Figure 15.1a   Modal split of business trips in Western Europe

Source: OECD (ed.), *The Future of European Passenger Transport*, Final Report on the OECD Study on European Intercity Passenger Transport Requirements (Paris 1977) p. 142.

correlation between mode selection and travelling distance which was ascertained on the basis of sample surveys and sample censuses for passenger traffic between the conurbations of the Federal Republic of Germany. A comparison shows that more than half of all journeys up to a distance of approximately 500 km (approximately 300 miles) are undertaken by car in the Federal Republic of Germany, which is equipped with an elaborate network of well-built overland routes, whereas the car loses this absolute dominance in the West European perspective even short of the 400 km (approximately 250 mile) mark. The varying modal split shown in these diagrams is also based, however – apart from differences in methodology that should not be underestimated – above all on the fact that it was only business trips that

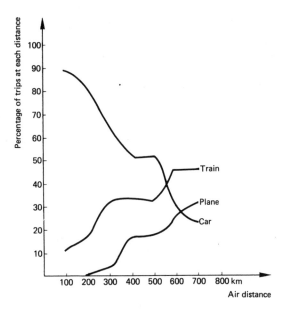

Figure 15.1b   Modal split of all interagglomeration trips in the Federal Republic of Germany

Source: Voigt, A., Die Personenverkehrsnachfrage in den Regionen der Bundesrepublik Deutschland 1970 und 1990, in Deutsches Institut für Wirtschaftsforschung, Beiträge zur Strukturforschung, H. 43/III, (Berlin, 1977), p. 122.

were covered in the West European study but all long-distance journeys in the German one.

This difference prompts further interpretations. It is to be assumed, for example, that the travelling expenses are of different significance for business and private journeys. It is only some of these expenses that are apparent to everyone, viz tariff-bound payments to be made for transportation by public or commercial transport services, and the costs of fuel for the car, whereas the other usage-dependent costs of the car are readily concealed in private calculations, though naturally not in business ones. The journey by car also gains significance for private travel purposes through the fact that the subjective evaluation of time difference from other, faster modes produces opportunity costs (costs of renounced time gain that a faster mode would offer) with a tendency towards zero. A quite different evaluation is applied to these time differences in business transportation in which, on the other hand, time savings prove to be much more easily expressed in terms of money than in private transportation ('renounced benefit' for the latter, 'renounced profit' or 'saved labour costs' for the former).

The influence, too, of those factors characterising travelling quality differentiates between the motives for the journey. Whereas comfort and reliability are important criteria for business travellers, making them firm clients of scheduled public transport facilities, it is rather the qualities of being independent of timetables and having a door-to-door connection that make the private traveller find car journeys more acceptable.

3 Criteria for assessment of the modal split

It is obvious that there can be no universal, ever-valid optimum value – possibly defined as a quotient of individual and public transport – for the empirical phenomenon of the modal split. Quantification of this ratio can be successful only with a maximum differentiation and concretisation of space and time. An attempt is nevertheless to be made to provide some axiomatic answers to the question of the optimum modal split. It should first be recalled that it is only within a welfare-oriented economic perspective that the overall social interdependencies and the totality of costs and benefits come into question for an analysis of this kind. Optimisation of the modal split can accordingly be seen not only in an increased profit-earning capacity of public transport (Figure 15.2, case A). Optimisation must also comprise more than the maximisation of the benefit-cost ratio of the traffic user (Case B). As transportation is a sector with great – and possibly the greatest – external effects, its optimum organisation also depends largely on those effects of an extra-sectoral nature (Case C). The manifold classification and assessment problems entailed in an incorporation of external effects into the overall cost-benefit calculus suggest that it may be advisable to develop detailed criteria for concrete situations only. In this paper, just three basic considerations which must be taken into account by any optimisation policy that has the modal split as its strategic variable are to be advanced:

(1) The modal split manifest between the transport operators in a traffic system must be based on an efficient intra-sectoral factor allocation. This implies exploiting the technical and organisational efficiency within one mode and among the modes (rationalisation and specialisation) with the aim of reducing transportation costs.

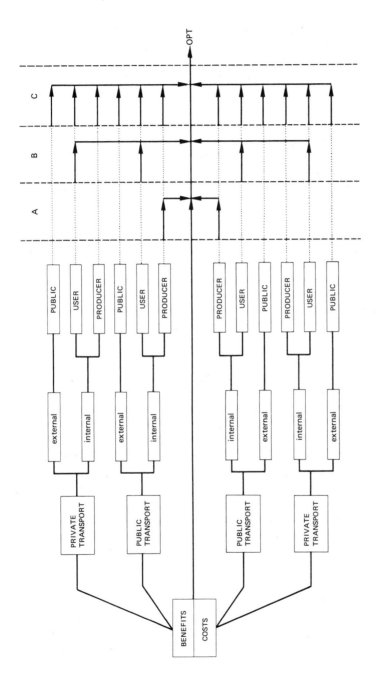

Figure 15.2 Evaluation of modal split

(2) The modal split of a traffic system must ensure an efficient intrasectoral benefit allocation. If, for instance, an unbalanced situation in favour of individual transportation is assumed to exist, then future increases in benefits must fall first and foremost to the users of public transport, e.g. in the form of

    (i) gained time (through improved operating frequency, greater speed, etc.);

    (ii) economies (reduction or disproportionately low increase in tariffs);

    (iii) increased quality (greater comfort, improved access or transfer facilities).

Apart from the possibility of providing an absolute improvement in the position of the public transport user, there is also the alternative of a relative improvement that can be attained with a benefit reduction in individual transportation:

(i) withdrawal of the time, cost and quality advantages enjoyed by individual transportation, through driving restrictions, tax increases etc. (see Nash, 1976).

This strategy of marginal benefit compensation is not inconsistent with the economic application of resources postulated under (1), as long as it is associated with overcompensatory positive effects in the spheres outside the transportation sector. This leads to the third principle.

(3) The maximum overall efficiency of a modal split is yielded only as the addition of internal production and distribution efficiency and of external efficiency. In this context, for instance, the time gains of car journeys that are reduced by speed limits (or increased transportation costs) can be overcompensated in the final result by

    (i) increased road safety;

    (ii) reduced noise emission.

The assessment of modal split effects in the sphere outside the transportation sector is first and foremost a problem of quantifiability. Many factors – such as psychological and aesthetic ones – still largely elude any form of measurement; trial quantifications, on the other hand, are available for other factors:

(i) spare requirements;
(ii) accessibility;
(iii) effects on supply industries.

It must be emphasised once again that the optimisation criteria given here cannot be more than rough guides. The individual conception of 'optimum' depends on a large number of national and regional circumstances and on social and individual preferences. The statements made by Koopmans in his Nobel Prize speech are valid here too: 'The economist as such does not advocate criteria of optimality. He may invent them. He will discuss their pros and cons, sometimes before but preferably after trying out their implications . . . But the ultimate choice is made, usually implicitly and not always consistently, by the procedures of decision-making inherent in the institutions, laws and customs of society. A wide range of professional competences enters into the preparation and deliberation of these decisions. To the extent that the economist takes part in this decisive phase, he does it in a double role, as economist, and as a citizen of his polity: local polity, national polity or world polity' (Koopmans, 1977, p. 272).

4 Alternative courses of action to influence the modal split

(a) Individual measures

State-controlled transportation policy tools offer a wide range of individual measures that can be used in different ways to influence the modal split:

(1) Investments in the road or rail network, in new or improved public transport facilities, in traffic-oriented facilities (car parks, bus stops, railway stations, airports) influence almost every cost and benefit item. They permit savings to be made in travelling time and travelling costs, improved accessibility and transportation quality and increased employment in the input sectors. These positive effects are offset by high to very high capital requirements that rapidly reach the budget limits. Infrastructural investments furthermore use up considerable land – a non-renewable resource.

(2) Price policy measures (fees, taxes, subsidies) exercise their effects on modal split by influencing the costs to producers and

consumers. In their current form they are directed above all against the car and aeroplane as primary initiators of subjective externalities (road tax, fuel tax) and promote bus and railway transportation (e.g. subsidies for the reimbursement of social services). In order to determine their overall effect, the necessary administrative expenditure must also be taken into account.

(3) Regulative measures (restrictions, prohibitions, standards) serve first and foremost to secure goals outside the transportation sector. Speed limits are intended to increase road safety and to reduce energy consumption; spatial and temporal driving prohibitions and emission standards are designed to increase environmental quality, etc. Administrative expenditure on regulative measures is likely to be considerable.

Apart from these measures within the transportation sector, which may effect direct modifications of the modal split via a change in the modal competitive position, public decision-makers also have at their disposal a series of extra-sectoral measures that can cause indirect split effects via a spatial and temporal differentiation of the transportation demand. Private long-distance traffic, for instance, is influenced to an increasing extent by holiday period controls, and the future volume of business traffic will partly depend on the extent to which it can be substituted by new long-distance communication technologies.

Public decision-making has a wide range of measures of varying practicability and efficiency at its disposal. Applied individually, however, these measures can produce only marginal effects: investment latitudes are restricted by tight public budgets, cross-price elasticities between private and public traffic modes are very low, and regulative measures alone would rapidly reach the limits of reasonableness (Baum, 1973). The diverse objectives that are to be attained with an optimum modal split must thus be faced with correspondingly diverse strategies: 'The meaning of transport strategy is analogous to that of military strategy: it is the co-ordination of major decisions affecting the transport system in order to achieve relatively long-term objectives. But whereas military strategy has one clear goal, victory, transport strategy has many diverse objectives which can never be fully attained, only approached' (OECD, 1977, pp. 335–6).

(b) Strategies

The growing political and economic integration of Western Europe has been accompanied by an increase in cross-border communication systems and a more pressing need for supranational or international co-operation. In order to investigate the extent of future demand for long-distance transportation and the possibilities of optimum compliance with their demand, the twelve European member states of the OECD in conjunction with the EEC and the ECMT produced a study in the years 1972–75 in which the development of West European long-distance traffic up to the year 2000 – depending on various strategies – is forecast (OECD, 1977).

(1) The Status Quo strategy implies that the demand for long-distance transportation continues to be fully met and the consequent problems are dealt with by means of anticyclical measures. The strategy is aimed primarily at meeting growing mobility in long-distance transport with an adaptive investment policy (above all: new roads, new airports) as far as public finance latitudes permit.

(2) The Controlled Mode strategy is based on the premise that an excessive demand for car and air transport services gives rise to the greatest problems and that these problems can be solved by diverting streams of traffic to the railways – whose attractiveness would need to be considerably increased. This strategy is simulated in two variants: in variant A it is built upon conventional railway technology together with an extensive improvement to and partial expansion of the existing railway network, whereas variant B implies the construction of a high-speed network. In both strategies the railway network is supplemented by an efficient road network (which, however, is kept smaller than in the Status Quo strategy) and the imposition of strict noise controls for cars and aircraft.

(3) The Controlled Demand strategy implies that the disproportionately high demand for car and air transport services cannot be taken over by other traffic modes and must therefore be regulated by means of direct measures. The primary goal of this strategy is effective exploitation of existing capacities. For this purpose, differentiated road taxes are to be levied and an intercity bus system introduced.

(4) The Planned Demand strategy implies that the problems of bottlenecks in long-distance traffic are due neither to an excessive demand nor to a basically unbalanced traffic mode selection but to spatial and temporal concentrations in demand. In order to split this demand more effectively, it is advisable to effect transportation investments above all in peripheral areas, to introduce motorway and airport taxes and to provide for improved temporal adjustment of holiday and weekend traffic.

Some results of the model calculations are represented in Figure 15.3. They show that those strategies related to the ratio 'internal benefits (producer benefits + consumer benefits) to investment costs' are almost comparable, so that preferences cannot be unequivocally founded. Regarding external effects, on the other hand, those strategies promoting railway transport are to be given preference. The strategy comparison therefore traces out these lines for a well-balanced development in the future.

The railways can maintain their important function in long-distance transport only if they succeed in attaining decisive improvements in their service without increasing fares: 'The key question for the railways is not whether they can afford to improve their service without raising their fares . . . but whether they can afford not to . . . If the railways can meet this challenge, they can continue to take more than 20 % of the growing market in long-distance travel. If they fail, however, . . . the resulting congestion . . . will pose a formidable problem to which there will be no easy solution. The American solution – to build more airports and large suburban motorway networks – would be difficult to achieve in the higher density conditions of more European cities' (OECD, 1977, pp. 586 ff). According to this study, one of the essential components of future railway policy should be an increase in rail transport speed to up to 250 km/h (up to 155 mph), a speed that can be achieved with conventional technology and a marginal expansion of the existing network. Railway technologies extending beyond this point, on the other hand, are considered to offer only slim possibilities of profitable application.

An increasing proportion of the future long-distance traffic volume will be absorbed by air transport, particularly if the options of

(i) expansion of conditioned tariffing (charter traffic),
(ii) decentralisation of the airline network, i.e. an increase in the number of direct flights,

Figure 15.3: Costs and Benefits by Strategy (in US $ 1973)

Strategy *Costs and benefits*	SQ^a	$CM(A)^a$	$CM(B)^a$	CD^a	PD^a
I. International costs:					
1. Investment costs	71.800	68.600	83.600	52.700	84.800
2. Operating costs	31.750	31.905	ca. 31.000	30.559	31.563
3. Users' costs	25.258	25.624	25.867	26.963	26.239
II. Internal benefits relative to the status quo					
1. Producers' benefits	—	162	1.158	−4.296	1.100
2. Users' benefits	—	−203	770	2.646	484

[a] SQ $\hat{=}$ Status quo
CM(A) $\hat{=}$ Controlled mode, variant A

CM(B) $\hat{=}$ Controlled mode, variant B
CD $\hat{=}$ Controlled demand
PD $\hat{=}$ Planned demand

Source: OECD, 1977, pp. 512–47

are realised. The first measure might manage to attract part of the increased demand for holiday and recreation transport, whereas an expansion of the airline network would primarily benefit business traffic.

All in all, however, it must be expected that only a small proportion of road traffic can be diverted to the railway. 'One is forced to the conclusion which, though far from new, is often questioned, that for the majority of out-of-town trips the car has no effective substitute' (OECD, 1977, p. 590). It is above all in the holiday and recreational sphere that the behaviour of car-owning road users is difficult to change. For this reason measures that serve the temporal and spatial deconcentration of private road traffic appear to be more promising than a strategy directed at essential changes in the modal split:

   (i) improved staggering of European holiday periods;
  (ii) inclusion of Fridays and Mondays in weekend rulings;
 (iii) replacement of some fixed national holidays by flexible ones.

III CONCLUSIONS

Optimality is a concept tending towards rigidity. It is used freely to characterise the quality of circumstances or completely controllable processes. Applied to transport – a system which is so dynamic in space and time and so versatile in its activities – optimality seems unattainable. We should reconcile ourselves to this and seek 'good' solutions to our transport problems; they may subsequently prove to be the 'best' ones.

REFERENCES

Baum, H. (1973). Free public transport, *Journal of Transport Economics and Policy*, 7, 3–17.
Koopmans, T. C. (1977). Concepts of Optimality and their Uses, *The American Economic Review*, 67, 261–74.
Nash, C. A. (1976). *Public versus Private Transport*.
OECD (1977). *The Future of European Passenger Transport*, Final Report on the OECD study on European Intercity Passenger Transport Requirements.

Discussion of Papers by Drs Bajusz, Lindner and Kakumoto and Professor Seidenfus

Opening the discussion, *Dr Goodwin* said that all the countries dealt with in these papers had their own specific historical and geographical differences, but it would be helpful to consider the papers on Japan and West Germany together, then the papers on Hungary and the GDR together.

The experience described very accurately by Professor Seidenfus and Professor Kakumoto was similar to that in Britain, America and several other countries (though not exactly the same as Scandinavia or France). The dominant trend had been the growth – at first slow and then accelerating – of private individual road transport. This had been caused mainly by a combination of increases in national and personal income, and the higher quality of service offered to the individual owner.

In the *first phase* of increase in private transport, public transport also grew, because it benefited from a general increase in travel and movement of goods. However, in the *second phase*, growth of private transport accelerated and the rise of public transport declined. There were six results: (i) inefficient use of energy: (ii) traffic congestion and time delays; (iii) increased accidents; (iv) increased pollution; (v) increasing public transport finance deficits (resulting in service cuts, fares increases, subsidy increases or all three); (vi) pressure for very large expenditures on road building. This might be described as 'social inefficiency' even though it had arisen from choices by individuals and enterprises in favour of what was – to them – a more efficient form of transport.

Dr Kakumoto and Professor Seidenfus discussed ways of solving this problem. He agreed that in many conditions it was necessary to give various sorts of priority to public transport – using various policy instruments such as capital investment, prices, tariffs, taxes, restrictions, and general planning measures. However, he thought they would agree that the reversal of a well-established trend was, at best, extremely difficult – some would say impossible.

Drs Bajusz and Lindner described a very different situation in two socialist countries. Superficially, there appeared to be a strong resemblance between the present stage of development of Hungary and the DDR and what he called the 'First Phase' of motorisation in capitalist countries, namely increased incomes and simultaneous growth both in public and private transport use. However, he thought both authors would argue that this was not a correct resemblance, for two important reasons – first, that central planning allowed decisions about transport to be taken in the interests of the whole economy, and secondly, that there was in both countries a firm plan not to go into the Western 'Second Phase', but instead to continue putting priority on public transport – to secure an 'optimum' balance in which public transport remained dominant.

Dr Goodwin said that he would like to comment on two problems that arose from this comparison. What did we mean by 'optimum'? This was a strict, scientific word which required a precisely defined objective function, a quantitative measure of 'goodness' which was maximised. All the authors implicitly agreed that measures of financial deficit or surplus were not adequate objectives of transport services, and there was discussion of wider economic and social aims. This approach suggested that tariffs, profits, etc. might be an important lever in achieving an optimum balance, but they were not a good measure of whether that balance had been achieved. How then could we continue good management discipline and efficiency (for which simple, financial objectives were very useful) with social objectives (which required very complex measures)? He wondered also if the word 'optimum' was not being used rather vaguely, simply to describe an approved transport policy.

Lastly, some technical laws of course operated alike in capitalist and socialist societies: for example, there were well-established relationships between increased traffic levels and reduced speed. Now, was it possible that such a tendency existed when we considered the *dynamic* effects of increased car ownership? In Western countries Governments had found it difficult to insulate public transport from the effects even when they had tried to do so, for three reasons: (i) traffic congestion made the quality of public transport service worse; (ii) the first groups to desert public for private transport were usually the adult, active, comparatively wealthy males – i.e. the financial core of the market; and (iii) in the long run, shops, workplaces, home and facilities were spread out in a way unfavourable to public transport.

In other words, the initial increase in car ownership created the conditions for its own acceleration. He hoped that this was *not* a tendency which would inevitably operate. But it would clearly be very difficult to maintain a growth in public transport provisions at the same time as a contraction of its market.

Discussion in this session focused on three main themes: (1) What was the appropriate definition of and influence on the 'optimum' mode split? (2) What was the most useful way of classifying 'public' and 'private' transport? (3) What were the specific institutional economic and policy factors? Although there was not a very sharp division, it was noticeable that most of the comments about centrally planned economies were made in the context of the first of these themes and about the market economies in the context of the third.

Dr Lindner referred to a difference of opinion within the GDR. At present, the overall mode split was approximately 70 per cent public transport, 30 per cent private. His view was that the optimum to aim for was 60:40, but some other people considered that the present ratio, 70:30, was already optimal. He agreed with Dr Goodwin that trends were quite different in socialist and capitalist countries, though it was interesting to note that a very similar debate was going on in both. Dr Tsankov had yesterday argued that the optimum was different for different journey distances, and he would like to agree with this. (The last point was subsequently endorsed by many later speakers, and challenged by nobody.)

Dr Bajusz said that in his paper he spoke of a level of car ownership in Hungary of 330 cars per 1000 population by the end of the century. Now this was not obtained by mathematical or theoretical analysis, but by statistical forecasts, and by analyses relating car ownership demand to the expected income and expenditure patterns of the population. These had led us to assess this as the optimal level – it implied that an average of 58 per cent of all traffic would be by public transport, though of course varying from place to place. Originally they had planned for cars to be developed to 'fill the gaps' where public transport was inadequate, though now they were planning for much higher levels of car ownership, which was influenced by general tendencies such as the transfer of shopping centres to the suburbs. These contributions caused some delegates to question the use of the word 'optimal'.

Dr Kakumoto said the 'optimum' should be calculated from some sort of benefit/cost ratio (though some people emphasised the top and some people the bottom of the ratio). But there was another aspect. Comparing two areas in Japan, one had a rail: bus: car split of 60:15:25, the other of 30:18:52 – completely different. Which was optimal? He did not know – but many Japanese were quite happy with this variety and thought that it was good. He did not believe that Dr Goodwin was helpful in talking of 'capitalist' and 'socialist' countries – similar problems applied to both.

Dr Leydon said that Dr Lindner referred to a 60:40 split between public and private transport. Was this 40 per cent predicted, or desired? If it were predicted, how could it be reconciled with such a huge growth in car ownership (sevenfold in seventeen years)? If desired, what were the policy instruments to achieve it? What were the *quantitative* criteria for an optimum, relating to waiting time, comfort and fare?

Dr Lindner replied that the 60:40 split was not a target, but a forecast of the combined effect of regulations and policies (such as were described in his paper – fares, traffic management, town planning, etc.) and the estimated trends in car ownership. The trends were influenced by economic, technical and engineering means – with the prime requirement that public transport would be dominant.

Dr Vitek said that they should start out with the basic requirements of transport for people to go to work, school, cultural activities, etc. In a socialist economy the Government had an obligation to provide these facilities: in Czechoslovakia this was done with two-thirds of the cost met by the State, and one-third from fares. Car ownership was increasing – they expected 3.3 persons per car by 1990 – but owners of private cars used public transport also.

Professor Wagener said that a different argument applied to long-distance and urban transport. For long-distance transport it was necessary to encourage private travel – this would relieve the load on public transport, which was operating at capacity. But the opposite was true for urban travel where substantial Government finance was necessary in order to minimise the use of individual cars, especially for the journey to work. In Dresden, for example, the 16 pfenning fare was so low that there was no incentive to use cars.

Dr Velikanov disagreed with Dr Leydon, and agreed with Dr Goodwin, on whether to distinguish between capitalist and socialist trends. He believed that in the USSR public transport must have the overwhelming dominance. People must become accustomed to the idea that public transport provided the best service, concerning waiting time, comfort and convenience. The optimum, or saturation, level of private car ownership was for the whole country about 250–350 cars/1000 population, but for cities, the larger the city the lower the level of car ownership – 160–80 cars/1000 was envisaged for Moscow.

Dr Goodwin thought it was better to distinguish between 'optimum' and 'saturation'. The 'optimum' level implied a deliberate judgement, a choice between alternatives. The 'saturation' level was better considered as the maximum level that people would try to attain, in given circumstances, whether this was socially optimal or not.

Professor Khachaturov expanded on the 'natural tendency' for people to want to buy cars, to live a fuller and better life. This happened as incomes increased; even though car prices were high, and petrol prices had doubled a year ago, there was still a waiting list to buy cars. Mostly, these were wanted not only for commuting to work, but also for Sundays, outings and so on. However, if we considered the social aspects, the provision of land for garages, capital investment for maintenance facilities, and so on all involved limited resources. In America the same features applied – but there, there was no public transport alternative. In the USSR fares were very low – the Metro in Moscow only cost 5 kopeks yet still made a profit, whereas in New York it was half-a-dollar. But the quality of service of public transport was still not nearly good enough to secure the optimum ratio in large, dense cities.

Dr Bajusz commented on the apparent differences between the socialist countries of the definition of optimum – he and Dr Vitek had been speaking of about 330 cars/1000, where Dr Velikanov spoke of 250/1000 in the USSR. But the difference was mainly due to different household sizes – the common point was the idea of one car per family in about the next fifteen years.

Dr Kozin, as chairman, made some final comments on this theme. They had not satisfactorily dealt with Dr Goodwin's point that to talk of 'optimum' required some quantifiable function to minimise. In passenger transport this was very complex. Perhaps they ought not to talk of 'optimum' at all, but use less strict terms like 'desirable' or 'rational' which enabled them to combine scientific, social and political requirements.

Professor Okano triggered off the next point of discussion, with a simple request for definitions of public and private transport. *Dr Bajusz* suggested that the main difference lay in ownership – i.e. private transport was owned by individuals, and public transport – in socialist circumstances – by the state. However, some public transport was used for 'semi-private' purposes, for example group excursions.

Dr Kakumoto considered that 'mass' and 'individual' were better classifications than public and private. Then buses were mass transport whether publicly or privately owned; rail was mass and public; cars were individual, even though taxis, for example, might be publicly owned. *Dr Kozin* agreed with Dr Kakumoto.

Dr Andruszkiewicz suggested a three-way classification. First, transport facilities owned by the state and available for anybody to use (i.e. 'common carriers'); secondly, both buses and cars which were owned by organisations such as companies, clubs, etc., which might only be used by specific groups; thirdly, the strictly family or individual car.

Mr Kaser concluded by raising a broader question. The appropriate share of individual and collectively financed passenger transport could be considered in the wider context of *all* private and social consumption, considered at another IEA Conference the previous month where economists from socialist countries advanced the same argument about the primary collective consumption. However, a recent study of UNESCO showed the interesting result that a high share of collective consumption was not necessarily confined to these countries.[1]

The conference turned to institutional, economic and policy factors, and *Dr Tsankov* asked Dr Kakumoto about differences between the price levels in state and private railway companies in Japan. Did different social obligations apply? How about labour productivity, especially in maintenance? *Dr Bajusz* followed up this line of questioning. In particular, what was the reason for paying for public transport out of the revenues of private transport.

Dr Kakumoto replied that they had two railways – a national system, and a 'private' system owned by companies but also by some municipalities and public organisations. The private railways carried more passengers than the public, on a quarter of the route mileage – mainly in and around the big cities. The social obligations were the same in both cases – i.e. essentially not to stop operations. Labour productivity was generally higher in the private enterprises. In 1960 Japan railways broke even, but by 1964 there was an increasing deficit – at the same time as the tax revenues from private cars were increasing, so there was a political decision to use the one to solve the other. Since then, urban public transport had also wanted subsidy.

Professor Khachaturov raised the question of energy use. Comparing Professor Seidenfus's 'four strategies', it was clear that there would be important changes by the year 2000. There would be substantial increases in fuel prices not only because of policy, but because of the depletion of oil resources.

Dr Bajusz commented that in the 1974–5 petrol crisis, railway traffic increased in a number of Western countries – America, France, Norway, Spain and Sweden. But in other countries, railway demand fell in spite of the petrol price increases. And 'free fares' experiments, for example in Rome, did not cause a great shift from car to public transport. Pricing seemed to have a limited effect on transport use.

Dr Tsankov asked about restrictions. Were there specific limits on the expansion of individual transport in West Germany? *Professor Seidenfus* replied that there were restrictions on car *use*, for example parking, pedestrian zones and speed limits; also restrictions on poll-

[1] See R.C.O. Matthews and B. Stafford (eds), *Collective Consumption*, Proceedings of a Conference of the International Economic Association at Cambridge (forthcoming) and V. Cao Pinna and V. Shatalin, *Consumption Patterns in Eastern Europe* (Pergamon, Oxford, 1979).

utants in exhaust, especially carbon monoxide and unburned hydro-carbons. But no other restrictions, for example on ownership. He added that buses and trains were not necessarily more energy-efficient than motor cars. In many cases, scheduled transport was less efficient, because average occupancies were much lower than full loads. This caused a complex trade-off between frequencies and load factors – energy savings could be made by reducing service frequencies, but if there was a private alternative this led to a loss of customers. He agreed with Dr Bajusz about the limited effect of pricing. In Scandinavia tax rates were 100 per cent, but there was still high car ownership and use. His experience was that car use grows less fast than car ownership, because 'second cars' were used mainly for shopping, with a lower average distance. Concerning the four strategies in his paper, he believed that we should reject strategy 1. Strategy 2 relied on a big unanswered question – would it be possible to *finance* new railway investment? If it were, this might result in overcapacity for many years, which surely could not be 'optimum' on any definition. He preferred to combine 2, 3 and 4, in order to ignore mode split.

Dr Kakumoto said that many people in Japan thought that railways should be used more if energy was short. However, fuel cost was only 10–15 per cent of total transport costs, and was therefore a small influence. The main point was a political one: in a democracy, it would be wrong for the leading class – which did use automobiles – to restrict their use by common people. Many, perhaps most of the people in Japan were satisfied with their present living conditions – and part of this satisfaction came from possession of motor cars. He did not know what the 'best' modal split was, but the split in Japan did seem to be popular.

Dr Kozin drew attention to a rather unexpected aspect of the discussion. Professor Khachaturov was rather dissatisfied with the mode split in the USSR, while Dr Kakumoto was rather satisfied with that in Japan. Passenger transport was very much more complicated than freight.

PART FOUR

Problems of Increasing Efficiency of Transport Modes

16 Impediments to the American Railroads' Achieving their Comparative Advantage for Long-distance Movement

GEORGE W. HILTON*

I INTRODUCTION

It is generally agreed that railroad transportation has a comparative advantage for long-distance inland movements of freight. It is also generally agreed that the American railroads are not realising this comparative advantage, though the reasons for this are in some dispute.

The American railroads themselves until fairly recently have argued that a major reason for this circumstance is subsidy to their rivals. The Interstate freeway system, they argued, is a right-of-way superior to the nineteenth century rights-of-way of railroads and user charges to truckers have not, in their view, been adequate. Similarly, the federal government's substantial investment in internal navigation facilities has been done in response to political pressures rather than from market evaluations. Until the present there have been no user charges whatever on internal navigation facilities, though an excise on towboat fuel and a trust fund for further navigational facilities have just been instituted.

Academic option has given a limited acceptance to these arguments. It is widely thought that the diesel tractor is such a technological

* Now at Department of Economics, University of California, Los Angeles.

221

improvement in intercity trucking that the excise on diesel fuel does not provide an adequate user charge for the use of facilities. It is thought, however, that any subsidy of trucking from this source is of relatively minor magnitude, not enough to produce any substantial misallocation of freight between modes on the basis of distance. The absence of user charges on the inland rivers undoubtedly has given rise to some considerable misallocations of freight by mode, but the diversion of freight and the depressing effect on rail freight rates has been borne largely by a limited number of railroads directly rival to the inland rivers system.

Rather, it is currently thought that the railroads' inability to realise their comparative advantage for long-distance movements stems from one or more of three considerations:

(1) a non-competitive economic organisation;
(2) a regional geographical pattern; and
(3) an archaic coupling-braking technology.

The relative importance of the three is in some doubt, though several recent studies have added to economists' knowledge of the subject.

II HISTORICAL BACKGROUND

As is well known, American railroads remain in private ownership but are organised in a compulsory cartel under the Interstate Commerce Commission, established in 1887. The statutory authority of the Commission at the outset was inadequate, but by 1910 it had been improved to the point that by the eve of the First World War, the Commission was stabilising the railroad cartels without pooling. The purpose of the collusion was to administer a discriminatory rate structure in which rates were set on the basis of an imperfect estimate of the elasticity of demand for various sorts of shipments. The elasticity of demand was estimated to be inversely proportional to the ratio of the value of the commodity to its weight. The other principal aspect of the railroads' tariff structure was discrimination against points which had inadequate water transportation. The railroads were subjected to occasional but not universal rivalry from steamboats on the inland rivers system. These steamboats were a competitive industry which charged rates on the basis of weight of cargo, in general without regard to the value of the shipment. Around 1914, trucks began to rival the railroads, with a comparative advantage for the transport of high-value goods. They were free of spatial limitations and capable of competitive economic organisation. As a consequence, the railroads were a declining industry by 1916.

Congress, which might have decartelised the industry by abolishing the Interstate Commerce Commission and relying upon the ubiquity of trucks to make the industry competitive, did the reverse. In 1920 it converted the Interstate Commerce Commission from a body which stabilised private cartels to an outright public cartelising body with powers of minimum rate regulation, target rates of return and restrictions on entry. Congress extended the cartel to truckers with the Motor Carrier Act of 1935. This statute enforced an economic organisation upon the truckers which was similar to that of the railroads, but it provided exemptions for private and agricultural carriage so that only about 39 per cent of intercity trucking has become regulated. In 1940 inland river navigation, which by now was mainly towboat-and-barge transportation rather than steamboat, was also brought into the cartel, though with even more exemptions. Only 6 to 10 per cent of inland river transportation has proved to be regulated.

The consequence was to make of American intercity transportation an incomplete cartel in which the cartelising body is unable to issue quotas. The consequence should have been easily predictable: efforts to make the cartelised portion of the industry prosper would inevitably stimulate the exempt portion. Furthermore, like other non-competitive organisations, this one stimulated strong unions throughout the regulated carriers, which made their operation relatively expensive.

The incentive to avoid the discriminatory rate structures and the enhanced cost of operation of regulated carriers by use of private trucking was very great. Consequently, private trucks became the comprehensive rivals to the railroads and to the regulated truck lines as well. The discriminatory rate structures became thoroughly inappropriate to the actual rivals which the regulated firms faced. Inevitably, the existence of the unregulated private trucks and the carriers of agriculturally exempt commodities, plus such illegal carriage as existed, combined with the discriminatory rate structures of the regulated carriers, gave an incentive to the use of private trucking which was probably excessive. The magnitude of the misallocation which came about as a result, as we shall see, is a matter of some academic controversy.

Integral with the cartelised economic organisation of the industry is its balkanised geographical pattern. The railroad cartels of the late nineteenth century were price-fixing associations of parallel railroads. As the industry matured there came to be three major regional groupings of cartelised railroads: the northeast, the south and the west. Within this grouping, subdivisions existed, such as the relatively self-contained New England railroads, the division between the grangers and the transcontinental railroads in the western region, and the Pocahontas carriers, the major coal-hauling railroads which formed an intermediate region between the northeast and the south. However, the only major exceptions to the regional grouping were the Wabash main line from Toledo to Kansas City and the Frisco secondary main line from Kansas City to Birmingham.

This geographical pattern of the industry had several consequences. Most important, it meant that technology had to be compatible between companies. Somewhat more than half of all American railroad shipments originate on one railroad and terminate on another. This requires a compatible coupling and braking system and this in turn requires major decisions concerning fittings of railroad cars to be decided upon jointly. Generally speaking, no one railroad can be allowed to make major changes in its car design because such changes might render the car more readily able to damage the cars of other railroads as trains are being made up.

III CONSEQUENCES OF THE ECONOMIC ORGANISATION OF THE RAILROADS

The economic organisation of this industry assures that railroads will continually be in the position of having to deal with one another as joint venturers. By application of Adam Smith's principle that entrepreneurs, even when they meet socially, are likely to begin colluding, if the entrepreneurs in this industry must continually meet to price as joint venturers, it would be exceedingly difficult to assure that they price independently when acting as rivals. The federal government since 1976 has been attempting such a differentiation.

The incentive structure within the industry is poor on a variety of grounds. When railroads are joint venturers in a movement, in general the originating railroad bears the damage claims which arise simply because it is usually impossible to determine which railroad inflicted the damage. The railroads in a joint movement split the fee in what is known as a division. A receiving railroad gets no higher fee for prompt delivery of a car and is not penalised for unsafe delivery, so it has a single-valued incentive to get the shipment to where it is going as cheaply as possible.

This entails letting cars sit around for long periods before making them up into trains and assembling them with heavy switching impacts simply because the railroad does not bear the cost of any damage which may come about. As could have been predicted, the railroads experience a high incidence of damage claims and a high degree of uncertainty in arrival times. This did not affect their ability to compete with the steamboats, but when the principal rival became the truck, which provides a superior quality of transportation, the problem became very serious indeed. Unfortunately, the problem is not being dealt with effectively. Railroad speeds, variance in arrival times, damage experience, and other major measures of the quality of service do not improve secularly.

IV GEOGRAPHICAL DISTRIBUTION, TECHNOLOGY AND RAILROAD DECLINE

The regional geographical pattern of American railroads renders them poorly able to adapt to changing regional demands for their services. From the 1830s it was recognised that railroads differed from other enterprises in the irretrievable commitment of their capital to a right-of-way. This situation had many consequences, but in particular it assured that the industry's decline would be long and arduous. A railroad is likely to be operated unprofitably for a very long period relative to other enterprises before being abandoned. Inevitably, given the distribution of industry in the United States in the late nineteenth century, the northeastern area would be plentifully supplied with railroads. The area was the seat of most general manufacturing in the nation. Goods moved out of the northeast in boxcars and agricultural products came back in the same boxcars. The cartel of the trunkline railroad produced the redundancy of investment which cartels typically produce, and eventually five major railroads connected Chicago with the important east coast ports. One area, eastern Pennsylvania, should be singled out as characterised by exceptional redundancy of facilities, because much of the investment was put in place to handle anthracite coal, which was then the dominant home-heating fuel. Equal redundancy was experienced outside the northeast by the granger railroads which connected the northeastern railroads with the Union Pacific.

Recent years have seen a decline in anthracite coal output, a dispersal of manufacturing about the country, a relative depopulation of the northeast in favour of the south and west and a greater use of trucks for agricultural haulage. All of this was to cause a severe problem of railroad unprofitability in the northeast and in the grain-growing areas of the midwest. Such manufacturing as remained in the northeast was increasingly of products high in value relative to weight, for which trucks had a comparative advantage in any case. As recently as the great depression, the northeastern railroads had been on the whole the most prosperous in the United States. By the 1970s secular forces operating against them had rendered them overall the least profitable. They had collectively suffered an absolute diminution in tonnage, whereas the southern and western railroads had a secular increase in ton-miles, though the composition of the ton-miles was moving adversely to the industry as a whole.

Compounding these difficulties was a distorted incentive to merge within the industry. Railroads had an incentive to merge with parallel railroads to reduce their costs even though there was a growing volume of empirical literature demonstrating that the savings from forming larger railroads were at best meagre and at worst negative (Healy, 1961). A disastrous merger in 1968 between the Pennsylvania and the New York Central into the Penn Central Transportation Company precipitated the so-called railroad crisis of the early 1970s. The merged Penn Central proved to be highly unprofitable from the outset, losing over a million dollars a day and physically deteriorating very rapidly.

Apart from the other disadvantages of the present technology of railroading, it entails dynamic problems which render the operations of a highly-deteriorated railroad both costly and unsafe. The natural frequency with which cars swing when in motion is augmented by the 39-foot rail lengths characteristic of American railroading, especially in a range of speeds between 10 and 30 miles per hour. About a third of the Penn Central became so deteriorated that the railroad was limited to 10 miles per hour in those areas. This resulted in astronomical labour costs. The technology is excessively labour-intensive in any case, requiring large numbers of men to tend the coupling and uncoupling operation and to couple up the brake hoses. This situation, incidentally, puts several groups in a position in which they may easily tie up the operation with a strike. Thus, the present technology has been in part responsible for the strong unions which have always characterised the industry.

V REORGANISATION OF THE RAILROADS

The federal government dealt with the weakness of the northeastern railroads with a planning operation in the mid-1970s. In the Regional

Rail Reorganisation Act of 1973, and the Railroad Revitalisation and Regulatory Reform Act of 1976, the federal government merged the six eastern bankrupt railroads into the Consolidated Rail Corporation or Conrail, abandoned a small portion of the redundant eastern package and turned other portions over to newly formed railroads which could operate under state and federal subsidies.

This planning operation tended to preserve most of what was undesirable about American railroading (Hilton, 1975). Most obviously, the planning operation preserved the regional pattern. The Act of 1976 did have some provision for partial decartelisation and partial deregulation, but these were not enough to bring about massive reorganisation of the industry. Rather, the industry remains in a compulsory cartel of firms which are simultaneously rivals and joint-venturers, stabilised and supervised by the Interstate Commerce Commission. Given the preservation of the geographical pattern of the industry, nothing could be done to reform the technology, for the firms remained joint-venturers as between areas.

The Carter administration proposed a deregulation of much the same character, though somewhat more far-reaching. The bill that the administration announced in March 1979 will allow railroads freedom to set rates within a range of 7 per cent, plus a compensation for inflation, for a five-year transitional period. Thereafter, they would have normal freedom of setting individual rates. They would lose their ability to apply for across-the-board rate increases after two years. After that two-year period the ICC would be prohibited from granting anti-trust immunity to rate bureau agreements that provide for general rate changes. Joint industry discussion of single-line rates would be prohibited. Rate bureau discussion of joint rates would be open to the public. Abandonment of rail lines would be facilitated, and shippers, local communities or state governments would be empowered to provide subsidies to maintain service on lines threatened with abandonment. All of these are essentially more extreme examples of the partial deregulation of the 4-R Act of 1976. In the proposed statute, jurisdiction over rail mergers would be shifted from the Interstate Commerce Commission to the Department of Justice.

Although the bill doubtless represents an improvement over present arrangements, it will probably also prove inadequate to allow the railroads to regain their comparative advantage over long-distance transportation. The changes in policy would still leave the industry one of firms which are simultaneously rivals and joint venturers with a compatible technology which the organisation of the industry helps to perpetuate.

The question whether a partial deregulation of this character could restore the railroads' comparative advantage for long-distance movements is integral with the original question of the relative importance of the reasons for the railroads' present handicap. Approximately a decade ago the first serious efforts were made at quantifying the costs of the cartelisation to the American economy. Thomas Gale Moore in a paper for the Brookings Institution endeavoured to assemble various estimates of the costs of the several aspects of cartelisation (Moore, 1975). He brought together a variety of estimates of the misallocation of freight between modes which had been made by various economists. These range from a cost of $300 million to 500 million per year (Friedlaender, 1969), to a range of $1 billion to $2.9 billion (Harbeson, 1969). These estimates were based on comparisons of the costs of freight movements by railroads and by regulated trucks. For long distances it appeared that rail costs were as little as a fifth of truck costs. From this it was deduced that the regulation imposed simply enormous costs to the economy from its observed tendency to cause goods to move too long distances by truck.

Subsequent scholarship has tended to reduce the magnitude of estimates of this character. First, these estimates made no serious effort at quantifying the effect of the difference in the quality of the service on the shipper. Professor Kenneth Boyer of Michigan State University endeavoured to quantify the costs mainly of holding inventories of shippers who habitually used rail as vs. truck (Boyer, 1977). He discovered that habitual users of railroads, owing to the high variance in anticipated arrival times, were forced to run larger inventories than habitual shippers by trucks. When he corrected estimates such as those of Freidlaender and Harbeson for this cost difference, he concluded that the tendency of the regulation to make goods move too long distances by truck was much less costly, around $126 million per year. More recently Richard Levin of Yale University has produced a similar study with an estimate of a welfare loss from rate regulation of $53 million to $135 million (Levin, 1978).

Equally important, recent literature has demonstrated that the cost advantage of railroads over trucking found by the researchers of a decade ago is overstated. Comparison of the costs of the railroads and ICC-regulated truckers is misleading, for they do not in general carry cargo for which the railroads currently compete. The railroads compete with exempt hauliers and owner-operators who drive under charter to holders of ICC irregular route authorisation. The railroads' cost advantage over such operators is on the order of 10 per cent, even on hauls as long as Chicago–Los Angeles (Hilton, 1978). Thus, cost considerations also lead to the conclusion that misallocation between railroads and trucks is not so great as it appeared in the late 1960s.

Consequently, the author concludes that even the rather substantial deregulation which the Carter administration proposes will not be adequate to deal with the railroads' present disadvantage. That disadvantage, in other words, stems from the most basic aspects of the industry's present technology and economic organisation. Rather, the industry has to be reorganised very fundamentally in its economic organisation, geographical pattern and technology, so as to be capable of operating as an ordinary competitive industry within the framework of the anti-trust laws. The outlines for such an organisation were set out by the engineer John Kneiling, and they have since achieved a considerable measure of academic acceptance (Kneiling, 1969).

The industry ought to be reorganised so that railroads will not in the normal course of affairs be required to interchange equipment with one another, as interchange tends to perpetuate the present technology, to produce a large number of damage claims, to facilitate collusive pricing, and to involve much of the excessive labour costs of the industry. Freed of interchange the industry would no longer require a technology compatible between firms.

As the massive conversion of technology in ocean shipping over the course of the last twenty-five years has demonstrated, containerisation is a simple technological change which minimises the costs of intermodal movement. If the railroads were reorganised as a small number of nationwide rival systems with containerised technology, the firms would use each of the three major modes of transport in accordance with the comparative advantage of each. That is, railroads would be used normally for long-distance movements and trucks for short-distance movements, including origination, termination and classification. Present railroad yard facilities would be replaced with intermodal transfer facilities analogous to present ocean container terminals. There would be free entry into trucking either for the integrated transportation companies or specialised firms, or individual owner-operators. Under these circumstances, the market would determine whether the integrated transportation companies or other operators would provide the origination and termination function. Any effort at exercise of monopoly power by the integrated transportation companies would increase the economic range of truck operation by the independent operators. The industry would be an ordinarily competitive one. In technology, the integrated transportation companies might differ from one another in their means of moving freight between cities. Kneiling proposes a technology of turbine-electric articulated units approximately one-quarter mile long with flat beds for the containers and multiple-unit operation to permit trains of infinite length. To pursue the analogy with the economic organisation of the merchant marine, Kneiling proposes special integral trains in the hopper car configuration for bulk commodities. His proposed technology of turbo-electric trains would be in rivalry with other forms of technology for moving the containers, many of which are not yet in existence, but there is no reason why a single technology such as this should not be used by all companies in an industry reorganised along these lines.

Such academic objection as has been voiced to this reorganisation of the industry has largely centred on the problem of whether this organisation could suit present traffic flows, which are highly diverse. There is admittedly a problem of determining the geographical patterns of the nationwide rail systems which this proposal envisions. A public planning operation to bring it forth is likely to be open to the sort of political pressures which were abundant in the recent planning under the 3-R and 4-R Acts of the 1970s. One virtue of containerisation is that if goods arrive in containers there is no obvious reason why one should have a strong preference whether they do so by rail or truck. However, political pressures for retention of rail lines or for special characteristics of the emerging patterns would undoubtedly arise. Similarly, given the distortions in the current incentive structure in the industry, simply letting the firms get together to determine how to merge is not certain to produce an optimal geographical pattern. In addition, the country remains dynamic and what is an optimal geographical pattern now gives no assurance of being so well into the next century.

The answer to these problems is a simple one: reduce the present railroads to leasing companies which would negotiate in a competitive market with integrated transportation companies for the use of their rails. There is no reason why trains must be operated by the owners of rails. Indeed, there are abundant situations in the present railroad network where ownership and operation are separate. Two or more companies can operate on the same rails. There are still rival rail routes between most major points in the United States, allowing for competitive bidding between specialised intermodal transportation companies and the railroads which own the rails. The contracts for the use of the rails would be of finite duration and thus as the geographical pattern of industry in the country changed, so would the pattern of routes in the intermodal transportation companies.

Containerisation in maritime transportation has demonstrated itself to be consistent with competition. Containerisation has tended to erode the power of steam-ship conferences and also of longshoremens' unions. A container may be moved at a flat rate by cubic volume or by weight. It is sealed so that value-of-service considerations should not enter and, indeed, in a competitive industry would not enter. Thus containerisation would be consistent with competition in product markets.

Containerisation would, as has previously been pointed out, be consistent with competition in the factor markets in initiating rivalry between various means of moving the containers. It would also be consistent with competition between railroads to provide their tracks to the intermodal container firms. Consequently, we have at hand a simple technological advance which renders the railroads in all major respects capable of competitive organisation and consequently capable of achieving their comparative advantage within a competitive framework.

REFERENCES

Boyer, K. D. (1977). Minimum Rate Regulation, Modal Split Sensitivities and the Railroad Problem, *Journal of Political Economy*, LXXXV, 493–512.

Friedlaender, A. (1969). *The Dilemma of Freight Transport Regulation* (Washington: Brookings Institution).

Harbeson, R. W. (1969). Towards Better Resource Allocation in Transport, *Journal of Law and Economics*, XII, 332–4.

Healy, K. T. (1961). *The Effect of Scale in the Railroad Industry* (New Haven: Yale University Press).

Hilton, G. W. (1975). *The Northeast Railroad Problem* (Washington: American Enterprise Institute for Public Policy Research).

Hilton, G. W. (1978). What Does the ICC Cost You and Me? – Currently, That Is, *Trains*, June 28–32.

Kneiling, J. G. (1969). *Integral Train Systems* (Milwaukee: Kalmbach Publishing Co).

Levin, R. C. (1978). Allocation in Surface Freight Transportation: Does Rate Regulation Matter? *Bell Journal of Economics*, IX, 18–45.

Moore, T. G. (1975). Deregulating Surface Freight Transportation, in Phillips, A. (ed) *Promoting Competition in Regulated Markets* (Washington, Brookings Institution).

17 The Development and Main Problems of International Transport Systems

R. SQUILBIN

I INTRODUCTION

The spectacular development of international exchange in recent decades makes it necessary for transport operators to examine carefully the matter of adapting their means to the demands of the loaders. The following considerations are concerned solely with rail transport and will be based mainly on experience drawn from railway operation in Europe, a continent with highly developed international rail links and considerable international traffic. The conclusions which will be drawn could be regarded as specific to this situation. Nevertheless, they will be suitable for wide consideration on the railways of other continents, perhaps avoiding certain errors of assessment for the railways concerned or indicating to them certain worthwhile steps.

Since the second half of the nineteenth century, which saw a prodigious expansion of the railways, great progress has been accomplished, firstly in establishing, and then in facilitating, international rail links. In fact, it should not be forgotten that originally the railway, developing within a national framework around the most important population and industrial centres of each country, was limited to a national service, and that it was not until the rails were ready to be joined on both sides of the frontiers that rail transport problems took on an international dimension.

One must bow to the wisdom and science of our predecessors who, with effect from that time, set to work to give the railway the necessary legal and technical instruments to establish international traffic.

The CIM and CIV Conventions, the RIC and RIV Regulations, the agreements within the CEH and CEM, and the provisions enacted by the UIC, gradually formed with effect from 1890 (supported moreover by periodical exchanges of information aided by international bodies such as the IRCA which took the initiative for this from 1885) the bases of a coherent international rail supply, and enabled the railway to meet demand correctly during the many years when it enjoyed a near monopoly as long-distance carrier.

The development since 1930 of increasingly active competition from other means of transport, particularly road, and the considerable increase in international exchange after the Second World War, have served to alter the problems facing the railways in many ways.

The competent international bodies[1] have untiringly continued their action to bring suitable new solutions to these problems.

Despite all their efforts, and although tangible results have certainly been obtained, the situation at present cannot be said to be entirely satisfactory, nor can it be said that the railway fulfils in the most efficient manner the role which it should play in the 'international transport' function.

The purpose of this paper is to analyse the weak points remaining in the accomplishment of this important function by the railways.

II TECHNICAL PROBLEMS ENCOUNTERED IN INTERNATIONAL TRAFFIC

To put international rail transport into effect satisfactorily means making use of and harmonising factors stemming from various sectors involving rail technology, as well as the co-ordination of commercial action and organisational measures. It is therefore these various fields which need examining. In addition, it should not be forgotten that although railway managers are certainly able, within the framework of their responsibilities, to overcome numerous questions, irrespective of the statutory system applied to them, there are still decisions connected with the responsibility, either of their own authority, or other national authorities. These external constraints will also need to be examined.

Once the legal bases of international rail transport were defined, it was

---

[1] In 1957, the OSJD was added to the older international bodies mentioned above.

obviously the technical field which first occupied the attention of the railways. In this field they endeavoured to achieve the most complete harmonisation of the practices in use on each system. Whether infrastructure, rolling stock or technical operating, the results obtained are remarkable, but there are still problems remaining.

1 Infrastructure

The European Railways have four different track gauges: 1435 mm, 1524 mm, 1600 mm, 1668 mm. This disparity, which there can be no question of eliminating, and which must therefore be accommodated, means that at the following transfer stations:

 (i) French–Spanish frontier for 1435–1668mm transfer,
 (ii) USSR frontiers with Poland, Czechoslovakia, Hungary and Rumania, and the Finnish–Swedish frontier, for the 1435–1524mm transfer,

it is necessary to effect, for each vehicle crossing the frontier, complex and costly operations in installations, staff and time, for changing bogies or axles, in order to avoid trans-shipping passengers or freight, a solution which, although more simple, is also very costly in time, unattractive to the passengers, and a possible source of damage to goods. The use of variable gauge axles makes it possible to improve the transfer conditions in certain particular cases.

The different clearance gauges adopted by the Railways have led to the definition, for international rolling stock, of a 'universal' gauge observed by all the European Railways, except in Great Britain. This gauge limits the width and height of the vehicles or loads, and thus involves certain restrictions in the degree of comfort desired for passengers or in the transport capacity of the goods. On the direct services with Great Britain, specialised rolling stock of still smaller dimensions than the 'universal' stock has to be used, which increases the constraints mentioned above for this traffic.

The recent introduction of containers, and the advantage of being able to transport lorries by rail, has demonstrated particularly the inadequacies of the 'universal' gauge, especially in height. The international organisations (UIC and OSJD) are studying the possibilities of achieving a new gauge offering increased possibilities for rail transport on essential routes.

Axle loads and maximum weight per linear metre permissible for each railway form, by the nature of their diversity, an additional constraint for international freight traffic. The equipping of international routes with uniform characteristics reduces the difficulties encountered to a certain extent, especially for transit purposes.

The electrification of the railways, which was undertaken with effect from the initial years of the twentieth century on some systems, and which is still continuing, was based, very logically and especially as it concerned internal relations only at the outset, on the use of the technique most developed at the time when the railway electrified its system. This has resulted in an European patchwork with four different co-existing systems of electrification, which means that the junction stations must be equipped with special changeover tracks where locomotives can be changed, or which give rise, if it is desired to avoid the lost time by such changes, to the use of multisystem locomotives, a solution which is technically very neat, but costly.

The different signalling systems used by the railways are also an obstacle to rationalising international operations: on the one hand, the drivers employed on a foreign railway must assimilate a particular set of regulations in detail; on the other hand, the traction units running in the foreign country must have the signalling monitoring equipment peculiar to that railway.

In addition to the technical problems just mentioned, the field of infrastructure cannot be left without mentioning the question of investments. Investment decisions do not generally lie within the power of the managing authority of the rail system, but are taken at a higher level, where the requirements of the rail transport sector must be assessed concurrently with those of the other economic sectors (transport and others), with a view to defining which share of a limited overall amount can be allocated to it. It is a fact that, in many countries, railway investments have remained limited to the barest minimum in recent decades, the political authorities having devoted their main investment in the transport sector to roads or waterways. This has resulted in the ageing of the railways, whose international traffic suffers the consequences: insufficient speeds on medium-distance passenger services, congestion of certain installations increasing the transit time of freight, increased competition from road transport possessing a network of motorways or modern roads over considerable distances, and accessible to the users at a cost often less than the operating, maintenance and depreciation charges.

A fair distribution of investments for transport purposes, based on multicriteria economic studies and a correct allocation of the infrastructure charges to the various users, would help in harmonising the conditions of intermodal competition, which would render the transport market, particularly the international market, more realistic.

2 Rolling stock

In connection with infrastructure, various problems also involving rolling stock were mentioned. No further reference to these problems will be made. However, the decisive importance for international rail traffic of a normalisation of rolling stock should be emphasised. This normalisation can attain various degrees ranging, without mentioning mere dimensional and qualitative normalisation, from capability to total standardisation, via interchangeability and unification. It can be limited, depending on the stock concerned, to one or other of these possibilities.

Obviously, it is the rolling stock, and within this the freight wagons, which require the most advanced degrees of normalisation for healthy international operating. The requirements can be considered less strict for traction stock, since the international operating conditions for this stock are usually related to specific circumstances governed bilaterally in each specific case between the railways concerned. The unification of rolling stock enables the railways to offer passenger or freight customers a well-defined technical supply, irrespective of the railway owning the stock used. Standardisation of this stock also facilitates group purchases (producing economies for the acquiring railways), and its maintenance away from the owning railway. With regard to their freight stock, the railways must certainly look towards standardisation, for within the international bodies to which they belong, unification is often regarded as sufficient for passenger stock, through the standardisation of certain components or groups of components, or at least their interchangeability.

3 Operating

Like their colleagues in the other branches of the railways, the operating specialists have contributed extensively to setting up the international rail service. It was first necessary for them to define the conditions for the exchange of stock between the railways. This was the task of the RIC and RIV Unions which, with effect from the 1920s, established – and are continually improving – the necessary regulations affecting the conditions of use, treatment, compensation and accounting for reciprocal services provided, and the technical regulations relating to the vehicles. However, it must be accepted that these regulations do not achieve optimisation of the conditions for reciprocal use of the stock. Operating pools involving a limited number of railways and a limited number of types of stock, such as the Europ and OPW pools for wagons, and the VL pool for sleeping cars, are aimed at this objective, and their extension should be pursued.

The compilation of timetables for international trains is another important concern of the operating experts. Their discussions within the CEH and the CEM, carried on in an atmosphere of reciprocal understanding, have always been successful. However, progress may still be made especially to ensure that the supply is adequately adapted to developments in demand, and to overcome certain national peculiarities in favour of national services standing in the way of the progress of international traffic.

But, however attractive it might be on paper, the international rail service supply and the development of international traffic requires an increased effort in the matter of timekeeping and guaranteed transits. Only the close co-operation of the railways concerned in the traffic and a structured exchange of information will improve a situation which, at present, cannot be considered satisfactory, particularly for freight traffic.

In connection with the problem of the exchange of information, the need for developing a system of centralised management system for freight traffic supported by an adequate transmission network should be stressed. Such a system is the cornerstone of efficient international operating, and the efforts at present deployed by the international organisations to set it up are particularly praiseworthy.

III COMMERCIAL PROBLEMS

Having considered the most important technical problems arising in international traffic, it is now necessary to examine the commercial problems. Generally speaking, it must be recognised that, at the commercial level, much remains to be done to improve the competitiveness of the railway in international traffic. Indeed, one cannot ignore the fact that, despite unprecedented expansion and the considerable development of international exchanges experienced by European economic activity during recent decades, the share of international freight traffic carried by the railway has not increased in the same proportion as transport as a whole. Of the causes which limit the development of international rail traffic, some are outside the organisation of the railways. Others are inherent in the railways and it is for them to eliminate them, by developing within their own organisations positive and effective action affecting both their working methods and the means available to them. This should centre around the improvement and unifying of international commercial collaboration, based on a common commercial strategy.

This action can have different aspects, which can be classified in two main categories:

(1) steps which the railways can take to improve their position on the international transport market, without any of them giving up individual responsibility, or freedom in the matter of rates or carriage conditions;

(2) steps which commit the railways to a process of integration which, to a greater or lesser extent, will cause them to lose their individuality, create an international entity – even partial – and remove from each railway a certain share of its autonomy and therefore of its individual responsibilities.

Among the measures stemming from the first category the improvement of knowledge of the transport market should be mentioned. Unreserved collaboration between the commercial departments and a systematic exchange of information, simplification and improvement of the supply to customers should not be limited to mere tariff questions but should present a single entity to the customers, and aim at achieving a 'door-to-door' service, realising a better quality of service, adapting international carriage charges to the particular requirements of such traffic, and extending and improving the system of tariff unions and the joint monitoring of the results of the action taken at international level.

The measures stemming from the second category concern even more complete co-ordination of the commercial action of the railways abroad, by the introduction of through rates, independent of national tariffs, and by the creation of pools for certain defined traffic or for all international traffic. These pools can take the form of operating agreements, or solely commercial agreements covering revenue or costs. A further measure is the formation of common subsidiaries, in the form of international companies for a very specific purpose, responsible for exploiting well-determined techniques or traffic. The development of such measures, particularly with regard to the second category, is a long-term exercise which is still far from being concluded, but which the railways should pursue with tenacity.

IV EXTERNAL CONSTRAINTS

The external constraints must now be considered. As already indicated, these constraints can emanate from the government rail authority or from other national authorities. The former stem from the status of subordination of the railways to their national community. In all states, the railways are subject to a certain amount of supervision by the public authorities, and pressure from national political or economic quarters, which influence their management in varying degrees. This situation is the result of historical, geographical, economic and political causes. Thus, there would be no point in imagining that a railway could take measures in its own interest which might be directly prejudicial to the national interest.

Similarly, a railway may be obliged to take, under government or political pressure, measures which do not conform to its own interests or to that of the other railways, but which benefit national activities while standing in the way of international rail collaboration. It can be taken for granted that these constraints will be relaxed, and that the railways will obtain greater freedom of action as the other modes of transport develop, offering the community alternative solutions to the use of the railway. However, total freedom from the constraints resulting from the supervisory role of the public authorities does not seem to be likely.

Other constraints are exerted on the railway by the public authorities, by reason of the requirements arising from other government authorities which are not directly responsible for rail transport. These concern particularly the provisions laid down by the regulations for the crossing of frontiers, whether consisting of rulings for the safety of the State or persons (police checks), the health of individuals, livestock or plants (health and phytosanitary inspections), or financial red tape, and the knowledge and/or monitoring of commercial exchanges (customs examinations). These regulations are all obstacles to the provision of a quality international transport service, through the loss of time they cause at frontiers.

The relaxing of these regulations, inter-State agreements enabling certain checks to be eliminated, and remaining frontier operations to be carried out jointly, checking passengers on the move, and transfer of certain formalities to internal departure or destination stations, are all measures which certain countries have developed on a fairly large scale with success and will constitute major factors in improving rail transport.

Finally, mention must also be made of the important shortcoming whereby in certain European States, particularly those under the market economy system, there is no real intermodal transport policy or no concerted common transport policy between the States. The distortions of competition rampant on the transport market and which are mainly to the detriment of rail transport (obligation to carry, tariff regulations, social conditions, infrastructure charges, etc.), are harmful to the competitiveness of rail, and hinder the progress of a mode of transport whose socio-economic qualities are nevertheless universally recognised; these include economy of space, respect for the environment (low atmospheric and acoustic nuisance), safety, economy of raw materials, economy of energy, possibility of using energy from various sources.

V CONCLUSIONS

As has been shown, the railways remain confronted with numerous problems in accomplishing their function as international carriers. However, one must not be discouraged. We must follow untiringly the path our predecessors have marked out for us, not without success, and find the necessary solutions to these problems. Achieving these solutions requires total co-operation, however, both at government authority level in the countries concerned and by the railways themselves. With regard to the latter, the concerted action they undertake within the large railway bodies to which they belong, strengthened by the direct contacts they can – and must – organise, constitutes the surest guarantee for favourable development of such co-operative action.

Discussion of Papers by Dr Squilbin and Professor Hilton*

Professor Wickham, opening the discussion, said that in previous sessions of the Conference a generally optimistic view on future railway development had been stated. Both of these papers stated a position which emphasised much more the past and present difficulties faced by the railways of Western Europe and of America.

Dr Squilbin discussed the heavy financial burden on taxpayers – even

---

* Neither author was able to attend the Conference.

the relatively efficient railway system in Switzerland imposed a burden of about $100 per head per year. This had led to a drying up of finance for other forms of transport, and for research. Similarly in France, money which was needed for research into new urban transport, was instead spent on the railways. In addition, there were inefficiencies on small lines, and decreased competitiveness of railways even for the long-distance and international traffic which previously was dominated by rail. Dr Squilbin pointed to the continued existence of four different gauges, a European patchwork of four systems of electrification, variations in maximum loads, and the absence of a common commercial strategy.

Professor Hilton was, if anything, even more gloomy about railways in the United States, with non-competitive economic organisation, an irrational geographical coverage, and archaic coupling and braking technologies.

There was some disagreement between the two papers on what to do. Dr Squilbin's argument was essentially one of moderation and caution. There should be more co-operation and fundamental work in study groups, limited international technical co-operation, and partial integration of the European railway networks. All should agree with this – though he would question whether it went far enough: for example, should we not try to apply the same argument to much bigger networks, including the USSR and Canada?

Professor Hilton's proposals related to US economic and financial institutions. He suggested what seemed to be a wild idea – restoring drastic, unlimited competition, not only between rail and other modes but also between different railway companies. This would mean dissolving the Interstate commissions, and new institutional arrangements such as one railway company leasing lines from another. There were some precedents for this – for example, in the operation of sea and airways which jointly used the same international lines.

In the general discussion *Dr Leydon* argued that Dr Squilbin's points could only be understood on the basis of what had been happening to market shares – in Europe, the general pattern was a radical shift with a decline in the share of rail and increase of road. Competition was not the only – or even the main – cause of this; rather, the nature of foreign trade was different. Probably about half of the decline in railway freight was due to the greater trade in light, high-value goods, and reduced trade in heavy, low-value goods. This trend would continue. He believed that in order to cope with it, the railways would need to change their strategy, putting an emphasis on long-term market analysis leading to specialised operation with clear market objectives. There would need to be some disinvestment, removing trucks, products and methods, and some investment especially in order to increase productivity. Social funds should be used for retraining some existing staff so that they could find other employment.

Mr Kovalev contrasted the situation in the USSR with that described by Dr Leydon. Instead of 'disinvestment' it would be necessary to double the capacity of the railways. He did not agree that, even in West Europe, the railways had outlived their welcome: the problem there was that customers who should be using rail, from the point of view of overall social efficiency, were actually using other modes. Public transport could compete, if it were developed. The railways needs were to co-ordinate shipping, offloading and line-haul to reduce delays, and standardisation with a unique gauge.

Professor Hunter said that standardisation, especially using containers, would increase the ease of combining the advantages of all modes. He particularly liked Professor Hilton's idea of a 'Transportation Company' which would organise carriage by rail, road and perhaps ships – that was, a company based not on mode, but on function.

Dr Kakumoto said there were three main conditions for the survival of the railways – large traffic volumes, containers and a stable origin-destination pattern. He believed that the planners had made a big mistake in exaggerating the reputation and expectations for railways. We should not consider 'The Railway System' as a whole, since some lines were profitable, and others uneconomic. There might be a case for subsidising passenger transport (fares covered 60 per cent of costs in Japan), but freight must at least cover direct costs, and this meant that traffic volumes would be smaller.

Professor Noortman agreed with Dr Leydon's point about the changing structure of demand – and this would not allow Dr Kakumoto's conditions to be fulfilled. To him, this meant that the solution was not technical, but organisational – i.e. to improve reliability.

Professor Khachaturov returned to Dr Squilbin's analysis. There was an extra problem that the vast network, built over decades to cope with coal, construction material and other bulk freight, now had excess capacity. Professor Hilton's idea for a 'Transport Company' was quite unrealistic concerning the separation of ownership of rolling stock and track – the alternative was a merger of railways, and increased state regulation – an idea which seemed to have few supporters there, but which he believed was necessary. The technical problems, especially of a unified gauge, would take a long time to solve – but at least the Association of Railway Companies should have a minimum goal of preventing new obstacles to technical unification.

Dr Lake pointed out that, while the USSR was different from 'America', Canada actually had more in common with the USSR on these issues, than with the US. They must consider the basic cost characteristics of railways: while the train was actually moving, the system was very different. But the terminals were very inefficient. It followed that for high loads on long distances, railways were difficult to beat – and also for very high loads on shorter distances. But when a long-distance journey was a series of short distances, the advantage was lost. The best experience they had had was when it was possible to organise for a direct haul from origin to ultimate destination, with the minimum number of interchanges. So he agreed with Professor Khachaturov on the need for mergers within the railway system.

Dr Tye said that there had been some improvements in the US, but even now there was a reputation that in any marshalling yard, you could find a wagon that had not moved for a year. Part of the answer was to have a good 'back-up' system – trucks as a back-up to rail, small parcels as a back-up to truck. This helped to minimise inventories, and to relieve temporary difficulties, using mathematical methods to achieve an optimal mix. In reply to Professor Khachaturov's criticism of Professor Hilton, he added that Hilton's views were not widely supported within the US, although he had generated much interest. It was interesting to note that in the very early days of railway development in Britain, there was a system of track-owners charging tolls to users, but this was rejected in favour of a unified system.

Professor Seidenfus reiterated the importance of the declining volume of 'mass' products, transported by rail. This would be reinforced by regional development policy, which often tried to organise manufacture using materials near to the place where they were produced. However, there might be some increase in coal transport due to difficulties of petrol supply. The question was, why had combined road-rail systems been so unsuccessful? Partly this was due to long-standing enmity, and to the separate development of the two systems in isolation from each other. But also there was a need for centralisation of operation (which would mean both railways and truckers losing some independence), and for the use of economic incentives to encourage co-operation, which were now lacking. One interesting problem was that the railways, when publicly owned, had 'social' goals but were still encouraged to act like a private enterprise.

Professor Hunter commented on the 'traditional enmity' between railroads and other carriers, indeed between rival railroads. Efforts to co-ordinate operations faced difficulties with human capital as well as physical capital. Trained people were stubborn, and it might be as difficult to change attitudes and methods of working, as it was to change technical aspects of the system. The merger of the Pennsylvania Railroad and the New York Central illustrated the problem.

Professor Wickham summed up the discussion. There was a widespread problem (everywhere except USSR and Canada) when long-distance hauls involved trans-shipments between railways. Strict technical standardisation was not wholly necessary – some improvements could be made even where the gauge was not standard, by international or interstate organisations. The main bottleneck was in commercial co-operation – the development of a single marketing organisation and common tariff structure. And the main operational problem was delay at interchanges.

18 Rational Policies for Development of International Air Transportation

JOHN R. MEYER AND WILLIAM B. TYE*

One does not assure the survival of a regime of competition by a policy of mere laissez faire: That is why we have the antitrust laws . . . The preservation of a competitive market structure sometimes requires us to protect some suppliers from the application by more powerful rivals of competitive tactics that deny them an opportunity to compete for reasons that have nothing to do with their comparative efficiency in serving the public.

Alfred E. Kahn, Chairman of the C.A.B. (1978)

The biggest cost of the commitment to subsidy and support of flag carriers is the restriction bred by concern over the amount of subsidy to be drawn from public treasuries. If nations are ever to forego restrictive policies, a change in attitudes with regard to subsidy support of flag carriers must occur first.

Mahlon R. Straszheim (1969)

* Much of the preliminary work done by Dr Tye on the issues discussed in this paper was funded by a research grant by Pan American World Airways to Charles River Associated Incorporated. Neither Pan American nor Charles River Associated bears any responsibility for the authors' conclusions. The authors are also indebted to Jane Piro, research assistant to the project, to Tom Wendel and James Murphy of Pan American for assistance in providing data on costs, and to Stanley Gewirtz for his comments.

I INTRODUCTION

In recent years international trade negotiations have been increasingly concerned with a series of closely related issues involving charges of predatory competition, 'dumping', etc. These issues usually involve a charge that political considerations sometimes take precedence over economics; for example, that costs and profits have been ignored in international trade decisions to the detriment of the functioning of the competitive marketplace. Perhaps the most widespread recent example of such a charge is that Japan has been disrupting international markets by 'dumping' manufactured products at prices below costs. Similar accusations have been made in recent years about US grain exports. Western maritime interests increasingly suggest that the Soviet Union, in entering international shipping markets, has failed to heed cost considerations and has cut rates below competitively sustainable levels. As still another example, the existence of highly-subsidised state-owned air carriers has been alleged to preclude the extension of the thus far successful US experience with airline deregulation to the international sphere.

A common thread in all these instances is the degree to which the multiple objectives of state-owned or controlled enterprises or other state agencies may come into conflict with what many consider to be the conditions for maintaining a workably competitive marketplace. The usual prerequisities listed for workable competition include an absence of pronounced economies of scale or other factors leading to market concentration and a sufficiently large number of buyers and sellers to deprive participants of undue power over prices.

General acceptance of profit maximisation as a primary business motivation is also usually implicit, although goals of state enterprises often involve employment maintenance, generation of foreign exchange, consumer interests or protection, showing the flag, national defence, etc. These multiple goals can be financed through direct subsidies or indirectly through cross-subsidies (on profits earned, for example, in certain protected markets). All this raises the intriguing question of the extent to which state-owned enterprises and private enterprise can coexist, let alone achieve a workably competitive accommodation, in an unregulated international marketplace.

This paper addresses this issue in the particular context of the international air transportation industry. An immediate impetus or incentive is provided by recent attempts to introduce more competition into this industry. Among the specific questions to be addressed are:

(1) Will the pursuit of non-economic goals by state enterprises, innocently or by intent, lead to a situation where fares, service and demand will depart significantly from the competitive outcome with potentially large efficiency losses?

(2) Would a relatively unregulated international market for air transportation lead state enterprises to engage in market practices such as predatory pricing as a means of passing on the costs of any inefficiency?

(3) Can private carriers survive in a market environment dominated by state-owned airlines or would conditions force their withdrawal or acquiescence to a non-competitive market structure?

(4) Do the special circumstances of international air transportation, particularly subsidies to state carriers and the lack of an enforcement mechanism to deter anti-competitive acts, suggest that a policy of *laissez faire* will not lead to more competition, but to substantial departures from competitive fares and service, thus arguing for regulatory safeguards to preserve the competitive process?

II COMPETITIVE GOALS AND FUTURE INTERNATIONAL AIR TRANSPORTATION AGREEMENTS

The announced goal of US international aviation policy is to achieve as close an approximation to open competition in international aviation markets as possible (Kahn, 1978). This goal would clearly appear to be in the US interest, whether viewed from a producer or consumer standpoint (as it would be for any efficient producer of such services, regardless of nationality). However, implementing this policy may be rather difficult. Specifically, the major device open to US policy for achieving this goal is to negotiate more competitive bilateral agreements and, in particular, agreements in which both governments stipulate that they would refrain from any support for their respective flag carriers and would permit the competitive process to determine market share.

Further complicating the task is the simple fact that international airlines differ greatly in their efficiency and therefore in their ability to compete for market share. Thus, governments with inefficient flag airlines may not readily embrace the competitive process. In essence, these governments must choose from among four distinct negotiating postures:

(1) accepting the possibility of their inefficient flag carrier withdrawing from the market in favour of more efficient rivals;

(2) agreeing to negotiate a competitive arrangement but with the stipulation that the state flat carrier can be subsidised so as to 'meet competition' if the need arises while otherwise abiding by the competitive rules;

(3) agreeing to a more competitive agreement (with continued right of subsidy) but looking upon this as a useful means of accomplishing anti-competitive acts; or

(4) finding the competitive objective totally unappealing and not agreeing to less restrictive bilaterals in any form.

From a pure efficiency standpoint the outcome of free competition with no government subsidies is the most desired state. However, such a course would require that many nations, indeed perhaps most, repudiate a long history of support for national flag carriers. This suggests that a 'second-best' solution in which some nations retain a limited or unlimited right to subsidise their carriers may be the best that is achievable.

Any such 'second-best' solution raises, however, certain questions as to whether competitive process can survive if the right of subsidy is continued. All else equal, subsidies will generally increase the incentives or ability to pursue uneconomic goals, in ways that may often be anti-competitive. Subsidies also greatly compound the problem of maintaining the competitive process in international air transportation because: (i) they increase the likelihood that a market structure will develop which is not conductive to competition, even without intentional predatory behaviour; (ii) they increase the difficulties of defining and detering predatory behaviour for regulatory purposes; as a result, they increase the desirability of restraining allegedly predatory behaviour prior to knowing the actual competitive impacts, thereby risking the deterrence in the meanwhile of legitimate competitive business decisions; and (iii) they increase the incentives for anti-competitive behaviour. These difficulties are considered in greater depth, in turn, below.

1 Increased likelihood of market structures not conductive to competition

The potential of economic injury from subsidies is real even if there were no threat of predatory acts. Subsidies usually represent conscious attempts by governments to modify a competitive market structure. The objective, for example, may simply be to subvert the competitive process by depriving more efficient carriers of market share. Behaviour in such circumstances may be only marginally concerned with predatory intent in the anti-trust sense. But the end result may be much the same if the resulting fare and service decisions are incompatible with the survival of private carriers. Many international airlines have been consistently unprofitable, indicating a willingness by the governments involved to sacrifice economic objectives to other goals. If the private carriers withdraw, the economic harm to consumers may be minimal if re-entry or entry by new competitors is easy. Political and economic impediments to entry exist in many international air markets, though, and are certainly higher than in the domestic US airline market, where many participants have been developed as a deliberate public policy. Thus, even if subsidised international airlines do not employ internationally predatory tactics, subsidies could well lead to a market structure not conducive to competitive fare and service decisions.

Of course, if the subsidised carrier does not engage in predatory activity, it can be argued that taxpapers in the country doing the subsidisation bear all the costs of the resulting inefficiency, with air travellers in general benefiting from lower fares.[1] Furthermore, if uneconomic decisions of foreign governments drive efficient carriers from the market or deprive them of market share, there may be a real cost to the efficient carriers and their employees which is not paid by foreign governments.

2 Subsidies and the problem of defining predatory behaviour

Grave doubts have often been expressed by economists about the desirability of enforcing strong safeguards against predatory behaviour because such safeguards smack of protecting competitors rather than the competitive process. In US domestic air transportation, for example, scepticism about claims of harm from predatory behaviour would seem thoroughly warranted. US domestic airlines are all private enterprises facing definite limits on how much profit they might sacrifice to finance predation. The anti-trust laws also apply and provide for triple damage remedies. In addition, regulation is a continuing, if permissive, reality in

---

[1] ' . . . . If foreign taxpayers want to subsidize the availability of low-cost air service to American and foreign travellers, I would not necessarily regard that as an unmitigated catastrophe, even though a privately-financed competitor would take a dimmer view' (Kahn, 1978).

the US so that predators need the acquiescence of the regulators to raise prices if and when they succeed in driving others from the Field. Finally, with several well-established trunk lines and larger regional carriers in the market, most cities are served by more than one domestic carrier. Entry into any market subject to predatory exploitation requires *at most* only CAB approval (and often not even that) and certainly nothing akin to negotiations between sovereign governments; indeed, re-entry by a US carrier into domestic markets it once served generally requires no government approval whatsoever.

Incentives to engage in predatory behaviour can, though, be far greater in international air transportation. To start with, there is generally no credible anti-trust or regulatory deterrent. Entry and re-entry would be the only real economic deterrents to predation in international markets and these are rather more difficult to execute in an international than in a domestic context. If a decision is made not to exercise prior restraint on predatory behaviour in international markets, it is at least possible that if predatory behaviour succeeds, a major irreversible change may take place in the number of competitors in some markets. Accordingly, the usual scepticism about the potential harm from predatory behaviour may not be quite as warranted in the circumstances of some international air transportation markets as in those for domestic aviation.

Differences in domestic and international aviation markets, particularly the power of governments to tax and to subsidise, may also call for a different, broader test for predatory behaviour than when purely private decisions are involved. Predatory pricing is usually defined for private enterprise competitiors according to the classic model of driving out one's rivals with the hope of recouping the losses by exercising future market power, that is, 'the deliberate sacrifice of net revenues in the expectation of greater future gains' (Scherer, 1976).

Some anti-trust experts have proposed a firm's own short-run marginal costs both as a standard for setting prices for regulated firms and for defining predation; for example, a test for predation would be whether prices were above or below the short-run marginal costs of the alleged predator (Areeda and Turner, 1975). Pricing below this level usually would be irrational (i.e. unprofitable)for a private enterprise, even in the short run, and the only rational reason for pricing at this low level would be to injure competitors. This standard has been questioned on several grounds (Scherer, 1976; Williamson, 1977).

One alternative cost standard for defining predatory pricing, often recommended as appropriate for regulatory ratemaking in mixed economies, (Meyer *et al.*, 1958), is long-run incremental costs. A major reason, among others, is that pricing according to short-run marginal costs ' . . . might constitute predatory pricing – driving out of business rivals whose *long-run* costs of production might well be lower than those of the price-cutter' (Kahn, 1970). Whereas there are arguments for allowing a regulated monopolist to reduce rates to account for excess capacity, 'the possibility that such reductions might be predatory or destructive makes this kind of pricing much more objectionable in a competitive situation. . . . Some dynamic loss if the result is the elimination of those competitors' whose stimulus is required for efficient performance of the industry is one reason for preventing predation (Kahn, 1970).

In defining predatory pricing in the context of international aviation, several distinct pricing motives might be distinguished. First, a carrier may conceive of itself as being in a declining cost industry and price below its own long-run average cost but at long-run incremental costs with the difference made up by a permanent subsidy. Second, temporary losses may be incurred, not with the intent to injure or force out competitors, but to meet competitors' prices, and looking toward a future when one's own costs are brought into line with lower cost competition; alternatively, such a relatively benign pricing policy might be pursued by an inefficient carrier subsidised by its government just to maintain a presence in the market, for national prestige or other non-economic reasons. Third, prices below a firm's own long-run incremental costs may be established as a more or less permanent policy, the difference made up by government subsidy[3] or from profits earned in protected or cartelised markets, with the consequence being elimination of competitors from the market by pricing below the competitors' long-run average costs. (Such a policy is obviously not economically rational in the profitability sense but might be motivated by employment maintenance or as a means of indirectly encouraging other industries, such as tourism or air frame manufacture.) Fourth, prices might be temporarily set below a firm's own costs and those of efficient competitors with the intent of forcing the competitors from the market and recouping losses by higher charges later or indirectly through taxes in the same market; this, of course, more or less includes classic

[2] The subsidy in this case might also be elsewhere recouped from air travellers through hotel or airport taxes or other such devices.

predation. Obviously, these four cases are not necessarily all mutually exclusive and might appear in different combinations or degrees of severity.

This first case is probably largely an 'empty box' in aviation since declining costs are seemingly experienced only at very low volumes. The predatory pricing label is thus perhaps best reserved to describe behaviour in cases like the third and fourth. A predatory price then becomes a price not only below a supplier's own costs but also consistently below the level sufficient to keep efficient carriers in business. It is approximately based on long-run average costs, with proper allowance for departures in the short run because of demand or cost considerations (and not otherwise justified as to achieve marginal cost pricing objectives). The test is whether subsidies are being used to set fares consistently below levels that would be justified in a competitive market (or below levels that otherwise would have prevailed) with the intent or possibility of preventing efficient carriers from recovering their costs over the life of their investments, and with the probable intent or possibility as well of recovering such a subsidy from consumers.

The identification of predatory competition may also need to take into account the motivation of the state in supporting its carrier, the controls on the use of subsidy and the state's willingness to reinforce predation through its taxation policies. Its willingness to discriminate against other carriers must also be considered when labelling an act 'predatory'. The subsidy mechanism itself would also have to be carefully considered to determine whether it facilitates predatory behaviour. The state may institute strict controls to ensure that a subsidy is used only for an intended purpose other than financing predation, for example (although this may be impossible in practice). These determinations, moreover, could often be complicated in many instances by unclear motives for subsidies or for certain taxes; furthermore, the motives could well change as time passed (e.g. starting with motive two above and 'progressing' to motives three or four).

A private enterprise predator is ordinarily assumed to suffer short-term losses, which must be measured against the discounted present value of the higher revenues to be gained after successfully eliminating competition. The calculation of expected benefits from predation obviously depends on the choice of the predatory tariff, the discount rate, the length of time required for rivals to withdraw, and the monopoly rents to be earned after withdrawal occurs.

State-owned enterprises may have, though, an opportunity for immediate recovery of the revenue losses from lower fares through 'squeeze' tactics, which are far less risky than waiting. This possibility, in turn, can enhance the attraction of engaging in predatory behaviour in some international markets, despite the fact that such predatory behaviour might at first glance appear irrational. In the special circumstances of international air transportation, it may be possible, for example, to recoup subsidies and to squeeze competitor's profits by raising landing or other such fees or by imposing special taxes on travellers (including artificially high rates of exchange for the local currency).

Of course, what a country may gain as an airline operator from these tactics may be lost as a tourist attraction. Any subsequent attempt to exploit position as a successful predator might detract from tourism objectives. But a country nevertheless could succeed in squeezing out an efficient carrier of different nationality at little or no cost to itself and with no benefit – indeed a probable loss (depending on the relevant elasticities) – to the air traveller. Indeed, a particularly alert government might impose special taxes on the business traveller (or others who are destination-insensitive or price-inelastic) to make the predation pay immediately and with little risk of tourism loss.

The popular image of a predator is generally that of a large, low-cost producer who cuts his rates to drive out his rivals and monopolise the market. Some have argued that it is not consistent for state-owned carriers to want restrictions on competition to hold down subsidy requirements and simultaneously to contemplate predatory competition. However, in the past the heavy burden of subsidies may have been a factor motivating anti-competitive market practices.

It is therefore pertinent that governments have frequently used discriminatory acts to favour their carriers and to discourage competitors. A recent US government report found that many countries place obstacles (such as quotas and minimum prices) in the path of charter operators to discourage entry (General Accounting Office, 1978) and cited numerous examples where US carriers were charged higher user charges and rental fees than the indigenous or native state airline. Other cited examples of discrimination were currency restrictions, requirements to use monopoly ground services, higher aviation fuel prices, arbitrary restrictions on operations, and preferential marketing advantages for the native domestic carrier.

The US Congress passed the International Air Transportation Competitive Practices Act in 1974 (P.L. 93–623, 88 Stat. 2102) as a step to protect US flag carriers from discrimination. This act allows US action against 'unreasonable' user charges, mandates observance of tariffs, and prohibits rebates on air freight. The act provides for an annual report by the CAB to Congress and, if necessary, compensating charges on foreign airlines to be rebated to US flag carriers. However, the difficulties of enforcing this provision, the problem of discrimination in forms other than user taxes, and problems in defining reasonable user charges impose great difficulties (Subcommittee on Aviation of the Committee on Commerce, 1974). Although annual CAB reports indicate the results of negotiations to reduce excessive user charges, the United States has never imposed compensatory charges (GAO, 1978). US carriers have criticised the process as being too slow to act as an effective deterrent.

Article 15 of the Chicago Convention (Convention on International Civil Aviation, 1944) requires that user charges not be higher for other nations than for the signatory's own aircraft engaged in similar international air service. This provision provides some protection against blatant discrimination, but the predator always has the choice of simply rebating the equal but higher user tax to the subsidised state carrier through higher subsidies. Furthermore, Article 15 considers only discriminatory user charges and not other forms of discrimination.

The direct gain to be derived from predation depends, of course, on any difference in fares achievable with and without rivals. If one assumes that prior to predation fares were determined by the low-cost carrier, the predator's potential gain is equal to the difference in costs of the excluded efficient carrier and the level costs of a new entrant. Even ignoring political problems and difficulties commonly encountered in international markets, these entry level costs will differ substantially with different routes and operating characteristics. For example, in high-density markets that can be well served by simple turnaround operations, especially vacation travel markets, charters will be a good substitute for scheduled service so that entry will be relatively easy, entry costs low, and the monopoly gains from predation correspondingly limited. On the other hand, where densities are either relatively low or volume depends on 'feed' from other origins or destinations, a network is required to achieve economical operations and entry will not be so easy or inexpensive; reservations systems and ground facilities for servicing several planes and large numbers of transferring passengers will be necessary. An efficient network operation may also require establishing a 'market presence', which again may require time and money (e.g. for advertising) to achieve. (See Meyer and Tye, 1981, for discussion.)

Typical of the complaints of US carriers about competition in 'network markets' internationally is the statement of Charles C.

Tillinghast, Jr., at the Annual Banquet of the Academy of International Business, 19 June 1979:

> With very few exceptions, the industry pattern in Europe and Asia is that internal airline services are provided by, or under the control of, the national carrier. Thus the flow of traffic from internal to international services is also controlled by the national carrier. It can easily account for 20 to 50 passengers per flight.
>
> Foreign airlines often control the local reservations systems, booking procedures, travel agents, tour wholesalers and freight forwarders — and often use that control to ensure that they achieve a disproportionate market share. The Russians are the extreme example. US carriers, of course, have been forbidden by law to own, or to exercise such control over, travel agents, wholesalers or freight forwarders.

In international aviation, moreover, the gains from predation may not be exclusively limited to 'the expectation of greater future gains' strictly in the market in which the predation occurs. For example, carriers operating under fifth freedom rights (the right of a carrier to pick up traffic at a point in a state other than his own and to set it down at a point in a third country) can sometimes pose at least a minor competitive annoyance to bilateral pooling arrangements entered into by other countries for flights between themselves. Certainly, these fifth freedom flights represent some alternative to the otherwise explosive position enjoyed by those in a bilateral pool. Accordingly, if any efficient 'outside' carrier has its basic economics undermined by predation on its major leg (i.e. third and fourth freedom traffic), then its fifth freedom presence in markets beyond can also be eliminated. If so, an additional benefit to suppression of competition through predation in major international airline markets could be the maintenance and strengthening of collusion elsewhere.

When the issue of classic predatory actions arises, the source of funds to finance the money-losing services is almost always a major issue. In essence, a predator must possess greater resources or 'financial staying power' than his rivals. In the case of foreign flag airlines, several sources of such funding may be available. As already mentioned, taxes might be imposed one way or another on competing airlines or on travellers. Furthermore, if the predators participate in pooling arrangements or other anti-competitive activities in certain bilateral markets, above-average profits from these markets may be available to finance predation in competitive markets. Finally, the ultimate source, of course, would be government subsidies from general funds.

Data on the revenues and profitability of route segments subject to pooling agreements are not generally available.[3] Many of these markets are characterised by uneconomic services and restrictions on efficient practices which may in part dissipate the effects of high fares. Nevertheless, as shown in Table 18.1, fares under these agreements are much higher than in competitive sectors, and these revenues are a potential source of funding for predation.

TABLE 18.1   SELECTED 1976 AVERAGE NORMAL ECONOMY
FARES PER PASSENGER KILOMETRE
(US cents)

			Distance (km)			
	250	500	1000	2000	4000	8000
World international						
average	15.6	13.3	11.4	9.7	8.3	7.1
Between Canada,						
Mexico and the US	12.3	9.6	7.5	5.9	4.6	–
Local Europe	19.8	16.1	13.1	10.7	8.7	–
North Atlantic	–	–	–	7.2	6.7	6.3

Source: ICAO (1978) *Survey of International Air Transport Fares and Rates: September 1976* (Montreal: ICAO) p. 13.

Willingness of governments to finance predatory acts from general tax revenues is even more difficult to assess. The most that can be said is that the means are available, and anti-competitive acts have been justified in the past by some governments as a means of reducing any subsidy requirements.

III INEFFIENCY AS AN INCENTIVE FOR PREDATORY BEHAVIOUR

The relative efficiency of various participants in a market is a major consideration in evaluating the likelihood of workable competition

---

[3] Routes serving North America appear to be generally more competitive and have a large share of the world market, but the size of the markets governed by restrictive agreements is by no means insignificant. The International Civil Aviation Organisation (ICAO) reported that in 1965 only a small number of bilateral agreements required prior determination of capacity. By 1976, 60 per cent contained provisions for prior determination of capacity (ICAO, 1977).

emerging. Furthermore, inefficiency is ultimately the potential burden that might be imposed on consumers by suppressing a competitive market outcome. Thus, the magnitude of differences in levels of efficiency are critical to the issues raised in this paper.

That various international carriers experience substantial differences in relative efficiency may be considered self-evident from the history of IATA fare 'crises' and disputes (Straszheim, 1969). Conflicts over the proper role of competition are also indicative of substantial differences in costs among the carriers.

One commonly used method of measuring the relative efficiency of airlines is the amount of financial aid required to keep inefficient carriers afloat. However, the subsidies may be necessitated by considerations other than technical inefficiency alone, such as maintaining service in markets without sufficient traffic or with tariffs that are below costs. Moreover, estimates of the burden of inefficiency using a subsidy measure are complicated by the fact that nations aid their carriers in ways that are often difficult to measure. (A recent CAB survey found only 8 of 55 foreign international airlines were wholly owned by private interests.) The preferences and benefits conferred by foreign countries on their respective airlines are many (CAB, 1974, 1975; Department of Commerce, 1976). Methods of support include outright subsidy, currency controls, favoured treatment of user charges, illegal rebating, provision of goods and services at below-cost prices, forgiveness of loans, assumption of debts, low-interest or no-interest loans, loan guarantees, and purchase of services at prices above the market price. Handicaps imposed by restrictive practices may also raise the costs of efficient carriers and must be taken into account. Finally, the profit and loss in one year may not necessarily be representative.

The second method of estimating inefficiency is to compare various measures of output (seat miles, available ton-miles, etc.) to inputs (labour hours, etc.). Unfortunately, different airlines generally do not provide similar services under similar operating conditions. Chief among the differences which must be taken into account are route structures and density, costs of resources, different environmental conditions, different accounting and operational procedures and the type of service involved.

The essential problem is how to identify sources of productivity differences among firms ('firm effects') after the operating environment is considered ('environmental effects'). Cross-section comparisons may not provide a valid basis for forecasting relative efficiency in a common competitive environment because some carriers often operate in highly constrained circumstances. Part of the poor performance of some European state carriers, for example, might be attributed to cabotage and fifth freedom restrictions in European markets, rather than inefficiencies inherent in the carrier's operating procedures. However, it has been estimated that the cost savings from eliminating these restrictions have been exaggerated (Gordon and DeNeufville, 1977). Illustrative of these difficulties is a recent study which compared British Airways' performance with that of US flag carriers and concluded that: (i) BA's productivity is substantially lower than that of US flag carriers; (ii) BA's costs and revenues are significantly higher; (iii) BA's fleet is more inefficient; and (iv) BA is subsidised through Public Dividend Capital (Taussing, 1977). However, the author was forced to hedge his conclusions because the merger of BOAC and BEA combined the overseas and European operations, making comparability with US carriers difficult. An appropriate definition of output was also deemed difficult to ascertain.

Another approach to evaluating international cost differences is to infer the relative efficiency of carriers by comparing the costs of performing comparable services, in lieu of trying to correct for differences in the operating environment. IATA cost data on scheduled services provide at least a basis for making such comparisons.

Tables 18.2 and 18.3 show the relative costs and load factors of the two US flag carriers reporting to IATA and comparable data for the average of all other carriers for the years ending March 1977, March 1978 and March 1979 (estimate). Reviewing the data for the years ending March 1977 and March 1978, these data suggest the following conclusions:

(1) North Atlantic operations were not profitable for the reporting non-US carriers *in toto*, since as a group they did not even cover operating expenses; realised passenger load factors were below the levels required to recover operating costs, which were in turn below the levels required to meet capital costs.

(2) US carriers reported costs both as a measure of passenger and freight capacity (per available ton-kilometre or ATK) and passenger capacity (per available seat kilometre) below the average for other carriers; the other reporting carriers as a group in 1976–77 experienced operating costs per ATK 10.4 per cent above those reported by US flag carriers and the figure for 1977–78 was 10.9 per cent.

(3) US flag carriers experienced breakeven passenger load factors for

TABLE 18.2 AIRLINE COST ANALYSIS–NORTH ATLANTIC REGION (All costs in US cents)

	Weighted US carrier average (PAA and TWA)		All other carriers	
	Year ending March 1977	Year ending March 1978	Year ending March 1977	Year ending March 1978
Passenger load factor percentage (First and Economy)	56.4	56.8	59.0	59.5
Operating cost coverage (Freight and Passenger)[a]	107.6	106.3	95.5	97.4
Operating cost/ATK	18.3	19.6	20.2	21.4
Passenger operating cost/ available seat kilometre (First and Economy)	2.19	2.35	2.43	2.55
Breakeven load factor to meet operating costs (First and Economy)	52.8	53.4	63.3	62.8

[a] Total revenue divided by operating costs
Source: IATA Cost Committee.

TABLE 18.3. AIRLINE COST ANALYSIS – NORTH ATLANTIC REGION ESTIMATES FOR THE YEAR ENDING MARCH 1979 (All costs in US cents)

	PAA & TWA	All other
Operating cost/ATK	20.7	24.6

Source: IATA Cost Committee, estimates as at January 1979.

Notes to Tables 18.2 and 18.3
1. Possible differences among carriers in accounting methods and procedures for allocating costs among regions must be considered in making these comparisons. A further difficulty with the data is that only two US carriers are included and British Airways data are not included. Seventeen carriers reported for the period ending March 1977, and eighteen reported in the following years. Changes in exchange rates over time can also affect estimated cost differences.
2. Although not reported in the tables, non-US carriers found among the low-cost carriers tended to be either airlines of other nationalities with substantial private ownership participation or airlines from countries outside Europe where wage levels are undoubtedly lower.

3. IATA data also report a percentage for 'capital charges allowance' for each of the reporting carriers. These charges are based on companywide percentage reported by the carriers and therefore may not be valid for individual IATA regions because of differences in equipment types and utilisation among regions. Career reporting and accounting practices also differ. The reported data on operating cost coverage clearly indicate that fully-allocated cost was not being covered in the North Atlantic region for the reporting carriers during the two years. One indication of the magnitude of the discrepancy is the difference between the realised 1976–77 passenger load factor for all reporting carriers (59.0 per cent) and the total cost break even load factor derived by IATA using the average capital charge allowance (13.9 per cent) for all reporting carriers. Using this capital allowance, the total cost breakeven load factor for all reporting carriers in the North Atlantic is 68.5 per cent in the year ending March 1977.
4. Revenue for military traffic is not reported to IATA by US flag carriers. Thus the realised load factors for US flag carriers are actually higher than those reported here. On the other hand, breakeven load factors for US carriers would also rise because of the lower yields on military traffic.
5. During the year ending March 1977 reporting US carriers supplied 39.9 per cent of the available seat kilometres in the North Atlantic provided by reporting carriers.

operating costs significantly below the average breakeven load factor for the other carriers taken as a whole.

(4) US flag carriers experienced actual load factors below the average for the other carriers.

Complete data for the year ending March 1979 are not available. However, one may speculate that the yields (passenger revenue per revenue passenger kilometre) have declined significantly because of recently introduced discount fares, thereby raising the breakeven passenger load factors. Actual load factors have undoubtedly increased significantly as well. US carriers apparently increased their advantage over the composite of all other carriers, as shown in Table 18.3. Part of the dramatic increase in non-US carrier costs in US dollars was undoubtedly attributable, though, to the devaluation of the dollar relative to other currencies during the year. In any event, the implied cost burden seems fairly large.

All carriers other than US carriers reported operating costs of almost $1.5 billion in the North Atlantic in the year ending March 1977. A 10.4 per cent cost burden would imply a relative operating inefficiency of over $150 million, not including any allowance for capital costs or indirect subsidies.

Use of the level of inefficiency dictated by the data for 1978–79 would have doubled this estimate. However, the large cost differential, 18.8 per cent, also reflects the weakness of the US dollar during this period. The

IATA cost comparisons reported here have certain deficiencies as measures of potential costs of predation:

(1) They measure the level of burden under past conditions of IATA ratemaking and restrictive agreements. More competitive markets might cause governments either to increase or decrease the level of inefficiency, and subsidised carriers might lose market share. The stimulus of more competition might cause subsidised airlines to cease many inefficient practices. After predation was successful, government decisions to pursue uneconomic policies might also change. Actual costs of a successful predator could rise after the stimulation of competition is eliminated. Or it may be the case that most of the subsidies are for 'public service' which is unrelated to market share.

(2) Only part of the costs might be passed on by a successful predator.

(3) The total costs of inefficiency are not just the costs of providing a given level of capacity ('X-inefficiency'). The costs of providing too much or too little capacity have not been considered, nor has the cost of inefficient utilisation of whatever capacity is actually provided ('allocative efficiency'). Recent large fare cuts after more competition emerged in the North Atlantic suggest that a more competitive market will induce higher load factors in international air transportation.

(4) A successful predator may be able to achieve certain economies of better utilisation, load factors, and marketing as a result of a greater market share. In particular, some of the high operating cost experience of state airlines may be from poor personnel and equipment utilisation arising from low market share. Successful predation might improve this utilisation and reduce costs.

(5) The IATA cost data show only the relative efficiency in the North Atlantic service, where there are substantial competitive pressures. Other areas might show different levels of efficiency.

Thus, the estimates of relative inefficiency should not be equated to the actual burden that a successful predator would impose, but rather regarded as an indicator of the adverse effect of subsidies in the marketplace. However, it would seem that firms in international air transportation are characterised by major differences in relative efficiency – with all that may imply in the way of incentives to avoid competitive markets.

IV SUMMARY

The interests of both consumers and efficient carriers would appear to be well served by creating a more competitive international air transportation market. Freer competition would benefit low-cost carriers and consumers would benefit from fares based on these lower costs. However, structural differences between the US domestic and international markets increase the likelihood that the competitive process will not be as self-enforcing internationally as it is domestically in the US.

Successful negotiation of openly competitive international markets will thus require a considerable effort. The international air transportation policies of some governments are opposed to accepting consumer interests as an objective or the competitive market structure as an outcome. Such governments may continue to seek restrictive agreements and use that less restrictive environment to achieve anti-competitive policy objectives. Governments may also attempt to pass the additional costs created by the pursuit of non-economic goals on to the air traveller. Preliminary estimates of the cost of this inefficiency in this paper indicate that these could be fairly substantial.

Once governments are granted the right to advance non-competitive objectives at their own expense (i.e. through subsidies to their own flag carriers), it may become difficult, if not impossible, to protect many legitimate consumer and producer interests. Subtle distinctions indeed may be needed to differentiate between departures from competition at general government expense and those ultimately passed on to travellers. In order to make this distinction, difficult judgements may be required about the intent of anti-competitive acts. In this connection, a concern about the survival of efficient carriers as a 'yardstick' may also be justified.

In general, scepticism regarding the likelihood of predatory and other anti-competitive acts cannot be naively extended from domestic markets to the entire international air transport sector. A unique regulatory problem arises when attempting to define 'predatory competition' when countries retain the right to help their state enterprises 'meet competition' through subsidy or other devices. The complexity is only compounded when it is recognised that sovereign governments may have many reasons for promoting the interests of their national carriers, many of which may be inconsistent with efficiency goals but nevertheless deemed legitimate by a society for other (non-economic) reasons.

Even if one is completely confident that subsidised carriers will not engage in predatory tactics and harm consumers directly, subsidies can be a threat to the competitive outcome. Subsidies increase the likelihood that a market structure will develop which is not conducive to competition, especially if efficient carriers are forced to withdraw. Also, it may prove impossible to insulate efficient carriers and their employees from the real economic costs of being deprived of the economic benefits of their relative efficiency.

Of course, it is one thing to identify the problem, another to make constructive proposals to solve it. Defining predation is not enough, since difficult problems of interpretation and enforcement will arise. For example, suppose a subsidised carrier chooses a policy of uneconomic overcapacity and in turn justifies low fares on the basis of excess capacity. Should regulators intervene? Will this inevitably lead to a 'slippery slope' of greater regulatory intervention? Should the controls be in the regulatory process or the subsidy process? Having defined the issue here, these are problems we hope to address in the future. (See Meyer and Tye, 1981.)

REFERENCES

Areeda, P. and Turner, D. F. (1975). Predatory Pricing and Related Practices Under Section 2 of the Sherman Act, *Harvard Law Review*, 88, 697 ff.

C. A. B. (1974). *Restrictive Practices Used by Foreign Countries to Favor Their National Carriers.*

C. A. B. (1975). *Government Ownership, Subsidy and Economic Assistance in International Commercial Aviation.*

Convention on International Civil Aviation (1944), 61 Stat. 1180, T.I.A.S. No. 1591, 7 December.

Department of Commerce (1976). *U.S. Service Industries in World Products: Current Problems and Future Policy Development.*

General Accounting Office (1978). *The Critical Role of Government in International Air Transport* (Springfield, Va.: National Technical Information Service).

Gordon, S. and DeNeufville R. (1977). Rationalization of the European Air Net, *Transportation Research*, August, 235–244.

ICAO (1977). *Regulation of Capacity in International Air Transport Services*, ICAO Circular 137-AT/43 (Montreal: ICAO).

Kahn, A. E. (1970). *The Economics of Regulation: Principles and Institutions*, Vol. I (New York: John Wiley).

Kahn, A. E. (1978). *Presentation by the Chairman of the C.A.B. Before a Symposium on the Changing Environment of International Air Commerce* (Georgetown University, Washington DC 4 May).

Meyer, J. R., Peck, M. J., Zwick, C. and Stenason, W. J. (1958). *The Economics of Competition in the Transportation Industries* (Cambridge, Ma.: Harvard University Press).

Meyer, J. R. and Tye, W. B. (1981). On the Problems of Maintaining

Competition in International Air Transportation, *Economic Regulation: Essays in Honour of James R. Nelson,* William G. Shepard (ed) (East Cansing, Michigan, Michigan State University).

Scherer, F. M. (1976). Predatory Pricing and the Sherman Act: A Comment, *Harvard Law Review.* 89, 868.

Straszheim, M. R. (1969). *The International Airline Industry* (Washington, DC: The Brookings Institution).

Subcommittee on Aviation of the Committee of Commerce, US Senate (1974). *Hearings on S. 3481, International Air Transportation,* Fair Competitive Practices Act of 1974, July 16 and 17.

Taussig, W. M. (1977). *British Airways – An Analysis of Efficiency and Cost Levels.* Prepared for US Department of Transportation, Office of the Secretary (Springfield, Va.: National Technical Information Service).

Williamson, O. E. (1977). Predatory Pricing: A Strategic and Welfare Analysis, *Yale Law Journal,* 284–340.

Discussion of Paper by Drs Meyer and Tye

Professor Sarkisian, in opening, said that this was an interesting paper, but one with which he wanted to disagree on several issues. The first question was that of the appropriate goal – the paper appeared to accept the goal of maximum profits, or something similar. But there were other goals beside profits – and finance for these goals often involved subsidy, which raised the problem of how state, subsidised and private companies could coexist in a regulated international market. Drs Meyer and Tye, while accepting the 'wider goals' in principle, stressed the problem of 'predatory pricing' caused by subsidies, which enabled companies to discourage competition in the long run by deliberate loss-making in the short run. Now he agreed that this could cause decreased efficiency and harm international and trade relations, but he did not agree with the proposed solution, i.e. deregulation aiming at achieving perfect competition. This simply encouraged the growth of monopolies. He believed there should be more regulation, not less, through bilateral treaties with controls on implementation. 'Dumping', or uneconomically low pricing, was a facet of competition, so it could not be combated by competition. The regime of 'free' competition would lead to large profits for large companies, and would especially oust smaller airlines from the North Atlantic market. This was not a theoretical issue, but a practical one. The paper also omitted consideration of the implications of demand forecasting and energy availability.

On a more general point, profit was often a necessary lever, but it should not be used as the basic criterion of efficiency. Profit maximisation often resulted in unjustified tariff increases, limited the scope of international trade, and reduced the efficiency of the economy as a whole. He agreed with Professor Mitaishvili, that the criterion of minimising transport cost (including wider effects) was a better criterion.

In the general discussion *Professor Okano* raised four questions. What were the factors affecting efficiency? What was the role of the 'protection of infant industries' argument for subsidy or regulation? What were the differences between domestic and international airlines? What was the relationship between bilateral agreements on air travel, and other issues? In general, he was sympathetic towards the case for competition made by Dr Meyer and Dr Tye, but there was a danger that it would lead to inconsistency between countries due to their different stages of development.

Professor Khachaturov said that they should also consider the interests of the consumers. These would not in general be advanced by 'competition' under a profit-maximising regime, if in fact the competition were between monopolistic companies. In this case, regulation was certainly justified. As to dumping, he thought that this could be resolved by agreement between countries.

Professor Hunter, replying to Professor Khachaturov, said he would stress that there was genuine competition among US airlines. Every three months, each carrier reported detailed statistics of passengers, and routes, which was circulated to all the rival airlines. They then made their detailed plans: there were never less than two, and usually three or four, airlines on each route – each one big enough to cover its costs – and the public's choices determined when and where to travel. The system served the public very well. A similar system of circulating a standard set of figures could be operated on an international level using standard agreed definition of costs, etc. This would protect each carrier from unfair competition, but would encourage fair competition.

Mr Kovalev said that he would like to raise a different question, ignored so far. Everybody had been treating international air transport as a single mode, unconnected with others – in contrast with all the previous discussions which had emphasised the close connections between modes. The same principle must be applied to air transport – namely, the important considerations related to *door-to-door* journey characteristics. This was very important, since the advantages of the speed of air travel were lost if the first and final stages of the journey were slow.

Dr Tye replied to the discussion, saying that they must distinguish between deregulation and competitive equilibrium. The main thesis was that certain sorts of regulation *were* necessary, in order to achieve a proper competitive equilibrium in which the price was determined by cost of the most efficient carrier, but was not subject to arbitrary influence from any one carrier.

Did economic forces exist which caused a tendency towards monopoly in air transport? It was an axiom of the deregulators – at least in the domestic market – that the opposite was true: there would be large numbers of competitors. In the international market there was at present excess capacity on too many routes, so there might be some routes which could not sustain competition. But most bilateral agreements were in fact based on keeping competitors out – he believed that the restrictive practices of IATA and Governments were anti-competitive and led to high fare levels. In this environment, he agreed that profit maximisation should not be the sole criterion. But he believed that in a competitive equilibrium profit maximisation would be appropriate.

On the other points, he accepted that they had missed some important aspects, especially fuel costs. He did not accept that bilateral agreements were the best way forward – they had resulted in a patchwork of inconsistent and inefficient negotiations.

Lastly, *Dr Tye* commented on Professor Okano's four questions. There did not appear to be important economies of scale linked to company size: route structure was very much more important to efficiency. The best operating strategy appeared to be a 'hub and spoke' arrangement, channelling traffic through a major centre. He did not think the 'infant industries' argument was valid for air passenger transport. There did appear to be possibilities for a different policy for domestic and international airlines, but experience had not been good – there was after all competition between *destinations*, especially for holidays. For a period it was cheaper to travel to Europe from the US than to stay at home! He thought that non-air issues were sometimes taken into account in bilateral agreements (for example in landing rights for Concorde) but this was not formalised.

19 Time as a Factor in Increasing the Economic Efficiency of Ports and Sea–Land Transport

WITOLD ANDRUSZKIEWICZ

I INTRODUCTION

The time taken in the transportation of cargo and passengers has become especially important in the economic evaluation of sea–land transport in the second half of this century. More attention is also being paid to the time which ships, barges, rail wagons and lorries spend in port. The increasing average value of cargo and the growth of international transport (Table 19.1) means that large amounts of capital are inactive during transport. It is therefore understandable that the average speed of cargo transport is increasing. By the early 1950s, most

TABLE 19.1   WORLD TRANSPORT BY SEA AND PORT THROUGHPUT (millions of tons)

Years	Transport by sea	Port throughput
1930	440	880
1946	360	720
1950	550	1100
1955	830	1660
1960	1100	2200
1965	1640	3280
1970	2605	5210
1975	3072	6144
1977	3475	6950

Source: United Nations Statistical Yearbook, 1948–78.

ships sailed at speeds over 10 knots, and by 1979 most of the world fleet has a speed of 20 knots or more. The speed of road, rail and air transport has also increased, and pipeline transportation is a recent development.

The technical and economic progress which made possible the marked growth of transportation speed in the whole transportation chain, has ensured quicker 'door-to-door' cargo delivery. This has resulted in many positive economic effects, with:

(1) quicker turnover of capital tied up in cargoes;
(2) lower losses resulting from cargo decay, specially of foods;
(3) the possibility of carrying two or three times more cargo during a year by the same means of transport.

Although a ship operator's annual costs are higher, he can provide more frequent services, and profits from freight have generally increased even more. This shows the economic importance of increasing transportation speeds.

Time savings have been experienced both by passengers and in freight transport. In the latter case, a monetary value can be placed on the time saved, as in the old adage, 'time is money'. These savings are most often calculated as interest on the cargo value for the time saved in transport. The effects of the reduction in voyage time can be presented in an even simpler way: by own costs or transportation production value per twenty-four hours for every day saved by ships, barges, rail wagons or lorries.

II THE REDUCTION IN TIME SPENT IN PORT BY SHIPS AND CHARTER PARTY CARGO-HANDLING STANDARDS

The sea port is a highly developed link in the transportation chain. Growth in the throughput of passengers and cargo and faster servicing of ships, barges, etc. mean that the average time spent in port by a ship can be reduced, with many positive economic results. Quick cargo throughput in port and efficiency of auxiliary services shortens the time during which the cargo stays in port and speeds up rotation of capital tied up in these cargoes. The development of the world merchant fleet is shown in Table 19.2. The increase in the number and average size of ships has led to intensive port development. Ships are now increasingly costly and thus more attention is devoted to minimising the time spent unproductively.

TABLE 2   WORLD MERCHANT FLEET DEVELOPMENT: 1890–1977

Year	Number of ships	Total capacity thousand GRT	Average ship capacity in GRT
1890	32,174	21,119	656
1900	27,840	28,957	1,040
1930	32,713	69,608	2,128
1950	31,832	85,303	2,742
1960	36,311	129,770	3,574
1970	52,444	227,490	4,338
1973	59,606	289,927	4,864
1977	67,945	393,678	5,794

Note: Fishing, auxiliary, research and other vessels are included in the data.
Source: *Morskie rocznik statystyczny* (*Maritime Statistical Yearbook*) (Wydawnictwo Morskie, Gdynia, 1960). *Rocznik Statystyczny 1978* (*Statistical Yearbook 1978*) (Glowny Urzad Statystyczny, Warsaw, 1978).

The speed with which a ship is serviced in port is of special importance. The total time spent by a ship between entering the roadstead and putting out to sea again, including all the services carried out in port, is called in Poland the 'roadstead–roadstead' time. A knowledge of this time is essential for freight calculation and programming the use of a ship. The time taken for loading or unloading cargo has been written into the charter party for many years. The roadstead–roadstead time is also a good measure of port efficiency, but unfortunately only a few ports publish this statistic.

It used to be considered that the larger the ship, the longer it could spend in port for cargo-handling services. As larger ships, especially bulk cargo carriers, were built, this traditional practice led to a marked increase in turnround time, without economic justification. For example, the throughput standard for grain in the port of Gdynia in Poland was 1000 tons per day for the largest ships, which were about 5000 to 10,000 tons. However, when ships of 45,000 tons were chartered, the old throughput standard was written into the charter party, which in practice meant a stay of nearly two months. Technical rationalisation reduced turnround time to about ten days, but although rebates were made, they did not represent the total overpayment, as shipowners had calculated costs on the basis of the throughput standard. This situation stimulated the introduction of higher throughput standards and thus lower freight charges for grain carried on large ships.

Selection of appropriate cargo-handling equipment depending on the size of ships to be serviced at a quay should be based on a typical ship's 'ton-metre'. This defines deadweight tonnage per metre of ship length, and is many times larger for big ships than for small ones. This means that cargo-handling equipment should be efficient enough to minimise turnround time.

By 1978 the time spent in port had been reduced to one or two days for most ships. This was due to liquid cargoes, dry bulk cargoes and containerisation.

III INFLUENCE OF CARGO AND PORT EQUIPMENT ON TURNROUND TIME

Oil tankers are now the world's largest, and most quickly serviced, ships (Table 19.3), which carry about half the total cargo transported by sea. Generally tankers spend no more than one or two days in port, and actual cargo handling normally takes only ten hours. The tanker terminal at North Harbour, Gdansk, which was opened in 1975, takes ships of around 150,000 tons. The roadstead—roadstead time for a large tanker is one to two days. The new deep-water harbour at Antifer, in France, offers very quick service for the largest tankers. For example, the French *Batillus* (554,000 DWT) stays in port no longer than small ships in other ports.

Modern berths for large ships carrying coal, grain, ore and other bulk cargoes can service a ship within one or two days. The guaranteed throughput of a coal base built at Gdansk in 1974 for ships of 100,000 DWT or more is 50,000 tons\124 hours/ship. Cargo-handling equipment includes two conveyor belts with a throughput of 2000 tons/hour each. An ore base is under construction at the same harbour for ships of a similar capacity, and servicing time will be two or three days at first and two days after further development. The growth in shipments of edible liquid cargo (palm oil, wine) and chemical cargoes has also led to the provision of new pumps and pipelines in various ports. However, at

TABLE 3   WORLD SEAGOING MERCHANT FLEET:
STATE AT 1 JULY 1978
(in thousands GRT)

Specifcation	1960	1970	1975	1977
Total	129,770	227,490	342,162	393,678
Of which tankers	41,465	86,140	150,057	174,124

Source: *Rocznik Statystyczny 1978 Glowny Urzad Statystyczny, 1978.*

traditional berths handling operations are slower, so the turnround time is longer. General cargo carriers normally spend the longest time in port. However, the servicing of ships carrying containers or pallets, and 'roll-on-roll-off' ships is quite quick, normally no more than one or two days.

IV UNDERINVESTMENT IN PORTS LENGTHENS TURNROUND TIME

Research at the Maritime Institute in Gdansk has shown that where berths are adequately equipped, an increase in the time spent in port is not necessary, despite the increasing size of ships. The author's research indicates large differences in turnround time for different types of ship. In 1978, time spent in port as a percentage of the total time the ships were used was:

tankers	7–11 %
bulk cargo carriers	22–31 %
traditional general cargo ships	45–62 %
modern general cargo ships	19–36 %.

Over the last thirty years, turnround time has been much higher in Third World ports in Africa, Asia and South America. These times are used by shipowners and shipping conferences to justify incommensurably high rates for freight to and from Third World ports. The throughput will have to be increased before freight charges for these ports can be reduced to the level set for similar distances but between efficient ports.

If waiting time before a ship is loaded or unloaded forms a significant proportion of the turnround time this is an indication of underinvestment in the port. Furthermore, if the average time spent by a ship is twice as long as in an efficient port, the number of ships in the port is doubled, and this leads to congestion.

V REDUCTION IN THE TURNROUND TIME OF BARGES, RAIL WAGONS AND LORRIES

Over the last thirty years there has been a marked reduction in the turnround time for rail wagons at ports. For example, coal wagons stayed at Polish sea ports for an average of 30 hours/wagon in 1960. This time has been reduced to 4 hours per wagon in the modern North Harbour in Gdansk, with a saving of one wagon-day for each wagon. Additional journeys can be made, thanks to the time savings, and 20 per cent more cargo can be transported. There has also been a reduction of 50 per cent in the turnround time for lorries at Polish sea ports between 1960 and 1978.

Two distinct groups of barges can be identified. The first group consists of barges belonging to port businesses and used as floating warehouses and as interport transport. In the second group are barges belonging to shipowners specialising in long-distance transport, including those carried on barge carriers. Time savings amounting to around two-thirds have been experienced for long-distance transport barges since 1950.

VI SUMMARY AND CONCLUSIONS

In 1977 the total amount of cargo handled by ports was over six times larger than in 1950. During the same period the average ship size increased from 2742 GRT to 5794 GRT. Many large ships have been built, and the largest tankers are already over half-a-million DWT. This forced further development of existing ports and also construction of new ports. In many ports, which were not ready with new cargo-handling and storing potential, the quality of ship and cargo servicing decreased. This was observed mainly in the form of longer turnround times, which led to congestion and longer waiting times in the roadstead.

Large ships should not have to stay in port longer than smaller ones. Regardless of size, ships could be serviced in 1–2 days. About half of the total world cargo is serviced at this speed. It is recommended that the total turnround time for ships should be measured in terms of 'roadstead–roadstead' times, and that these times should be compared. The shortest turnround times are generally for tankers, ferries, 'roll-on-roll-off' ships and container ships. A reduction in turnround times leads to a reduction in freight charges, and high throughput standards should be written into the charter party.

REFERENCE

Andruszkiewicz, W. (1966). *Problemy ekonomiczne zwiekszania szybkosci obslugi statku w porcie* (Instytut Morski, Gdansk).
Ashton, H. (1947). Time Element in Transportation, *American Economic Review*, 37.
Funck, R. (1968). Die okonomischen Aspekte des Zeitproblems im Verkehr, *Zeitschrift für Verkehrswissenschaft*, Nr. 3.

Metodika razczotow i ekonomiczeskije pokazateli dla razpredelenija perewozok miezdu widami transporta, Moscow.

Robert, J. (1973). *Elements d'une politique des transports maritimes* (Paris: Editions Eyrolles).

Tarski, I. (1973). Czynnik czasu w procesie transportowym, Wyd. Komunik. i Laeznosci (Warsaw).

20 Port Congestion or Port Dysfunction?

S. WICKHAM AND N. TIEN PHUC

I INTRODUCTION

The expansion of world trade and rate of growth of industrialised countries from 1945 has been reduced in the last few years, first with the upsurge in oil prices in 1974 and then with the events of the so-called oil crisis. Shipping appeared to be severely hit, with fleets laid up, even if only temporarily. However, traffic congestion in ports did not disappear. Tremendous waiting times and stockpiling occurred in many new ports in developing countries, and at the same time, delays, excess costs and dysfunctions persisted in many old ports in industrialised countries with a long maritime tradition, such as Italy, France and Great Britain.

Is traffic congestion the incurable counterpart of world economic progress? Or are our ports far too small and calling for heavy additional investments, as generally claimed by port managers? Or are ports simply out-dated, an inheritance from the days of sail, to be widely reconsidered for the next generation?

II IS THERE A WORLD CRISIS IN MARITIME TRANSPORT?

In examining the situation of the different flags, it can be seen that the crisis which seems to condemn to death certain flags enables others to have a tremendous development. Taking two maritime nations, Norway and Sweden, as an example, the Norwegian flag lost 700,000 DWT in 1977 and more than 8 million DWT in 1978, beside the fact that roughly 25 per cent of the ships flying the Norwegian flag are laid up – as against a world average of 9 per cent. The Swedish flag also dropped during the last two years from 14 million to 7 million DWT; among OECD member countries which recorded significant reductions, Japan and UK are also the most prominent.

France, as an average maritime nation, is in the same situation: for the last three years only 20 new ships amounting to 2000,000 DWT entered under the French flag while 191 vessels disappeared either by sale to other flags or released for scrap, amounting to 3,250,000 DWT.

During the same period several main facts should be noted:

(1) The British flag of Hong Kong grew from 27 million to 37 million DWT.

(2) The three well-known flags of convenience, Liberia, Panama and Singapore, have continued to expand. The growth of the Liberian flag is not less than 10 per cent per year with the addition of large tankers, bulk carriers and gas carriers, despite the world crisis. Panama and Singapore both grew very much faster: Panama recorded in 1977 in both absolute and relative terms its greatest increase in a single year; over half of Singapore's fleet is new, and over 80 per cent of its tanker tonnage is less than five years old.

(3) The East European fleets have grown significantly during this period. In terms of gross tonnage, the USSR fleet, which represents 74 per cent of the whole East European fleet, showed an average increase of 5 per cent per annum while the other Eastern flags, although of course starting from a smaller base line, have average growth rates of 12 per cent for Poland and 21 per cent for Romania.

Compared to these developments in the Hong Kong and convenience flags, it could be stated that the growth is rather limited; in fact the key points are that the East European fleet has concentrated on the replacement of old, slow vessels by fast versatile carriers, unit-load vessels, roll-on-roll-off, barge carriers and container ships. This leads to far higher productivity than was previously attained.

(4) The fleets of the developing countries have continued to figure prominently in the development of the world fleet. Brazil, even with a drastic cut in government expenditure last year, will have a fleet of 10 million DWT by the early 1980s, of which 4.6 million are under construction in Brazilian shipyards.[1]

---

[1] The most significant comment on these newcomers came not from a layman but from a specialist, Dr H. Shinto, President of the Shipbuilder's Association of Japan: 'I consider that it is historical inevitability that Brazil and other rising shipbuilding countries of the world will in due course come to lead the world shipbuilding industries. . . . '

Indian has continued to reinforce its general cargo fleet which has increased over the last two years by 29 per cent. The rapid growth of the Chinese fleet is maintained with a large utilisation of the second-hand market. Last but not least is the growth of fleets of the Middle East and North Africa. In 1977, the Arab and Iranian tanker fleet amounted to 12.5 million DWT compared to only 1.5 million by mid-1974. The oil crisis and the reopening of the Suez Canal led to a steady and cautious expansion in their tanker fleet but, as far as general cargo and gas carriers are concerned, the Gulf States and Algeria have been expanding their fleet quite extensively.

If the development of the world fleet as a whole over the last twelve years is considered, it can be stated that there is no world crisis in maritime transport but only a change in the regional pattern, associated with the fact that the oil crisis and the reopening of the Suez Canal have induced a slowing down of the growth of the tanker fleet.

TABLE 20.1   DEVELOPMENT OF THE WORLD FLEET 1966–77

Types of fleet	In 10^6 GRT 1966	In 10^6 GRT 1977	Average growth 1977–66
Total world fleet[a]	171.1	393.7	7.87
Total active world fleet[b]	161.9	372.3	7.86
Ratio Active/Total	0.946	0.945	–
Total world non-tanker fleet[a]	110.9	219.6	6.41
Active non-tanker fleet[b]	102.4	214.5	6.95
Ratio Active/Total	0.923	0.976	–
Total world tanker fleet[a]	60.2	174.1	10.14
Active tanker fleet[b]	59.5	157.8	9.27
Ratio Active/Total	0.988	0.960	–

[a] The world fleet includes United States and Canadian Great Lakes fleets and the United States Reserve fleet.
[b] The active fleets exclude the laid-up tonnage and the United States Reserve fleet.
Source: Lloyd's Register of Shipping.

Table 20.1 indicates the growth of the world fleet between 1966 and 1977, and the following points should be noted:

(1) The total world fleet and the total active world fleet have increased

during this period 1966–77 despite the oil crisis, by roughly 7.8 per cent.

It should be noted that the ratio active/total remained constant during this period, which means that the percentage of US Reserve fleet and laid-up tonnage has not changed significantly. Therefore, on the whole one cannot state that there is a world crisis in the maritime world.

(2) The non-tanker fleet, mainly general cargo and dry and liquid bulk, has shown a reasonable average annual increase of 6.4 per cent from 1966 to 1977; moreover the ratio active/total has improved during recent years.

(3) The tanker fleet has shown a fairly high increase, around 10 per cent per year during the whole period.

This was mainly due, before the reopening of Suez Canal, to intensive development of VLCC (very large crude carriers up to 1 million DWT) using the Cape route, a development which was dictated by the decrease in cost of transport versus increase of capacity.

The high increase in the tanker fleet was also due to a boom in oil-producing countries which ordered new vessels most probably without cognisance. Therefore the ratio active/total dropped from 0.988 in 1966 to 0.906 in 1977, resulting from the lay up of half the Libyan and a third of the Saudi tanker fleet, as well as two of the eight Arab Maritime Petroleum Transport Company's vessels.

(4) In fact with the exception of the tanker fleet, there is no crisis for the time being, in maritime transport, but there is a change in regional pattern. The traditional maritime nations, mainly western countries and Japan, have lost their supremacy and are being replaced by convenience flags or newcomers from developing countries.

This major event is explained only by the differences in operation costs. The difference between the daily operating cost of a ship manned by Chinese or Pakistani or Indian seamen and that of an identical ship manned by Norwegian or Swedish seamen is rather heavily in favour of developing countries, with a ratio of roughly 1 to 3.

Western countries, despite the switch to more automation, more capital-intensive types of ship and even the reduction of profits, cannot compete. There is a direct, disagreeable link between the operation costs of a flag and its decline or its development.

III WHAT IS BEHIND PORT CONGESTION?

It is not realistic to state that the maritime economy has suffered in recent years the most fundamental crisis ever to strike this sector. But it is true to confirm that one of the major problems of maritime transport which has existed for some years and will certainly prevail for some time more is endemic port congestion in the majority of the developing countries; and considering that those countries are raw material producers for all developed countries, port congestion will also reflect on the economy of developed countries. Just three years ago, in all Middle East countries, especially oil-producing countries, but to a lesser extent in all developing countries, port congestion was tremendous.

Taking as examples in 1976–77 Dammam Port, Jeddah Port in Saudi Arabia and Lagos in Nigeria: on average not less than 100 vessels were waiting in each port with an average waiting time of 50 days per vessel for Dammam, 100 days per vessel for Jeddah and 150 days for Lagos. So in the case of Dammam, assuming that the daily cost of a vessel was roughly 5000 US dollars per vessel/day, due to demurrage and congestion overcharges applied by the shipping conferences and paid by the importers, the loss for the country was:

$100 \times 5000 = 500,000$ US dollars/day.

Apart from the cost of congestion, it also induced a high rate of inflation (not less than 25 per cent per year in Saudi Arabia during the period 1976–77) and has negative effects on the whole economy, such as delay in project implementation.

1 Port congestion comes from inadequacy of port infrastructure and the demand for shipping services

For ages, ports have been built for general cargo, mainly for manufactured products. Bulk traffic was transported in bags and was handled therefore as general cargo; the concept of the bulk carrier is a recent one and derived from the oil carrier. But with progressive economic development, general cargo traffic has become less important.

Within world seaborne trade, general cargo traffic accounted for 38 per cent of tonnage in 1965 but nowadays for something around 30 per cent; in ton-miles, the decrease is more significant: from 26 per cent in 1965 to 18 per cent in 1977 (cf. Appendix 1). During the same period 1965–77 world seaborne trade for solid and liquid bulk increased considerably:

(1) roughly $1000\,0.10^6$ tons in 1965 against $2300\,0.10^6$ tons in 1977: more than twofold;
(2) and roughly $4,300\,0.10^9$ ton-miles in 1965 against $14,600\,0.10^9$ ton-miles in 1977: more than threefold.

Given this fundamental change in maritime traffic, the main existing international ports are based upon a traditional concept coming from the beginning of this century:

'Gares maritimes' was the phrase used previously in France where sea transport was connected with the new prestigious railways, incurring large port investments; modern ports built or enlarged on specific sites, with heavy breakwaters, multitraffic accommodation, multimodal interconnections, multiple port operators and agents, marshalling areas or dock facilities, and the dignified financial and managerial autonomy of a Port Authority. With the fast growth of world trade which started in the 1950s, the larger harbours were the better they were. Each state tried to refrain from dispersing its harbours, and to concentrate its maritime investments in its larger ports or largest diversified port complex.

Moreover, this inheritance from the past has been transferred to developing countries as a perfect model. Developing countries have been induced by international experts to give priority to a main port complex, near the capital, as an attraction to heavy industries and with exclusive access to the world international freight transportation network. This historical view of ports as a transit meeting place, a 'Gare', now raises acute difficulties in newly industrialised countries, with limited managerial capacities to run such heavy complexes, and limited capacity to finance them at high interest rates.

The situation can be summarised as follows: ports were built mainly for general cargo traffic; handling equipment has been designed to cope with general cargo. With the decrease in general cargo and the increase in bulk traffic the only solution which was found to avoid congestion was to enlarge the port by adding to general cargo berths, berths equipped for liquid or solid bulk traffic. Ports then became large complexes with heavy financial investments, high bureaucratic costs, sensitive social problems and inertia in spite of sophisticated computerised gadgetry.

2 The inadequacy of ports could become more acute in the future due to the volatile character of maritime traffic

It should be remembered that in ton-miles, bulk traffic represents some 82 per cent of total traffic. The maritime routes for bulk traffic are not stable, as is shown by examining shipping distances (cf. Appendix 2) which have increased for iron ore, coal, bauxite/alumina and crude oil, and decreased for phosphate rock and grain, over a quite short period from 1965 to 1977. Bulk traffic is mainly using the tramp business which is in a random traffic. Depending strictly on demand and supply of liquid and solid bulks, the tramping business is dominated by short-term traffic rerouting.

So, for instance, the world seaborne trade in iron ore underwent notable changes in the years 1975–76: a drop in the transport requirements generated by the US trade as a result of lower shipments from South America, a higher trade from Canada to the US and Europe, as well as increased shipments from South America to Europe and Japan.

Coal tonnage movements are also changing: a large part of EEC imports were moved overland and besides traditional importing areas such as Japan, which absorbs some 50 per cent of the overall seaborne trade, seaborne imports were reported from developing countries such as India, Pakistan, North Korea, Brazil and Argentina.

Grain traffic has also shown constant changes in route patterns; an unfavourable harvest in one country leads to a new configuration in seaborne trade: the USSR in 1977 became the world's largest grain purchaser with the result that certain countries normally taking USSR cereals had to rely more heavily on imports from the US, Canada and Australia; the same year, rice was also shipped to Indonesia from Japan, Korea and the Philippines, three countries which normally do not export rice.

The volatile character of maritime traffic is also reinforced by hard competition between shipowners utilising all the flexibility offered by maritime transportation technology. Reverting to bulk traffic again, the OBO (ore, bulk and oil) vessels introduced on the market in the late 1960s allow either ore, bulk or oil to be carried and therefore bulk traffic could escape the non-economic one-way traffic. Thus large Brazilian OBO vessels are using the Mindanao port to stockpile iron ore for trans-shipment to smaller Asian ports which cannot receive large ore carriers. For their return journey it is planned that these vessels will transport oil to Brazil.

Thus port congestion is due to two main factors: they have not been constructed to handle bulk traffic, which is now the most important seaborne trade, and they are built as large complexes facing great fluctuations in traffic. The future of ports has to be considered with these factors in mind, but the trend in the size of ships should also be considered.

Present socio-technological factors (including safety and ecological problems raised by large oil carriers) lead one to expect that during the last quarter of this century the increase in the size of ships will slow down if not stop altogether; and the high price of energy will prevent the search for additional shipping capacity through higher speeds. A slower but steady increase of the world merchant fleet is to be expected: an increase of 50 per cent of the number of merchant ships circulating throughout the world from 1977 to 2000 might appear likely. This expected increase in maritime circulation, coupled with the previous remarks, induces us to question the future ability of our major international ports.

IV RELIEF FROM PORT CONGESTION

The future of ports could be improved on one hand by proved technologies of fast building systems, but in the long run we are convinced that the port as a 'system' has to be reconceptualised. To solve the port congestion problem, several solutions have been implemented.

(1) The most economical way is to improve at least the administrative procedure in ports, mainly customs clearance and dispatching of goods from the berth to the final destination; some countries have been obliged to tax importers who utilise the port as a warehouse and goods are put up to public auction after a certain time in port.

(2) To improve the throughput of the port, better handling equipment is implemented and priorities for loading are given to door-to-door services such as 'roll-on-roll-off' vessels.

(3) Heavy investments have been made in new berths, warehouses, etc. This solution, so called port extension, is a traditional one, and the most evident. This has been accompanied, when necessary, by the construction of breakwaters. This conventional solution is obviously a good one if the country is not facing two main parameters of choice of investment: availability of financial resources or availability of time; this last parameter is in fact the main one.

Usually it needs roughly one to two years to build concrete berths and associated infrastructure, and once finished it can happen that the congestion disappears either by the rerouting of maritime traffic or by a reduction in imports.

(4) When the harbour congestion is such that it cannot wait ten to twelve months for any sort of additional berth to be installed, an immediate way of increasing the discharge capacity is the use of mobile jack-up platforms used as crane barges. The mobile jack-up platform would be installed at a suitable place where all kinds of cargo would be handled, discharged and taken direct to an inland dry port. The location of the barge would be chosen away from the present port installation, and it would depend basically on the availability of wide open spaces, on flat, solid soil, relatively close to a main road. Cargo is unloaded on to the shore, directly on to trucks, or else on to barges.

The solution of the prefabricated pier is based on the idea of prefabricating nearly 100 per cent of the final pier and installing it in a very short time on site using an air-operated jacking system.[2] This type of pier can be generally commissioned within one year, which means the saving of roughly a year compared with any other conventionally designed and built pier. Self-installing, it does not require the costly help of any floating or jack-up derrick barge, and therefore the installation costs and the hazards are kept to a minimum. It can be installed in protected or totally open waters. When the harbour development scheme incorporates the construction of a breakwater, the pier can be installed simultaneously, thus saving on the overall delivery time.

Extending the pier is very easy to accomplish by the addition of one or several new modules. Quickly built, quickly moved, the installation procedure is fully reversible, making the removal of the pier as easy as its installation. This is of particular importance when the piers are needed quickly at a first location and have to be moved to a final location according to the development of the complete harbour scheme including land access, storage and handling facilities. By reducing the delivery by half, it procures a great saving in the operational cost of the harbour and speeds up investment return.[3]

This technique is largely utilised for oil terminals. The two main reasons are:

[2] Originally developed for the US Army in 1951 in Thule, Greenland, the Delong Pier System was quickly adapted to civil and commercial needs where the development of a harbour was required in a very short period of time. The major application is for oil terminals.

[3] A marine oil terminal for tankers up to 250,000 DWT was built using this process at Novorossiysk. The contract was signed on 23 July 1977 and the first tanker serviced on 26 October 1978.

(1) The technical priority is the closest connection between oil carriers and the inland oil transportation system. The gains from the proximity of other berths for general cargo are zero, if not negative.
(2) The integrated and automated trans-shipment process of oil makes the connection between maritime and inland transportation a technical linkage (as between two workshops inside a plant).

While long-distance seaborne transportation involves more and more technical differentiation between ships, handling equipment and inland transportation means, the terminal oil model may have some relevance for other integrated world transportation chains: coal, wine or fruit, containers and so on.

If one conceptualises the transportation of a product as a 'system', meaning by this concept that the targets are on one hand the maximum steady flow of traffic and on the other hand the maximum flexibility due to the volatile character of maritime traffic, then the port concept for one given product should be purpose-built berths with proper handling equipment. There is no need to integrate this concept or these berths within a large port complex.

Small, specialised and widespread terminals with low-cost investments, even removable terminals, will cope more efficiently with maritime traffic than large port complexes, with their administrative inertia and their possible social conflicts.

V CONCLUSION

International integrated cargo transport chains will increasingly imply differentiated ships and complementary inland transport equipment. The connection between maritime and inland transportation networks at ports will have to be reconsidered and partially redistributed for the common benefit of developing and industrialised countries on the basis of maritime networks of specialised terminals.

Port Authorities, as public intermediaries in the transport chain, have proved highly rigid during the recent years: small organisations and light institutional structures of terminals should help international flexibility in the future. A maritime economic policy will then emerge. Let us remember that the maritime world is one key to international economic relationships: 'Whoever commands the trade of the world, commands the riches of the world, and whoever is master of that, commands the world itself' (Evelyn, *Navigation and Commerce* 1674).

Appendix 1

WORLD SEABORNE TRADE
(million tons)

Year	Total trade	Liquid and solid bulk in %	General cargo in %
1965	1,638	62	37
1973	3,120	70	30
1977	3,420	68	32

WORLD SEABORNE TRADE
(thousand million ton miles)

Year	Total trade	Liquid and solid bulk in %	General cargo in %
1965	5,849	74	26
1973	15,403	83	17
1977	17,785	82	18

Liquid and solid bulk includes crude oil, oil products, iron ore, coal, grain (wheat, maize, barley, oats, rye, sorghum, soya beans, etc . . .).
Source: Fearnley and Eger's Chartering Co. Ltd.

Appendix 2

Development of Liquid and Solid Bulk Cargo

Liquid and solid bulk	Years			1965 = 100
	1967	1973	1977	
Iron ore				
−tonnage	108	196	186	
−shipping distance	114	135	143	
Coal				
−tonnage	114	176	212	
−shipping distance	110	123	128	

Development of Liquid and Solid Bulk Cargo

Liquid and solid bulk	Years			1965 = 100
	1967	1973	1977	
Grain				
–tonnage	101	169	174	
–shipping distance	102	100	97	
Phosphate rock				
–tonnage	112	172	164	
–shipping distance	108	109	99 (estimate)	
Bauxite/alumina				
–tonnage	115	181	210	
–shipping distance	113	160	172	
Crude oil				
–tonnage	118	225	242	
–shipping distance	123	146	156	

Source: OECD, *Maritime Transport 1977*

Appendix 3

IMPORTANCE OF MARITIME TRANSPORT FOR FRANCE
(average percentages 1974–7)

Types of transportation	Imports	Exports
Maritime transport	75·3[a]	22·7[b]
Road transport	8·8	20·7
River transport	6·8	21·5
Railroad transport	8·9	35·1
Air transport	0·2	0·1

[a] Of 75.3 per cent, roughly 63 per cent represents bulk traffic, crude, iron, ore, etc.
[b] Of 22.6 per cent, roughly 6 per cent represents bulk traffic, crude, iron, ore, etc.
Source: Ministry of Finances and Economic Affairs.

21 Inland Waterways and Long-distance Freight Traffic[1]

D. M. HAYTER[2] AND C. H. SHARP[3]

I INTRODUCTION

It may seem surprising that a paper written in Britain and intended for an international conference should deal with inland waterways. This form of transport has been very much neglected in the UK and our canal system still consists mainly of waterways built in the late eighteenth and early nineteenth centuries. However, recent research carried out at Leicester University (Garratt *et al.*, 1979) has suggested that there would be some advantages in using rivers and waterways to allow sea-going vessels carrying long-distance traffic to provide a direct service to inland areas. The Leicester research was based on the River Trent but some of the conclusions may be of more general application.

II BACKGROUND

Despite their initial importance in supporting and promoting industrial development and internal trading during the eighteenth and nineteenth

[1] This paper is based on work carried out at the Public Sector Economics Research Centre, University of Leicester during 1977–78 and funded by the Nuffield Foundation. The authors are indebted to all who participated in the various phases of the project and particularly M. G. Garratt who was responsible for much of the development and preparation of the published final report. The authors, however, bear total responsibility for this paper.
[2] Public Sector Economics Research Centre, University of Leicester.
[3] Department of Economics, University of Leicester.

centuries, British inland waterways now play a relatively insignificant role in domestic freight transport and, in terms of tonnes lifted, have accounted for less than 1 per cent of total domestic freight lifted for many years. In addition, waterway traffic volumes (tonnes lifted) have declined on average by 4.3 per cent over the period 1951–77 (see Table 21.1).

TABLE 21.1   FREIGHT TRAFFIC BY TRANSPORT MODE, ALL COMMODITIES, TONNES LIFTED

	Road	*Rail*	*Coastal shipping*	*Waterways[a]*	*Pipe-line*
(a) *All models*					
1967 { million tonnes	1651	204	52	7	26
%	85.1	10.5	2.7	0.4	1.3
1972 { million tonnes	1629	178	47	5	45
%	85.5	9.4	2.4	0.3	2.4
1977 { million tonnes	1422	170	49	4	75
%	82.7	9.9	2.8	0.2	4.3

(b) *British Waterways[a]*

Year	1951	1955	1960	1965	1960	1975	1976	1977
million tonnes	11 723	10 645	9 775	8.537	6.197	4.1	4.357	3.74

[a] These figures cover waterways under the control of the British Waterways Board only, which represents some 35.50 per cent of all commercially used waterways depending on the definition of 'inland waterway' used.

During the last decade though, there has been an upsurge of interest in inland waterways (led by their increasing use for recreational purposes and a concern over the environmental impact of freight movement by road) and many suggestions have been made for a diversion of freight traffic (back) to waterways.

However, it is the authors' contention that under existing and forseeable economic circumstances, waterway improvement to promote the internal carriage of freight in Britain will not provide any significant economic benefit. Instead, given likely budget constraints, investment should be concentrated on those waterways which can be readily improved to promote the long-distance movements of sea-going vessels between inland manufacturing and consuming areas in Britain and the European mainland. The objective of this paper is therefore to justify these contentions with the main findings of work recently undertaken to assess the potential for improvement to the River Trent which is presently used as a commercial (inland) waterway over its 131 km length between Nottingham in the East Midlands and the Humber estuary, linking to the East Coast of Britain.

III THE RIVER TRENT

The location of the River Trent is shown in geographical perspective on Figure 21.1 while Figure 21.2 specifies and locates in detail the main track and associated features. Sea-going vessels of up to 2000 DWT

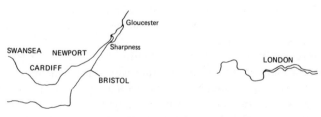

Figure 21.1 The River Trent in geographical perspective

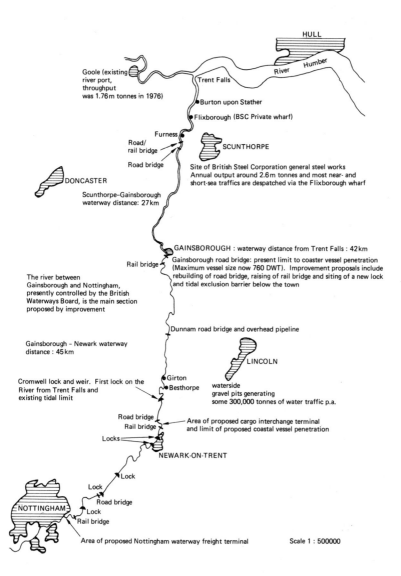

Figure 21.2   Representation of the River Trent

regularly navigate the first 15 km from the Humber Estuary to wharves in the Scunthorpe/Keadby area. A road bridge and shallower water then restrict vessel access, but Gainsborough, a further 27 km on, is served by vessels up to 700 DWT. Here, another road bridge forms the navigable limit to all but two purpose-designed vessels built to serve a nearby grain milling complex with imported cereals. Otherwise, from the road bridge to Nottingham (94 km) the river is controlled by the British Waterways Board and freight movement is by waterway barge. Barge capacity limits vary from 190 tonnes at Nottingham to 200 tonnes at Newark and 500–600 tonnes at Gainsborough.

The decline in traffic levels on the Nottingham-Gainsborough (barge only) section is shown in Table 21.2. Aggregates moving between waterside pits and Humberside landing points represent some 87 per cent of total traffics, the remainder consisting of petroleum products (5 per cent) delivered to Newark and cereals (6 per cent) delivered to Gainsborough. These traffics are representative of previous traffic types (i.e. wet and dry bulks) and, in line with experience elsewhere, manufactures (i.e. break bulks) form a very low proportion of movements (1 per cent in 1978).

TABLE 21.2   RIVER TRENT (NOTTINGHAM—GAINSBOROUGH) TRAFFIC

(a) Tonnes Lifted

Year	1968	1970	1972	1974	1976	1977	1978
tonnes ('000)	741	723	401	434	381	381	359

(b) Commodities Moved

Commodities:		Cereals oil seeds nuts	Petroleum products	Sand and gravel	Other minerals	Other (incl. manu- factures)	Total
Tonnes:	1976	42	29	313	5	–	391
('000)	1977	24	20	303	–	4	381
	1976	23	18	314	–	4	359

In contrast, traffic on the lower Trent (Gainsborough–Trent Falls) has remained steady at around 1.5 to 2.0 million tonnes p.a. over recent years. Most movements are imports of bulk and semi-bulk products landed over private and public wharves. The largest single traffic is in steel product import and exports generated by a steel works at Scunthorpe and steels from the Sheffield/Rotherham area. Some 96 per cent of traffic flows are within near and short sea trade areas.[4]

However, it is the barge only (Nottingham–Gainsborough) section of the river which is under consideration for improvement and before turning to the assessment of potential process the factors which have contributed to the traffic decline are outlined. These can be presented in three main categories as follows. First, a significant proportion of traffic up to the mid-1960s had been generated by the overside loading/unloading of deep-sea vessels calling at the main Humber port (Hull). This was eliminated as UK trading patterns altered in favour of near and short-sea areas while the remaining UK deep-sea services, influenced by vessel and cargo-handling technologies, switched from multiport to mainly single port of call itineraries, serving the entire UK market from the one or a few ports rather than only the regional port hinterland as before.

Second, excluding activities around the lower reaches of the Trent, the river does not provide water access to any major existing industrial areas. New light industrial works, manufacturing/processing plant and power stations in the river basin area have been located away from waterway sites, thus increasing dependence on road and rail modes to avoid freight trans-shipment. Third, and most important, is the changed competitive relationship between water and alternative freight transport modes. Over time, the cost structures according to road, rail and pipeline transport have been influenced by investment in new and/or upgraded track and associated infrastructure provision, while technological and operational changes (including labour/capital ratio cost and utilisation changes) have significantly altered overall capacity utilisation capabilities. Over the same time, the waterway network has remained fixed and navigation has been constrained by a lack of dimensional standardisation on the interconnected waterway routes and has been compounded by an inability to navigate around the clock and often by severe tidal fluctuations. Consequently, the physical or economic use of the same craft over various routes has been restricted (and the available length of haul shortened). The necessity to build or purchase craft for a specific waterway limits optimal vessel size and/or potential utilisation, resulting in 'inflexible' freight costs and the loss of traffic flows to alternative modes where the annual volume amounts to less than the annual capacity of a single barge.

It is reasonable to note that the main competitor to waterways for

---

[4] Near-sea areas are: W. Germany, Netherlands, Belgium, Luxembourg, France, Irish Republic. Short-sea areas cover Scandinavian and Baltic, Iberian and Mediterranean countries.

high volume bulk flows, the railways, has for some time enjoyed an indirect subsidy for freight. This is through a government subsidy to support passenger services but which forms a contribution towards freight track costs. In addition, some large rail customers are allowed a 50 per cent rebate on terminal and rolling stock capital equipment investment with the result that a number of large flows (particularly of petroleum products) have been attracted away from water and potential flows 'lost'.

IV RIVER TRENT DEVELOPMENT POTENTIAL

The possibility of improving the barge-only section of the upper Trent to a consistent 'coaster' (i.e. 1000–1800 DWT sea-going vessels) standard was not the only possibility considered and in the evaluation process the familiar elements of transport investment appraisal were covered, including eight improvement standards for barge and/or coaster vessels relating to a range of technical options regarding vessel and handling systems.

Initially though, a coaster improvement standard was suggested by a number of observations. These were: the use of the lower Trent for traffics delivered by ship to/from Scandinavia and Europe (and in the case of the latter, direct movement inland via the Rhine to the Ruhr district ports); the importance of European inland waterway ports in handling internationally traded goods; the continuing growth of UK– European trade and the consequent importance of UK east coast transport facilities in dealing with trade growth. Also earlier UK inland waterway users dependent on a few staple traffics were attracted to alternative modes, which implied that any improvement standard should attempt to satisfy the movement demands of a broad range of commodities with diverse origins/destinations, handling and cost requirements. A barge standard development did not appear capable of achieving this flexibility.

The work carried out on analysis of modal cost structures, potential freight demand and cost modelling to identify potential resource savings over and above existing transport methods (and thence calculation of Net Present Values for the investment options and rate of return), supports this thinking. Some of these findings are now presented.

1. Freight mode characteristics and costs

The conventional waterway barge is capable of carrying a relatively large volume of goods in one unit with little labour and low fuel costs.

Their use is best suited to commodities which can be cheaply and rapidly handled and require movement over long distances in large volumes. This is primarily a function of restricted speeds allowable on waterways which encourages the use of large vessels but causes longer periods to be spent during cargo handling. Consequently, average throughputs over time need to be large to provide economic employment of a barge. Where the length of haul is constrained, the cargo cannot be handled rapidly (in excess of 100 tonnes/hour) or when the annual volume of traffic is low or irregular the barge faces severe competition from road and, in some circumstances, rail transport, unless both origin and destination are waterwide. Even with improvement of the river the length of haul cannot be increased or access provided to new industrial areas. Trans-shipment costs cannot be absorbed on short-distance journeys for most commodities (excepting, say, bulk liquids, powders, cereals, which can be rapidly pumped or sucked) and it would be illogical and expensive to have a situation where vessel size is increased by capacity improvement but one to three days are involved at each trip end during cargo handling.

The push-tow tug and dumb barge systems, increasingly used on waterway and river systems in Europe and America, offer the advantage of grouping individual traffics which might be of insufficient volume to employ a conventional barge for movement at a reduced unit cost. Their drawback though is that relatively high capital and operating costs require intensive usage rates and in operation they appear only to approach the costs of a conventional barge over long hauls, at high volumes and where large flotilla flows are feasible.

Consequently, while the push-tow system might more readily compete with rail for some traffics (sharing the rail advantage of not having to tie up the tractive/pusher unit during loading and unloading operations) and possibly even might be able to penetrate road transport markets which rail cannot (i.e. part-loading work using dumb barges as storage), the restricted length of haul and overall traffic market available to either conventional barge or push-tow system appeared inadequate to justify development to these standards.

The alternative then remains with increasing both length of haul and potential traffics by allowing sea-going vessels to penetrate inland. Such vessels, in serving international traffics, would use an inland waterway for the purpose of maximising the distance travelled by water and, in reaching as close as possible to the final destination/initial origin of cargoes, minimising the distance required to be travelled by other modes while at the same time reducing overall trans-shipment costs. There is a penalty involved though, in that the costs per tonne nautical mile are reduced by optimising vessel size according to length of haul and cargo-handling rate. If either increases (assuming a large enough traffic market is available) then ships' size will increase, whereas inland navigation (according to track capacity) constrains vessel size.

Fortunately, two factors work in favour of the Trent. The first is that for most near- and some short-sea trades optimum vessel size would appear to lie between 700 and 2000 DWT, assuming cargo-handling rates of 50–100 tonnes/hour (steel, coke, clay and forest products would fall in his category). The second is that vessel operators face a strong incentive to use vessels which can compete for a variety of traffics rather than for a specific traffic on a specific route. Vessel life is approximately fifteen years and this is often beyond the duration of an individual traffic. A review of the UK registered dry goods and coasting fleet shows average vessel deadweight capacity to be 1302 tonnes at present and this has declined from 1546 tonnes in 1968. Depending on vessel design, a coaster standard development for the Trent would allow vessels of up to 1800 DWT and exceptionally 2000 DWT to navigate inland.

Finally, a Barge Carrying Vessel (BCV) system such as LASH (Lighter Aboard Ship) might provide an alternative technology to link sea and waterway. Potentially, it could allow international traffics handled at inland areas to take advantage of economies of scale on the sea leg of the journey, but the high capital costs of the mothership (£10 m for a 6000 DWT, sixteen LASH barge vessels at 1977 prices) and barge sets (a further £6.3 m for five sets to serve two inland areas) would require very intensive use to keep the system fully employed and the flows required appear beyond the capacity of two port hinterlands to generate. A multiport itinerary would be necessary (but so would extra barge sets) and this would produce logistical problems where flows were in any way unbalanced. In comparison, if coasters can reach inland they would provide a superior transport option.

2 Potential freight demand

In the absence of comprehensive origin/destination data on domestic and international traffic flows the identification of potential waterway freights is not an exact science. However not all traffics will be attracted to water and it is possible to isolate appropriate commodities and generating/consuming industries. Survey work carried out among such industries within a corridor running between South Wales, the Midlands and Humberside/Yorkshire produced valuable data on origin/destination, annual commodity tonnages, present transport and handling modes and ports of entry/exit and this was supplemented with various statistical data collected on port, trade, industrial and regional activities and discussions with road, waterway and ship transport operators resulting in the tonnages shown in Table 21.3.

TABLE 21.3 POTENTIAL WATERWAY TRAFFICS, DOMESTIC AND INTERNATIONAL (1977–78 LEVELS)

Commodity	Tonnes	Foreign origin/destination	UK origin/destination
(a) International traffics			
Manufactured fuels	228816 (X)	/LC WG SB	EM/
Timber	229300 (M)	SB P/	/EM WM
Paper and board	144000 (M)	SB /	/EM WM
Fertiliser raw materials	50000 (M)	LC WG/	/HW EM
Non-ferrous metals	36500 (M/X)	SG LCS/WG LC	WM/WM
Iron and steel	250000 (M/X)	WG LCS/WG LC S	WM/WM
Container traffic	252000 (TEU) (M/X)	WG LC F/WG	
		LCF[a]	WM EM/WM EM
(b) Domestic traffics			
Chemicals	6500	–	HS/EM WM
Petroleum products	620000	–	HS/EM
Aggregates	332000	–	EM/HS
Minestone	2700000	–	EM/HS[b]
General merchandise	10000	–	HS/EM

[a] Includes Rotterdam transit traffic to deep-sea areas.
[b] Includes coastal land reclamation and open-sea tipping.
M: Import, X: Export; LC: Low Countries; WG: West Germany; SB: Scandinavia/Baltic; P: Poland; F: France; EM: East Midlands; WM: West Midlands; HS: Humberside.

This constitutes a total international traffic potential of 938,616 tonnes and 25200 TEU of containers, and domestic traffic potential of 3,727,500 tonnes (of which 360,000 tonnes is existing traffic), giving a total traffic potential of 4,666,116 tonnes as of 1977–78.

Other traffics may exist either at present or in the future (as the result of industrial relocation or changed trade opportunities) but only those shown satisfied the various criteria of our cost-modelling process in that the sum total of vessel, vehicle, handling, collection/distribution and port costs would be less via an inland waterway than under the (estimated) costs of existing transport methods.

Of the potential domestic traffics the largest new flow would be the movement of minestone waste by sea-going, bottom-opening barges from Newark to coastal- and sea-tipping sites. There are other considerations though which may make inclusion of minestone traffic premature or prevent the traffic from eventuating. Otherwise, the petroleum products and aggregates have both waterside origin and destinations and the chemicals a waterside origin and such traffics would not be unusual on any major continental waterway system.

Of the international traffics (forest products, manufactured solid fuels, metals, fertiliser raw materials and containers) only the container traffic can be considered, in the light of current shipping practices, to be controversial. Containers moving between the East and West Midlands and Germany, East France and the Low Countries are presently directed through a limited number of east coast ports (Hull, Teesside, Felixstowe, Tilbury) and one Welsh port (Newport) to achieve an economic use of specialised terminals and vessels, and services are mostly concentrated on trans-shipping in the Europort (Rotterdam) area. Such a route structure does make sensible use of vessels and terminal equipment but results in the length of water-borne haul being minimised at the expense of additional road and rail movements. In contrast, the use of two inland port terminals, one at Newark on the Trent, the other at Düsseldorf or Cologne on the Rhine, would save considerable inland haulage costs which in turn would be sufficiently large to outweigh the penalty of restricted vessel size (at 100 TEU capacity), longer round trip time and, to maintain service frequency, an additional vessel (three vessels would be needed) and vessel operating costs.

On the assumption that the appropriate waterway improvement of the Trent did take place (opening in 1985) then allowance must also be made for traffic growth over the lifetime of the development (50 years). Previous mention has been made of the recent growth in UK near-sea/short-sea trade in comparison to deep-sea trades. Table 21.4 shows that between 1972–77, total UK trade (excluding fuels) with near short-sea areas has increased by 16.6 per cent overall (a growth of 3.2 per cent p.a.) as opposed to total trade growth of 8 per cent overall (1.5 per cent p.a.). In turn, near-sea trade growth has been a remarkable 58 per cent

TABLE 21.4   UK FOREIGN TRADE (EXCLUDING FUELS)
(million tonnes)

Year	All areas	Deep-sea	Near-short sea	Near-sea
1972	99.0	45.7	53.3	18.1
1973	113.1	50.6	62.5	23.5
1974	110.7	45.0	65.7	29.2
1975	97.4	38.6	58.8	28.2
1976	108.1	43.5	64.6	29.3
1977	106.9	44.7	62.2	28.7

overall (or 9.6 per cent p.a.), with the major growth impetus coming from trade with West Germany and the Netherlands, the same two areas being the source of much of the international traffic generated for the River Trent.

V POTENTIAL RESOURCE SAVINGS FROM A COASTER STANDARD IMPROVEMENT TO THE TRENT

After calculation of trade and commodity growth rates and increased movement, handling and distribution costs, the resource savings according to traffics assigned to the river were calculated to identify the level of revenue, as of 1985, available for the repayment of capital and operating costs. The results are shown in Table 21.5.

Thus, if all traffics were attracted to the river, this would imply that improvements of up to £172.9 m (covering both capital and annual running costs) would be justified with a rate of discount set at 5 per cent, or £74.8 m at a 10 per cent of discount.

Both the capital costs and the annual running costs were identified in a separate engineering study. These were £43.4 m for track improvement; £4.37 m for terminal and handling facilities and £1.285 m p.a. for

TABLE 21.5 FIRST YEAR VALUE OF IMPROVEMENT £m 1985

Commodity	*Thousand*	*Existing cost*	*Trent cost*	*Saving*	*Net Present Value at 5% (£m)*	*at 10% (£m)*
(a) International						
Manufactured fuel	431.3	3.904	3.578	0.326	8.866	3.578
Forest products	405.7	6.965	6.264	0.701	19.559	8.135
Fertiliser inputs	76.9	0.4397	0.281	0.116	3.388	1.389
Metals	381.1	3.12	2.412	0.708	20.567	8.467
Containers	501.8	6.451	44.846	1.605	46.632	18.830
(b) Domestic						
Chemicals	100.7	0.336	0.292	0.044	1.623	0.567
Petroleum products	620.0	1.490	0.896	0.594	13.600	6.665
Aggregates	323.0	0.453	0.210	0.243	7.161	3.378
Minestone	2700.0	7.884	5.815	2.079	48.213	23.348
General merchandise	11.5	0.065	0.037	0.028	1.146	0.475
TOTAL	5552.0	31.065	24.621	6.444	172.955	74.832

running costs. When the latter costs were capitalised over the life of the development (50 years at 10 per cent p.a.) and added to the initial capital cost, a net present cost of £63.46 m is arrived at which, when compared with the traffic savings benefit (see Table 21.5), generates a net surplus of £11.34 m. This is equivalent to an internal rate of return of some 12.0 per cent. However, if the two traffics mentioned as being sensitive to other 'forces' (i.e. containers and minespoil) did not eventuate, the rate of return would fall to around 5 per cent, but if only minespoil traffic were eliminated the rate of return would be 8.6 per cent.

An evaluation along similar lines was made for alternative improvement standards and the next best option to coaster development appeared to be a barge standard (based on half-LASH dimensions) over the total river length to Nottingham (whereas the Coaster standard development would finish at Newark, 44 km downstream and thence a barge improvement to Nottingham), however, this would rely on a BCV system operating from Hull to Rotterdam for international traffics and doubts exist on the viability of such a system for this type of operation. In addition, a number of the domestic traffics appear susceptible to alternative mode competition (rail) and, on the basis of the narrow traffic market available, the future of such an investment is considered to be unsound, despite a net surplus of £8.9 m over net present costs of £7.61 m.

Apart from the two alternatives mentioned above, no other improvement standard generated a significant level of benefits. Consequently, the total result of our investigation leads the authors to believe that if the River Trent were to be considered for improvement, then the greatest potential benefit would be achieved by undertaking developments for coaster vessel access rather than as an inland waterway for barges only. The analysis, however, cannot readily take account of the reactions of existing transport operators providing services to the traffics identified as potential waterway traffics. Coastal ports already vigorously compete for traffic shares and would not enjoy the prospect of being by-passed, while railways and other transport operators (particularly for the unitised traffics) are faced with considerable and expensive investments to protect and the power to cross-subsidise, in the short term at least, between traffics or over market areas may be used to deter potential waterway users or operators from setting up services. There is also no way of ensuring that traffics which presently move in a suboptimal manner and could achieve a level of resource savings by switching to a waterway would do so, or that future traffics would realise optimal savings potential by using the waterway. This will continue to be the case while the *prices* charged by competing modes do not totally reflect their true resource costs.

VI CONCLUSIONS

If the conclusions drawn from the River Trent Study are correct, then they could also apply to other rivers and waterways in Britain and some areas of mainland in Europe. Most of the commodities which would make up the bulk of the flow on the improved River Trent (petroleum products, manufactured fuels, iron and steel, timber and aggregates) are likely to be prominent amongst the transport requirements of other areas and countries. The only traffic that may be specific to the Trent is the minestone from the proposed Vale of Belvoir coalfield. But the removal of this colliery waste without any replacement by alternative bulk traffic flows would reduce the expected rate of return and the economic viability of any scheme requiring new investment on the scale of the Trent Project.

One disadvantage of the Trent scheme is that there is little industry producing or consuming large traffic flows situated directly on the banks of the river between the Humber Estuary and Newark. This means that goods must be trans-shipped and this reduces the cost advantage of water-borne traffic. In the long run new industry receiving large inputs of materials from mainland Europe, or exporting to Europe, might be developed on waterside locations if a direct service were available to European destinations.

The costs per loaded ton kilometre of direct long-distance waterway–sea–waterway link for European waterways that already have significant industrial development on their banks would probably be lower than those found in the Trent study. Long-distance waterway–sea–waterway transport would obviously compete more effectively with other modes where trans-shipment could be avoided at one or both ends of the journey.

An important problem, both at national and international level, is that of the impact of government policy and the extent to which conditions of competition are harmonised. The subsidisation of some forms of transport, such as the railways, could drastically reduce the rate of return earned by waterway investment. Similarly, differential pricing policies adopted by port authorities could distort competitive conditions and result in misleading pricing signals being given to transport consumers. In this case any advantages of waterway–sea–

waterway long-distance transport could be lost and traffic might continue to be carried by rail or road, even where these modes are less efficient in using scarce resources.

REFERENCE

Garratt, M., Hayter, D., Gibson, M. and Sharp, C. (1979). *The Potential for Commercial Waterway Investment* (PSERC, University of Leicester).

Discussion of Papers by Dr Andruszkiewicz, Professor Wickham and Dr Phuc, Messrs Hayter and Sharp

Professor Zaleski began by saying that sea and river transport was important because of its effect on international relations and division of labour, and the stimulus it could provide for economic and scientific development. Maritime transport was a factor of integration in the world economy – but also a factor of disintegration, if it reinforced traditional models of specialisation.

The paper by Dr Andruszkiewicz concentrated on the time spent in ports. It used to be the case that big ships stayed longer than small ships, but the increase in liquid cargoes and containers and unitary instead of general cargoes, had made possible quick servicing with new techniques (pipelines, and roll-on-roll-off). It would be increasingly important to shorten associated delays in waiting time, bureaucratic hold-ups, and manoeuvring time of lorries and barges – especially in some developing countries where underinvestment caused very long delays.

Professor Wickham and Dr Phuc had also examined port congestion, caused by the use of ports which had not been designed for bulk traffic (now the most important part of their trade), and the volatile nature of demand. Shipping capacity and the number of ships had each increased by a factor of two or more since the Second World War, and this growth would continue, though at a slower pace. In the long run, it would be necessary to redesign the whole port system, including administration, handling, berths and warehouses, and combined facilities at inland ports. Smaller specialised ports could also help to deal with volatile traffic demands.

The paper by Messrs Hayter and Sharp, by contrast, suggested that there might be advantages in using inland waterways, so that ocean-going ships could penetrate nearer to their final destination. Their research, based on the River Trent, might be of wider application, although there were great problems due to the lack of standard dimensions, round-the-clock navigation, and tidal flows. The railways had had an indirect subsidy for freight, so perhaps waterways should also.

In the general discussion *Dr Andrusciewicz* said that in ports where freight traffic was not intensive there was no possibility of new equipment, though some administrative improvements could be made. Where traffic was intensive (and the port authorities were rich) modernisation must be introduced. In Poland there was no deep berth suitable for ships of over 100,000 tonnes – which were used for grain – and they would have to find a source of funds to pay for this. The other main problem was that of delays – time was money, and the price of delays at present was too high.

Dr Antal suggested that a more complex approach was necessary. For example, Hungary imported phosphates from the USSR, but these could not be discharged from the Soviet ship in Poland because of a shortage of railway wagons. So they had to take the cargo to Hamburg, which was more expensive – the bottleneck was not directly shipping, but connected with the railways.

Mr Hayter commented that 'Time was money', but it cost money to save time. It was a waste of money to invest very heavily in new port facilities, if there were bigger delays in other parts of the system, such as customs. In that case, it was more important to reduce administrative delay.

Professor Khachaturov suggested that on the same point, they should look more at cheap *ad hoc* measures – such as the reference to methods used by the US army in Greenland. In the long term this could cause problems.

Dr Phuc said he agreed with Mr Hayter that removing administrative delay was cheaper than new investment – but changing people's minds could be very difficult. Professor Khachaturov's point was a good one. He thought that the military systems had three advantages – they were easily built (less than fourteen months to build a berth in a shipyard, and tow and set it up on site); they could be cheaply built because of the depressed activity in the shipyards; above all, they could be moved from place to place if the pattern of trade changed. Their argument was that there were new parameters. First, maritime transport was the only economic sector where no one country could dominate another – this would oblige nations to co-operate. Secondly, the increase in fuel prices would put greater pressure on reducing all costs, but make it more expensive to travel faster – therefore the only way to improve overall times was in port. Thirdly, the changing structure of costs of long-distance journeys would make, for example, the large iron-ore deposits in Senegal economic to mine.

Professor Wickham mentioned that the potential for economies of scale was frequently overstated. *Dr Tye* agreed. There was little advantage in owning large fleets. The US Congress continued to subsidise them in the belief that they got commercial and military advantages, but neither applied.

Professor Khachaturov and *Dr Phuc* both questioned details of Messrs Hayter and Sharp's paper. What was the basis for the economic calculations? What about river investment which was not totally dedicated to transport (e.g. flood defences) – how did they allocate such costs? How about availability of capital?

Mr Hayter said the capital investment required would be £47.8m – a very sore point, because of the administrative framework which prevented the British Waterways Board from raising money by loans. The procedure they adopted was to calculate a discounted net present value for the first year of operation. Certainly they had tried to take account of the allocation of flood prevention costs, drainage costs, etc., though in the final event this was determined by the operators, and might lead to tolls.

He was not sure how widely their results should be applied – this was only a study of one very specific situation, and they must remember that in the UK inland-waterway traffic hardly existed any more – it was only about 1 per cent of the total traffic. Could the existing waterways once again play a major role? As in many other discussions, the answer seemed to depend on the characteristics of the overall door-to-door journey. However, nothing was immune to change and we should not write off any mode, however little it might be used. Lastly, it seemed to him very important that prices should adequately reflect the *true* resource costs of using the different modes – this might well favour inland waterway transport.

PART FIVE

Transport and Production: Organisational Aspects of Transport Development

22 Spatial Distribution of Productive Powers and Socialist Transport Policy

GERHARD REHBEIN

I INTRODUCTION

Development of the powers of production, with a planned increase in the productivity of labour, will always have positive effects for society, with an increase in social wealth. The statements made by Lenin (1961a) on the importance of increasing labour productivity for the construction of a new social order are as valid today as they were over fifty years ago.

The location of production, and of political, social and cultural facilities, is an important factor in the planned proportional development of a national economy, which is a prerequisite for an effective increase in the productivity of labour. In order to solve a variety of problems connected with these questions a knowledge of the fundamental principles is necessary. These principles explain:

(1) the historical formation of the powers of production which produce the means for satisfying the growing needs of society;
(2) the direction and rate of growth of their future development;
(3) the economic-political decisions which influence the location of the powers of production.

The resulting spatial distribution is defined as a process of planned spatial organisation of social production processes, which may be based on regions or include the whole country. Increasing integration of planned economy countries means that for more and more fields of production, location is planned not only within one country, but also goes beyond national borders.

In this respect the distribution of productive forces is an important means of achieving the political, economy and cultural goals of socialist society in a planned and comprehensive way. As productive forces are the most mobile element of production the theoretical knowledge and above all the practical consideration of conditions generating them and influencing their development are of great importance for society. Their degree of action has a great bearing on state, economy and population.

For these and other reasons, the increase of regional concentration in economic development and in social life which may be observed in our time calls increasingly for new considerations to be taken into account by economists aiming at an efficient increase in productivity. The general theory of location with regard to productive forces may be fully applied to the transport system – the generic term for transport and communications. However, problems of location are of specific importance to the transport system.

II THE ROLE OF TRANSPORT IN THE NATIONAL ECONOMY

Transport and communications are productive factors within a planned economy (Rehbein and Wagener, 1968). The movements of goods and people are essential in production processes, such as industry or agriculture. Transport links occur in all areas of the state and the economy independent of their management responsiblity and organisational affiliation (e.g. transport processes used by anybody as a public transport service; those processes which only apply to a limited group of users, such as works transport service, commercial transport, non-public communications, etc. or those which are simply intraplant transport processes but have the same economic aims). When considering the degree of labour division achieved so far no member of society is, after all, able to fulfil his tasks without transport. Transport requirements therefore exist for people, goods and information. Improving the performance of the transport system will lead to increased efficiency of economic, national and social institutions, and thus the development of the economy will raise living standards.

By satisfying such needs of existence the transport system does not only fulfil its operational tasks but at the same time carries out fundamental social functions. The social role of the transport and communication system is demonstrated by its contribution to increased social labour productivity which is a prerequisite for improving the working and living conditions of man. The basic importance of transport for society also becomes apparent in the course of daily life, when, for example, critical economic situations, or even severe weather, demonstrate that a smooth-running transport and communications system is indispensable.

In developing productive forces, transport beyond the borders of a country becomes increasingly more important. In this respect the range of international transport directly depends on social conditions and their advancement. By utilising its means and possibilities transport is thus able to contribute to an improvement of international co-operation both in a national and economic life and also to a considerable deepening of personal relations between men.

However, national and international tasks can be realised only when the location of productive forces working in the transport system is in accordance with social requirements. The location of technical productive forces resulting from a long historical development must be used more efficiently within the framework of social requirements. There are many cases where they must be extended and adjusted to changing conditions. This may lead to considerable technical and economic requirements for the transport system which often may only be realised within long periods of time. In this connection the technical and economic problems of transport facilities scattered over a large area but nonetheless dependent on close co-operation must especially be considered. On a long-term basis new locations must be created depending on the development aims of the national economy.

III THE CONSEQUENCES OF THE FUNCTION OF TRANSPORT

With regard to the development of productive forces, transport has a social function of great importance, designated as a connecting function of socialist society. What are the consequences of the connecting function of transport and in which way does it influence social practice?

In the first place the social need for transport and for the development of its productive forces must be mentioned. In a classical way Marx (1959 edn) pointed out the reasons proving the importance of transport for the development of society. He stated that the more production was based on transport and thus on exchange, the more important became the physical conditions of exchange, i.e. the means of communication and transport. He further remarked that capital according to its very nature surpassed spatial barriers. The creation of physical conditions of exchange, i.e. of means of communication and transport, he said, thus became a necessity for it in a quite different degree resulting in an annihilation of space by time. Furthermore, he argued that production of cheap transport and communication means was a precondition of production based on capital and was, therefore, produced by it. Marx also stated that the spatial condition, i.e. putting the product on the market, belonged, from the economic point of view, to the production process itself. The product was only then really finished when it was on the market. The socially connecting position of transport with regard to all other fields of national economy, however, not only characterises economic position with the development of technical productive forces (transport and communication means), but also has an effect on the location of the totality of productive force (see Lenin's speech of 1919, in Lenin, 1961b) and the means of production present differing requirements for transport. While, for instance, industrial production is generally bound to a specific plant, transport is a different matter, being clearly characterised by a chain-like interaction of productive forces. Due to the functions of transport within a given area the different transport chains must be linked up to allow transport to become effective in space and time.

The transport system formed in this way may be compared with a network spreading throughout the whole country (as far as inland transport is concerned) or even developing into a world transport network. A system is necessary which is able to act in a uniform way and which is considered to be part of a whole, otherwise the transport chain would be interrupted. Only on this basis will modern transport, which may cover large areas, be realised and be able efficiently to fulfil these functions which are important for people, state and economy.

That is why interrelations between productive forces and transport processes are characterised by a number of specific conditions. To know them and to take them into consideration ensures a transport system which is well-organised and fulfils the needs of the national economy and its contribution to the development of the whole society. These are the conditions which form the basis for the organisation of productive forces:

(1) The tasks of the transport system are realised on transport routes according to lines forming the basis of transport practice and thus of utilisation of the necessary productive forces.

(2) Transport routes in their turn run into transport junctions. The

location of productive forces is especially stimulated and concentrated at these points.

(3) Transport junctions as a whole form the basis of the transport network. The networks of different transport carriers (railways, road transport, air service, etc.) require the development and utilisation of special productive forces for the purpose of transport handling. Accordingly, due to the practical requirements of transport and communications, high qualitative demands are made on science and technology.

(4) In order to avoid national economic losses the co-ordination of transport networks on a national and international scale is necessary. This is true both for the installation and for the extension of connections as well as for the transitions from one network to another. Transport handling in practice must be carried out on the basis of the closest co-operation of transport carriers concerned.

(5) The fulfilment of transport tasks will only be ensured by the interaction of productive forces which are scattered over a large area but are utilised both a national and more and more at an international level.

The theoretical and practical problems resulting from these five conditions apply to all fields of national economy characterised by the division of labour and by the task of changing the place of goods, persons and communications. Thus transport can be differentiated from other sectors of the economy, such as industry and agriculture. The special characteristics of the transport and communication system identify its own sphere of social production.

For the transport system to operate efficiently it is essential:

(1) to organise the productive forces in an optimal way; and

(2) to make sure that the chain-like connection of all installations with transport functions will form a close network.

All theoretical considerations and practical steps must be based on the fact that the efficiency of national and international transport depends to a high degree on the joint harmonious action of all elements in the transport chain. This chain is jeopardised by interruptions even at a single point.

In international technical literature there are comments on those factors which were specifically instrumental in the location of productive forces. There are rarely any doubts about the inseparable interrelations which originated from the course of historical development. This led not only to the formation of various transport networks but also to different trends of development. The location of productive forces is, therefore, a historical process. Consequently it changes in the course of development of society leading to the conclusion that there is a direct interrelation between the location of productive forces and the development of the ownership of means of production. A planned economy allows for a new stage of location of productive forces, and thus transport can be developed in an an appropriate way.

IV TRANSPORT POLICY IN A PLANNED ECONOMY

The measurements of socialist transport policy are based on the fundamental functions of society expressed in the basic economic law of socialism. As transport cannot be separated from social conditions, the general basic social lines and the aims of the whole society as well as the provisions of the national economy regarding the development of productive forces must always be applied to transport and transport policy. The connecting function of the transport and communication system relating to a planned economy is demonstrated, therefore, as a partial function serving to achieve the main social task.

It is due to T. S. Khachaturov who, among other Soviet economists, carried out research in the field of transport economics, that the correlations between transport processes and location problems have been pointed out (Khachaturov, 1959). The following factors of location of productive forces under socialist conditions are essential:

(1) the aim of distributing production over the whole country;
(2) the guarantee of bringing about the economic and cultural advance of each region of the country;
(3) location of industry with regard to raw material resources and consumption areas aiming at a reduction of transport routes;
(4) planned division of labour according to national regions;
(5) increase of national defence;
(6) growing international division of labour.

Practice demonstrates that, due to the connecting function of the transport and communication systems, the location of productive forces in many cases is the essential point of existing transport facilities or those to be developed. Transport is influenced according to its past development, its present situation and, last but not least, its future trends by the following factors:

(1) technical and technological requirements of production processes;
(2) spatial distribution of productive forces;
(3) urbanisation including the development of conurbations;
(4) development of labour division, specialisation and co-operation at a national and international level.

Therefore, appropriate decisions relating to transport policy must be based on these and other factors (for instance, requirements of geographical environment) if transport is to be developed in such a way that it will meet the growing demands of state, economy and population regarding quality and quantity of transport services.

REFERENCES

Khachaturov, T. S. (1959). *Ökonomik des Transportwesens* (Moscow: Akademie der Wissenschaften der UdSSR).

Lenin, W. I. (1961a). Die grosse Initiative, *Werke*, Vol. 29 (Berlin: Dietz Verlag).

Lenin, W. I. (1961b). Gesamtrussischer Kongress fur ausserschulische Bildung, *Werke*, Vol. 29 (Berlin: Dietz Verlag).

Marx, K. (1959 edn) *Grundrisse der Kritik der politischen Okonomie* (Berlin: Dietz Verlag).

Rehbein, G. and Wagener, H. (1968). Das Transport – and Nachrichtenwesen als Produktivitats – und Wachstumsfaktor der sozialistischen Gesellschaft, *Staat und Recht*, Nr. 12, 1932–40.

23 Organisation of Transport Enterprises

H. J. NOORTMAN

I INTRODUCTION

A paper on the organisation of transport enterprises requires an explanation of the direction from which this topic will be approached. Although the organisational aspects of individual transport companies will be given proper attention, it is nevertheless also necessary to broaden the scale of the analysis. Specifically because of its strategic importance, passenger as well as freight transport has always attracted a great deal of attention, not only at the management level of individual companies, but also from governments. The planning of economic development necessitates involvement of governments in the organisational aspects of transport services. After the Second World War, involvement at the political level was further expanded, with many aspects of this involvement being centred in the hands of international organisations.

Special attention will be given to the many important impacts of political involvement on the management of individual transport companies. Finally, it seems desirable to comment on those specific aspects which tend to make the setting up of an efficient organisation more complicated for transport companies than for other sectors of the economy.

II TRANSPORT AS AN INSTRUMENT VARIABLE FOR PUBLIC AUTHORITIES

Undoubtedly, transport facilities have always played a very important role in the development of political unity and so there is hardly a country where the organisation of the supply side of the transport market has been left on its own. Governments were too dependent on this

312

organisation. Here the primary governmental interest may perhaps have been concentrated on the infrastructure facilities for transport. However, infrastructure facilities without a well-organised transport industry which is supposed to make use of this infrastructure, hardly makes sense. Therefore, government involvement in transport has almost always two dimensions; one concentrating on infrastructure planning and construction, the second on the actual operational side of the transport companies.

Considering this governmental involvement with the transport services, it does not matter whether government intervention is primarily directed towards infrastructure or towards the operational side of the transport industry. This difference in impact is perhaps stronger in private enterprise economies than in economic systems with state-owned or controlled transport companies. In general it can be stated that, as far as the infrastructure is concerned, governmental responsibility for infrastructure investment decision-making is without question independent of the political structure of the country.

Having said this and leaving aside the political structure of the country, the next interesting point seems to be whether the strategic relevance of infrastructure investments is self-evident in the economic development of areas under discussion. Given the experiences of the last decades this point should be treated with caution. This applies both to the more developed parts of the world as well as to the less developed. Generally, it can be said that the contribution of infrastructure facilities to the economic development of the area they open up is a function of the level of economic development that has already been reached. The socio-economic impact of a transport facility is in general much larger in less developed areas than in highly developed countries. In the latter case, infrastructure facilities are not the motor for further development, but are only conditioning for that development. However, even in less developed countries it is still not clear why transport infrastructure investments have effectively led towards a higher level of economic activity in some cases and not in others.

In estimating the relevance of infrastructure investments as an instrument variable, it is desirable to take care in classifying the various parts of the world. The importance of infrastructure cannot be gauged by the classification of countries into two broad groups: developed countries and the developing countries. Our patterns of economic development are too complicated to allow for such a simplistic view. Western Europe could serve as an example here. The strategic value of infrastructure policy is quite different in the central part of Western

Europe, from the more peripheral areas. As far as the central part is concerned, new infrastructure facilities can hardly be of vital importance for the take-off of new economic development, and quite different incentives are needed. On the other hand, there are many peripheral areas in Western Europe, where better transport connections with the centre of Western Europe and/or other parts of the world are vital for overcoming the gap between their economic development level and that of the central part of the EEC.

Government involvement with the actual operational side of the transport industry has much stronger impacts on the management of the transport industry than in cases where the public authorities focus their attention on infrastructure. This difference is most apparent in countries with a private enterprise economy. There the government involvement in the provision of transport services is in general most apparent in the operations of the railway companies. At least as far as Europe is concerned, the governments have used this mode of transport as a tool in many areas of government responsibility. As a consequence, two main lines of development can be distinguished as having important effects on the management of transport companies.

First, considering the railway companies themselves, it should be pointed out that the strong involvement of national governments with this mode of transport has blurred the borderline between governmental responsibility and the management responsibility of the governing boards of the railway companies. This 'clouded area of responsibilities' has resulted in the railways having a rather weak competitive position, compared with the other modes of transport. However, government involvement in railway operations also has an impact on those modes of transport that are in competition with the railways. For instance, many road transport regulations are justified by the competitive position of road transport in relation to the railways, rather than by competitive conditions within the road transport industry.

Until now, government intervention in the provision of transport services has been approached by way of the involvement of national governments in the management of the railway companies as a tool in stimulating economic activity in underdeveloped areas. However, in the very densely populated areas of the world, government involvement with the operational side of the provision of transport services has created a different incentive. Here we enter the area of government involving itself in the provision of transport services in order to cope with the negative impacts on transport resulting from economic activities at a high level of development. Here the negative environmental effects of private motorised passenger transport are dominant in political discussions. Government involvement in the operational side of the transport companies is therefore in this case concentrated on the provision of public transport services as a substitute for private passenger transport.

III SOME SPECIFIC ASPECTS OF TRANSPORT COMPANIES

Dealing with the management aspects of transport companies makes it desirable to keep in mind that the companies providing transport services possess specific characteristics that further complicate any management system. Three such characteristics may be distinguished:

(1) A tendency towards diseconomies of scale in surface transport. Although there may be reservations about the slogan 'the bigger the better', there is nevertheless an emotional resistance to statements like 'diseconomies of scale'. However, as far as surface transport is concerned, this trend towards diseconomies of scale is very serious. In the first place we are confronted with the practical point that, given a certain demand for transport services, the provision of these services has to be disaggregated into demands per geographical unit. Thus, the scale of services rendered per geographical unit is much smaller than might perhaps be expected, given the aggregated demand. The possibilities of making use of large transport units are further diminished by the distribution of the demand for transport services over the various seasons, the days of the week and the hours per day. These characteristics of the demand side limit the technical possibilities of acquiring economies of scale. However, besides this, the supply side of the transport market has its own tendencies towards diseconomies of scale.

Here it should be remembered that the diminishing costs per unit of output via an increase in production capacity result from a change in the labour/capital goods ratio. In surface transport this change in ratio is limited to road transport and often also to inland navigation. These limitations result from the capacity of the infrastructure facilities or from traffic regulations.

When the maxima set for the dimensions of trucks, buses, trams and barges have been reached, a further enlargement of the supply of transport services by a company can only be attained via fleet enlargement, keeping constant the labour/capital goods ratio at the operational level of the company. At the same time, however, there is a very strong trend towards a more than proportional increase in overhead costs (Noortman, 1971).

(2) The absence of a uniform unit of production. There are two critical points for management decision-making in the transport industry. The first is closely connected with decision-making about future plans, where expansion and penetration into new market segments are under discussion. The second is the evaluation of the results of previous actions. For both areas of evaluation it is of vital importance to compare profits and costs. The absence of a uniform unit of production implies that the transport industry management needs a rather sophisticated flow of information concerning the interrelation of costs and the various outputs of transport services. The availability of such information flows is not common in 'average' enterprises.

(3) The geographical decentralised demand for transport services. Apart from limiting the scale of the provision of transport services, geographically decentralised demand for transport services lends an additional dimension to the management of a transport company, because it seriously limits the possibilities of a direct visual control of the transport services production process. The management of a transport company therefore needs indirect forms of observation.

Given these three specific characteristics of many companies providing transport services, what are their impacts on management? It seems that they complicate management in two respects. First of all, consider the market approach. In those cases where the transport company is confronted with a tendency towards diseconomies of scale, the widening of its market is a very difficult task. For if such a tendency exists then it seems to be a good question: why there are not only small and medium-size companies in those sectors of the transport industry, but also quite often transport companies which are very large? Looking in more detail at those sectors of the transport market, it can be concluded that the various suppliers of transport services, although differing in size, are generally not competing for the same clients. This is because the difference between the companies is not purely a matter of size. The services they can offer are different as well. In general terms one may perhaps characterise this difference in the following way:

(1) The small transport companies have a relatively low cost level, and are very flexible in their decision-making, but can in many cases provide only a relatively simple transport service.

(2) The big transport companies, on the other hand, can usually provide a much more complex transport service with a more differentiated fleet and with a larger and more specialised staff that enables them to offer a product-mix of physical distribution services. This larger organisation results, however, as far as the transport services as such are concerned, in a relatively high cost level and often makes them more inflexible than the small companies.

Given the highly heterogenous structure of the demand for transport services, the small, medium-sized and the big transport companies can all operate at the same time in the same geographical area. Because of the lack of economies of scale there is in these sectors of the transport industry no optimal company size. Given the structure on the demand side of the market, there can only be an optimal distribution of the supply side over the various company sizes. It will be understood that in a dynamic economy, the structure of the demand for transport services changes over time. This means that the structure of the supply side has to adapt itself to these changes in the demand pattern. In general for an area with an increasing GNP this results in an upward shift of the supply side of the transport market, as far as the distribution of the companies over the various sizes is concerned.

How can and should this phenomenon of the lack of economies of scale be integrated in the planning of the transport companies? It seems in this connection wise not to plan on the basis of general macro indicators for the growth of economic activities. Further information is needed on the planning of the company expansion as well as on the changes in the structure of the demand for transport services. Such changes not only influence the potential market shares for the various modes of transport, but per mode to the potential market shares for the various company sizes.

Now if these are market developments in a direction where the demand characteristics give openings for an enlargement of the market share of the bigger companies, it is not enough for the management to find these openings. Planning for the future asks at the same time for a very careful analysis of the historical market sectors, where the expanding company has operated up to now. The expansion of the company into new sectors makes an enlargement of the size of the company possible, but brings the costs of the transport services to a higher level in the cases where the company is confronted with diseconomies of scale. If the historical market sectors ask only for relatively simple transport services, this means in a private enterprise economy that the freight rates will be fixed in relation to the cost level of the smaller companies. So in order to avoid the risk of structural losses in such historical market sectors, a plan for expansion asks not only for planned penetration into new market sectors, but at the same time for planning of the cut-back in the actual service rendered to the sectors which will no longer be profitable.

The impact is different in economic systems with state-owned or state-controlled transport companies. In fact we have the same situation as in all those cases in a private enterprise economy, where the government uses the services provided by transport companies as an instrument variable in such a way, that price-setting forms part of the political decision-making process. In these cases the equilibrium between revenues and costs no longer indicates whether the structure of the supply side of the transport market is in harmony with the characteristics of the demand side.

Some possible management consequences of the phenomenon of diseconomies of scale have been discussed. The two other mentioned specific characteristics, the absence of a uniform unit of production and the geographically decentralised demand for transport services, complicate management in a different way. Both characteristics make it very important to have a good management information system available within the company.

IV THE RELEVANCE OF DISTANCE FOR THE MANAGEMENT OF TRANSPORT COMPANIES

Some special characteristics which perhaps make the management of companies in the transport industry more difficult than in other sectors of the economy have been mentioned in the previous section. Apart from these more or less 'mode-inherent' characteristics, it seems desirable to reflect upon two distance dimensions of the transport services. In the first place the impact of distance in terms of miles should be considered. From the management point of view it can be stated, that an increase in the transport distance in terms of miles means at the same time an increase of the management tasks. This is due to the fact that, considering the door-to-door aspects, an increase in the transport distance very often implies the involvement of a larger number of companies providing the required service, and this opens up many possibilities for diminishing the quality of the service offered.

The second dimension of distance concerns the time horizon. Living in an age of uncertainties, it is very difficult for the management in transport companies to arrive at proper decisions. The management cannot be certain about their cash flow for a period of much more than one year ahead, and as a result will have to follow the lines set by the system of process planning. This kind of planning may appear rather opportunistic to the outsider. However, there is not much scope for alternatives as long as there is no certainty about future lines of development. Under these conditions the managers as well as the political authorities have to make use of simulation systems that indicate the impacts of alternative lines of development.

V POLICY ORIENTATED SIMULATION SYSTEMS AT THE MACRO LEVEL

As an example of a simulation system for transport planning, mention should be made of the freight transport simulation system for Western Europe, developed for the planning of the infrastructure investments in the coming decades (Netherlands Institute of Transport, 1978). The objective of this study was the preparation of estimates of community infrastructure requirements for freight transport on principal routes for road and rail transport and for inland navigation, in the years 1985 and 2000.

To be able to make such estimates, a simulation model was developed, by which forecasts of future freight flows can be produced, given various scenarios for economic development between now and the year 2000. It will be understood that the simulation model approach was chosen because of the uncertainties involved in the prediction of the future level and structure of the economic activities of Western Europe. The model enables the freight transport demand consequences of different assumptions concerning this economic development to be evaluated. In addition, the model offers the possibility of determining the infrastructure consequences of various transport policy strategies, given a certain economic development in future periods.

Figure 23.1 gives an idea of the basic elements of the simulation system. As can be seen, the model system is fed by four groups of data. Two of these groups, 'objectives' and 'exogenous transport variables', are derived from the scenarios. A third group of data originates from the strategies. The fourth group of data, the transport data, is produced by the transport model, given certain expected economic developments in the study area, the expected development in the exogenous transport variables and the transport policy to be followed. The structure of the transport model is presented in Figure 23.2.

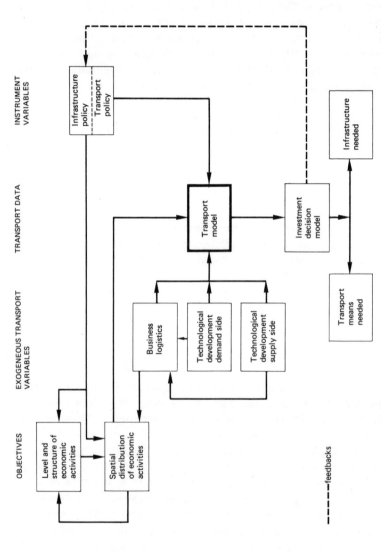

Figure 23.1 Basic elements of the freight transport simulation system, for the European Community and Spain

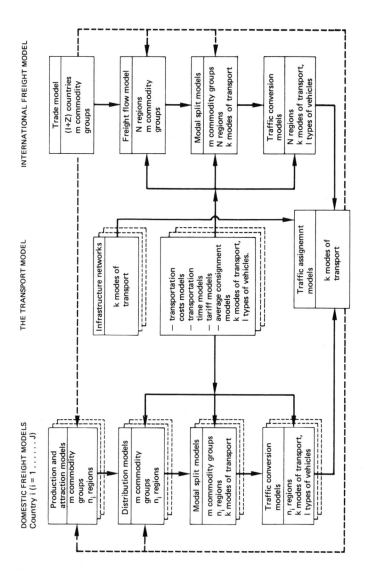

Figure 23.2 The transport model

This kind of simulation system is not only needed for decision-making by political authorities for their infrastructure planning, but is also of vital importance for planning in the transport companies. For the information that this type of model can provide gives managers an idea about the developments on the demand side of the transport market. With the help of sensitivity analyses they can further determine which scenario elements have the greatest influence on the development of freight transport demand with regard to its volume and structure. It is this information that they need in order to estimate what potential market chances their companies will have, given their strong and weak sides per mode of transport and within that mode, the characteristics of their company size.

VI A (PUBLIC) TRANSPORT MANAGEMENT INFORMATION SYSTEM

In Section III of this paper some specific aspects of the supply side of the transport market were described that make the availability of advanced management information systems desirable. It was also stated that there is an extra need for such an information system in those cases where the provision of transport services is used as an instrument variable by the political authorities. In Western Europe this is especially the case with the public transport companies. Here it is desirable to have available in *one* system concept all the elements needed at the political level to come to a proper decision-making process, when using the public transport services, and at the management level to have good control over the planning and realisation of the transport services.

The Dutch Ministry of Transport requested the Economic Bureau for Road and Watertransport (EBW) in Rijswijk, The Netherlands, and the public transport companies of Amsterdam, Rotterdam, The Hague, Utrecht and five smaller cities, to investigate the possibilities of developing a Management Information System (MIS) to tackle these problems. As a result of this investigation a combined management and policy information system (ANALAD) has been developed as a tool for policy-making and management at all levels. This system is now operational not only in the Netherlands, but also in Switzerland for a group of subsidised private railway companies, while its applicability has been tested in various other countries as well, both in private enterprise economies and in countries with state-owned or controlled transport companies.

The Management Information System ANALAD may be visualised

as a pyramid with information at increasing levels of detail as one moves from the apex to the base. The system is designed not only to provide up-to-date statistics on the operation of the company but also as a means of translating policy decisions into definitive figures on source, objectives, performance characteristics, costs and revenues. As such it implies a close comparison of budget and realisation, not only in terms of costs and revenues, but also on the performance on each subdepartment within the company. The complete system is rather complex and cannot be fully described within the context of this paper. However, a brief description of the Basic Policy Model and the Cost Control System can give some impression of the model approach. For a more detailed description see Economic Bureau for Road and Water Transport (1979).

Figure 23.3 illustrates the basic policy model. In order to reach the

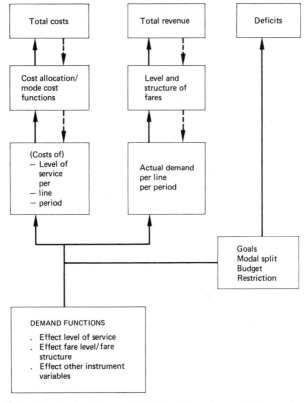

Figure 23.3   The basic policy model of the Management Information System
ANALAD

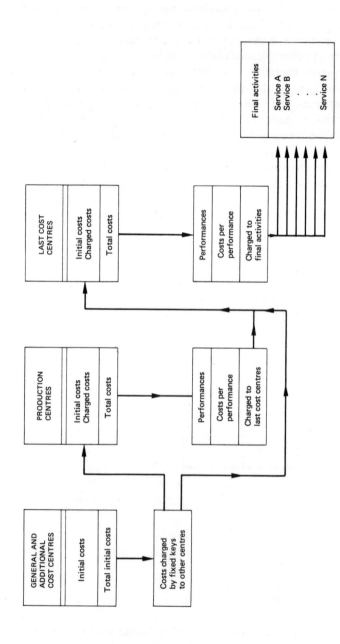

Figure 23.4 General principles of a cost centre system

goals of the public transport policy, certain instruments are available such as level of service to be offered, fare scales and other instrument variables in the sphere of public and private transport, including infrastructure facilities and the parking policy. In addition there are financial restrictions. Using an iterative approach, in theory, the best set of policies can be derived and implemented. However, in reality, the information on some vital elements in the data needed to come to the decision on the best set of policies is incomplete or completely unknown. Here for instance the causal relationship between costs and level of service should be mentioned, keeping in mind the lack of a uniform unit of production. In such a situation it is hardly possible to formulate an integral public transport policy, let alone monitor and control the execution of such a policy. It may be clear that to set up, implement and control such policies, the information needed by the company management and at the various political levels is in principle the same. Only the degree of required detail differs. Now the implementation of this approach demands an integral system with one central part: The Cost Centre System. The essential purpose of this system is to determine the causal relationship between the initial costs per cost type and the final performance on the network.

Figure 23.4 gives an idea of the general principles of this Cost Centre System. As the relations that exist between cost centres are rather complex, they are laid down in a mathematical model for the larger companies, programmed on the computer. With this system, a view can be taken on the causal relationships between the initial costs and the final performance. At the same time a task-setting budget is created for the company. Moreover, a basis is formed for a consistent MIS that can be linked to the other aspects of management and policy.

REFERENCES

Economic Bureau for Road and Water Transport (1979). *A public transport management information system* (Rijswijk, The Netherlands).

Netherlands Institute of Transport (1978). *A freight transport simulation system for the European Community and Spain* (Rijswijk, The Netherlands).

Noorman, H. J. (1971). Some organisational aspects of public transport, *Fourth International Symposium on Theory and Practice in Transport Economics* (ECMT, the Hague).

24 International Transportation Systems

RICHARD BURKE

I INTRODUCTION

The theme of this paper is the role of economics in the development of transport policy within the European Economic Community. The best available advice and information is necessary in preparing the political actions of the European Commission in this important field. However, before the uses of economics in the development of the common transport policy are discussed, it would be useful to outline the framework within which Community policy develops.

II FRAMEWORK OF THE COMMUNITY'S APPROACH TO TRANSPORT

The guiding principle underlying the common transport policy, since its inception in 1961, is that transport undertakings and users should benefit from the advantages of competition. It is through competition therefore that we seek to have an efficient transport industry, operating at least cost to the Community by:

(i) meeting users' needs in an optimal manner;
(ii) favouring development of trade and industry in an economic union;
(iii) furthering economic relations and better adjustment between regions; and
(iv) contributing to better conditions of life and work for people.

These general principles must of course be translated into detailed policies and implemented gradually by both Community and national authorities. In implementing this action, there are roles both for the public authorities, including the Community, and for transport enterprises themselves.

The role for Community action is seen primarily in the development of infrastructure, in assuring the complementarity of the different modes of transport. Transport is not an isolated industry and has an important part to play in the development of environmental and regional policy and in the important field of energy policy.

Community policy relating to transport enterprises seeks, on the basis of progressive steps, to bring about freedom in the markets with respect to capacity and pricing – public authority intervention in the markets being limited to that required to correct serious disturbances, lack of competition or the provision of essential public services. The public authority is also concerned with the reconstruction of different sectors of the industry. The implementing policy instruments fall under two headings:

(i) those relating to infrastructure; and
(ii) software policy

Dealing with infrastructure policy, the Commission is concentrating on:

(i) consultation concerning investments;
(ii) transport system development plans;
(iii) exchanges of information;
(iv) co-operation between national authorities;
(v) appropriate Community financial means for support of key projects;
(vi) development and role of new transport techniques.

Turning to the 'software' policy instruments, the Commission is concerned with:

(i) helping the markets to function freely, an objective to be achieved progressively, passing through interim phases of some controls or guidance on capacity and aspects of prices and conditions;
(ii) in the longer term, replacing quantitative controls on access to the transport business by introducing qualitative criteria, i.e. competence, knowledge of the industry, etc.; and
(iii) establishing comparable standards where governmental regulations significantly affect competition.

The concern of transport policy is with meeting users' needs through a mixture of competition and co-operation looked at from a multimodal point of view and interrelating transport to other fields of policy. The guiding principles set out above have their origin in the treaties establishing the Communities.

Transport itself, however, is also an important user of economic resources: land, skilled manpower, energy and finance. If our people are to be assured of a high standard of living, we must seek to make transport as efficient as possible and to assure the optimal utilisation of our economic resources.

A few statistics will illustrate the importance of transport in our Community of nine countries. Commercial transport represents something in the order of 6 per cent of GNP. This is an average figure which varies between 5–10 per cent of national GNP in individual countries. Adding own account transport for freight traffic and private motoring results in an average figure of 15 per cent or more.

Transport represents approximately 30–40 per cent of public expenditure on gross fixed capital formation. About 10 per cent of total public expenditure goes towards transport infrastructure. Similarly, about 10 per cent of total household expenditure is on transport. The annual turnover of shipowners and airlines is something above 19 billion European units of account (over 25 billion US dollars). Community ports account for about 40 per cent of total world oil and bulk freight movements, served by the world's shipping industry, of which the Community's fleet constitutes some 21 per cent.

III WHAT ECONOMICS CAN DO FOR THE POLICY-MAKER

Economics should help the policy-maker in five ways. Perception: first of all, it is important that policy problems are set out as far as possible in a quantitative manner so that the different elements of a particular problem can be seen clearly within this framework.

Analysis: secondly, one looks at some tools for estimating the size and extent of the problem. These can include market research, investment analysis and cost benefit analysis at both the micro and macro level.

Developing options: having outlined the problem and researched the different causes, one arrives at the first step towards its solution, which is the establishment of the different options which are open to the policy-maker.

Decision theory: economics through cost effectiveness analysis can help to quantify the cost implications of particular options. Once a particular course of action has been decided on, a system for monitoring the attainment of the option chosen, through such means as, for example, planned programmed budgeting, can be particularly helpful.

Finally, in order that particular problems which arise for detailed analysis can be seen in a wider perspective, it is useful and perhaps essential to have a regular monitoring of the activities of the transport market, with forecasts of future expectations to permit assessment of both the magnitude and the appropriateness of solving the problem by different options within a wider framework.

The art of economics is very wide. Transport policy itself covers a wide field. It would not be useful to try to cover all the areas where these two activities interlink. This paper therefore concentrates on a number of areas which are particularly important at the moment.

IV MARKET OBSERVATION

Reference was made earlier to the interrelationship between economics and policy formulation. A practical expression of this interrelationship is now considered. The Commission has, over the years, presented the Council of Ministers with a number of policy initiatives dealing with freight transport between the Member States. This has raised the opportunity of incorporating economic analytical methods directly into the formulation of new Community policy in an important area.

Agreement has been reached with the Council that the Commission's services should establish over a three-year period an experimental system for monitoring the economic trends for the carriage of freight by road, rail and inland waterway between the Member States. Here, our economists and statisticians have the opportunity of developing, with national experts, an information system which is orientated towards policy formulation on both the Community and national levels. This will also be of interest to transporters in improving their knowledge of their business environment.

This challenge of relating economics and policy can be seen in the following way. Public authority surveillance of the transport industry should be sufficiently flexible to ensure rapid reaction to changes in the needs of users while at the same time strengthening the framework for a healthy industry. Such a requirement implies the provision of up-to-date and comprehensive information on the progress of the economy in general and of the transport markets in particular. The basic objective is the creation of a framework in which market developments can be analysed in a format which can directly assist policy discussions, particularly policy dealing with:

(i) bilateral freight licences for traffic between Member States;
(ii) the Community freight licences for traffic between Member States;
(iii) road freight pricing regulations;
(iv) commercial co-operation between railways;
(v) inland waterway capacity.

In designing and building the system recommended, it is necessary to identify the information needs of the different parties involved in policy discussions. The needs of public authorities, including the Commission, are the monitoring of short-term trends, and information for medium-term planning. Enterprises need general market information, and information on medium-term developments as an aid for investment planning. In addition, the availability of better information will be equally useful to trade and industry and to representatives of transport workers' unions.

Of the different policy instruments available to public authorities in structuring the transport market, perhaps those concerning pricing, capacity and crisis management are of the most immediate relevance. It is to these instruments that most consideration has been given in developing the initial scope and structure of the indicator system. As the detail of these instruments will continually evolve, it has been necessary to anticipate the range of information which might be required in future years. However, while it is important to anticipate future information requirements, it is equally important to know the current state of the market. Since the accuracy of the indicator system improves with experience, it is more efficient to begin immediately and to allow the system to evolve on the basis of both practical experience and the changing policy framework.

In order to meet the information requirements of the different parties involved, and to ensure that this information is directly relevant to the three policy instruments, indicators of market structure, enterprise performance and social trends, especially employment, are necessary. The simplest and most effective way of presenting the essential information is by means of three reports:

(i) a quarterly transport report on the current situation;

(ii) an annual report assessing both the recent trends and forecasts for the following year;

(iii) a periodic medium-term report, presenting forecasts for a five-year period.

Table 24.1 shows the interrelationship between the users' requirements, the reports which will be presented and the indicators.

TABLE 24.1   MARKET OBSERVATION: INFORMATION AND PRESENTATION

Public authorities as 'users', require	Reports presenting essential information	Indicators required to meet needs of 'Users'
(i) To know current trends quickly	Quarterly Transport Report	(i) Based on the proposed Transporter Inquiry Survey and other indicators available quickly
(ii) To assess the overall balance between supply and demand		(ii) Comprehensive analysis based on market structure enterprise and social indicators
(iii) To know the changes needed in capacity	Annual Report (current trends and demand forecasts for one year ahead)	(iii) Trends in current utilisation of existing capacity linked to forecasts of likely changes in foreign trade
(iv) To know the trends in prices		(iv) Enterprise indicator (price and input cost indices)
(v) To monitor secular changes in freight transport between member states	Medium-term report	(v) a periodic five-yearly strategic analysis

V   ECONOMIC COST

In Community policy, competition is the basis for assuring the best allocation of economic resources in meeting society's transport needs. The corollary of this is:

(i) free choice for the user;
(ii) autonomous decisions by transport enterprises operating on commercial profitability;
(iii) freedom of establishment.

Transport activity takes place in the context of free movement of goods and people within the Community and free currency convertibility. Underlying these commercial activities is the acceptance of certain notions of financial and economic costs. These notions are shared by the Community's Member States in common with other members of the OECD. Other economic systems do not necessarily share this market structure or apply the same notions of economic costs. This difference in approach in economic philosophy causes friction in commercial life where economic agents of different systems meet.

The shipping sector is an example of an area in which practical difficulties are being encountered. The European Community is concerned with the question of how to come to grips with non-commercial shipping competition from state trading countries. The Community's shipowners and indeed shipowners in the whole of the OECD are faced with the enormous expansion of the general cargo fleet of some state trading countries and the aggressive competition practices which only state trading enterprises can apply over a long period of time. The objective of these practices seems to be to penetrate Community liner shipping markets.

In the bilateral trades the USSR applies the principle of selling CIF and buying FOB. This restrictive practice is reinforced by the fact that Community shipping companies cannot establish their own agencies in these markets. Everything is channelled through state transport agencies. At the same time, state trading shipping agencies may establish themselves in the Community. Consequently, as far as bilateral trade is concerned, Community carriers are placed in a totally artificial and restrictive position.

Competition between Community carriers and state trading companies is equally severe in other market areas. It is not unusual to find that price competition from state trading enterprises is artificial with some conference rates being undercut by more than 40 per cent. This 'loss-leader' or 'traffic-creaming' approach can be carried on for as long as it is necessary to build up the traffic volume required to fill the ships serving a particular trade. Furthermore, the importance placed by state trading countries on foreign exchange leads to an artificially high shadow price.

The consequences of these practices are, first of all, to inflict direct loss of income on competition, with a consequent gradual erosion of financial resources; and secondly, there is a weakening of the liner conferences to which most of the companies belong. The discipline of the market, operating on a profit and loss basis, does not apply to state trading shipping companies. They operate in an environment where costs and prices are centrally determined and where the notion of competition is non-existent. Furthermore, many of the cost elements borne by a private shipping company are, in those countries, borne by the state.

The present situation is not acceptable to the Community. It is necessary, therefore, to find some adjustment factors which will put competition between private enterprises and state trading shipping lines on a more equal footing. As a first concrete measure in seeking this new accommodation, the Transport Council has decided that from 1 January 1979 the Member States will monitor the liner trades between the Community and Central America and between the Community and East Africa. All liner operators in these trades, whether members of liner conferences or not, are asked to supply information regularly on the establishment, motivation or expansion of liner services. They must also provide information on the cargo carried and the average freight rates by carrier paid for selected commodities which are important in these trades.

Further action is to see how national legislation can be utilised in common to achieve a balance and to reduce the unacceptable levels of penetration by non-commercial practices. In other trades between OECD countries and state trading countries, a quota system applies.

VI AIR TRANSPORT

Last June, the Commission approved a memorandum to the Council on air transport services within the Community. This memorandum deals with the question of how air transport services within the Community can be improved and developed. It starts from the view that the time is right for a series of initiatives which can help adapt air services to suit modern conditions and to take advantage of recent important changes in civil aviation on a world scale.

Four broad objectives underlie the suggestions made in the memorandum. The first is the development of the most comprehensive possible network of air routes accompanied by efficient services at prices as low as possible without discrimination. The second concerns the development of a sound financial basis for the airlines, reducing their operating costs and increasing their productivity. Thirdly, the interests of workers employed in the industry should be safeguarded in the general context of social progress, including the elimination of obstacles to free access to employment. Finally, air transport should develop in ways which take account of public concern with the environment (and particularly noise), regional development and the rational use of energy.

The memorandum deals with five types of implementing measures for short- and medium-term action aimed at achieving the four objectives mentioned above.

1 Lower fares and greater flexibility in services

The Commission has suggested that as an initial step, the Member States should ask the airlines to introduce travel arrangements permitting a reduction of tariffs on the most important air routes, preferably in a multilateral framework. These arrangements could provide for:

(i) the introduction of a third class fare;
(ii) special fares for a limited number of seats on condition that the fare is paid in advance and is not refunded or only partly refunded if the passenger decides to postpone his flight;
(iii) a basic no-frills point-to-point ticket for which additional services such as reservation, interchangeability, etc. could be purchased;
(iv) the offer of a specified percentage of weekly capacity available on certain routes at a fare not exceeding 50 or 60 per cent of the economy class fare;
(v) a European roundtrip ticket;
(vi) general implementation of standby tariffs.

In Community arrangements, it would be envisaged that if airlines are reluctant to introduce these reduced tariffs, the governments responsible should allow the establishment of a limited number of services at these tariffs by other operators on the routes in question.

One radical means of opening the way for innovation in scheduled air services between the Community countries might be arrangements to grant rights to an airline of a Community country, which was prepared in its own commercial judgement and with the consent of the licensing authorities of its own country, to introduce new links with another country or to offer services of a new type (accompanied by fare and marketing innovation). The receiving Community country should not, after a certain consultation period, be able to refuse permission.

Under the heading of 'increased flexibility', the Commission is also examining possible steps for the development of new cross-border services connecting a larger number of regional centres in the Community countries. In the area of non-scheduled services (charters, etc.), it is hoped to find ways of extending their scope and removing obstacles, thus increasing the range of cheap travel opportunities available.

2 Competition rules

The Commission at present lacks the means to ensure that the airlines regularly and effectively comply with the rules of competition which apply to air transport. In this sector, unlike other economic sectors, there is no regulation providing for an investigation procedure and penalties for conduct causing distortion of competition. To remedy this, the Commission intends to propose the adoption by the Council of an appropriate implementing regulation, which would facilitate the investigation of restrictive practices or abuse of dominance on air transport markets where there is little or no State intervention. As regards air services affected in various degrees by State intervention, the Commission's endeavour to bring greater flexibility into the structure of civil aviation will correspondingly broaden the scope for competitive conduct on the part of both airlines and States.

Other measures which could be taken under the heading of 'lower fares and more flexibility' include a common approach to co-ordination of State aids for airlines, respect for the principle of right of establishment in the air transport sector, the reduction of directional differences in tariffs arising from exchange rate fluctuations and a compensation scheme for passengers affected by overbooking by airline companies.

3 Measures to reduce operational costs of airlines

Under this heading, the Commission intends to promote the simplification of procedures and documents used in international air freight transport especially in the framework of the programmes for the achievement of customs union and fiscal harmonisation. Further possibilities for cost savings by airlines lie in the field of technical standard harmonisation for aircraft and work has already started in this sector.

4 Action affecting staff

The Commission has initiated a comparative study on working conditions in the air industry within the Community and will decide on what action to take in the light of the results of the study. Steps will also be taken to bring about the mutual recognition of qualifications of aircrews and ground staff.

5 External relations

The Commission believes that it is important to identify in good time the problems of common interest which could arise in relations between Member States and third countries in air transport. This is why it has proposed that the Council set up a consultation procedure between Member States and the Commission on air transport questions dealt with in international organisations and on negotiations with third countries.

6 Implications for the aerospace industry

An increase in air transport activity should give rise to additional demand for aircraft of which the European aircraft industry should be able to take advantage. The Commission seeks to encourage and support research connected with the development of new aircraft. It will also stimulate contacts between the airlines and the manufacturers to allow the industry to benefit from the operating experience of the airlines and to take account of their future requirements.

VII TRANSPORT INFRASTRUCTURE

Turning to transport infrastructure, the time horizon changes. Market observation covers a period of from one to five years ahead. Transport infrastructure analysis requires a time horizon which can, in some cases, stretch into the early years of the next century. Major constructions often take a decade or so to complete so that the assessment of their costs and benefits has to deal with factors and influences which come into play at points well into the future. Even the construction cost analysis, which in traditional terms is the easier part of the exercise, often becomes extremely difficult because the cost will run over a long period of time. Operational costs enter into force only after the basic construction has taken place and these, together with the benefits accruing from the new infrastructure, have to be assessed a long time into the future. Infrastructure investment usually deals with a considerable sum of resources. The executive decision must be taken at a given point in time. Given the great unknowns and, until recently, the lack of analytical tools, these decisions were often based on considerations more closely linked to contemporary influences at the moment of decision than on the likely outcome of the actual work in question.

The nature of the influences operating on infrastructure decisions has changed and indeed widened in recent years. The traditional task of decision-makers in this area was to meet the growing demand for transport in an optimal manner, given the available resources. Infrastructure decisions dealing with particular modes of transport were often taken in isolation and were concerned essentially with the capacity requirements for the particular mode now and in the future. Now the trend is towards a multimodal approach and an assessment of the overall infrastructure requirements created by the growing demand for transport in an integrated manner.

The complexity of the task facing the decision-maker is increased by the uncertain economic environment in which we live. One can envy those who in the past had to take similar decisions in an atmosphere of steady and continually rising economic growth. Now, we are faced with uncertainty not only about the demand for transport but about such fundamental inputs as the availability of energy and its cost.

Public opinion is increasingly concerned with environmental conditions. The simultaneous execution of projects for different modes of transport in regions with high population density can raise concern about basic land use considerations. Considerations such as these have lent greater emphasis to the integration into the decision-making process of objectives other than those related solely to transport demand.

Transport infrastructure investment is often influenced by economic policy dealing with the trade cycle. In a period of recession, infrastructure investment can be used as a boost to the general level of economic activity. This economic role for such investment can be broadened when new infrastructure is used as an instrument for promoting economic development, as for example in helping disadvantaged regions to 'take-off industrially'.

These instances, which are by no means exhaustive, serve to illustrate the growing complexity of what was originally purely a transport decision. Our greater consciousness of the economic forces at work and the widening of the policy considerations have served greatly to increase the complexity of the analysis underlying any major infrastructure project. The economist is therefore faced not only with trying to estimate the long-term demand for infrastructure but also with reconciling the frequently conflicting objectives which must be taken into consideration in making the initial decision.

VIII TRANSPORTATION MODELLING

Some of the work done for the Community on the estimation of the long-term demand for freight transport and the consequences of this demand for infrastructure requirements will now be examined. However, it would first be useful to recall the Commission's role in infrastructure development. The Commission concentrates on looking at infrastructure at the Community level. This requires consultation about national investment plans and co-operation between different Member States.

The Council of Ministers' decision in February 1978 has widened the scope of the Commission's action in the field of transport infrastructure. Amongst other tasks, the Commission has the obligation to formulate a response to infrastructure needs at the Community level. Furthermore, there are new possibilities for financial intervention at Community level which can help in the execution of infrastructure projects.

A major study to provide estimates of Community infrastructure requirements for freight transport on principal routes (road, rail and inland waterways), in the years 1985 and 2000 was begun in 1976. In this study, technical assistance was provided by the Netherlands Transport Institute (NVI). The structure of the model and the methodology used are discussed elsewhere in this book (Noortman, p. 322). The study gave an indication of the total growth in freight transport divided into growth for different commodity groups and for different modes. These forecasts were then translated into traffic movements from which the assignments were determined. Some of the results are shown in Tables 24.2–24.4.

The growth of total freight transport amounted to 70 per cent on the more pessimistic scenario of a 2 per cent GDP growth to the year 2000. The more optimistic scenario of a 5 per cent growth suggested an

TABLE 24.2 TOTAL FREIGHT TRANSPORT IN THE STUDY AREA (in million tonnes; 1974 = 100)

Category	1974		1985		2000/(2%)		2000/(5%)	
	Absolute	share	Absolute	share	Absolute	share	Absolute	share
Domestic transport								
absolute	8,168	95	11,383	94	14,020	92	21,336	87
index	(100)		(139)		(172)		(261)	
International transport								
absolute	400	5	716	6	1,256	8	3,067	13
index	(100)		(179)		(307)		(767)	
Total transport								
absolute	8,568	100	12,099	100	15,276	100	24,403	100
index	(100)		(141)		(178)		(285)	

TABLE 24.3   GROWTH FACTORS OF TRADE PER COMMODITY
GROUP 1963–72 AND FORECASTS 1974–85, 2000/(2 %), 2000/(5 %)

Period of growth	1963–72	1974–85	1974–2000/(2 %)	1974–2000/(5 %)
	%	%	%	%
1. Agricultural	14.53	5.67	3.78	6.72
2. Foods	10.00	5.90	4.20	6.89
3. Fertilisers	1.37	2.59	1.69	3.09
4. Minerals	8.99	6.55	4.51	7.44
5. Ore and metal residues	0.32	−1.37	0.47	2.49
6. Chemical products	17.96	13.56	9.00	14.32
7. Products of metal industry	7.57	3.93	3.76	7.37
8. Other agricultural products	5.48	5.86	4.04	6.48
11. Oil products	16.59	8.38	6.45	11.19
12. Cement lime	7.90	5,13	3.51	5.94
13. Other fabricated building materials	9.79	8.26	5,63	9.41
14. Other articles	12.55	9.19	6.26	10.14
Total all commodities (excluding 9 and 10)	9.86	7.15	5.37	9.44
Gross domestic product	4.56	3.84	2.78	4.51

TABLE 24.4   TOTAL TRANSPORT VOLUME AND NUMBER OF
TRAFFIC MOVEMENTS FOR INTERNATIONAL FREIGHT
TRANSPORT (units: in million: 1974 = 100)

	1974	1985	2000/(2 %)	2000/(%)
Rail transport:				
transport volume				
absolute	91.2	124.9	191.5	454.2
index	(100)	(137)	(210)	(498)
loaded-wagon movements				
absolute	3.9	5.9	9.0	20.9
index	(100)	(150)	(230)	(533)
Road transport:				
transport volume				
absolute	117.3	263.7	466.0	1,121.5
index	(100)	(225)	(397)	(956)

TABLE 24.4 (*Continued*)

	1974	1985	2000/(2%)	2000/(%)
loaded-lorry movements				
absolute	5.7	10.9	17.5	37.6
index	(100)	(191)	(307)	(656)
total lorry movements				
absolute	8.8	16.7	26.7	56.6
index	(100)	(188)	(302)	(641)
Inland waterway navigation: transport volume				
absolute	190.8	327.4	567.9	1,490.6
index	(100)	(172)	(298)	(781)
loaded-vessel movements				
absolute	0.3	0.5	0.7	1.4
index	(100)	(155)	(229)	(455)
total vessel movements				
absolute	0.4	0.6	1.0	2.0
index	(100)	(157)	(237)	(490)

increase of 185 per cent in total demand. There is an important implication for freight transport deriving from the two different scenarios. Within the total forecast, international freight transport always increased faster than domestic transport and this is independent of the formulated strategies.

Given the economic situation today and the uncertain prospects for the medium term, the interesting element is not the precise growth rates themselves but the sensitivity of the freight transport forecasts to the assumed economic developments. Important changes are possible in the different growth levels for major commodity groupings. With few exceptions, these developments are the continuation of structural changes in the production structure of Western Europe, changes which have already begun to take place. If these already apparent trends continue into the future, they will have a major influence on the structure of freight transport demand.

An important consideration in the development of policy is the modal split. The increase in the transport volume in each commodity group and the resulting changes in the composition of total freight transport demand have important implications for the modal split structure. The study assumed that price developments in the different cost categories will not give rise to changes in relative real transport costs. Consequently, the resulting estimates in changes in the modal split were limited to being a function of the change in the transport volume itself. An increasing transport volume can affect the modal split for each commodity group in two ways. Firstly, an increase in volume may be accompanied by an increase in consignment weight. Secondly, an increase in transport volume can by its scale affect the use of transport modes which have a relatively high technical transport capacity.

Based on these estimates, the transport volumes, by commodity grouping and by geographic relation, were translated into loaded traffic movements. This permitted estimates to be made for the infrastructure network through the assignment models. These basic results allowed us then to look at the sensitivity of different assumptions.

IX CONCLUSIONS

This paper began by emphasising a particular approach to the theme of international transportation systems. This approach is that of a user of economics and economic systems which can be directly applied in formulating policy initiatives particularly in that area of the common transport policy which deals with freight transport between the Member States. The paper has concentrated on two time horizons corresponding to market policy and infrastructure investment.

What has been described is a brief summary of a great deal of analysis being developed by the Commission's services and the Member States' experts and drawing on the technical expertise of a number of major research institutes throughout the Community. Emphasis has been laid on the need to integrate economic expertise directly into the policy process, both in its early formulation and in its later development. Such close integration is necessary for participants in the arts of decision-making and of economic analysis.

Discussion of Papers by Professors Rehbein and Noortman and Mr Burke*

Professor Wagener, opening the discussion, said that these papers treated their problems from the viewpoint of a capitalist market

* Mr Burke was not present at the Conference; his paper was presented by Dr Leydon.

economy or a socialist planned economy, with fundamental differences of opinion. He proposed to comment on some main themes in the papers – from his own viewpoint, which was not neutral but based on socialist economies.

Mr Burke defined the guiding principle of transport policy to be competition, with limited intervention by public authorities mainly in infrastructure. Professor Noortman however regarded railways as an instrument of Government. Neither paid adequate attention to the satisfaction of social needs by a planned and co-ordinated development of transport. One illustration of this was the contrast between reliance on political *responses* by the State to market information on stochastic processes in a capitalist economy, and transport science used as a planning instrument in a socialist economy. There were thus different accountancy and statistical requirements. Of course, if a socialist transport enterprise competed in the international transport market, it would find itself requiring the same sort of information as that described by Mr Burke.

Professor Rehbein examined the interrelations between location policy and transport from a socialist viewpoint. In freight transport it was necessary to minimise the total expenses of production plus transport. For passenger movement in towns, it was necessary to integrate location planning, general development plans, and transport plans. Both required infrastructure decisions in a long-term, social context. This did not correspond with the planned reduction of unprofitable transport branches as postulated by Professor Noortman.

Both Mr Burke and Professor Noortman emphasised problems of international transport policy, especially that of the EEC. Mr Burke listed the principles of free market economy; free choice of mode of transport; free access to markets; free conveyance; free convertibility of currencies. He was quite right in suggesting that socialist economic systems did not apply these principles. Professor Wagener was quite astonished at his view that this was not acceptable for the community – why should he be surprised that socialist shipping companies made use of their competitive advantages on the market? In fact, Mr Burke's suggestions amounted to a form of discrimination which was inconsistent with his own principles.

It was interesting to contrast the long-term forecasting methods used by Mr Burke and Professor Noortman, with methods that the GDR used – primarily because the Germans were able to base forecasts on processes relatively free from cyclical fluctuations. They did not, in fact, distinguish between planning and prognosis, since they were seen as part of the same process. As a result, even quite simple forecasting methods were able to achieve a high degree of accuracy ($\pm$ 10–20 per cent) except where economic problems such as energy shortages had not been foreseen, or when as sometimes happened technological enthusiasm led to ignoring the inertia of transport systems to rapid changes.

Professor Noortman examined the high degree of state involvement in transport enterprises, especially railways, which restricted competition within a free market economy. This raised some questions of interest also to socialist economies – if there were regional cost differences, how could one cope with a common tariff? What social-political and economic development functions should transport prices have?

Although the subject matter of the papers overlapped, in the event the subsequent general discussion on each of the three papers was distinct, starting with Professor Rehbein's paper. *Dr Tye* said that in his firm, they had recently discussed whether to have one single pool of typists, or spread the typists around the firm. There was an analogy here with the problems in Professor Rehbein's paper – should transport in society be allocated to individual organisations? This caused problems of excess capacity and shortages. Or should they combine into one big pool? This caused problems of large and bureaucratic management structures.

Professor Hunter noted that economic location theory had a long history, originating in German work; in modern form this theory could still be very useful. The aim of 'minimising transport' had been a Soviet objective for half-a-century, and one of the rules for achieving it was to minimise cross-hauls, e.g. goods wagons carrying steel passing each other en route. But such 'cross-hauls' might be necessary and sensible. Often they arose because one wagon was carrying – say – girders and the other carrying plate; these were different commodities. Even if the products were apparently the same, other conditions of the shipments might make them thoroughly justifiable from an overall economic point of view. So achieving the aim of minimising transport in practice required careful scrutiny of product categories and careful study of all relevant costs.

Mr Hayter queried whether major industrial concentrations should be planned around transport facilities, or vice versa. *Dr Andruszkiewicz* argued that the tendency for railway wagons, trucks, barges and ships all to increase in size and speed required a different policy to the relation between location and transport.

Dr Tsankov said that the most important difference between socialist and market economies was the way in which economic laws were applied in practice. For example, in socialism tariffs were used as an economic instrument for co-ordination, whereas in the market they were used as an instrument of competition.

Professor Rehbein had stressed that capitalist and socialist countries often had similar problems, but chose different solutions. In socialist countries research work – by Professor Khachaturov and others – had established a set of factors of location, with aims of distributing production and securing economic and cultural development over the whole country. The biggest difficulty was to balance this against the requirements to reduce transport costs by obtaining a location of industry closer to the raw materials, and also to utilise the advantages of planned regional and international division of labour.

The discussion next turned to Professor Noortman's paper. *Professor Noortman* himself commented that this research was all policy-oriented, so he had to accept that there would be different political approaches. But he was not convinced that there was a large gap between capitalist and socialist societies – either in their problems or their solutions. The philosophy in his paper (and that of Mr Burke) was that it was necessary to have an integrated model for long-term planning, involving national, sectoral and enterprise level simulation. The basic unit was that of the enterprise – and in both socialist and capitalist societies the biggest problem was labour management, not technology. There were no major differences in Government responsibilities for regional planning, location or minimising costs – Professor Rehbein's principles applied in West Europe also.

Decentralisation of transport was different from decentralisation of industry – the former depended very much on indirect management information because, inherently, management could not *see* transport as it was happening. His view was that the diseconomies of scale were more important than the economies.

Mr Hayter took this point further. The UK road haulage industry had many small units – which fitted in well with the very dispersed spread of origins, destinations and journey distances. Perhaps the implication was that we should be *promoting* small units.

Dr Lake said we should distinguish between economies of scale (e.g. an enterprise functioning in many areas) and economies of density (e.g. a railway running twice as many trains on a specific route). In general there were economies of density – certainly this was the Soviet experience – but not of scale.

Dr Tye commented that in the US the tendency was for the small independent operator to beat the large operator in competition. Public transport could not compete with the car, and railways could not compete with a single driver working his own truck – 20–30 per cent of US operators. However, even the capitalist economy was not entirely dominated by the market – for example, decision rules *within* enterprises were rarely based on market principles.

Professor Okano said that probably the transport sector within a market economy was the one in which there was least difference from a socialist economy. Specifically state regulation, and forecasting errors, affected them both.

Professor Wagener replied that he agreed that there were some common problems. On models, they often manipulated similar models on the same sort of computers. But the input data to such models were very different – more so for freight, less for passenger transport. Freight data were not 'forecast' but 'planned'.

Dr Bajusz pointed out that in Hungary national development plans had the same sort of 'binding' force as in other socialist countries, but plans at the enterprise level had a greater degree of choice of charter, employment of different transport agencies, etc. As a result, direct regulation was impossible, and there were some effects such as a recent spontaneous rapid growth in vehicles owned by enterprises so that they could move their own freight. From a social point of view this was a waste of resources, but very difficult to control – tariffs had little effect. Eventually they had success by persuading enterprises with their own fleets to join with each other – thus encouraging more effective management.

Professor Noortman said that there was no single answer to the optimum distribution of company sizes – it would be influenced by the structure of demand, economic growth, the nature of the commodities, and so on. To understand these problems properly required highly accurate, but highly disaggregated, information.

The conference came finally to Mr Burke's paper. *Dr Leydon* said that this paper outlined goals and the instruments to achieve them – considering competition as a means, not an end. The paper was basically an application of scientific method, involving models using statistics, econometrics and common sense. Professor Wagener's criticisms of the paper were not satisfactory, since they did not relate to the scientific aspects of the argument. Now it was not their intention to discriminate against the ships of the centrally planned economies, but he would say that competition was not necessarily comfortable, and it could happen that there were some knocks before the efficient solution was reached. He also disagreed with Professor Wagener when he implied a divergence between this paper and that of Professor Noortman – there was no conflict. For air transport, they had four objectives; lower fares; more flexible services; a competitive framework; care for the effects on transport employees.

It seemed ironic to him that the 'free market' economists were those who were most concerned with developing planning techniques. However, these techniques were not to dictate centrally, but so that they could influence the organic development of the economy.

Dr Antal queried the implications of the Treaty of Rome for maritime and air transport. *Dr Leydon* confirmed that the Treaty mainly concerned surface transport, though if there was unanimity air and sea problems could begin to be tackled.

Professor Seidenfus argued that it was not correct that the Commission should undertake political decisions in this area. Only the Council of Ministers had that right. The Commission should confine its role to preparing memoranda – actually most of its suggestions had not been accepted by the Council. There were still major unsolved problems – traffic licences, pricing, subsidies. 'Competition' could not be achieved because the underlying conditions had not been fulfilled. With the exception of West Germany, not one single member country had a properly integrated multimodal policy at Government level. Nor did a 'Common Transport Policy' exist. Mr Burke's paper reflected the ideas of some of the Commission's economists, but was no help for policy.

Dr Leydon replied that Professor Seidenfus had ignored progress achieved in the Common Transport Policy. For example, road tariff rules (both obligatory and reference) and legislation touching on railways. The Commission was part of the policy-formulating institutions of the Community and therefore had need of the best information systems in executing its role. There was however a need for healthy scepticism when working with sophisticated models. Good data were essential, but there was a danger of 'horse and rabbit stew'[1] – spending 90 per cent of the effort on data collection and only 10 per cent on analysis. It should be the other way round.

[1] *Editor's Note.* A traditional recipe for horse and rabbit stew: one horse, one rabbit. The point is that the rabbit does not greatly influence the taste.

25 The Importance of Organisational Forms of Integration in the Field of International Transport

STEFAN TSANKOV

I INTRODUCTION

Transport appears to be the material basis for the processes of the international division of labour and the constant expansion of economic, political and cultural links between states. Apart from this function of integration, transport also influences economic results. The degree of this influence depends on different characteristics of transportation such as speed, regularity, the preservation of the use value of transported goods and services offered to passengers.

With the growth of speed of transported goods, conditions are created for intensification of the reproduction processes in international terms and for economy of working capital invested in transported goods, thus increasing the economic efficiency of international division of labour. An increase in the speed of passenger transport leads to extra working and/or free time, which increases the potential wealth of man and of mankind. The absolute and relative reduction of transport expenses in the transportation of goods and passengers furthers the growth of economic efficiency in international division of labour.

Therefore it is clear that the improvement of the different qualities of transport connections between separate countries positively influences the results of their multilateral relations. Transport brings closer the different peoples and in this way fulfils a peaceful historical mission in world development.

As transport links are improved, there is an increase in the economically justifiable distance over which goods, especially bulk, cheap cargoes, can be moved. Taking into consideration the positive results obtained by improving transport links, the following question arises: what measures have to be taken and in what way so that the positive influence of transport on economic and other relations between different countries can be increased? One of the basic measures that could contribute to this is integration in the field of international transport, i.e. the establishment of close bilateral or multilateral production co-operation between two or more transport enterprises of different countries. The organisation of different forms of integration will enable each partner to achieve its goals more successfully and with a reduction in operational expenses. When production forces are organised at an international level, they can be used more rationally, and at the same time integration brings closer co-operation between the transport enterprises involved.

The organisation of joint activities in the field of transport is also connected with scientific and technical progress. This progress breeds a number of technical problems for the national transport enterprises which may be solved more successfully on an international basis. This is so because the development of science and technology in modern times requires considerable financial means, a modern experimental basis and highly qualified scientific cadres. The provision of these conditions is beyond the powers of small countries, so it would be more profitable if these problems were solved jointly. That is why integration and co-operation in scientific-research activities in the field of transport between the planned economy countries is of vital importance.

The necessity of establishing co-operation in the field of international transport proceeds from the essence of its production process and from the spatial parameters of its organisation and management. This kind of co-operation is necessary because transport means of one country move on the territory of other countries. Thus, relationships between the respective transport enterprises have to be established, and periodically reassessed.

II INTEGRATION OF TRANSPORT IN PLANNED ECONOMY COUNTRIES

As the transport of goods and passengers increases, it is necessary to improve the quality of transport. At the same time, conventional forms of co-operation should be replaced by modern forms, with the integration and joint operation of international road, water and air services. The nature of the relationships between socialist countries offers many opportunities for the development of integration within the field of transport.

The co-ordination of international transport plans between planned economy countries is aimed at the rational use of transport, the reduction of transport expenses and an increase in the speed of delivery. The co-ordination is expressed in the optimal distribution of goods transportation between the different modes of transport. The cargo flows: the physical volume of goods, their structure, seasonal character and directions are compared with the existing production capacities of the different modes and, according to the needs for development, a system of undertakings is envisaged with a view to ensuring the necessary traffic, handling and transportation capacity for the realisation of transport-economic connections between the different socialist countries. Thus the co-ordination of transportation plans contributes to establishing and maintaining optimal proportions between the development of national transport systems, the different modes of transport in the socialist countries, and the needs for international goods and passenger transportation. According to the spatial flow of cargo and passengers, the co-ordination of transportation plans is done on a bilateral basis for neighbouring countries and at a multilateral level for transit and combined transportation.

Different forms of joint operation are used in road, water and air transport. In international railway transport the following more important forms of joint operation of transport and equipment are used: common wagon stock, the ferryboat complex 'Varna-Ilichovsk', the joint operation of containers and the European pallet pool.

One of the most important forms of integration is the common wagon stock, founded in 1964. The goods wagons are of the same technical-operational qualities, as this is a necessary condition for the principle of 'natural compensation' in their joint operation. Each railway administration preserves its right of property ownership, but operational ownership is internationalised. When wagons pass on to the railway lines of other administrations, they fall to the operational ownership of that railway administration. This form of integration contributes to a reduction in the empty running of goods wagons, both in international and domestic traffic, and also their circulation is accelerated. This brings additional production advantages in the more rational use of the traffic capacity of the respective international railway lines and of the crossing border points, and the transportation capacity of railway transport increases. All these advantages lead to reduction in the prime cost of railway transportation.

Another organisational form of integration is the international society for the transportation of goods in large containers, called 'Intercontainer', founded in 1967. This society includes railway administrations of both planned and market economy countries. Its purpose is to assist the development of container transportation. The society owns container carriers and grants them to its members for the transportation of large containers. The internationalisation of production forces creates conditions for their rational use.

The organisation of forms of joint operation in international airlines is widely used between the aeronautical enterprises of the socialist and capitalist countries. The pool is the legal basis of integration between airlines. It represents a contract between two or more aeronautical enterprises, by means of which the principles and conditions for joint operation of given air services are determined with a view to creating possibilities for two-way, rational use of the passenger capacity or the cargo capacity of aircraft, thus achieving maximum economic results for each pool partner. The pool form of joint operation of a given air service prevents competition between enterprises participating in its operation and creates conditions for the establishment of co-operation between them. This co-operation finds expression in a co-ordinated commercial and tariff policy, mutual assistance, etc. With this form of integration it is very important to design the economic mechanism of the pool correctly, i.e. to determine the system of economic and operation indices and targets which stimulate each partner to participate actively in the fulfilment of the pool programme, and to achieve a fair distribution of the economic results among the pool partners.

Another organisational form of integration is the joint construction of projects of international transport importance. One of the first projects, built by the CMEA countries, is the 'Bridge of Friendship' on the Danube river between Russe–Giurgeu. This bridge increased the traffic capacity of the railway border point tenfold, and contributed to the further development of transport-economic links between the People's Republic of Bulgaria and other countries. The road networks of the People's Republic of Bulgaria and the Socialist Republic of Romania are also connected by the bridge.

III CONCLUSIONS

The different forms of joint activities in the field of international transport are being constantly improved with a view to adjusting them to current conditions. In future it should be possible to internationalise not only the operational, but also the property ownership of transport means which will lead to increased production cooperation between the different transport enterprises.

The same is valid for the development and improvement of the integration of separate modes of transport. It is possible and at the same time necessary gradually to integrate the national transport systems of the socialist countries into a unified international socialist transport system. This system will be built by means of co-ordinated development of the material and technical basis of the national transport systems in the socialist countries, which will make it possible to establish and maintain optimal operation interaction between them. This interaction is an important condition for the satisfaction of the constantly growing needs of goods and passenger transportation between socialist countries, and in the further deepening of the international socialist division of labour.

The development and improvement of the different integration forms in the different modes of transport, and the gradual building of a unified international socialist transport system will turn international transport into an important factor which will ensure normal integration processes between the respective branches of the people's economies in the socialist countries, and increase their economic efficiency.

26 Material Relations and Transport Policy in the Czechoslovak Socialist Republic

KAREL VITEK

I INTRODUCTION

Planned and effective supply is an essential component in the development of planned economies. It is a subject of great importance and the most recent congresses of the Communist Party of Czechoslovakia as well as the plenary sessions of the Central Committee of the Communist Party of Czechoslovakia have stated the need for improvement in this area. Similar situations exist in other centrally planned states, and the Xth International Symposium of Material and Technical Supply is just one example of the way in which COMECON countries are co-operating in finding solutions to technical problems of improving supply.

The volume and importance of the circulation of means of production is increasing due to the following factors:

(1) The continuous development of production leads to intensified social division of labour.
(2) The volume of merchandise in circulation is increasing steadily.
(3) The increasing volume of production is characterised by a continuous extension in the range of products.
(4) Planned expansion in international specialisation in production, including both economic integration between planned economies and increasing international trade, leads to qualitative and quantitative alterations in the circulation of goods.

The development of the flow of materials in the Czechoslovak Socialist Republic is shown in Figure 26.1.

In the Czechoslovak Socialist Republic, the index of material flow in relation to national income is much higher than in other countries. This is due to a high level of consumption of materials, a high number of materials transport cycles during processing, irregularity in the sequence of production and usage and the regional structure of production and consumption. In view of this situation, the government has implemented a programme to rationalise handling, transport, packaging and storage. Transport policy plays an important part within this programme.

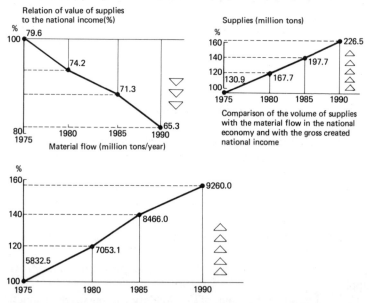

Figure 26.1   Development of supplies in the Czechoslovak Socialist Republic

II MAIN PRINCIPLES OF THE GOVERNMENT'S TRANSPORT POLICY

Division of labour has proceeded rapidly within transport during the twentieth century with the development of new means of transport: road, air, city mass transportation and pipelines. A special form of the division of labour is between public and works transportation. As specialisation continues within individual transport sectors, productivity increases but at the same time management becomes more complex. Management of the total transport system is carried out with the aim of satisfying the transport requirements of the national economy and of the population with maximum social effectiveness. This represents a considerable challenge, not only because of the intricacy of the system, but also because of the organisational structure of transport.

The basic content of the government's transport policy is to intensify the integration of transport by creating a unified transport system within the State, which will also link up with the systems of COMECON and other countries. A unified transport system is a planned, optimally developed system of the modes and sectors within public transportation, regardless of the technology involved and of the role played by transport (whether it contributes to production or consumption).

The basic purpose of transport policy is to create conditions for an optimum division of transport labour among the individual sectors and forms of transport and also for their development as organic links of the uniform transport system. At the same time, it is necessary to remember the non-economic factors, such as comfort, speed and frequency of service, which influence the choice of mode in passenger transport.

The government's transport policy involves action in the following areas: management and organisation, the introduction of progressive transport systems, the development of transport in conurbations and the nationalisation of suppliers' and customers' relations. The introduction of transport systems involves co-operation between single forms of transport. In this context, containerisation and the movement of part-loads are of special importance. The rationalisation of goods transport calls for the creation of closed transport systems so that transport requirements throughout the State are met. This involves the introduction of unconventional means of transport, which at present play only a small part in the total transport system. The rationalisation of public road transport organisation is to be investigated, especially the possibility of integrating public road transport and city mass transportation into a common-interest group which would jointly organise transport.

III SOME TRANSPORT SYSTEMS IN THE CZECHOSLOVAK SOCIALIST REPUBLIC

In Czechoslovak terminology, a transport system is a higher level of the organisation of a form of transport in a given region which will constitute an element in an integrated transport system. The whole

TABLE 26.1 GOODS TRAFFIC AND SERVICES OF PUBLIC CONVEYANCE AND WORKS TRANSPORTATION

Index	1965	1970	1975	1976	1977
	metric tons (thousands)				
Total goods traffic	800,259	944,656	1,274,072	1,329,779	1,364,258
of which: public conveyance	418,185	467,375	579,380	598,381	599,018
of which: Czechoslovak State Railways	218,527	236,876	271,413	275,548	274,319
Czechoslovak State Automobile Transport	195,578	226,011	302,284	316,940	318,256
river tranposrt	4,056	4,464	5,654	5,866	6,418
air transport	24	24	29	27	25
work transportation	382,074	477,281	694,692	731,398	765,240
	ton-kilometres (millions)				
Total services in ton-kilometres	66,079	73,556	86,913	89,649	91,607
of which: public conveyance	62,677	68,301	79,192	81,434	82,756
of which: Czechoslovak State Railways	56,904	60,995	69,271	70,748	71,550
Czechoslovak State Automobile Transport	3,573	4,838	7,296	8,076	8,454
river transport	2,172	2,434	2,580	2,568	2,709
air transport	28	34	45	42	43
works transportation	3,402	5,255	7,721	8,215	8,851

TABLE 26.2   PIPELINE TRAFFIC

Index	Metric unit	1970	1972	1973	1974	1975	1976	1977
Oil pipeline Družba								
Total tons transported	thous. tons	13,371	16,817	15,673	14,665	14,868	17,164	17,749
of which: for Czechoslovakia	thous. tons	9,236	11,963	14,091	14,141	14,239	16,562	17,127
Total tkm performed	mill. tkm	6,364	7,867	8,029	6,772	4,404	8,663	8,990
of which: for Czechoslovakia	mill. tkm	4,994	6,265	7,507	6,599	4,197	8,464	8,785
Transit gas line								
Transport of gas	mill. m³	—	—	—	—	—	—	19,608
of which: for Czechoslovakia	min. m³	—	—	—	—	—	—	1,009

TABLE 26.3   TRANSPORT OF GOODS ACCORDING TO TYPE OF PRODUCT

	Transport of goods, 1977 (thousand tons) by:			Average transport distance (km) by:		
	Rail	Road (CSAT)[a]	Works road transport	Rail	Road (CSAT)[a]	Works road transport
Total traffic	228,629	318,256	765,240	229.1	26.6	11.6
of which:						
(0) solid fuel	81,065	9,226	30,573	214.1	20.4	8.8
(1) crude oil, tar and tar products	14,007	622	8,774	243.8	64.3	37.7
(2) ores, metallurgical and engineering products	37,344	5,676	23,521	301.2	81.0	22.0
(3) minerals	9,506	3,950	28,807	219.7	14.2	4.6
(4) building materials	44,099	241,463	501,692	173.8	12.4	7.7
(5) timber	8,675	1,048	20,592	235.4	127.7	20.1
(6) grain, foodstuffs, livestock	6,552	16,381	47,033	265.9	50.8	27.7
(7) root fruits	2,545	6,816	1,920	129.5	18.6	15.4
(8) other goods	23,144	27,452	102,328	265.5	114.4	19.9
(9) part loads	1,692	5,622	—	205.8	85.4	—

[a] CSAT – Czechoslovak State Automobile Transport

process involved in the movement of goods from shipper to consignee, including tariffs, means of transport and technical conditions, represents an integrated transport system. The development of the transport system in Czechoslovakia is shown in Tables 26.1–26.3. The State programme designed to develop progressive transport systems and to improve materials handling lays special emphasis on the following points:

(i) the development of containerisation and palletisation;
(ii) centralised loading and unloading of railway trucks;
(iii) the collecting service of the Czechoslovak State Automobile Transport for part-loads.

Total investments in this programme during the seventh five-year plan will amount to 2200 million kcs, of which about two-thirds will be devoted to transport. Reductions in costs of 50 to 80 kcs/ton should be achieved for internal transport, and 100 to 300 kcs/ton for international transport.

Apart from the transport systems mentioned above, attention is being paid to the development of a complex transport service for industrial centres and for regions, entailing the centralisation of reloading and warehouse facilities. Pipelines are also growing in importance, and the use of belt conveyance for bulk cargoes is increasing. Research into further unconventional forms of transport is continuing. Finally, internal forwarding is an important element in the development of transport systems. This activity is being developed on the basis of the principle: 'freight forwarder = designer and producer of transportation'.

IV CONCLUSION

The further development of transport systems in Czechoslovakia is based on the application of technology appropriate to the needs of the Czechoslovak economy. The exchange of information and experience with other COMECON countries continues, and has proved very valuable. At the same time, Czechoslovak practice has a number of practical results which might be of interest to other countries. For example, the Czechoslovak Association of International Hauliers – CESMAD – is an organisation of individual transport concerns involved in international truck transport. The management system of this organisation has led to a very rapid advance in this form of transport. KOMBITRANS is a common-interest association of manufacturers, forwarders and shippers, which is implementing the results of research, especially in the development of combined transport systems.

The planned economy offers optimum conditions for the development of progressive transport systems within the overall unified transport policy, and there is still much scope for further development.

27 Principal Problems of the Development of International Relations in the Transport Sector

G. ANTAL

I INTRODUCTION

A discussion of general current problems of international transport policy involves questions of the transport of people and goods, especially across national boundaries. This paper is concerned with aspects of international trade policy, and thus is confined to a discussion of freight transport.

The basic tenet of this paper is that international exchange is advantageous for everyone. No country, not even the greatest, can be economically self-sufficient. Participation in international division of labour is necessary, even for large countries, to sustain profitable production. Furthermore, the development of weapons has reached the stage where mutual destruction is possible. Sanity requires that arms are not used, leaving peaceful co-existence as the only alternative. The economic consequences of this are that national borders should not be closed; instead, international relations should be developed as far as possible in all fields of life. This was confirmed by the Helsinki Conference in 1975, and this paper concerns two questions which arose there: the need to intensify international economic and commercial relations, and the related problems of international transport relations.

The energy problem and the consumption of raw materials are two further aspects to be taken into account in considering the political and economic reality of our age. It has been predicted that oil resources will be exhausted within fifty to sixty years. At the same time, diminishing resources and growth in consumption, not only of oil but also of many other raw materials, are in inverse proportion to each other. The age of production based on cheap energy and raw materials is over. Production must now minimise the use of energy and raw materials, regardless of the ownership of the means of production. Finally, higher productivity is necessary to meet expectations of better living standards, with increased personal consumption, and the growing demand for more leisure time. All these factors lead to the conclusion that future economic development should be based on international trade.

International transport must exist to meet the needs of international trade. Therefore, international transport policy should be considered as part of the international economy.

II INTERNATIONAL TRANSPORT POLICY

Within any country, the transport policy implemented by the Minister of Transport will be concerned with the control and co-ordination of individual transport undertakings and the development of infrastructure to provide an appropriate transport system for the country's needs. The movement of imports, exports and transit goods completes the transport needs of a country's economy. Thus separating a country's international and national transport policy is merely an abstraction, as virtually every country has its own foreign trade and transit traffic.

It is obvious that international transport policy can differ greatly, depending on the part played by foreign trade in the national economy. Hungary, for example, realises about 50 per cent of her national income from foreign trade; this means that about half of the new values produced in a year are sold abroad and raw materials, means of production and consumption goods to an equivalent value are imported. At the same time the geographical position of our country offers an excellent possibility for carrying out East–West and North–South trade. The result is that the demand for transport within the country for international foreign trade, besides transit traffic, differs substantially.

The theoretical side of the question is covered by Marx (1907).

Quantities of products are not increased by transportation. . . . . But the use-value of things is materialised only in their consumption, and their consumption may necessitate a change of location of these things, hence may require an additional process of production in the transport industry. The productive capital invested in this industry imparts value to the transported products, partly by transferring value from the means of transportation, partly by adding value through the labour performed in transport.

If transport, as a labour activity necessary to be society, is a process which increases value, the values of goods and their price increase also. It is however understood that, as in any production process the social and not the individual value has to be considered, consequently not the greatest, but the least, possible use of labour is desirable.

Let us return to the original statement, that international transport policy has to be investigated not apart from, but in relation to, its aim, namely the change of location of goods. It is quite evident that transport companies must have an appropriate income for their activity. But on which level? The problem is equal for domestic and international transport in countries with both market and with planned economies.

There seems to be no real problem in this respect under clear market conditions, but practice has shown that even in planned economies there can be a discrepancy in the interests of the carrier and the owner of the goods. This is especially valid with respect to the import-export and transit traffic of a country. If there are no established multilateral tariffs which are applied, the level of rates can have a decisive influence on freight movements. Even the level of multilaterally determined tariffs is relevant in the question of whether that country purchases or sells a higher quantity of ton/kilometre services, calculated on the basis of that tariff level.

The interests of the cargo-owner are thus different from those of the carrier. The owner endeavours – and due to his position in the market he could not do otherwise – to decrease the freight costs borne by the goods.

It is virtually impossible to find a definition of freight policy in the international literature. However, freight policy is defined here as the totality of activities which aim to create the possibility of transporting goods from the place of despatch to the destination, by choosing the route, the means of transport and the intermediaries in order to minimise freight costs. These activities together constitute the forwarding industry.

International forwarders, by making use of the laws of the freight market and with the help of well-trained staff, are able to pursue a more efficient freight policy with better results than that of the single owner: in other words, they can secure a lower level of costs. However, their contribution still has to be paid for, but the total of freight expenses will be lower than if the cargo-owners had concluded the contract of carriage without the freight forwarder.

Therefore, each cargo-owner is exercising a freight policy, but the forwarder does this with a greater expertise, with a higher degree of knowledge and can also solve problems which could not be overcome by the cargo-owner alone. He can thus also discover new markets especially in international trade. The difference between the carrier and the cargo-owner is known as the discrepancy between transport policy and freight policy. This difference is settled as soon as the freight contract has been concluded between the carrier and the cargo-owner or, in other words, the principles of transport policy and those of freight policy have come to an identical denominator.

The question when, under which conditions, and in favour of whom the discrepancy between international freight policy and transport policy can be solved, depends on the combined influence of many factors. It depends basically on whether the total effects of the freight market and the goods market are resulting in a sellers' or a buyers' market. When trade is influenced by a sellers' market and, at the same time, the necessary transport capacity is not available, freight costs will increase. When there is a buyers' market and transport capacity is ample, this will of course result in the decrease of costs. In practice however there are many different combinations of these situations.

The basic task and the aim of transport policy is to meet the demands raised by freight policy. This signifies that in a planned economy, the objective laws of a planned and proportional development have to determine the dynamics of development of transport capacity in proportion to the increase in goods traffic. On the other hand, under market conditions the demand for transport capacity by the cargo owners should be met by the supply offered by the owners of transport firms.

It seems interesting to observe the present (1979) situation in Europe in this respect: it can be stated that the ideal mentioned above is not fully realised in either of the economic systems. In East European socialist countries the dynamics of economic development surpass the development of infrastructure and of transport capacity in general, whereas in Western European countries, especially since 1974, transport capacity exceeds the demands of cargo-owners.

The situation of international transport policy will now be investigated from the point of view of:

(i) tariffs,
(ii) the legal conditions governing transport, and
(iii) movement of goods,

with respect to different transport sectors.

III TARIFFS

1 Railways

Railway tariffs are generally set by the government. This situation is due to the position in the last century and early in this century, when railways were essentially in a monopolistic position. It is well-known that many countries consider the establishment of export-import tariffs promoting foreign trade as one means of protectionism. This can actually be considered as a new distribution of national income promoting capital invested in foreign trade. At the same time it should be remembered that there is great competition between the railways and the road haulage industry, and in most countries with market economies, the railways are in deficit. In planned economies, railway tariffs form part of the price policy implemented by the state, which is the owner of the means of production. In general, every country makes efforts to procure transit traffic, as this means an additional income with relatively low prime costs.

The Uniform Transit Tariff (ETT) is an achievement of countries with planned economies. It came into force in 1951, and was replaced in 1977 by the International Transit Tariff (MTT). The ETT not only promoted freight traffic between socialist countries, but also with those capitalist countries where it was implemented. The tariff level of the new MTT is in general double that of the former ETT and consequently has resulted in an increase of foreign trade costs for the cargo-owners. However, the general increase in prices which took place over the last twenty-five years inevitably had to be taken into consideration in these tariffs.

2 River navigation

In this context, discussion will be confined to the Danube. Countries on the Danube have created a uniform freight tariff, similar to the railway ETT tariff, signed in 1955 in Bratislava. The tariff is obligatory for transports of CMEA-countries on the Danube, but Yugoslav, Austrian and Bavarian navigation companies also comply with the agreement.

3 Road transport

Road transport constitutes a special case, as no obligatory tariffs have been established for international transport, so market competition is decisive.

4 Maritime navigation

In general, freight rates for bulk cargo carriers are agreed in the shipping exchanges, while for linear trade, navigation companies have joined in freight conferences. These conferences generally give good services, but sell their services at high prices with a monopolistic character. These high rates can only partially be offset by so-called outsiders, or in special cases, such as the traffic between Europe and the Far East on the Trans-Siberian route. The Code of Conduct for Liner Conferences set out by UNCTAD has not yet come into force, but if it is ratified, the author's opinion is that it will not eliminate the problems which it was intended to solve.

5 Air transport

The transport of goods by air is carried out on the basis of tariffs laid down by IATA. However, the situation is greatly confused, especially with the deregulation of tariffs decided recently in the USA. The airlines of CMEA-countries use a special tariff, called EAGT, for their mutual traffic.

On the whole, carriers are willing, depending on the prevailing market situation and the quantities of goods offered for transport, to grant rebates, reductions or reimbursements from the published tariffs.

IV LEGAL CONDITIONS GOVERNING TRANSPORT

The legal conditions which govern the rights and responsibilities of carriers are important in determining whether the interests of the carriers or of the cargo-owners have priority, or in other words, whether the interests of transport policy or of freight policy predominate.

1 Railways

Rail transport in Europe is governed by two conventions: the CIM and the SGMS. All European countries, apart from the Soviet Union and Albania, and some countries in the Middle East, are members of the CIM, which dates back to 1890. It gave great assistance to international trade, although in its earlier stage, it revealed signs of the railways' monopolistic situation. Even today the CIM can be considered disadvantageous for the owners of the goods. The change in the railways' position has not been recognised and thus there is scope for further responsibilities to be accepted by the railways.

The SMGS regulates the international transport contracts between the European CMEA and the Asian socialist countries. Compared with the CIM, the SMGS is in many aspects more advantageous for the cargo-owners, despite the fact that in this area road is obviously of less importance and represents no or very little competition to the railways. Otherwise, there are no important differences between the two conventions and soon after the SMGS came into force in 1951, it was suggested that they should be brought in line with each other or replaced by a single convention. The question has been dealt with by several authorities, including the Economic Commission for Europe of the United Nations, but for the time being it is rather difficult to tell when a positive solution can be expected.

2 River navigation

The Bratislava Convention regulates transport on the Danube, but it also regulates the responsibility of carriers.

3 Road transport

The CMR has been generally accepted in Europe. It ensures the co-ordination of the interests of carriers as well as cargo owners.

4 Maritime navigation

The Brussels Convention of 1924 regulates the worldwide responsibilities of maritime navigation companies. The convention is unilateral, basically protecting the carriers' interest, and therefore it is quite understandable that in 1978 a new convention, the so-called Hamburg Rules, was created, which – considering the development in technology – greatly widened the carriers' responsibility. This new convention has not been ratified as yet, but it can be considered a step in the right direction. In other words, transport policy yielded to the pressure of foreign policy.

In this context, the convention proposed by the UNCTAD to deal with multimodal transport should also be mentioned. The development of containerisation made this convention necessary. The draft of a convention will be considered in November 1979 by a Diplomatic Conference, but it will be several years before the convention is ratified.

5 Air transport

The legal conditions for air transport are regulated by the Warsaw Convention of 1929, revised in 1955 at the Hague. The alterations of 1955 took into consideration technological developments and they have considerably widened the carriers' responsibility with respect to flight safety.

V THE MOVEMENT OF GOODS

The effective change of location of goods, as an activity, the necessary social labour invested as a value-creating economic process and the legal expression of this, the contract of carriage, all represent the movement of goods. Transport policy will be considered here for different modes, bearing in mind that transport policy should correspond with the needs of freight policy. It is above all in this area that the difference between transport policy and the needs of cargo-owners, both in planned and market economies, becomes clear.

Railways

In planned economies, problems are arising due to the peak in demand for rail transport in the last quarter of the year. The important role of agriculture in these countries and the necessity to fulful the year's plan mean that the railways cannot meet the demands of cargo-owners. However, if sufficient rolling stock were acquired to meet the peak demands, it would be underutilised during the rest of the year.

In Western European countries, on the other hand, general overcapacity has resulted in the last few years, as the growth of commercial traffic was lower than estimated.

Diesel and electric locomotives are replacing steam locomotives in both planned and market economies. This is not only advantageous for the moment of goods, but also beneficial for the environment. Replacing the track is also necessary in some areas, so that the full capacity of trucks can be utilised. A further problem concerns transport between railways of different gauges, where appropriate transloading facilities are necessary. Arrangements should also be made by railways in co-operation with shippers and consignees to build railway sidings so that freight does not have to be unloaded twice.

2 River navigation

There is scope for increasing navigation on the Danube, but there is already a need for increased port capacity. The Danube will be connected to the Rhine by canal, probably in 1985. Problems will arise over tariffs and the control of traffic, and up to now the countries involved have made only negative statements. It is hoped that the parties involved will reconcile their differences so that the problems can be solved by the time construction is completed.

3 Road transport

The rapid increase in motorisation since the Second World War has forced individual countries to make large investments in the construction of highways. At the same time, lorries of a very large capacity are being built. Thus road transport represents strong competition to the railways, and has been especially successful in attracting general cargoes. Since the costs of building and maintaining highways are essentially borne by the state, road carriers are able to undercut the railways, and this has been compounded by the fact that road transport is much faster, and transloading is not necessary. The TEEM trains have proved to be successful, and the railways are undertaking modernisation programmes in their attempt to re-establish their position.

Maritime navigation

The situation prevailing in worldwide maritime navigation has proved that the forecasts of world development made by the shipping companies of countries with market systems prior to the crisis of 1975/76 were unrealistic. Tankers and bulk cargo carriers have the greatest overcapacity, and if the whole shipping market is considered, excess capacity amounted to 100 million tons deadweight in the summer of 1978, despite the fact that some vessels were not using their full speed, and that there had been recent improvements in the situation. The disproportional development in shipping capacity is largely due to the Western European shipping companies. However, the Soviet union and, to a lesser extent, Poland and the GDR have also developed their fleets. The tension in the shipping market has prevented an excessive increase in linear rates and, as far as the movement of goods is concerned, the demands of the cargo-owners have been met.

5 Air transport

The difference between development in Eastern and Western Europe can also be identified in air transport. Air transport in Eastern European countries is still in its early stages, and for several reasons, little cargo is carried as yet. With the exception of the Soviet AEROFLOT, airlines of socialist countries do not have large fleets at their disposal, and the increase in tourist traffic means that the capacity available is used mainly for passenger transport. Western European airlines handle much more cargo, especially on intercontinental flights. There is no doubt that this sector of transport has a good future, although freight costs are naturally much higher than surface transport.

VI CONCLUSIONS

A brief outline of transport policy relating to freight transport in Europe has been given, with the aim of showing the links between transport policy and international trade. The author's opinion is that these links exist within planned and market economies, and it is necessary that carriers and users should be aware of them.

The users generally make use of the services of a separate branch of the economy: the freight forwarders. The latter, while generally owning neither goods nor means of transport, act towards the cargo-owners as intermediaries of the services offered by the carriers: they are thus the cargo-owners' representatives and protect their interests. It could appear as though the freight forwarders were adversaries of the carriers.

This is of course not correct, as they are only in opposition to the carriers inasmuch as the natural interests of cargo-owners create a situation, where their interests differ from those of the carriers. The freight forwarder is of course in the same position, but at the same time his role as an intermediary and counsellor has the result that he is often able to arrive – based on the reasonable flexibility of both partners – at reciprocal concessions. In this way the transport of goods can be affected which – owing to the high transport costs – would not have found buyers without his contribution and thus no sales contract and no transport contract could have been concluded. The conscious freight policy made by the freight forwarder is therefore an indispensable factor in the international division of labour, and forwarders can be confident in their future.

REFERENCE
Marx, K. (1907). *Capital*, Volume II.

Discussion of Papers by Drs Tsankov, Vitek and Antal

Professor Rehbein, opening the discussion, said that transport policy, its theory and the relationships between transport and production were becoming much more important in socialist countries. These three papers, from Bulgaria, Czechoslovakia and Hungary, had some common findings. In summarising the findings put forth in the different papers he took the view that the following problems be discussed. There was a first group of five problems.

(1) Transport policy should never be treated exclusively in an abstract sense, but rather using a scientific approach in order to achieve transport/political objectives.
(2) As a consequence of increasing labour division and of co-operation resulting from this, interrelations between transport and production became more and more close and needed to be considered properly in all further investigations of transport science.
(3) Transport policy was of fundamental importance for state management and especially for the transport enterprises. Yet transport policy must always be based on integration into national economic policy.
(4) Transport and production must increasingly co-ordinate their relations according to *long-term* concepts and plans in the interest both of the whole national economy and of their own specific (technical and economic) requirements. Co-operation must then

not only be reached with regard to fundamental questions but also in practical and operational fields (for example co-ordination of different goods transport requirements).

(5) It was one of the utmost objectives of transport policy to increase the efficiency of the transport system. But this could only be achieved if the latest findings of science and technology were permanently applied to practical operations as well as to theoretical considerations regarding co-operation between transport and production.

A second group of problems referred to the internationalisation of production and transport relations.

(6) Transport, fulfilling its basic function of changing the place of goods, reached more than ever far beyond the borders of national transport systems, thus making higher demands on them and contributing to promote co-operation between the nations. National transport systems co-operated with transport systems of other countries having the same social foundation, but in addition they also co-operated with transport systems of different social orders according to the policy of peaceful coexistence.

(7) The international production and transport relations, based originally on linear routes, developed to cover a whole area. This required a combined utilisation of different transport modes (rail, road, water and air).

(8) Where social, technical, enterprise and economic conditions had matured, international enterprise ownership came into being and developed dynamically serving the purpose of an efficient utilisation of national means of production by the community of the respective transport administrations or countries concerned. The combination of national ownership of transport infrastructure with international enterprise ownership – in the socialist countries demonstrated by the common rolling stock of railway administrations, but increasingly also in other fields of the Council of Mutual Economic Aid – would become more important.

(9) The higher efficiency generally required in the utilisation of transport modes inevitably called for more rational utilisation of transport capacity, and reduction of idling on an international level.

(10) An all-round improvement of co-operation between transport

and production was of paramount importance for national and international transport policy. Such a concerted action would influence the national and international goods exchange in all branches of transport.

In a very short general discussion, most interest centred around Dr Antal's reference to the 'Freight Forwarder'. *Professor Seidenfus* said the freight forwarder was on the boundary of the transport system. He agreed with Dr Antal's description of his interests – but what was the difference for the forwarder between transport policy and freight policy?

Dr Antal replied that he thought the Freight Forwarder would have an enormously important and quite new role. He was typically an important and intelligent man, performing almost a magic function – unlike other agents, he did not solely represent one side's interests, but was able to resolve conflicts and smooth international trade.

Short comments on this issue were added by the following speakers, who also referred to transport and production relationships (*Professor Noortman*); progress towards integration (*Dr Bajusz*); the importance of sea ports (*Dr Andruszkiewicz*); relationships between western and eastern countries (*Professor Khachaturov* and *Dr Tsankov*); interaction between public transport and individual institutions (*Dr Vitek*).

The conference then moved to a final session where *Dr Goodwin* and *Professor Khachaturov* presented summaries of the papers and discussion throughout the whole meeting.

28 Themes and Conclusions of the Conference

THE DISCUSSIONS: P. B. GOODWIN

A recurrent motif in the conference was the need to consider very specific circumstances. The transport problems considered are special because of:

(1) Geographical conditions, which have their counterpart in the technical solutions which may be found.
(2) Socio-economic systems, which influence theories, aims, organisations, constraints and the institutional framework.
(3) Transport functions, arising from a specific structure of production and consumption, nature of commodities, length of journey, need for interchange and pattern of origins and destinations.

At each session, delegates pinpointed the distinction and differences peculiar to their own problems. It is quite clear that in many respects the problems found in the different countries are very different – and in some cases diverging, for example in the future role of rail transport.

However, it is always true to say of any problem that the answer 'depends on specific circumstances'. This is not always helpful, because any analytical approach depends on some degree of generalisation. Therefore the areas of common experience have a particular importance. Five general conclusions emerged so strongly and consistently that it is fair to describe them as being a consensus view. These were first, there is a need to consider transport as an integrated *system*, all the way from door-to-door, from origin to final destination. Therefore the relationships between air, sea, river, rail, road, pipeline, bus, metro and car transport – all of which were discussed – are particularly important.

It is necessary to make an efficient selection of which mode is most appropriate for a specific task, or – very often – which combination of modes. The latter condition requires efficient arrangements for interchange as an integral part of the transport system.

Secondly, it is necessary to consider transport in some way as part of the economy as a whole, with effects on the cost of production, economic growth, quality of life, protection of the environment and scarce resources, especially fuel.

Thirdly, new technologies and technical needs are becoming increasingly important – both those based on investment in large, advanced new infrastructure and those based on new, smaller, flexible ways of coping with the essentially *volatile* character of international trade.

Fourthly, human attitudes are important motors of change (and sometimes a barrier to it), whether in the management of institutions, selections of methods, desire for private cars, and so on. Finally, it is necessary to select carefully a cost structure which will promote efficiency, economic growth and other objectives.

Some of these points of agreement are at a very general level (though not trivially so: there are real questions of content involved, which are in some cases not even agreed in principle in national transport policies). Delegates did not reach agreement on all solutions to these problems. Indeed, a very healthy mark of the constructive and free nature of the discussions was the amount of disagreement expressed between and within national delegations. Four areas of difference appeared particularly important.

(1) How to *achieve* the desired efficient and integrated transport system. Some delegates from both West and East considered that the best way was by a high level of planning and regulation, arguing that only by such methods would it be possible to consider social (as distinct from commercial) costs, the needs of the economy as a whole, and the abolition of commercial antagonism between modes of transport and sectors of the economy.

Other delegates considered that the best way is by increasing competition, arguing that this would ensure that prices reflect costs, lead to a flexible and dynamic system, and automatically contribute to the development of the economy. These delegates argued that central planning may involve bureaucratic and slow practices.

The underlying question for both views is: under what conditions do decisions taken by individuals or firms in pursuit of their narrow aims, add up to the social optimum? It may well be that the attempt to impose competition when it does not naturally grow may involve an even greater bureaucratic and regulatory machine.

(2) There was disagreement on the role and methods of precise quantification and measurement of economic costs and benefits of transport investment. One group of delegates was particularly interested in the exact relative ratios of cost and benefit for alternative plans. For these, questions of how precisely to define 'optimum', 'costs' and 'profitability' arose sharply.

Other delegates were much more concerned with *general* strategic and political judgement of practical transport policies: such an approach is not antagonistic to measurement, but does not rely in the same sense on formal decision rules.

It was of interest that delegates from the market economies appeared to be more interested in the quantitative tools of economic evaluation of transport policies – even though sometimes those economies do not have the institutional framework enabling the easy application of their results.

(3) An area where agreement was only very superficial was that of prices. Most delegates stated that prices should be at a 'proper' level – but this was interpreted in many, incompatible, ways. It was suggested that prices be set according to: short-run variable costs; long-run costs including capital, social and external costs, values and effects; or simply at that level which achieves a planned level of consumption. There was also disagreement on what action should follow if a transport service is unprofitable or uncommercial.

(4) The last area of disagreement was about the reasons for the other disagreements. One approach was that the differences primarily arise from the socio-economic differences between planned and market economies and the attitudes and viewpoints of economists coming from the two social systems. The other was that in *both* types of economy there are tendencies of thought emphasising 'social' and 'market' approaches. The latter view is partly supported by consideration of who said what at the conference. Certainly it is quite impossible to be a transport economist in any country without coming sharply up against the same problems of pricing policy, conflict between individual and social objectives, and economic efficiency.

THE PAPERS: T. S. KHACHATUROV

The Conference considered many important questions concerning the economic development of transport in socialist and capitalist countries. In particular, we considered the reasons for the rapid expansion of road and air transport and the way it is edging out rail transport in internal communications. We also talked about the development of new means of transport, particularly pipelines, slurry pipelines, hovercraft and others. We touched upon the relationship between private and public transport. We discussed problems relating to the development of transportation methods for fuel and energy, and the opening-up of new areas by means of transport. We examined important tasks concerned with the increasing of efficiency in sea transport, and considered also the major organisational problems of transport.

The first group of papers was devoted to an analysis of the changing relationships between various forms of transport. Papers given by Professor Voigt (W. Germany), Professor Pegrum (USA), and Professor Okano (Japan) demonstrated the way in which transport by rail is being edged out by road transport for internal communications in the developed capitalist countries. The authors of these papers considered the reasons for this development and, in the case of the USA, of the squeezing out of railways by river transport. It was seen that this was a logical development. Moreover, it was the opinion of these speakers that this process should not be hindered. In Western Europe and in Japan, rail transport is largely in the hands of the State, or is at least supported by it. The speakers considered that the effectiveness of every mode of transport should be estimated in the light of real costs, and in particular that state intervention should cease, and that railways should be allowed to cut unprofitable lines and services. But unprofitable lines can be necessary sometimes for national economic needs. It was suggested in the discussion that modes of transport and their economic effectiveness should be evaluated not only according to the criterion of profitability. And it may be that the relative increase in road transport will be restricted by possible further increases in the price of fuel.

Professor Mitaishvili (USSR) and Professor Wagener (DDR) provided in their papers an analysis of transport planning in the socialist countries. Professor Mitaishvili demonstrated the role of the 'balance' method of accounting and the computation of costs in transportation planning, and dwelt on the prospects for their further development, taking into account new forms and means of transport. Professor Wagener explained the bases used in directing and planning a socialist transport system, and the subsystems of which such a system is formed, according to functional, territorial, technological, organisational and economic criteria, together with an explanation of various spheres of co-ordination and temporal horizons. As transportation in the USSR is distributed between various forms of transport, measures destined to improve planning and strengthen the effects of economic mechanisms, including the problem of increasing profits, assume a great importance. As far as the bases for management are concerned, then while one must on the one hand bear in mind those principles common to all socialist countries arising from socialist ownership of transport and national economic planning, one must equally consider the differences determined by, for instance, the various stages of completion of the transport system and variations in the degree of centralisation of management and planning.

One group of papers concerned itself with the theme of fuel transportation; these were given by Professor Hunter, Mr Dienes and Mr Bettis (USA), Dr Ivantsov (USSR), and Dr Lake (Canada). In the first of these an analysis was given of the importance of transportation of fuel and energy, of the factors affecting their economic viability in the context of growing consumption – and depletion – of fuel resources, and of alternative methods of conveying fuel and energy over long distances. The point is to find the best relationship between methods of transport and the areas of production and consumption of fuel and energy. Mentioned in the discussion were the possibility of moving energy-intensive industries nearer to fuel sources, the task of economising fuel and stockpiling resources with this aim in mind, as well as the possibility of using other types of energy, such as atomic and eventually thermonuclear energy, as well as solar, wind, tidal and other forms of energy. All this may have a significant influence on all questions concerning the transportation of fuel.

Dr Ivantsov's paper on the effectiveness of gas pipeline transportation in the USSR provoked a lively discussion. Questions were raised about the comparative effectiveness of pipeline and other forms of transport as far as cost and capital investment were concerned, about permissible pressure-levels in pipelines and their optimum diameter, about the construction of slurry pipelines, the possible distances over which slurry can be transmitted, and also about pneumatic container pipelines. Discussion arose also from Dr Lake's paper on the effectiveness of fuel transportation over long distances. Attention was drawn to the fact that in Canada a number of railway lines are running at less than full capacity, so that the installation of slurry pipelines and the introduction of new lines of communications are not viable.

There were many contributions in the group of papers dealing with transport in inaccessible regions. Professor Zaleski (Poland) and Professor Burkhanov (USSR) gave papers on transport in the Arctic; and we also discussed papers from Dr Ginn, Dr Kresge and Dr Gray on 'Alaska: planning a transport system and development'. During the discussion we heard about working conditions as far as land and sea transport in the Arctic are concerned, building railways and pipelines in permafrost, navigation in the Arctic seas and transport underneath the ice. Questions were raised about the economic viability of conquering the Arctic, the required capital investment, and the use of natural resources, the need for which is becoming more and more acute.

Professor Seidenfus (FRG), Dr Bajusz (Hungary), Professor Lindner (DDR), and Professor Kakumoto (Japan) spoke on the theme of the best correlation between private and public transport for passenger traffic. The speakers pointed to the considerable growth in private transport both in towns and in intercity passenger traffic which has been fostered by road construction. Using data from West Germany, they determined the spheres in which various forms of transport are used in relation to the distances covered – the proportional decrease in road transport with increase in distance, the increase in air transport and proportional rise in rail transport over distances up to 600 kilometres and its decline over distances beyond 600 kilometres. The criterion to be used for evaluating the distribution between the various modes of transport is that of keeping transport costs to a minimum. The American version, which is to build airports and an extensive network of highways, cannot be applied in Europe because of the density of the population there. Any rise in the national income has a considerable influence on the growth of private transport. Dr Bajusz described models for computing the provision of the population with road transport in relation to its national income. It is on this basis that attempts can be made to compute perspectives for the future. Much depends on the density of road transport already attained. In Japan, for instance, it is expected that growth in road transport will decline; and Hungary itself is also reaching saturation point.

During the debate doubt was expressed about the feasibility of determining an optimum correlation between private and public transport. Certain speakers were of the opinion that the very notions of private and public transport needed more precise definition. The correlation between the two types of transport depends not only on levels of production but also on consumer satisfaction. Expanding the use of road transport involves not only the acquisition of cars, but also the construction of garages and repair centres, and it is affected also by the price of petrol. Once a certain degree of congestion in town streets and roads is reached, public transport becomes preferable – and the insufficiency of it in certain countries is beginning to make itself more and more acutely felt. The conditions for developing private and public transport in various countries differ according to a range of economic indices, current capital outlay, the speed of communications, etc.

A range of papers considered the question of how to increase the effectiveness of various forms of transport. On rail transport, we heard papers from Professor Hilton (USA) and Dr Squilbin. Professor Hilton's paper examined the reasons for the chronic crisis of the railways and their unprofitability even with government subsidies. Amongst these reasons are rivalry from road transport, changes in regional economic structures, and obsolescence of technical equipment. The author proposed that container transportation should be expanded, and that transport companies should be so organised as to allow for the use of the same railway lines by two or more companies, as well as an end to the practice of trading in carriages en masse, which apparently serves to perpetuate existing technology. These proposals are very controversial, and seem scarcely likely to eliminate the real reasons for the critical condition of American railways, especially their surplus capacity.

Dr R. Squilbin, general secretary of the Association of International Railway Congresses, analysed in his paper the weak points of railways as far as international communications are concerned, as well as the problems involved in the improvement of international transport systems. There are significant differences in the technical equipment of various countries, as regards width of gauge, clearance, systems of electrification and signalling, types of freight cars, as well as in allocations for major construction work. Measures were proposed to eliminate the shortcomings mentioned, as well as to improve information about the transport market, to co-ordinate commercial activity, and to reduce restrictions at frontier stations, etc.

A lively discussion took place with regard to both papers, and a number of proposals were made for eliminating the faults in rail transport, and for devising technical and organisational measures to increase the utilisation of the railways and to distribute transportation more expediently between the railways and other forms of transport. Proposals were put forward about the merging of some railway lines, the closure of unprofitable ones, and the improvement of management.

The paper by Professor Meyer and Dr Tye (USA) on national policies towards international transport stressed the importance of free competition on the international air market. This allows for consumers' interests to be defended against state policies. The authors came out against the right of the state to give aid to its air companies. However, the more powerful air companies in the world probably do not even need state assistance. On the other hand, it is hard to believe that it is a characteristic of monopolies to defend the interests of consumers.

Two papers – by Professor Andruszkiewicz (Poland) and by Dr Wickham and Dr Phuc (France) – were devoted to the problems of sea transport and of ports. The questions covered were the expansion of sea-going fleets and the even more rapid growth in transportation by sea. Even though in recent years a series of nations (Sweden, Norway, Great Britain, France and Japan) have reduced their tonnage, this does not mean that we have a crisis in world navigation. Far more ships are now flying the flags of Liberia, of Panama, and of Singapore, and also those of the Soviet Union, Poland, and Rumania. With the growth in turnover of the developing countries, it has become apparent that their ports are not adequate to accommodate the volume of traffic, and there have been too many unnecessary delays. Many ports need considerable development; but the traditional method of enlarging them is a very slow one. It was proposed that floating cranes should be used, and that piers should be assembled from prefabricated sections. Small and cheap specialised terminals are more flexible and effective in satisfying the needs of maritime shipping than huge port complexes. Poland has achieved considerable success in cutting down delays of ships and wagons in port. In particular, barges are being used there as floating warehouses.

Dr Sharp and Dr Hayter's paper examined the use of inland waterways in Great Britain for the long-distance transportation of goods, using the example of the River Trent. This could be deepened and adapted for navigation by vessels of 1000–1800 tons deadweight, which can go out to sea and travel as far as, for instance, Rotterdam, and then up the Rhine to Cologne or Dusseldorf. The River Trent can also be used for transport up adjoining inland waterways. The cost of such transport can be extremely low and, so long as the state does not subsidise rival forms of transport, investment in waterways can be very rewarding.

Two other papers – by Professor Noortman (Holland) and by Mr Burke (EEC) – discussed the organisation of transport companies. Professor Noortman drew attention principally to the following points:

that intervention by the state in transport management is greater than in other branches of the economy; that it is impossible for management to have direct visual control over work in transport; and that there is a great variety in the quality of the services offered by small, medium or large transport companies. In the paper he introduced the model devised by the Rijswijk Institute of Transport simulating freight transport in the EEC, as well as an information system for management in public transport (ANALAD).

Mr Burke and Dr Leydon examined the role of economic factors in decision-making concerning transport, including information about markets, and variations in certain economic indices such as the unit cost of transport. Questions raised by the EEC with regard to air transport were mentioned; these were, for example, the rules governing competition, measures to reduce costs, etc. Attention was drawn to the problem of investment in the infrastructure of transport. They examined the problems of making transport models, its methodology, scenarios, and variants in transport policy. In conclusion proposals (prognoses) were made about the growth of freight transport and its composition in the next few decades, up to the year 2000, according to two possible assumptions of growth (2 per cent and 5 per cent). The paper provided information about transport policies in the EEC, and was therefore also of interest from the factual point of view.

There was also a group of papers about transport policies and the organisation of transport. Professor Rehbein's paper was about the connection between the location of productive forces and socialist transport policy, based on Marxist-Leninist theory. He considered the question of the distribution of productive forces within and between countries, as well as the various factors determining such location, the natural conditions governing the development of production, and socio-economic requirements and their interrelation with the development of transport.

Professor Tsankov of Bulgaria gave a paper where he examined various ways of integrating international transport; the co-ordination of plans for joint use of wagons, containers, airlines or ferry-boats.

Dr Vitek (Czechoslovakia) gave a paper where he expanded on the question of state policies in socialist countries with regard to transport, using the model of Czechoslovakia. This paper elaborated on the organisation and management of the socialist transport system, to which were devoted the aforementioned papers by Professor Mitaishvili and Professor Wagener.

Transport policies were also the theme of a paper by Dr Antal

(Hungary); he touched in particular upon certain points which had not been examined in the other papers such as tariff policy, the legal aspects of transportation and the whole question of liability, and points concerning the organisation of operation.

In the discussion of these papers a whole range of questions were elaborated upon and defined more precisely, both concerning transport policy and the organisation of management.

Index

Entries in the index in bold type under the names of participants in the Conference indicate their Papers or Discussions of their Papers. Entries in italic type indicate contributions by participants to the Discussions.

Air transport, international, policies for, 245–64, 264–6

Alaska, development of transport for, 112–33

Andruszkiewicz, W., *72*, *161*, *215*, **267–73**, **300–2**, *344*, *373*

Antal, G., *71*, *73*, *301*, *347*, **361–71**, **371–3**, *373*

Arctic, transportation in, 97–105

Areeda, P. and Turner, D. F., 250, 263n.

Arndt, O., 35, 48n., 186n.

Ashton, H., 272n.

Bajusz, R., *70–1*, *162*, **167–78**, **210–17**, *346*, *373*

Baum, H., 206, 210n.

Becker, G. S., 53, 63n.

Bettis, L., 89, 92n.; Hunter, H. and Dienes, L., **81–93**, **94–6**

Bokserman, I. U., 89, 92n.

Boon, C. J., 149, 155n.; Schwier, C. and Lake, R. W., **143–56**, **157–63**

Borisenko, T. M., *158*, *161*, *163*

Boyer, K. D., 228, 231n.

Burke, R., **326–42**, **342–7**

Burkhanov, V., **106–11**, **156–63**

Cao Pinna, V. and Shatalin, V., 216n.

Campbell, R. W., 85n., 86n., 92n.

Coal, US Western, modal selection of transport of, 149–55

Comparative advantage, of US railways long-distance, 221–31, 240–4

Conference, conclusions of, 374–83

Co-ordination, of road and rail in GDR, 38–48

Corneil, E. R., Lake, R. W., Helmers, H. O. and Law, C. E., 145, 156n.; Lake, R. W., Law, C. E. *et al.*, 144, 155n.

Czechoslovak republic, transport policy in, 353–60, 371–3

Dantzig, G. B., 82, 92n.

DeNeufville, R. and Gordon, S., 258, 263n.

Development, of Alaska, transportation and, 112–33; transport a necessity for, 106–11

Dienes, L., 86, 92n.; Bettis, L. and Hunter, H., **81–93**, **94–6**; and Shabad, T., 87, 92n.

Dorfman, R., 82; Samuelson, P. A. and Solow, R. M., 93n.

Efficiency, of road and rail in W. Europe, 12–21

Engelbloom, G. M. and Lake, R. W., 147, 155n.

Friedlaender, A., 228, 231n.

Fuel transportation, long-distance, 81–95, 142–56, 156–63

Funck, R., 272n.

Furman, I. Y., 87n., 135n., 136n.

Garrett, M. G., Hayter, D., Gibson, M. and Sharp, C., 286, 300n.
German Democratic Republic, experience of, 179–86, 210–17; transport planning in, 34–48
Gibson, M., Sharp, C., Garrett, M. G. and Hayter, D., 286, 300n.
Goldsmith, O. S., 115, 133n.
Goodwin, P. B., *210–13, 214, 373,* **374–6**
Gordon, S. and DeNeufville, R., 258, 263n.
Goreux, L. M. and Manne, A. S., 83, 93n.
Gray, J. T., Kresge, D. T. and Royce Ginn, J., **112–33, 156–63**
Grounau, R., 53, 63n.

Harbeson, R. W., 228, 231n.
Hayter, D., 344, 345; Gibson, M., Sharp, C. and Garrett, M. G., 286, 300n.; and Sharp, C., **286–300, 300–2**
Healy, K. T., 231n.
Heggie, I. G., 49n., 54n., 63n.
Hicks, J. R., 82, 93n.
Hilton, G. W., **221–31, 240–4**
Hotelling, H., 84, 93n.
Hungary, development of transport in, 167–78
Hunter, H., 96, 93n., *156–7, 158, 160, 242, 244, 265, 344*; Dienes, L. and Bettis, L., **81–93, 94–6**

Individual transport, or mass, 167–78, 210–17
Inland waterways, and long-distance freight, 286–300, 300–2; network of in USSR, xv–xvi
International air transport, policies for, 245–64, 264–6
International transport, importance of forms of, 348–60, 371–3; problems of, 232–40, 240–4, 326–42, 342–7
Isard, W., 82, 93n.
Ivantsov, O. M., **134–41, 156–63**

Japan, motorisation in, 187–96, 210–17; transport policy in, 49–64
Judge, G. G. and Takayama, T., 83, 93n.

Kahn, A. E., 247, 249n., 251, 263n.
Kakumoto, R., *73,* **187–96, 210–17,** *242*
Kantorovich, L. V., *70,* 82, 93n.; and Zhuravel, A., 83, 93n.
Kaser, M., *73, 158, 161, 162, 215–16*
Khachaturov, T. S., **xiii–xvi,** *71–2, 73,* 82, 83, 93n., *96, 158, 160, 161, 163, 214–15, 216, 242–3, 265, 301, 302,* 310, 311n., *373,* **377–83**
Kneiling, J. G., 229, 230, 231n.
Koopmans, T. C., 205, 210n.
Kovalev, I. V., *72, 73, 242, 265*
Kozin, B. S., *94–5, 215, 217*
Krell, K., 21n.
Kresge, D. T., Morehouse, T. A. and Rogers, G. W., 115, 133n.; and Roberts, P. O., 93n.; and Royce Ginn, J. and Gray, J. T., **112–33, 156–63**

Lake, R. W., *73, 243, 345–6*; Boon, C. J. and Schwier, C., **143–56,** *157–63*; and Engelbloom, G. M., 147, 155n.; Helmers, H. O., Law, C. E. and Corneil, E. R., 145, 156n.; Law, C. E., Corneil, E. R. *et al.,* 144, 155n.; and Macdonald, J. A., 147, 155n.; Maughan, R. G., Smith, J. S. *et al.,* 147, 156n.; and Schwier, C., 151, 156n.; Schwier, C. and Macdonald, J. A., 148, 155n.
Lammert, U., 180, 186n.
Lange, O., 82, 93n.
Law, R. W., Corneil, E. R., Lake, R. W. and Helmers, H. O., 145, 156n.; Corneil, E. R. and Lake, R. W., 144, 155n.
Leibenstein, H., 64n.
Lenin, V. I., 305, 308, 311n.
Leontief, W. W., 82, 93n.
Less accessible regions, transport in, 81–163; trunk lines in, 106–11
Levin, R. C., 228, 231n.
Leydon, K., *160, 213, 241–2, 346–7*

Lindner, W., **179–85**, **210–17**; and Schleife, H. W., 42, 48n.
Losch, A., 82, 93n.

Macdonald, J. A. and Lake, R. W., 147, 155n.; Lake, R. W. and Schwier, C., 148, 155n.
Manne, A. S., 84, 93n.; and Goreux, L. M., 83, 93n.
Marx, K., 307, 308, 311n., 371n.
Mass transport, or individual, 167–78, 210–17
Matthews, R. C. O. and Stafford, B. (eds), 216n.
Maughan, R. G., Smith, J. S., Lake, R. W. *et al.*, 147, 156n.
Meyer, J. R., 82, 83, 93n.; Peck, M. J., Zwick, C. and Stenason, W. J., 263n; and Straszheim, M. R., 93n.; and Tye, W. B., **245–64**, **264–6**
Mitaishvili, A. A., **3–11**, **64–77**
Modal split, of transport, in Japan, 49–64; in USSR, 3–11; optimum, 167–78, 210–17
Modes, of fuel transport, in USSR, 87–91; changes of, 22–33
Moore, T. G., 228, 231n.
Morehouse, T. A., Rogers, G. W. and Kresge, D. T., 115, 133n.
Moses, A. L., 82
Mote, V. L. and Shabad, T., 87, 93n.

Nash, C. A., 204, 210n.
Natural gas, pipeline transportation of in USSR, 134–41
Noortman, H. J., *96, 242*, **312–25**, **342–7**, *373*
Nordhaus, W. D., 84, 93n.

Okano, Y., **49–64**, **64–77**, *215, 265, 346*
Optimum modal split, of transport, 167–78, 210–17
Optimum ratio, of public and private transport, 179–86, 197–210, 210–17
Organisation, importance of forms of, in international transport, 348–60, 371–3; of transport enterprises, 313–23, 342–7

Peck, M. J., Zwick, C., Stenason, W. J. and Meyer, J. R., 263n.
Pegrum, D. F., **22–33**, **64–77**
Phillips, A. (ed.), 231n.
Pipeline development, in Arctic, 98–9
Pipeline transportation of natural gas, in USSR, 134–41
Pipelines, capacity of in USSR, 135–41
Planning of transport, in USSR, 3–11
Ponsonby, G. J., 60, 64n.
Ports, congestion of, 267–73, 274–85, 300–2
Private transport, optimum ratio of, 179–86, 197–210, 210–17
Public transport, optimum ratio of, 179–86, 197–210, 210–17

Rail and road services, comparative efficiency of in W. Europe, 12–21
Railway network, extent of in USSR, xiii–xiv
Railways, US, impediments to achieving long-distance advantage, 221–31, 240–4
Rehbein, G., 180, **305–11**, *311–13*, **342–7**; and Wagener, H., 306, 311n.
Road transport, scale of in USSR, xv
Robert, J., 273n.
Roberts, P. O. and Kresge, D. T., 93n.
Rogers, G. W., Kresge, D. T. and Morehouse, T. A., 115, 133n.
Routes, Arctic transportation, 97–105
Royce Ginn, J., Gray, J. T. and Kresge, D. T., **112–33**, **156–63**

Samuelson, P. A., Solow, R. M. and Dorfman, R., 93n.
Sarkisian, S., *264–5*
Scherer, F. M., 250, 264n.
Schleife, H. W. and Lindner, W., 42, 48n.
Schwier, C. and Lake, R. W., 151, 156n.; Lake, R. W. and Boon, C. J., **143–56**, **157–63**; Macdonald, J. A. and Lake, R. W., 148, 155n.
Scott, M. J., 124, 133n.
Sea transport, scale of in USSR, xvi

Seidenfus, H. S., *64–9*, *95*, *158*, **197–210**, **210–17**, *243–4*, *347*, *373*
Shabad, T. and Dienes, L., 87, 92n.; and Mote, V. L., 87, 93n.
Shafirkin, B. I., 48n.
Sharp, C., Garrett, M. G., Hayter, D. and Gibson, M., 286, 300n.; and Hayter, D. M., **286–300**, **300–2**
Shatalin, V. and Cao Pinna, V., 216n.
Shepard, W. G. (ed.), 264n.
Smith, J. S., Lake, R. W., Maughan, R. G. *et al.*, 147, 156n.
Socialist transport, planning and management of, 34–48
Solow, R. M., 84, 93n.; Dorfman, R. and Samuelson, P. A., 93n.
Spatial distribution of production, transport and, 305–11, 342–7
Squilbin, R., **232–40**, **240–4**
Stafford, B. and Matthews, R. C. O. (eds)., 216n.
Stenason, W. J., Meyer, J. R., Peck, M. J. and Zwick, C., 263n.
Straszheim, M. R., 257, 264n.; and Meyer, J. R., 93n.

Takayama, T. and Judge, G. G., 83, 93n.
Tarski, I., 273n.
Taussig, W. M., 264n.
Tien Phuc, N. and Wickham, S., **274–85**, **300–2**
Time, as factor in efficiency of transport, 267–73, 274–85, 300–2
Transport:
changes of modes of, 22–33
and development of Alaska, 112–33
development in USSR, xiii–xvi
development, organisational aspects of, 305–42, 342–7
enterprises, organisation of, 313–23, 342–7
by inland waterways, 286–300, 300–2
in less accessible regions, 81–163
international, importance of forms of, 348–60, 371–3
international, systems of, 326–42, 342–7

long-distance, of fuels, 81–95, 142–56, 156–63
mass or individual, 167–78, 210–17 and production, 305–42, 342–7
socialist planning and management of, 34–48
socialist policy for and spatial distribution, 305–11, 342–7
time as factor in efficiency of, 267–73, 274–85, 380–2
systems, international, problems of, 232–40, 240–4
Treml, V. G. (ed.), 82, 93n.
Tsankov, S., *216*, *344–5*, **348–52**, **371–3**
Turner, D. F. and Areeda, P., 250, 263n.
Tye, W., *69–70*, *159*, *243*, *265–6*, *344*, *346*; and Meyer, J. R., **245–64**, **264–6**

USSR, long-distance fuel transportation in, 86–95; modes of fuel transport in, 87–91; pipeline transportation of natural gas in, 134–41; planning of transport in, 3–11; state of need for transportation, xiii; transport development in, xiii–xvi

Velikanov, D. P., *214*
Vitek, K., *72*, *73*, *214*, *373*, **353–60**, **371–3**
Voigt, A., 201n.
Voigt, F., **12–21**, **64–77**

Wagener, H., **34–48**, **64–77**, *162*, *181*, *214*, *342–44*; and Rehbein, G., 306, 311n.
Waterways, inland and long-distance freight, 286–300, 300–2
Wickham, S., *72–3*, *94*, *160*, *240–1*, *244*; and Tien Phuc, N., **274–85**, **300–2**
Williamson, O. E., 250, 264n.

Zaleski, J., **97–105**, *156–63*, *300–1*
Zhuravel, A. and Kantorovich, L., 83, 93n.
Zwick, C., Stenason, W. J., Meyer, J. R. and Peck, M. J., 263n.